P9-CAD-107

THE STATE
AND REVOLUTION
IN EASTERN AFRICA

THE STATE
AND REVOLUTION
IN EASTERN AFRICA

ESSAYS BY
JOHN S. SAUL

1979

MONTHLY REVIEW PRESS
NEW YORK AND LONDON

Library of Congress Cataloging in Publication Data
Saul, John S
   The state and revolution in eastern Africa.

   Includes index.
   1. Mozambique—Politics and government.
2. Tanzania—Politics and government. 3. Africa,
Eastern—Politics and government. 4. Africa,
Eastern—Economic conditions. 5. Africa, Eastern
—Social conditions. I. Title.
DT463.S35   309.1'67   79-11458
ISBN 0-85345-487-6
ISBN 0-85345-508-2 pbk.

Monthly Review Press
62 West 14th Street, New York, N.Y. 10011
47 Red Lion Street, London WC1R 4PF

Manufactured in the United States of America

10 9 8 7 6 5 4 3 2 1

CONTENTS

Contents

Part III
Eastern Africa:
Social Forces and Political Alternatives

Postscript

INTRODUCTION

This volume represents the continuation of work begun over ten years ago with Giovanni Arrighi, work which took published form in an earlier, jointly written volume, *Essays on the Political Economy of Africa*.[1] Substantively, these further essays seek to convey something of the reality of external control and internal inequality which still stalks most of the countries of Eastern Africa and impedes their progress. They seek also to convey something of the drama of those revolutionary endeavors on the perimeter of the region—in Mozambique and beyond—which makes the struggle for Southern Africa so important a contemporary undertaking. In fact, Eastern Africa offers ideal terrain for sustaining this kind of analysis of the political economy of Africa. For the range of experiences the area encompasses is striking, running as it does from Kenya's relatively stable peripheral capitalist regime, to Uganda's bizarre and terrible collapse into Aminism, to Tanzania's flawed and controversial attempt at a "transition to socialism," to Mozambique's more genuinely radical development effort, one first broached in the liberated areas and now carried over into the postcolonial, postguerrilla phase. An understanding of such an apparent diversity of experiences—an understanding not readily available from the slogans of either bourgeois development theorists or left rhetoricians—is of obvious relevance to all who see in revolutionary socialism the most promising escape route from the syndrome of African underdevelopment and who aspire to know the forces which impede or facilitate the mounting of such a project.

Analytically, the book does have a somewhat narrower focus. As its title suggests, it aims, first and foremost, to bring the political dimensions of such broad concerns into firmer focus. This seems important since all too often in Marxist and other radical literature on African dependence and underdevelopment a rather crude form of economic determinism distorts the discussion of politics. There are reasons for this, of course, not least the fact that African conditions make such reductionism particularly tempting. After all, there can be little disagreement concerning the continuing and often quite overwhelming centrality of the imperial economic presence in postcolonial Africa, or the tendency for the indigenous (and politically dominant) petty bourgeoisie to assume the role of mere "intermediary" (in Fanon's phrase) between Western capitalism and the domestic social formation.[2]

Moreover, the reality of the most extreme and manipulable kinds of dependency in Africa has been quite openly underlined by the imperial planners themselves. In this matter there is a marked continuity between the views of the more farseeing of British decolonizers in the 1950s and those of Andrew Young, United States Ambassador to the United Nations, at large in Southern Africa in the 1970s. Listen to Arden-Clarke, governor of colonial Ghana, suggesting of African nationalism that "you cannot slow down a flood—the best you can do is keep the torrent within its proper channels," or Sir Andrew Cohen, in his book *British Policy in Changing Africa*, writing that "successful cooperation with nationalism is our greatest bulwark against Communism [read: any kind of radicalism] in Africa."[3] Then move ahead twenty years and ask Andrew Young what logic underlies his attempts to ease Ian Smith out of power in Rhodesia in the interests of moderation and black nationalism. This question was put to him recently: "Some foreign-policy observers have said that the U.S. has two foreign-policy options in Southern Africa, one being neocolonialism and the other being outright support of the minority government of South Africa. Could you just comment on this idea and what kind of options we have in Southern Africa?" Young's answer?

I don't even see that many. I don't think that the United States has but one option and that's neocolonialism. As bad as that has been made to sound, neocolonialism means that the multinational corporations will continue to have major influence in the development and production capacities of the Third World.[4]

To such actors the handing over of the state—the ceding of formal political power—to Africans has seemed a mere bagatelle, the giving up of a dispensable pawn in the ongoing imperial game. Even more positively, such a move could be expected to have the benefit of *legitimizing*, by appearing to democratize, the imperial linkage—thereby helping to forestall an escalation of such dangerous stirrings of mass resistance to colonialism as temporarily coincided, within the nationalist movement, with the far more muted and negotiable demands of the system's petty-bourgeois critics. Clearly, this has been an important dimension of the situation, one undoubtedly implied in Arden-Clarke's formulation but also underscored by Frantz Fanon with characteristic pithiness:

> . . . a veritable panic takes hold of the colonialist governments in turn. Their purpose is to capture the vanguard, to turn the movement to the right and to disarm the people: quick, quick, let's decolonize. Decolonize the Congo before it turns into another Algeria. Vote the constitutional framework for all Africa, create the French *Communauté*, renovate the same *Communauté*, but for God's sake let's decolonize quick. . . .

Here it bears noting that another eloquent critic and revolutionary, Amilcar Cabral, attempted to illuminate just this pattern—that of Africa's false decolonization—precisely by focusing upon the state itself:

> We are not interested in the preservation of any of the structure of the colonial state. It is our opinion that it is necessary to totally destroy, to break, to reduce to ash all aspects of the colonial state in our country in order to make everything possible for our people. The masses realize that this is true, in order to convince everyone that we are really finished with colonial domination in our country.

Some independent African states preserved the structures of the colonial state. In some countries they only replaced a white man with a black man, but for the people it is the same. You have to realize that it is very difficult for the people to make a distinction between one Portuguese, or white, administrator and one black administrator. For the people it is the administrator that is fundamental. And the principle—if this administrator, a black one, is living in the same house, with the same gestures, with the same car, or sometimes a better one, what is the difference? The nature of the state we have to create in our country is a very good question, for it is a fundamental one. [5]

Cabral went so far as to insist that "the problem of the nature of the state created after independence is perhaps the secret of the failure of African independence." Was Cabral mistaken to see "the state" as being central in this way? Certainly much of what Cabral terms to be the "failure of African independence" seems already to be structured by the hard global realities of class and dependence, with the African state to that extent merely registering and consolidating such forces. For this reason, some observers might argue that too great a preoccupation with the political realm and with the state *per se* may merely blur the necessary focus on such crucial underlying variables— and in particular on the preponderant role of the foreign bourgeoisie in all its manifestations. [6] Is this a real danger?

Danger it may be, yet I am confident that the essays which follow do not discount the vital and continuing role of Western imperialism (the multinational corporation, the existing networks of trade, the so-called multilateral agencies like the World Bank and International Monetary Fund, the "aid" and other apparatuses of advanced capitalist countries) in structuring the accumulation process in Africa and in warping social, cultural, and political developments there. This was the ground that Arrighi and I attempted to map out in our previous volume, ground that has also been carefully explored by other writers, and such an emphasis continues to premise my work here. Yet this kind of outward-looking underdevelopment theory can sometimes seem almost too powerful (and too blunt) a tool. Handled carelessly, it can degenerate into a sterile determinism, overwhelming the specificity of different concrete experiences in Africa and devaluing the importance of domestic actors. The fact is that the imperial linkage is not as straightforward—neither as neatly facilitated nor as smoothly functioning—as is sometimes assumed. Moreover, it is precisely in the political realm that the full range of complexities and contradictions that characterize dependency in Africa have manifested themselves most clearly. It is here, then, that Cabral's emphasis on the nature of the state that emerges out of the decolonization process promises to be a fruitful complement to the global perspective offered by a broadguaged understanding of the workings of imperialism.

For the state does loom large domestically in the countries of Eastern Africa with which we are primarily concerned in this volume. Indeed, in the absence of any indigenous economically dominant class—bourgeoisie or landed aristocracy—anchored in the production process, the state can be said to have a particularly *central* role in the economy and society and a role that is not paralleled in more fully developed capitalist systems, where the state (and those classes and "social categories" which cluster around it) exists primarily to service the activities of an already dominant domestic bourgeoisie. Some of the ways in which the functions assumed by the postcolonial state define its centrality are spelled out in subsequent essays. There we will also see that reproducing the conditions for continued accumulation on behalf of international capitalism under very trying conditions (including the necessity of acting upon and orchestrating a diverse range of modes of production and the constraint of operating with what is often a very rudimentary measure of legitimacy) remains of the greatest importance. Nevertheless, the postcolonial state is different from that of colonial days, however many important elements of continuity there may be between the two. Crucial in this respect is the fact that indigenous classes now have much more direct access to the state—and very much heightened expectations with regard to it. And, given the centrality of such a state within the newly independent social formations we are examining, it is not surprising that various classes and fractions of classes are tempted to seize hold of it and to use it for their own ends.

The truth is that the activities of indigenous classes—even those in power—are not entirely predictable, from the standpoint of imperial interests, differing in this respect from the activities of the expatriate civil servants who staffed the colonial state. To be sure, an Andrew Young can, with some reason, draw the lesson from Africa's decolonization experience that such inheritors of power are *predictable enough*, and can then attempt to whistle up more of the same for Rhodesia/Zimbabwe. Yet there is a measure of "openness" to the situation which must be understood if we are to draw a clear bead on the nature of postcolonial politics and on such opportunities as might exist for the insertion of more revolutionary undertakings in contemporary Africa. One crucial clue to such an understanding is the nature of the most important of Eastern Africa's indigenous classes—the petty bourgeoisie.

My most developed attempt, following Cabral and Poulantzas,[7] to delineate the nature of this class is presented in essay 13 in the course of an analysis of Uganda, but the theoretical content of that essay casts retrospective light on a number of the earlier essays. In it I have suggested that Poulantzas's distinction between "old petty bourgeoisie," active in the private sector, both urban and rural, and "new petty bourgeoisie," the "nonproductive salaried employees," including "civil servants employed by the state and its various apparatuses," is particularly suggestive when adapted for use in the scientific analysis of African settings. Moreover, the latter element—the new petty bourgeoisie—is seen to be of special importance precisely because of the centrality of the state under African conditions, the state around which, in significant measure, the new petty bourgeoisie actually forms.[8]

Not that all the ambiguities of this emphasis are resolved here. For example, more might be made of the existence of stratification within the petty bourgeoisie itself, a reality that has led others to seek fresh terms for conceptualizing the upper echelons—those closest to the real levers of power—of such a class (with the term "bureaucratic bourgeoisie" as the most ubiquitous, though not necessarily most precise, of such terms). More thinking is also needed on the nature and significance of the overlapping between "new" and "old" petty bourgeoisie in Africa, between public and private spheres of power and influence, and more thinking, too, on other kinds of division that cut vertically across the class a a whole. Nonetheless, enough can be determined about the peculiar characteristics of the petty bourgeoisie (here again Poulantzas is helpful) to provide a convincing explanation of the (relatively) unpredictable political process which it sustains. And this in turn is important since the character of petty-bourgeois politics is a vital factor in throwing up such diverse results as the straightforward servicing of imperialist activity of a Malawi, the extreme fragmentation and virtual socioeconomic breakdown of a Uganda, the quite dramatic Africanization of the private sector of a Kenya (the petty bourgeoisie as aspirant national bourgeoisie, as some would have it), and the fragile attempt to mount a socialist project of a Tanzania.

As hinted at the outset of this introduction, it would be a poor theory that did not facilitate our making distinctions among such diverse cases, especially since these different situations have, on the one hand, varying implications for the workings of imperialism, and, on the other, provide quite distinct kinds of terrain for the activities of revolutionary socialists in Africa. In consequence, several subsequent chapters will attempt to demonstrate the proposition that an understanding of the nature of "petty-bourgeois politics" does provide a significant key in analyzing such situations. But—equally important—it will become apparent that this kind of approach can also help us to make sense of the process of liberation further south in Africa. For "petty-bourgeois politics" characterizes important phases of the liberation struggle as well, with the "new petty bourgeoisie" in a pre-independence Zimbabwe or Mozambique beginning to take shape as a class around the *future prospect* of its members' control over the postcolonial state in their country as well as around the existing structures of the liberation movement as a kind of state-in-the-making. Indeed, in Zimbabwe it can be seen that for many years the extreme fragmentation spawned by a familiar kind of petty-bourgeois infighting sharpened ethnic and other such wasting divisions in the African camp, preempted ideological and organizational advance, and spared Smith any very serious military challenge to his rule. On the other hand, such is the character of this petty-bourgeoisie-in-the-making that under other circumstances its openness to diverse pressures and influences may actually allow some of its members to play a genuinely revolutionary role (Mozambique being a case in point).

Of course it must be noted at once that any such emphasis on the importance of petty-bourgeois politics cannot stand alone. By linking the relatively indeterminant nature of the petty-bourgeoisie-in-the-making to the "relative autonomy" of the postcolonial state, I am not arguing that all things are possible to the petty bourgeoisie or that what is needed in order to realize socialist objectives is merely a "good leader" (a Nyerere, for example). To argue so would be nonsense.[9] As noted, the range of variation permitted by the playing out of petty-bourgeois political processes is not inconsequential. But we have already seen that such politics moves within the orbit of imperial preeminence, a preeminence that continues to set significant limitations upon the initiatives of the petty bourgeoisie. In addition, it is of at least equal importance in this regard to consider the role of the subordinate classes—the peasantry and the proletariat—who are by no means passive spectators to the underdevelopment game.

They are not passive spectators, though subsequent essays (numbers 10 and 11, for example) will also demonstrate that it is not enough merely to invoke the presence and radical vocation of such classes in a ritualistic manner. There are, not surprisingly, very real constraints upon their spontaneous contribution to a revolutionary process in Africa. Nonetheless, it was their first stirrings, and the fear of their more self-conscious entry into the political process as classes, which hastened the day of the decolonization bargain between colonial masters—the Arden-Clarkes, Cohens, and Youngs to whom we harkened earlier—and indigenous petty-bourgeois politicians. Similar calculations continue to inform the policies of most independent African governments, the tendency being for those members of the petty bourgeoisie in power to seek to preempt such dangerous possibilities by means of occasional concession, by repression, and by the ubiquitous attempt to deflect popular consciousness into more palatable grooves (the blandest forms of "African socialism" and nationalism, for example, or such blind alleys as ethnicity and religious communalism). It is sufficient to note here that even when such ploys can be made to work, the adjustments which the petty bourgeoisie must oversee in order to accommodate the presence of subordinate classes do affect the character of the postcolonial state. In this sense, too, petty-bourgeois politics can be seen as not proceeding in a vacuum. Moreover, the need to avoid any underemphasis on the popular term in the political equation will seem all the more pressing when one considers that, in future, the deepening economic contradictions attendant upon neocolonialism are likely to offer an even more pressing invitation to the exploited in "independent" Africa to come to a better understanding of their position and to act to change it. The degree to which the workers and peasants are merely instrumentalized by the petty bourgeoisie, the degree to which, even short of full revolutionary mobilization, they are able to thrust their way positively into the political arena—clearly, these are crucial factors in defining the concrete reality of diverse neocolonial situations.

This is one side of the coin. The other side is equally important: a parallel awareness of the importance of the role of subordinate classes to any serious discussion of the transition to socialism in Africa. For it is only a regime in which workers and peasants become the paramount actors that can hope to sustain a real challenge to imperialism. Without that development and, concomitantly, the emergence of a very different kind of state than the familiar postcolonial one, it is obvious that any left project which then remains primarily petty bourgeois in its provenance (Ghana or Tanzania, for example) will ultimately yield to the blandishments of an ever active imperialism and to the lowest common denominator of petty-bourgeois aspirations.

Not that the petty-bourgeois term drops out of the revolutionary equation altogether. East African experience does suggest that an active role for the subordinate classes is likely to grow out of a complex dialectic established between themselves and the petty bourgeoisie. As noted, such interaction usually finds the latter class working to repress or distort the input from worker and peasant into the political arena. The classic case of a different kind of dialectic at work is Mozambique, where one wing of the petty-bourgois leadership did move to crystallize active and class-conscious peasant involvement in the liberation struggle, and in the process found itself embedded in a developing popular movement, whose ideology and organization came in turn to evoke from that leadership an ever firmer commitment to the revolutionary project. This was the process through which such leaders came, in Cabral's memorable phrase, to "commit suicide" as members of the petty bourgeoisie and become instead a vanguard for the workers and peasants; this latter result emerged both from a fierce struggle within the petty bourgeoisie over the form that political mobilization, economic reconstruction, and military activity should take, and from the growing presence of the subordinate classes within the liberation movement, both processes evolving simultaneously and, in the Mozambican case, reinforcing each other.[10]

It has been suggested that such a positive result is most likely under the circumstances of protracted guerrilla warfare and in resistance to a straightforwardly colonial oppressor, and this is probably true. Yet part of the intense interest spawned by Tanzania's experience lay in the fact that, at least momentarily, it posed the possibility of establishing such a dialectic, in cold blood as it were, in the context of the more oblique struggle against neocolonialism and dependence. In that country there were hints that some fraction of the petty bourgeoisie was prepared to contemplate "suicide" by working to raise class consciousness and release mass energies, clear signs too of the emergence of subordinate classes increasingly aware of the full implications of their demands and ready to meet and to reinforce any positive initiatives that might be forthcoming from the petty bourgeoisie (the working-class response to the officially sponsored TANU Guidelines of 1971 being a case in point). But this kind of cumulatively revolutionary process was never fully realized, and it must remain merely a matter of speculation as to whether it ever could have been, within the framework of Nyerere's quasi-socialist strategy.[11] What is less speculative is the point presented here (essay 10) in the course of criticizing Cranford Pratt's facile defense of "democratic socialism" in Tanzania: the crucial index of failure in Tanzania and of the winding down of petty-bourgeois socialism well short of revolutionary transformation is to be found in the ultimate preemption of anything like a real and radical democratization of the system there. At the various points when subordinate classes seemed poised for progressive action in that country—the peasants of Ruvuma, the workers of Dar es Salaam, even the students of Ubungo—they were crushed.

Thus it remains the case that, to date, *revolution* in Eastern Africa has been part and parcel of the liberation struggles, as Part I of this book seeks to document. Amilcar Cabral, writing of developments in Guinea-Bissau in West Africa, helps bring the discussion back to the question of the state, arguing that:

> Our fortune is that we are creating the state through the struggle. We can now have popular tribunals—people's courts—in our country. We cannot create a judicial system like the Portuguese in our country because it was a colonial one, nor can we even make a copy of the judicial system in Portugal—it is impossible. Through the struggle we created our courts and the peasants participate by electing the courts themselves. Ours is a new judicial system, totally different from any other system, born in our country through the struggle. It is similar to other systems, like the one in Vietnam, but it is also different because it corresponds to the conditions of our country. If you really want to know the feelings of our people on this matter I can tell you that our government and all the institutions have to take on another nature.[12]

This aspiration is a world away from the milieu of even the most "progressive" of petty-bourgeois regimes—and suggests the extent to which the state-in-the-making in the liberated areas of Portuguese Africa was, in juxtaposition to the colonial state, creating a situation of genuine "dual power." This is the reality which Samora Machel also underlined in discussing the future of an independent Mozambique on that country's Independence Day, June 25, 1975:

> The State is not an eternal and immutable structure; the State is not the bureaucratic machinery of civil servants, nor something abstract, nor a mere technical apparatus. The State is always the organized form through which a class takes power to fulfill its interests. The colonial State, an instrument of domination and exploitation by a foreign bourgeoisie and imperialism which has already been partially destroyed by the struggle, must be replaced

by a people's State, forged through an alliance of workers and peasants, guided by FRELIMO and defended by the People's Forces for the Liberation of Mozambique, a State which wipes out exploitation and releases the creative initiative of the masses and the productive forces.

In the phase of people's democracy in which we are now engaged as a phase of the Mozambican revolutionary process, our aim is to lay the material, ideological, administrative and social foundations of our State. We need to be aware that the apparatus we are now inheriting is, in its nature, composition and methods, a profoundly retrograde and reactionary structure which has to be completely revolutionized in order to put it at the service of the masses. . . . The new battle is only beginning.[13]

The reality that premises Samora Machel's statements is something that I have witnessed for myself in two visits there, visits recounted in this book. Despite the great difficulties facing a poor and dependent Mozambique, it is hard not to feel that a good start has been made toward casting the newly liberated state outside the petty-bourgeois mold and upon a base of consciously active peasants and workers. However, as Machel indicates, the struggle for such a positive blending of state and revolution is, in Mozambique too, a continuing one.

In our earlier volume Arrighi and I quoted Amilcar Cabral's observation that "the crisis of the African revolution . . . is not a crisis of growth, but mainly a crisis of knowledge. In too many cases the struggle for liberation and our plans for the future are not only without a theoretical base, but are also more or less cut off from the concrete situation in which we are working." While this may overstate the case for theory somewhat, it remains an important emphasis and one that continues to provide a touchstone for the essays in the present book. In addition, it may help account for the specific format of a number of these essays, their adversarial posture vis-à-vis the formulations of others, their *critical* slant. Since ideas *do* have consequences—positive and negative—in the African struggle, it is important to contest the various formulations which claim to structure an understanding of development on that continent and which guide the actions both of African militants and of their supporters.

This is not only true for ideas and approaches which, willfully or otherwise, sanction the *status quo* and undermine class struggle: the sinister manipulations of a Richard Gibson (essay 1), the well-meaning but one-dimensional nationalism of the Dar es Salaam historians (essay 7), the social-democratic apologetics for "Tanzanian socialism" of a Cranford Pratt (essay 10). It is often equally true of other, more ostensibly "left" formulations, many of which, in my judgment, oversimplify African developments in the interests of *a priori* and abstract models—models that are sometimes only tangentially Marxist, whatever claims may be made on their behalf. Here the reference is, obviously, to those sectarians who chose to play demogogic games with the fate of the Angolan people during that country's time of travail under the pressure of American and South African intervention (essay 4). But some reference is also intended to such writers as Issa Shivji and Mahmood Mamdani, whose books (published, like the present one, by Heinemann and Monthly Review Press) have gained deserved attention, but whose rigid approach all too often bends East African reality out of recognizable shape in ways that cannot but stand in the way of effective political practice (essays 8 and 13). Of course, in the latter case in particular, there is a great deal of room for continuing debate, and I trust that my criticisms will be received in the comradely manner in which they are intended. Only a debate that is at once searching and honest can ensure that revolutionary practice, not academic gamesmanship, will be the ultimate beneficiary of our scientific differences, and I have no wish to reinforce the second of these alternatives.

It might also be emphasized here that the escalation of the struggle in Southern Africa lends a particular urgency to such intellectual undertakings. Indeed, the essays in Part I of this book spill over into that latter arena, with Mozambique providing a crucial link between the eastern and southern parts of the continent. Such a sense of urgency may also account for the fact that several of the essays in that first section are less overtly theoretical than later essays, and in consequence, perhaps, more directly accessible to that broader audience of people in North America potentially available for work around Southern African issues, for whom they were originally written. Yet it is the case that the

ongoing fight for Southern Africa, the drama of which is immediately apparent, also underscores the necessity of furthering
an understanding, in Western capitalist countries, of the nature
of neocolonialism in Africa. For, as noted above, it is increasingly apparent that in Zimbabwe and Namibia "false decolonization" has become the preferred solution of the Kissingers and the
Carters to political unrest. This, in turn, may be seen to lend an
added dimension to the interpretations of the politics of
neocolonialism in Tanzania, Uganda, and Kenya presented in
Parts II and III. The slogan "one struggle, many fronts" has never
been more true than in contemporary Africa, and what one
learns of developments in East Africa (useful, one hopes, to
revolutionaries there), also seems likely to illuminate such matters as the nature of the aforementioned "petty-bourgeois politics" within the Zimbabwean liberation camp (essay 5), or the
challenges that confront a socialist project in Mozambique and
Angola, or the character of imperial strategies farther south.

This much having been said, it becomes obvious that the
essays which follow make no pretense at being "neutral" regarding developments in either Eastern or Southern Africa. Nonetheless, I trust it will be equally apparent to the attentive reader from
the essays themselves that such a forthrightly committed
approach—premised, as Arrighi and I wrote in our earlier preface, on "an attempt to identify with the oppressed in their
struggle"—does not reduce the scientific quality of the work here
presented, or transform it into "mere" polemic. On the contrary,
I have found that such a commitment serves to structure, in
dialogue with other Marxists similarly engaged, a range of crucial
questions and plausible interpretations, which are merely muted
or displaced by alternative and more conventional approaches.
These essays thus represent one further attempt to contribute to
an undertaking that is now, fortunately, the task of many more
hands and minds in Africa than it was a decade ago—"the development of theory and analysis at once intellectually more
satisfying and strategically more relevant."

This, in turn, leads me to strike one final, more personal note.
Clearly, such an approach cannot be sustained in isolation. Of
course, it is conventional in such an introduction to thank one's

family, friends, and colleagues for encouragement and assistance. I continue to have more reason to do so than most, but, most important, I am especially fortunate that in all these categories I can number many who are also comrades. Thus the seven years I spent in Tanzania were turbulent ones—the "Arusha Declaration" years, years in which everyone was thrust, willy-nilly, into that country's "silent class struggle" (to borrow Shivji's evocative phrase). Moreover, the University of Dar es Salaam, where I taught, was unlike universities in most Western countries, an institution central to the society and a key arena for contestation. I am in considerable debt to many people who were on "the Hill" and engaged in that contestation during the period, but, most markedly, this volume bears the stamp of close collaboration with a small band of expatriate radicals who then frequented the university and who are still among my closest friends: Giovanni Arrighi, Jonathan Barker, Manfred Bienefeld, Lionel Cliffe, Peter Lawrence, John Loxley, Roger Murray, and Pat Saul, among others. In addition, it is of considerable importance to the shape my work has taken that I have been able to continue my collaboration with a number of the above as fellow editor of the *Review of African Political Economy*: indeed, it was in the pages of that journal that several of the essays contained in this volume were first published.

It is also the case that without the constant stimulus of my students at the university—drawn as they were from all over Eastern Africa—my understanding of that part of the world would have been much poorer. Their recognition and acceptance of the honest efforts of an "outsider" to struggle alongside them in the tasks of understanding and changing their societies, and their openness to critical debate about the most searching of questions concerning East African realities, provided a sharp contrast to the attitudes and activities of bureaucrats and politicos further up the heirarchy in Tanzania and were a source of considerable inspiration to me. In particular, the intellectual undertakings of a group of Marxist-oriented East African students and faculty—those whom I have characterized elsewhere in this book as the "*Maji Maji* socialists" (essay 9)— provided an important touchstone for my developing views. Even when I have been critical of what I conceive to be the "ultra-left" nature of some of their emphases, I remain, more than anything else, their student.

Two additional sets of political involvements have been of critical importance to the preparation of this volume. First, I am indebted to the comrades in the Front for the Liberation of Mozambique (FRELIMO) who from the first encouraged and welcomed my support for their cause and gave me every opportunity to make some small contribution to it. In the course of my years of contact with FRELIMO—including a 1972 trip, at the movement's request, to the liberated areas and combat zones of Tete province and a 1975 invitation to a newly freed Mozambique to participate in the independence celebrations and witness at first hand the transition to self-rule (see essays 2 and 3, below)—I experienced more of the meaning of comradeship and learned more about the real world of revolution in Africa than I have as yet found the words to convey. Nonetheless, my writings would be much poorer and much less real without that experience.

Furthermore, it was Samora Machel, president of FRELIMO and now of Mozambique, and his colleague in the movement, Jorge Rebelo, now Mozambique's Minister of Information and FRELIMO's Secretary for Party Ideological Work, who most actively encouraged me to become involved in Southern Africa support work on my return to Canada, and this advice has been of great value to me. For the second of my political involvements mentioned above has been with the Toronto Committee for the Liberation of Southern Africa (TCLSAC—formerly TCLPAC, the Toronto Committee for the Liberation of Portugal's African Colonies), founded by a group of us in 1972 and able to sustain a wide range of political activities since that time. Once again, the opportunity to work closely with a dedicated group of comrades has helped sustain my creativity, and the opportunity to engage in real political activity around African issues has served to keep my continuing scientific interest in Africa from becoming as abstract and vicarious as might otherwise have been the case. It has also served—and I have included here the essay on "Canada and Southern Africa" precisely to underscore this point—as a means of contributing to the development of a left analysis and practice relevant to the transformation of Canada itself.[14] I think this important since it suggests one way links can be forged which embody real, rather than merely charitable, solidarity with struggles in Africa. In short, to those with whom I have worked in TCLSAC I owe a very great deal.

With more immediate reference to this volume itself, there are also debts which must be recorded. I feel it a great honor to publish once again with Monthly Review Press. At MR Paul Sweezy and Harry Magdoff have been a source of essential encouragement and support over the years (support which has included the first publication of several of the present essays in their magazine). At the Press itself, I am greatly indebted to the late Harry Braverman, to Jules Geller, and to Judy Ruben, among others; in particular, I must thank Susan Lowes, whose crucial role in bringing into being Arrighi's and my *Essays on the Political Economy of Africa* has been duplicated in the present case. And at Heinemann, James Currey's active and sympathetic interest in my work, as well as his friendly but persistent insistence that this project be completed, have been equally important.

Finally, I would like to dedicate this book of essays to the memory of four comrades whom I came to know and respect while living in Dar es Salaam: to Eduardo Mondlane of Mozambique and James Birihanze of Uganda, revolutionaries who sacrificed their lives combating imperialism and tyranny in two different parts of Africa, and to Borondire Moronda and Hamisi Omari, militants for a socialist Tanzania who died too young.

Notes

1. Giovanni Arrighi and John S. Saul, *Essays on the Political Economy of Africa* (New York, 1973).
2. See Frantz Fanon, *The Wretched of the Earth* (Harmondsworth, 1967). It bears noting here that some brief sections of this introduction are drawn from my draft manuscript for the editorial, "The State in Africa," in *Review of African Political Economy*, no. 5 (1976).
3. These two quotations are cited from Gary Wasserman, *The Politics of Decolonization* (Cambridge, 1976), ch. 1.

4. This interview was reprinted in *Southern Africa* (March 1977).
5. Amilcar Cabral, *Return to the Source* (New York, 1973), p. 83.
6. This seems to be one main thrust of the observations of Colin Leys on my approach to Tanzania in his critical article "The 'Overdeveloped' Post-Colonial State: A Re-evaluation" in *Review of African Political Economy*, no. 5(1976). Wasserman, in passing, is critical of my approach to Mozambique on what appear to be somewhat similar grounds (p. 178).
7. See Amilcar Cabral, *Revolution in Guinea* (London, 1969, and New York, 1972), especially the essays "Brief Analysis of the Social Structure of Guinea" and "The Weapon of Theory," and Nicos Poulantzas's various works, especially *Classes in Contemporary Capitalism* (London, 1975).
8. This is a way of making the point which is obscured by Leys in his article cited above, in part because of his somewhat narrow definition of the petty bourgeoisie.
9. Yet this is the way my argument has been caricatured by Gavin Williams in his rather demagogic note, "There is no theory of petit-bourgeois politics" in *Review of African Political Economy*, no. 6 (1976).
10. This process is documented for ex-Portuguese Africa in essay 1, but a more detailed analysis of its earlier phases in Mozambique appears as ch. 8 in Arrighi and Saul, *Essays on the Political Economy of Africa*.
11. An earlier overview of the positive and negative features of Tanzania's *ujamaa* appears as ch. 6 in ibid.
12. Cabral, *Return to the Source*, p. 83–84.
13. Samora Machel, "The People's Republic of Mozambique: The Struggle Continues" in *Review of African Political Economy*, no. 4 (November 1975), pp. 19–20.
14. See also the Committee's book, *Words and Deeds, Canada, Portugal, and Africa* (TCLSAC, 121 Avenue Rd., Toronto, 1976) and my *Canada and Mozambique* (Toronto, 1974).

PART I

MOZAMBIQUE AND THE STRUGGLE FOR SOUTHERN AFRICA

The essays in this section set out, in the first instance, to explore those processes which can transform a national liberation struggle into a full-fledged revolution, and they take as their primary point of reference in Eastern Africa the experience of Mozambique. Here the focus is precisely upon the kind of dialectical relationship between petty-bourgeois leadership and popular classes—alluded to in the introduction—that can contribute to the preemption of a neocolonial denouement to the drive for independence. As the first essay indicates, this result was facilitated in Portuguese Africa by the peculiarly inflexible nature of Portugal's colonial posture, resistance to which forced upon the liberation movements a pressing need to clarify the direction their struggles should take. The Portuguese attitude also facilitated the active entry into the political arena of more class-conscious peasants and workers, strata with a growing interest in driving these movements even further in a progressive direction.

In the case of Mozambique, the crystallization of such developments enabled FRELIMO to bargain from strength with Portugal after the 1974 coup in the latter country, and ultimately to take power on its own terms. The second and third essays record my own on-the-spot impressions of the consolidation of these positive trends in Mozambique, first

19

in the liberated areas during the phase of guerrilla warfare, and second, at the moment of FRELIMO's formal assumption of power in the entire territory in June 1975. Of course, the struggle must also be a continuing one. Mozambique's inherited situation of extreme dependence (especially upon South Africa) and gross underdevelopment has led some observers to question the ability of FRELIMO to sustain its radical project, achieved most prominently to date at the level of politics and ideology, in the face of such grim realities in the productive sphere.

A warning of this kind is quite in order, but it must not be allowed to degenerate into a rigid determinism. Certainly the FRELIMO leadership has been quite frank about the nature of the constraints that confront it, while moving slowly but surely to fashion a socialist strategy that might remove them. This leadership has also been conscious of the dangers of its own possible bureaucratization. Thus, in 1973, at the height of military activity, Marcellino dos Santos (FRELIMO vice-president) was reminded by an interviewer that "in a war situation it is easier to get people to accept a certain type of communal effort, even by those who are ideologically not committed to this as defining the form of a future society." Agreeing, dos Santos responded that there is nonetheless "a strong possibility that in the course of the collectivist effort a situation is created from which it will be difficult to withdraw. If our organization maintains a true revolutionary leadership, the special circumstances of the process of our liberation open up real possibilities for an advance from liberation to revolution."

But how does the movement make sure that this is achieved? "The main defense must be to popularize the revolutionary aims and to create such a situation that if, for one reason or another at some future time, some people start trying to change their aims, they will meet with resistance from the masses. This must be the defense until the situation has been achieved where the truly revolutionary classes dominate all levels of power." The need for such a deepening commitment to democratization in the transition to socialism is a theme to which we will return in the next section of this book, that on Tanzania (see essay 10). Here it can be emphasized that an ongoing study of independent Mozambique's attempts to build socialism—from a running start, as it were—promises to be an instructive one.

However, even FRELIMO's experience to date—the transition from "primitive" or "bourgeois" nationalism to "revolutionary nationalism" (the phrases are again those of dos Santos) and thence to the postindependence declaration of a Marxist-Leninist project for Mozambique—is instructive enough. If Mozambique is viewed as a kind of gateway to Southern Africa, developments there can provide a touchstone for understanding processes which are in train elsewhere in the latter region. Thus essay 4 demonstrates the ways in which a parallel analysis of the Angolan situation underwrites a positive evaluation of MPLA's claim to represent the genuinely revolutionary stream of development in that country. The difficulties which some Western radicals (not to mention most Western liberals) had in grasping this reality during the period of "civil war" in Angola suggests the dangers of an approach to Africa which premises itself upon an exclusive preoccupation with global contestation rather than an understanding of the dynamics of revolutionary politics within Africa itself!

In a related manner the analysis of Zimbabwe in essay 5 demonstrates, largely by way of negative example, the dangers inherent in the degeneration of petty-bourgeois politicking within the liberation camp (including a heightening of factionalism and ethnic tension) and the costs incurred when, in consequence, the establishment of a positive dialectic vis-à-vis the African population as a whole is not facilitated. For it is not just that the task of removing the Smith regime from power has been rendered more difficult under such circumstances. In addition, the chances of avoiding a neocolonial denouement to his ultimate removal has also been reduced—this latter being a possibility whose significance has recently (as the essay emphasizes) been quite clearly grasped by imperial strategists.

In the camp of the latter one finds Canada, and essay 6 is included here not because Canada is the most important of the countries involved, but because a concrete case study can help to underscore the saliency of the imperial connection to developments in Africa. Equally important, it demonstrates the necessary interplay between anti-imperialist work in Africa and in "the West" and the real bases for solidarity in what is clearly a common struggle. It bears noting, parenthetically, that more recent developments in Canadian policy toward South Africa itself (*circa* December 1977), which reaped some global publicity and considerable liberal approval, have not affected the activities of Canada's private sector in any way. In fact, the measures involved represent a quite marginal gesture designed merely to encourage—in line with parallel American intentions—a modest measure of "reformism" on the part of the South African state.

1

THE REVOLUTION IN PORTUGAL'S AFRICAN COLONIES

The coup in Portugal and the subsequent movement toward the independence of that country's three erstwhile colonies has served finally to underscore for all what more knowledgeable observers have understood for some years—that the black challenge to white minority rule in Southern Africa is of great depth and seriousness and that, ultimately, it can and will succeed. Perhaps, in consequence, we will see less in future of the kind of academic superciliousness which has dictated that the bland and misleading—but "objective"—analyses of conservative writers be granted greater credence in Africanist circles than the writings of committed and activist—hence "nonobjective"—writers! For, as several of the books to be examined here demonstrate, much was known about "Portuguese Africa"—long before last year's dramatic coup—which "informed opinion" in Western countries (including Canada) chose, quite simply, to ignore. Nor have books such as those by Minter, Davidson, and Cornwall, even though written prior to the coup, been altogether outstripped by events. There remain lessons to be learned from a careful examination of the struggle which has taken place in Guinea-

This essay was originally presented as an extended review article, dealing with the following books: William Minter, *Portuguese Africa and the West* (London, 1972), new edition, with a fresh postscript entitled "The Nixon Doctrine: What Role for Portugal?" (New York, 1973); Basil Davidson, *In the Eye of the Storm* (New York, 1972); Barbara Cornwall, *The Bush Rebels* (New York, 1972); Richard Gibson, *African Liberation Movements* (London and New York, 1972). It first appeared in the *Canadian Journal of African Studies* 9, no. 2 (1975).

Bissau, Mozambique, and Angola—lessons relevant not only to the future of these three societies as they move to chart their postcolonial futures, but lessons which are also relevant to the continuing struggle for liberation which now escalates in Zimbabwe/Rhodesia, in Namibia, and in South Africa itself. To some of these lessons we shall turn in this essay.

I

In an admirably clear if somewhat abbreviated form, William Minter's *Portuguese Africa and the West* provides an exemplary overview of the situation which made Portuguese Africa a forcing-house for revolution. The three major sets of actors are present and well accounted for in his volume: Portugal itself, those Western interests, state and corporate, which became its allies in empire, and the African people of the colonies—seen, primarily, as they came to organize themselves for successful struggle within their own liberation movements. For present-day purposes it is perhaps fortunate that Minter's major emphasis is on the Western—and especially American—interests which have been implicated in Portugal's African wars. Since these interests are very far from having disappeared from the scene in post-coup Southern Africa, the continuing relevance of the book is underscored. But Minter also provides a thumbnail sketch of Portuguese "ultra-colonialism," a phenomenon which is even now of more than historical interest if only because of the nature of the African opposition—profoundly more radical than that which emerged elsewhere in colonial Africa—to which it has given rise. As we shall see, the pattern of development of the several impressive popular movements which have liberated the Portuguese colonies cannot be understood outside an analysis of the peculiarly intransigent colonialism they were forced to con-front. In addition, there is a second reason of almost equal importance for our continuing interest: It is precisely the blighted legacy of the colonial experience—Portugal's warping of the Guinean, Mozambican, and Angolan economies in particular —which now defines the enormous challenges confronting these same liberation movements as they come to power. Consequently, it seems appropriate to say something further about Portugal in Africa here.

For the Portuguese record was a particularly grisly one, even when measured against the flagrant racism and blunt exploitation which has marked other colonialisms on the African continent. Its history stretches back to the fifteenth century, when Portuguese ships first began to touch the African coastline, and forward, through the brutalities of the slave trade, to a twentieth-century pattern of forced labor and entrenched hostility to African demands for self-determination even at a time when other colonial powers were granting formal independence to their own African colonies. It was Perry Anderson who first described this record as being one of "ultra-colonialism"—"at once the most *primitive* and the most *extreme* form of colonialism"—and traced its roots to the peculiar character of Portugal's own status as an imperial power.[1] For Portugal itself is a poor, underdeveloped country, and for centuries has been as much a colony of stronger countries, most notably Britain, as it has been a colonizer in its own right. More recently, it was to become the associate of others—of the United States, of West Germany, and of South Africa—and one of the chief merits of Minter's account is to trace in great detail the nature of these links. But Portugal's own record, its refusal to yield for so long to the tide of recent history and to the just demands of the peoples under its colonial sway, remains worthy of careful analysis.

It is true that the Portuguese first came to Africa as early as the fifteenth century, but for a very long time their presence was mainly confined to the coastline, with occasional sallies into the interior to bolster trading networks or to set one tribe against another in the interest of strengthening their own hand—a policy of "divide and rule" which the Portuguese pursued, though with diminishing success, to the 1970s. For much of this period the economic key was the slave trade, which continued within the Portuguese empire until 1869. It has been estimated that the Congo-Angolan states lost over 7 million people during four and a half centuries to this cruel traffic, including most of the 3.6 million who wound up in Brazil. The record of this trade, which was only marginally less horrific in Mozambique on the east coast, should itself have been sufficient to undermine Portugal's claims to a "civilizing mission" in Africa. But Portuguese exploitation of their African wards did not end with the conclusion of the slave trade.

Instead, the framework of further exploitation was to be provided by outright occupation and the institutions of formal colonialism. Thus, it was not until the latter part of the nineteenth century that Portugal finally moved to consolidate its grip in Africa, and then under the threat of its eclipse as a colonial power by other, even more active and effective, imperialisms. Then, while Africa was being carved up by Britain, Germany, France, and the rest, the territorial boundaries which now demarcate Angola, Mozambique, and Guinea were blocked out. At that time, too, Portugal finally began to bring the African population to heel in all corners of these territories—with characteristic ruthlessness and against bitter resistance. Indeed, it was only in 1913 in Angola, the 1920s in Mozambique, and 1936 in Guinea that African resistance can be said to have been at last crushed, a fact conveniently forgotten by recent apologists for Portugal who have spoken of that country's five-hundred-year "presence" in Africa. Moreover, by these late dates there were already stirring those territorial-wide nationalisms which came to present an even more effective challenge to Portuguese hegemony than such early, dramatic, but often localized resistance to the imposition of colonial rule. It is the liberation movements which, in giving effective expression to this new nationalist consciousness, have now brought to a close the Portuguese chapter in Africa.

We shall return to a discussion of the rise of African nationalism and of the liberation movements. Here we must note that even as Portuguese colonial rule was being thus established at bayonet point, the particular character of Portuguese domination was reaffirmed: "Portuguese colonial policy to this day has been moulded by the early patterns of slavery, trade and pacification."[2] As noted, this policy in turn owed a great deal to Portugal's own poverty and underdevelopment. From a very early point in the modern era, Portugal had developed a relationship with the rest of Europe whereby it supplied raw materials to advanced countries and imported manufactured goods. Typical of this pattern was the Treaty of Methuen, which in 1703 granted Portugal entry for its wine into the British market, while Britain in return received privileged entry for its textiles. Through such a network of relationships, surpluses reaped in the colonies, including gold from Brazil, merely passed through Portugal and were in effect accumulated and put to productive use in Britain and other parts of Western Europe. While these latter countries then experienced industrial revolutions, Portugal remained under the domination of an old-fashioned landed oligarchy linked to the Church and the military and hostile to the emergence of an independent and effective capitalist class. The country became a stagnant, quasi-feudal backwater. This meant that the form of liberal democracy whose development accompanied the further evolution of capitalism in many parts of Western Europe and North America did not take root in Portugal. Evidence for this is provided by the convulsive and short-lived history of the Portuguese republic, in existence only between 1910 and 1926. Fascism was more successful: in 1925 the military overthrew the republic and, shortly thereafter, dictator Antonio Salazar came to power. His *Estado Novo*—New State—was a corporate state, setting itself firmly against "modernism" and democratic trends. In its broad outlines the Salazarist system remained entrenched under Salazar's successor, Marcelo Caetano, right up to the day of the coup. Accordingly, elections were rigidly controlled and carefully orchestrated, trade unions were government sponsored, and most forms of dissent were ruthlessly crushed by a highly developed network of political police. The liberation movements in Africa were never to lose sight of the fact that in Portugal itself most Portuguese also suffered under an oppressive, dictatorial regime, and the support which they were eventually to receive from popular forces within Portugal in the wake of the 1974 coup amply demonstrated the wisdom of this perception.

However, it was in the colonies that the logic of oppression worked itself out most relentlessly. All colonialisms have used some measure of constraint to pitchfork Africans into the labor force, particularly during the initial stages of colonial rule. But the impact of dynamic economies like those of Britain and France was dramatic. In their colonies, precapitalist patterns were eroded, and soon the lure of economic incentives began to replace this initial application of force in providing the colonialists with necessary manpower. Not so with Portugal. As Anderson has noted, "the most notorious single feature of the Portuguese African colonies is their systematic use of forced labor. It is this which immediately identifies the Portuguese variant of colonialism as against all others." The infamous decree of 1875, defining labor policy, was little more than an attempt to guarantee retention of the master-slave relationship, despite the formal abolition of slavery. And this attempt has lain at the heart of Portuguese practice to the present day. A decree of 1899 captures the characteristic tone of Portuguese legislation on the subject: "All natives of Portuguese overseas provinces are subject to the obligation, moral and legal, of attempting to obtain through work the means that they lack to subsist and to better their social condition."

Over the years an entire range of techniques were found to accomplish these ends: correctional and obligatory labor, contract labor, and, of course, "voluntary labor," the latter entered into under the threat of punishment if an able-bodied man were found to be "idle." Even when Africans were left on the land, as in the cotton-growing areas of northern Mozambique, enforced cultivation has been the rule rather than the exception; in these cases, the price structure also was manipulated against the African cultivator, enabling the colonial government to skim off most of the proceeds from such production. Small wonder that in 1954 Marcelo Caetano could summarize the philosophy underlying Portuguese colonial practice in the following succinct manner: "The natives of Africa must be directed and organized by Europeans but are indispensable as auxiliaries. The blacks must be seen as productive elements organized, or to be organized, in an economy directed by whites." To be sure, some marginal adjustments were made in this system in recent years: slightly higher wages, the removal of some of the most glaringly anomalous legal compulsions from the statute books. But the essential nature of the colonial economy is clear. The overall system worked to press Africans into the economic service of the Portuguese, of the South Africans (who draw labor from Mozambique in particular), and of those multinational corporations which operated in the colonies. Moreover, "the violence it [forced labor] introduces into the society is a contagion. . . . it settles on everything and deforms it. In the end, violence tends to coincide with the very notion of social relations themselves."[3]

All colonialisms exploit African labor, Portugal's more than most; this in itself provided sufficient reason for militant resistance to the continuance of foreign rule. But there has been a second, equally fundamental, aspect of the colonial impact which must be discussed. For all colonialisms also warp the African economies they touch in another way, by imposing upon these economies a subservient position in the world economy. From this position of dependence springs economic activity which serves first and foremost the needs and interests of the colonizer, rather than meeting the long-term requirements of the colonized territory for its own sustained transformation. Colonial economies are forced to produce raw materials for the "mother country," with their lines of communication all directed outward to the sea instead of facilitating the kind of internal economic links which might trigger off real development. Under such circumstances, too, capital is accumulated primarily in the metropolitan center and full-fledged industrialization is facilitated only there.

In recent years, of course, radical economists have come to see this continuing pattern of dependence and subordination, rather than merely the shortfalls of technology and capital emphasized by more conventional economic theories, as being the major constraint upon economic transformation in the "Third World." It is this pattern, in fact, which Andre Gunder Frank and others have spoken of as guaranteeing only the further "development of underdevelopment." The liberation movements are themselves well aware of this reality; just such an insight has been one of the elements which has lent urgency to their demands and which has given them an increasingly revolutionary character. Amilcar Cabral, leader of the struggle in Guinea-Bissau until his untimely assassination at the hands of Portuguese agents, summarized this point succinctly: "We therefore see that both in colonialism and in neo-colonialism the essential characteristics of imperialist domination remain the same: the negation of the historical process of the dominated people by means of violent usurpation of the freedom of development of the national productive forces." The conclusion which he drew from this analysis is equally significant: "If we accept that national liberation demands a profound mutation in the process of development of the productive forces, we see that this phenomenon of *national liberation* necessarily corresponds to a *revolution*."[4] At stake, quite literally, was the right of Africans in "Portuguese Africa" to *make their own history*—politically, culturally, economically.

In the meantime, the "development of underdevelopment" in Portugal's African colonies continued, a pattern most evident in Mozambique, where the two main sources of territorial revenue were the remittances of Mozambicans recruited to work in the mines elsewhere in Southern Africa (particularly in South Africa itself, through the Witwatersrand Native Labour Association), and revenues from the carrying trade between South Africa and Rhodesia and the sea. In addition, Mozambique's exports are all agricultural: cashew nuts, sugar, tea, sisal. There has been little chance that a balanced and self-sustaining development effort could arise from such a situation. Angola, forced into a similar mold, was even more lucrative for the Portuguese, its trade providing much of the revenue which financed the Portuguese war machine. Coffee was crucial, the major earner from Portugal's African colonies, but minerals became increasingly important, diamonds joined by iron ore and especially oil. Finally, in Guinea, it was the trade, carefully controlled and milked by the Portuguese, in groundnuts, palm kernels, and vegetable oils which built similar distortions into the economy—though in the Guinea case this pattern began to be undermined some years ago by the liberation of a large proportion of the territory and its coming under the soon-to-be-proclaimed Republic of Guinea-Bissau.

Sometimes this colonial pattern serviced Portuguese industrialization at the expense of the colonies; thus cotton from Mozambique and Angola was processed by Portugal's textile industry and returned (like some other Portuguese manufactures) to a protected market in Africa. But more often the effective economic links have been with more advanced capitalist centers,

Portugal reaping its benefits—foreign-exchange earnings from coffee sales abroad, for example—by playing a virtual middleman's role in the outside world. If anything, this pattern intensified in recent years, the stepping up of expropriation by foreign firms of nonreplenishable resources (the iron ore and oil just mentioned) represented not only a virtual theft from the African population of their birthright but also another way for the Portuguese to gain a middleman's profit—this time from capital inflows and from royalties, profits tax, and rents. The huge hydroelectric schemes at Cunene in Angola and Cabora Bassa in Mozambique were equally directed outward, representing once again a "violent usurpation of the freedom of development of the national productive forces." For these schemes were designed primarily to service the energy needs of South Africa and Rhodesia, and involved vast commitments of resources by the Portuguese to a particular pattern of economic policy and economic change for the future which in all probability would not have been chosen by the Africans themselves.

This was the underlying economic reality. Caetano's statement, quoted earlier, demonstrated the Portuguese long-time rationale for the existence of such a relationship between Portuguese and African in the colonies. However, this was not a particularly attractive rationale. More often the Portuguese tried to tell a different story, saying that, unlike other colonialisms, they were working toward the unified and multiracial society of the future. In fact, this became a part of the whole myth of imperial destiny which played so prominent a part in Portuguese rhetoric; it also informed the doctrine of "luso-tropicality" developed to prove that the Portuguese had a peculiar vocation for "working with" different races in other corners of the world. Yet, even if it were true that the fanatical extremism on the race question which marks South Africa's ideology of *apartheid* was not quite so prominent in "Portuguese Africa," the Portuguese approach was actually no less insidious. It constituted an ugly paternalism which looked only to the "assimilation" into the Portguese community of those few Africans who could become as much like the Portuguese as possible.

Prior to the 1960s this approach was actually enshrined in law.

An African could become an *"assimilado"* by passing the requi-
site language examination, earning a certain income, paying a fee
(even though no such barriers to citizenship were placed before
the often-illiterate Portuguese settlers coming to Africa). Needless to say, the vast mass of the African population were to be
classified instead as *"indigenatos"*—"natives." In the glare of world
opinion in the sixties, this distinction was quietly dropped, but
the underlying premises remained; the African population was by
definition "uncivilized," their cultures worthless, their aspirations, insofar as they deviated from the desire to become "honor-
ary whites" (in the phrase of FRELIMO's late president, Dr.
Eduardo Mondlane), to be considered aberrant. Moreover, even
if one were to overlook, for the moment, the racist premises
underlying the very notion of assimilation, certain figures were
revealing: by the 1950s the *assimilado* category encompassed only
thirty thousand of the African population in Angola and in
Mozambique five thousand, or .007 percent of the African population! Thus Portuguese colonialism, poverty-stricken as it was,
neither would nor could provide the amount of education necessary to realize even its professed aims of assimilation—let alone
provide the level of literacy and range of skills which would allow
the African population to develop itself. So much for the myth of
multiracialism. So much, too, for those other adjustments of the
1950s and 1960s by means of which the colonies were even more
directly linked to Portugal as "overseas provinces," becoming an
integral part, it was argued, of the Portuguese state. Manipulative
formulae all, continuing evidence of the doomed Portuguese
attempt to have their presence in Africa both ways—privileged
exploiter and helpmate to the African. A much more accurate
indication of their true position vis-à-vis the African population
was, of course, their violent and contemptuous rejection of those
African demands for self-determination which came to the fore
during this same period.

   We return by this route to an earlier question: Why did Portugal, alone of the traditional colonial powers in Africa and
unlike Britain, France, Belgium, and even Spain, grimly hang on
to its colonies against the seeming tide of history and the mounting demands of the people in those colonies? Our analysis

suggests an answer to this query, albeit a complex one. Most important, perhaps, was Portugal's continued economic weakness. Other imperial countries could hope to maintain their powerful voice in the affairs of their former colonies even after the granting of formal political independence. This is the so-called "neocolonial solution" and is best exemplified by the fate of the former French colonies, most of which France continues to dominate to the present day, more than ten years after independence. But, as Minter states, "Such influence depends on economic power; the ability to provide aid; to control enterprises through technicians as well as investment; to maintain good trade relationships by pressure on susceptible governments; to support with open or covert action the removal of governments that prove troublesome." In contrast, it was only its direct hold on the lever of power in the colonies—upon the colonial state—that enabled Portugal to profit from the economic exploitation of Angola, Mozambique, and Guinea—by claiming a percentage of the action, as it were. Even were a "false decolonization" to produce a very pliant and subservient African government in any of these territories, such a government would most likely deal directly with the strongest of economic powers—with South Africa, with the United States, with West Germany, and the like—rather than with Portugal. Under such circumstances, Portugal would be deprived of even those benefits attendant upon the middleman's role which it has claimed for itself. In consequence, the granting of independence seemed a much more costly option to Portugal's rulers than it did for other colonial powers.

In addition, there are other, noneconomic, factors which can be mentioned, the political realities of Portugal for example. That country was, of course, an overtly authoritarian society. In consequence, not only was it difficult to theorize a logic of freedom for the colonies in Black Africa, but also potentially dangerous to consider establishing a democratic precedent there. The Portugese people might then have been encouraged to intensify their parallel demands for self-determination in Portugal itself! There was also a third, cultural-ideological, factor. Authoritarian regimes are particularly in need of myths to legitimize their continuing usurpation of power both to themselves and to others. History decreed that Portugal's myth should be that of empire, "luso-tropicality," and mission. The constant reiteration of such slogans suggests the extent to which they provided a certain glue for the system; they could not, for that very reason, be readily reevaluated by the powers-that-be. It is even possible that some of the rulers had come to believe them themselves!

Of course, the coup in Portugal has since demonstrated the importance of these latter points: the retreat from colonialism did indeed involve a complete overthrow of the Portuguese system domestically. But for a very long time there was little reason to anticipate any such denouement. As the liberation movements developed their critique of colonialism, they saw that the mold of Portuguese colonialism was not about to crack from within in any significant respect. Despite some real costs, the ugly and anachronistic use of systematic violence to shore up racism and colonialism continued in Portugal's African colonies and, from the African perspective, seemed likely to do so until the perpetrators of that violence were forcibly driven from the field. This in turn was the task that the liberation movements in Angola, Mozambique, and Guinea-Bissau reluctantly but resolutely set for themselves.

Unfortunately, it was equally apparent that the liberation movements would have to fight not merely Portugal but also that country's powerful allies. At first, at the outset of the liberation struggles, the pattern was not quite so clear-cut. Thus there were early indications that Western governments, perhaps even South Africa itself, could have swallowed the notion of black governments coming to power in an independent Angola or Mozambique. Indeed, the United States, particularly in the very earliest days of the Kennedy administration, seemed to be actively pressing for decolonization of Portugal's African colonies (this on the then-current assumption that quite moderate and pliable black governments would inherit power, of course). But the intransigence of the Portuguese, analyzed earlier, made any such smooth transition to neocolonialism impossible. It became necessary for the Kennedy team and subsequent administrations to accommodate themselves to Portugal's position and even to cultivate an active partnership with that country. And this arrangement in turn became all the more attractive as the liberation movements themselves were radicalized and developed into much less certain guarantors of some future "false decolonization."

As Minter makes quite clear, the twin pillars of such Western support for Portugal were the existing networks of Western defense, notably the NATO alliance, without which Portugal could not have sustained its expensive military effort on three fronts, *and* the prevailing pattern of trade and investment. The economic link, in particular, merits some further comment here. As noted above, Portugal's position in the imperial hierarchy had granted it the status of a mere "middleman" with respect to Angola, Mozambique, and Guinea. Indeed, the threatened loss of this status was one of the most important reasons for Portugal's reluctance to seek a "neocolonial" solution and to begin the dismantling of the structure of formal colonialism. In so characterizing Portugal as an "imperial middleman" we refer not merely to its ability to earn from the export of African primary products (and African labor) to the outside world. Portugal had also forged a historical partnership with other Western interests in carrying out colonial designs right inside the African territories themselves. This is not surprising when one remembers that foreign capital has dominated a large proportion of the productive sectors of Portugal's own domestic economy. Similarly, from an early date, Portugal "contracted out" a range of colonial economic activities, including numerous large estates in Mozambique—the British-owned Sena Sugar Estate, for example—and Angolan enterprises like the Benguela Railway and the Angolan Diamond Company (Diamang).

To be sure, under Salazar's "New State," Portuguese policy reflected an uneasiness with such a state of affairs; the government actually mounted a vigorous effort to counter these trends by sealing Africa off for Portuguese enterprises, restricting foreign investment (other than that from Portugal!) in the colonies and placing highly restrictive tariffs upon foreign imports. But this attempt did not survive the rise of the African challenge to colonialism. Reversing its position in the early sixties, Portugal encouraged the flow of foreign capital into the African colonies, intending not only to reap economic benefits from the fresh supply of capital and revenues, but also to tie these large foreign companies, and ultimately their home governments, into an even more vigorous defense of the Portuguese position in Africa. "Today the foreign firm is given guarantees . . . better than the potential investor from Portugal itself, such as guarantees for the repatriation of capital, profits and dividends, and customs exemptions on plant and raw materials."[5] To a very late date this tactic worked well. To take but a single example, it was precisely in such realities as the active role of Germany's Krupp empire in the exploitation of Angola's Cassinga iron deposits that one will find the roots of Chancellor Willy Brandt's tortuous pre-coup formulation (trotted out when countering the excessive zeal for liberation expressed by some officials in his own Social Democratic Party): "The Federal Government cannot back the Portuguese point of view that Angola and Mozambique are one indivisible entity with Portugal. However, this is an internal problem of our ally Portugal, a problem which we must not interfere with"!

In agriculture, in mineral extraction, and in the light industrialization of the colonies, one soon saw busily at work a full range of corporations from Western countries, from Japan, and of course from Rhodesia and South Africa (the latter country also being deeply involved in those aforementioned huge and menacing hydroelectric projects—Cunene and Cabora Bassa, in Angola and Mozambique respectively). Most ominous of all, perhaps, was the growing economic involvement of the United States, dramatically exemplified in the absolutely crucial role played by the Gulf Oil Company, which by 1973 was draining off almost 150,000 barrels of oil per day from Cabinda in Angola. Not only were the Portuguese thus furnished with vital revenues, but the white Southern African redoubt as a whole was being given a safe source of potential oil supply for facing down any further sanctions or oil blockade. Moreover, as Minter demonstrates, the involvement of American corporations stretched beyond Gulf to companies such as Bethlehem Steel, which was, at one point, developing concessions right within the battle areas of Mozambique.

It seemed clear that the activities of these corporations provide particularly important reasons why United States' backing for Portugal intensified in recent years. In fact, Richard Barnett, citing this and other evidence of growing American military and economic support for Portugal in a 1972 survey of American policy toward Southern Africa, could conclude that, "The United States (under the rhetoric of containing violence and preventing war) now appears ready to step up its assistance to the minority racist and colonial governments in beating back challenges to their rule."[6] This is also a reality which Minter explores with great care in the postscript to the second edition of *Portuguese Africa and the West.*

Needless to say, it is now clear that this entire structure of domination was much less stable than it sometimes appeared. Minter presents its major weakness clearly—the fact that the liberation movements were too strong to be defeated militarily. This was an insight which General António de Spinola— sometime military governor of Guinea-Bissau (where he master-minded the assassination of Amilcar Cabral) and ultimately an important actor in the post-coup drama in Portugal—came to share, as witnessed in his book, *Portugal and Its Future.* In that volume, published early in 1974, Spinola brought out into the open the military weakness of the Portuguese position, counsel-ing instead a political solution—one which would judiciously Africanize colonialism and manipulate federal formulae to a point where a line against genuine liberation might more easily be held.

It was also apparent that in so arguing, he spoke for a broader constituency. Perhaps it is here—with, to be sure, the benefit of hindsight—that Minter's book can be most easily faulted. For he gives too little sense of the growing contradictions within Por-tugal itself. There a measure of economic development found many important Portuguese trusts increasingly orienting them-selves toward Europe and the EEC, while also regretting the costs to "economic rationality" of an anachronistic fascist system at home and those wasting colonial wars abroad. Not for nothing had Spinola been a director of the powerful Champalimaud group! Simultaneously, social and economic change and a continuing state of war (involving massive conscription) had also undermined the acceptance of their lot by broader masses of the people—one important manifestation of this dissatisfaction being the large-scale migration of workers to neighboring European countries. In these and other ways crucial props for the Portuguese system were being eaten away. When younger officers than Spinola pushed the regime it came toppling down.

Of course, no one could have predicted what was to follow. Spinola, now brought into the junta in order to legitimize the April coup as well as provide a symbol of moderation for Portuguese trusts and Western interests alike, sought to contain the situation. Until his unceremonious departure from power in September, he worked not only to slow down the pace of events at home but also to find the key to a neocolonial solution for Portugal in the colonies. Unfortunately for Spinola, however, a combination of developments—including the further revelation of a radical vocation on the part of the Armed Forces Movement (which had spearheaded the coup) and a release of popular energies beyond anything expected by even the most sanguine observers—confounded these aspirations. None of which is to argue that the situation has permanently clarified itself in Portugal. There a struggle is certainly ongoing. What does seem to have happened, however, is that breathing space has been created by progressive forces, sufficient to lift the dead hand of Portugal from Africa once and for all. As a result, in September 1974 Guinea's independence was recognized—*by the Portuguese* —and plans were soon afoot to facilitate the transfer of power in the Cape Verde Islands as well. That same month, Mozambique under the Frenté da Libertacão de Moçambique (FRELIMO) began the transition to its own promised independence on June 25, 1975. More recently, a settlement has been reached in Angola, with November 11, 1975, named as the date for the final transfer of power. *Sic transit* Portugal.

Not so Portugal's erstwhile allies! The NATO powers, the multinational corporations, South Africa (all so well described by Minter)—these continue to hover close to the scene. It can be assumed that the extreme nature of the denouement of the Portuguese coup—an unpredictable and accelerated pattern of change domestically, a remarkably unequivocal decolonization in Africa—has caught all of them off guard. Dramatic departures emerged so quickly and from such unpredictable quarters—from within the army, for example—that there was at first relatively little that could be done to affect the direction of events. Instead, these Western sponsors and Southern African allies would have to live with the changes and, as the dust settled, attempt to tame them. Moreover, in so doing they could have some degree of confidence. It is only necessary to remind ourselves of Portugal's role as imperial middleman. With Portugal out of the game, such forces will merely bring their undoubted power to bear more directly, if still quite subtly. Portugal, in the person of General Spinola, has been denied a neocolonial solution; that country's former sponsors will now try their hand.

The key to such an attempt is also clear from our earlier discussion. It is precisely the crippling imprint of Portugal's bankrupt colonialism upon the economies and social structures of the former colonies which now threatens to impede the logical extension of those colonies' revolution-in-the-making. For example, Pretoria can hope that the "spontaneous" tendencies of a Mozambican economy warped, as we have seen, by the Portuguese to service South Africa's needs will lock the new country into a position of subservience.[7] Similarly, the multinationals (and such subimperial potentates—General Mobutu, for example —as they have also created in the area) will seek to use their powerful purchase on the Angolan economy to bend any post-colonial government to their will.[8] Undoubtedly the ground for such results has been well prepared by five hundred years of "ultra-colonialism." Nonetheless, this is not the whole story by any means. "Ultra-colonialism" has had a second legacy, already hinted at: the creation of *strong, popular, ideologically advanced* liberation movements, movements which have defeated the Portuguese and which alone provide some firm prospect of preempting a neocolonial anticlimax in "Portugal's African colonies." It is to these movements that we must now turn our attention.

II

The history of African resistance to the imposition of Portuguese rule is as old as the history of that rule itself. We have already cited the fierce initial resistance offered by the African population in many parts of the three colonies and noted just how recently it is that Portugal can be said to have "pacified" all the peoples involved. As Minter observes in his book, "The history of the wars of resistance . . . is hardly more than two generations removed from the present liberation movements, and the memories are alive today." Yet these exemplary struggles in the past did remain localized, defining themselves in regional or tribal terms. The significance of contemporary liberation movements has been the new sense of territory-wide nationalism which they represent.

The immediate protagonists of this new nationalism were men and women of the cities, employed nearer the center of the colonial system and often possessing some minimal formal education (yielded, albeit grudgingly, by colonialism). In this situation they were better able to perceive the overall nature of that system and to understand the means necessary for challenging it. At first their mode of challenge tended to be cultural, vaguely reformist, even elitist, only gradually taking on a more effective and broadly political expression as the pace of change in the rest of the continent picked up and as the full meaning of colonialism was more clearly graspsed. But demands for reform were scotched by the Portuguese much more ruthlessly than by other colonial powers. Moreover, when pressure for change from the broad mass of the population also began to surface, the Portuguese response was even more brutal. In Guinea, at Pijiguiti in 1959, fifty striking dock-workers were shot down by the Portuguese; at Mueda in northern Mozambique in 1960, six hundred Africans were killed while peacefully protesting Portuguese handling of agricultural matters; the same year in Angola, at the village of Catete, two hundred were killed or wounded while demonstrating peacefully against the arrest, public flogging and imprisonment of Dr. Agostinho Neto, the prominent nationalist leader. This was precisely the point in the history of other colonialisms when the imperial power usually chose to negotiate with the spokesmen of nationalism—gambling, in part, on the elitism of these same spokesmen to restrain any radicalization of nationalism and intending to co-opt them into a smoothly functioning system of continuing economic dependence. However, we have seen that the possibility of such a response was not open to the Portuguese. Turning a deaf ear to peaceful protest, the Portuguese chose instead to perpetuate and intensify the violence of their colonial presence. They thus forced the Africans to take up arms to bring that presence to an end.

Here Basil Davidson's brilliant account (in his *In the Eye of the Storm: Angola's People*) of the emergence of such a struggle in Angola—an account which blends in its writing profound historical depth with on-the-spot immediacy—is required reading. He recounts clearly the manner in which this festering colonial condition first exploded in Angola. The Popular Movement for the Liberation of Angola (MPLA) had been organized as a nationalist movement in 1956, but was driven underground by general harassment and by the actions of PIDE, the Portuguese political police. However, in early 1961 a series of dramatic events brought the Angolan struggle to the attention of the world. Resistance to enforced cotton growing in Kasanje led to "Maria's War"—overt action by peasants in the area. At about the same time, MPLA attempted to free political prisoners being held in Luanda, the capital. The Portuguese response to the February initiatives, and to a rebellion in northern Angola launched by the União de Populacões de Angola (UPA) a month later, was particularly ruthless. It has been estimated that some thirty thousand to fifty thousand Africans died in the savage Portuguese "pacification" program which followed these events. Yet at this stage, as in the past, the African challenge was still largely spontaneous and localized. The mounting of coordinated and effective guerrilla warfare was to take more time and face real setbacks.

At first the UPA, soon to form a government-in-exile (GRAE) and ultimately to change its own name (to FNLA), seemed the most active agent of Angolan nationalism and continued for a time to have a marginal guerrilla presence in the north. But, as Davidson shows, its strength was sapped by the opportunistic leadership of Holden Roberto, by too close ties to Mobutu's Congo (and hence, it would seem, to American influence) and too narrow an identification with a particular ethnic base, the Bakongo people. The União para la Independencia Total de Angola (UNITA), a third movement, which emerged with Jonas

Savimbi's splitting away from UPA in 1964, professed readiness to launch a struggle in eastern Angola which would be more closely linked to popular aspirations and popular participation. The extent of its actual success to date remains a matter of controversy, although Davidson's conclusion that, at best, it had remained very small and had been effectively stalemated up to the time of the coup seems a sound one. However, both movements lingered on—to become much more active and salient protagonists in the complicated post-coup situation.

Of far greater significance was MPLA itself, which finally did begin to regroup itself and demonstrate renewed strength. At first it concentrated its activities on the small enclave of Cabinda because of the difficulties of linking up, via an unfriendly Congo, with those of its units which continued to operate in the Dembos forest north of Luanda or, clandestinely, in Luanda itself. Logistically, therefore, Zambia's independence in 1964 was a key development and meant both that preliminary political mobilization of the people could begin in the eastern regions of the country and that fully effective guerrilla warfare could be launched in Moxico district in 1966. From there the struggle was to be pushed into ten of Angola's fifteen districts, with MPLA managing to withstand general offensives launched by the Portuguese in 1968 and subsequently. As a result, Basil Davidson could conclude in 1970 that while "the guerillas have formidable problems still ahead: in military reorganization, in logistics across huge but widening distances, in building mass support in the central and western districts . . . yet they are moving on. Steadily, if slowly, they are 'marching to the Atlantic.' Already . . . they are west of the Cuanza river, pushing deeply into the 'colonial heartlands' of the Portuguese."[9] It is true, as we shall see, that even after 1970 difficulties continued to plague MPLA, and determined that its advances would be less dramatic than those achieved in Guinea-Bissau and in Mozambique. Nonetheless, despite the Portuguese deployment of some sixty thousand troops, a significant proportion of the country had been liberated prior to the coup—and the struggle was advancing.

The Partido Africano da Independencia da Guiné e Cabo Verdé (PAIGC), organized in 1956 under the brilliant leadership of Amilcar Cabral, a Cape Verdean trained as an agronomist in Lisbon, and drawing on the support of urban workers and *assimilados* in Bissau (the capital), also learned its lesson from the results of peaceful protest—at Pijiguiti and elsewhere—and moved toward armed struggle. Profiting from the Angolan experience, the PAIGC chose to prepare carefully for military action by first developing an efficient organization, mobilizing popular support through clandestine political work, and establishing firm international contacts. When guerrilla action began in 1963 with the opening up of fronts in the south and the north, the situation was ripe; by 1965 half of Guinea could be considered part of the liberated area. In 1966, despite the increase in Portuguese troops from ten thousand to twenty-five thousand (to rise to eighty-five thousand in the 1970s), a third front was opened in the east. Even within earshot of the capital, armed attacks began to occur, and by 1973 the guerrillas had obtained control of *80 percent of the territory*.

The Portuguese continued for some time to command the air, often with devastating effect, and could maintain fortified towns and bases. In the last years of the war, however, even this began to change as the military capability of PAIGC was strengthened further through the introduction of more autonomous regional commands, the promotion of many junior officers, and the acquisition of important new weapons. During a period of six months in 1973, PAIGC shot down more than twenty-five planes. With local peasant militias (FAL) established to defend the liberated areas, the regular army (FARP) was able to tighten its ring around many of the fortified bases (bases which had served in the past as launching pads for counterinsurgency patrols and as overseers of *aldeamentos*—strategic hamlets), and to occupy such large centers as Guiledje, abandoned by the Portuguese in May 1973 after a long siege and the ambush of supply convoys. By then, PAIGC could itself move more freely, with heavy vehicles in some cases, and even attack the towns still held by the Portuguese. Thus, when Guinea-Bissau declared its national independence on September 24, 1973, it did so from a position of considerable and growing military strength. Here, certainly, was one very important nail in the coffin of the Portuguese.

FRELIMO grew from the same social roots as the other movements and represented at its founding in 1962 a coming together of a number of nationalist organizations primarily operating in exile in neighboring African countries. FRELIMO, under the leadership of Dr. Eduardo Mondlane, a Mozambican who had worked at the United Nations and as a professor of anthropology in the United States before returning to Africa, requested the Portuguese to grant independence. Predictably the Portuguese response was to crack down on African activities, especially in the urban areas. The absolute necessity of military action became perfectly clear, and FRELIMO prepared for this carefully, beginning the fighting on September 25, 1964. Progress in the two northern provinces of Cabo Delgado and Niassa was sufficiently marked by 1968 that FRELIMO was able to launch armed struggle in a third key province, Tete, where once again the Portuguese were slowly but surely driven back.

Thus, by 1972 Cabo Delgado and Niassa were liberated areas, except for a few posts, towns, and concentrations of strategic hamlets. The same was true for much of Tete, where FRELIMO soon breached the natural barrier of the Zambezi River, previously a major factor in Portuguese strategic thinking, and where guerrillas began to harass effectively transportation into the area of the Cabora Bassa dam site. Both 1972 and 1973 provided even more dramatic evidence of progress. For in mid-1972 FRELIMO announced the opening of a front in the strategic and densely populated province of Manica e Sofala in the very heart of Mozambique. Soon the war hovered close to the important port of Beira and brought successful assaults upon Rhodesia's road and rail links to the sea; there were also attacks on the pylons and transmission lines designed to carry Cabora Bassa power to the south.

Equally impressive, and paralleling the Guinean situation, was the increased ability of FRELIMO to carry the fighting directly to the Portuguese in their fortified bases. Mid-September 1972 saw a raid, involving use of 122-millimeter rockets, on Mueda airstrip which destroyed nineteen planes, and also saw a growing number of direct attacks on military posts in Cabo Delgado province and elsewhere. In Tete province, Chingozi airbase near Tete town suffered a similar attack, seventeen aircraft being destroyed. And in June 1973, only weeks after General Kaulza da Arriaga (then commander-in-chief for Mozambique) had assured his men that the Cabora Bassa zone was impenetrable, FRELIMO attacked Chitima, the command center for Portuguese forces guarding Cabora Bassa. In desperation during this period, the Portuguese turned, as they had in Guinea-Bissau and Angola, to strategic-hamlet campaigns, to fruitless "great offensives" (involving the use of massive bombing, napalm, herbicides, and other artifacts of counterinsurgency) and, concomitantly, to the grossest kind of intimidation of the African population. Witness the massacre at Wiriyamu in December 1972—the essentials of the story so brazenly questioned by much of the North American press at the time but now admitted to by the Portuguese themselves. Yet all such attempts failed. Fully one-quarter of the country could be said to have been effectively liberated by the time of the coup. Moreover, it was FRELIMO's dramatic drive farther south, from 1972, which, above all other factors, sapped the will of the Portuguese soldiers to continue their wars.

In sum, the military picture became one of an increasingly successful challenge to Portuguese military rule. However, it would be misleading to leave the discussion of the liberation movements at this point; developments in the political and socioeconomic spheres were of at least equal importance, and in fact help furnish an explanation for the degree of military success which could be achieved. Though this is a complex story, it is nonetheless one which must be sketched out here, however superficially, in order that the nature of the revolutions which have been taking place in Portugal's African colonies be better understood.[10]

Politically, an instructive point of departure is a comparison with the pattern which has emerged in much of independent Africa. As President Nyerere of Tanzania, the most insightful of postindependence leaders, has argued, the nationalism which won independence in Africa in the 1950s and 1960s was in some senses a superficial accomplishment. In its aftermath, the leaders too easily entrenched themselves as a new privileged class, and the masses of Africans too easily lapsed back into apathy and cynicism. To obtain "real freedom" in all spheres of life, and to claim control over the productive forces (in Cabral's phrase), some form of "socialism" is required; at the very least, "to build . . . real freedom" there must be "a positive understanding and positive actions, not simply a rejection of colonialism and a willingness to cooperate in non-cooperation."[11] In Nyerere's Tanzania this kind of self-criticism had led to a real attempt in the postcolonial period to move beyond a superficial kind of nationalism to a more revolutionary version of it, a version which emphasizes genuine "self-reliance" and attempts to express and to meet the real needs of the vast majority of the population. The striking feature of the kind of struggle which the people were forced to fight in Angola, Mozambique, and Guinea was that such a struggle had already begun to reshape the conventional pattern of African nationalism, dictating, *in the nationalist phase itself*, an attempt to restructure social, economic, and political relationships in a fundamental way.

Inevitably, some of the nationalists who emerged in Angola, Mozambique, and Guinea favored the familiar pattern. Conservatively, they were prepared to pursue their own privileges as actively as they pursued independence, and to play down the importance of mass involvement, using vague appeals which asked no basic questions about the nature of the society which was to be brought into being. Unfortunately for them, in the context of a genuine liberation struggle this kind of nationalism *did not work* as it had for African leadership groups elsewhere on the continent. For a successful liberation struggle required that the energies of all the people be released in a new way. For example, the freedom fighters have had to rely on the peasants as active partners in the struggle—to protect them, to help in carriage and supply of produce, and to serve as a popular militia. Obviously, these duties have required more from the people than "a rejection of colonialism, and a willingness to cooperate in non-cooperation." Instead, they demand "a positive understanding and positive actions," a level of popular consciousness and commitment which is unlikely to emerge unless the leadership has forged a closer, more effective link with the broad mass of the people fighting for their liberation.

For these reasons, genuinely democratic methods of political work were necessary to close any possible gap between leaders and people. The entirely new programs and institutions in the spheres of health, education, production, and trade which developed in the liberated areas to service the peoples' needs and aspirations may also be cited in this connection. In launching such novel activities, crucial choices were being forced upon the movement, choices which ultimately came to feed the further democratization and radicalization of their struggles. Thus new patterns of education had to be developed which attack elitism and preempt privilege as effectively as they communicate skills; similarly, the collective practices which are emphasized increasingly in the economic sphere—marketing, distribution, production—serve not merely to pool popular energies but also to combat any temptation toward entrepreneurial aggrandizement on the part of the leadership. Nor is it accidental that within this overall process many of the hard problems of liberating women from the bonds forged by tradition and by colonialism were being confronted in a striking manner. And that concerted and quite self-conscious efforts to transform other aspects of traditional cultures were also in train in order to meet the requirements of a new society, without, however, entirely denaturing those cultures.

Here it is essential to stress that these emphases were very far from being mere theorizing: the concrete record of accomplishment on the ground was an extraordinarily impressive one. Though a number of other first-hand accounts might also be cited, it is with respect to these realities that Barbara Cornwall's book, *Bush Rebels*, makes its greatest contribution. Writing in a highly personal vein, she does capture something important, too, about the impressive quality of the FRELIMO and PAIGC cadres who are leading that transformation. Certainly her account of visits to the liberated areas of Mozambique and Guinea-Bissau at a relatively early date (1968) squares well with my own experience of a similar trip to the liberated areas of Tete province, Mozambique, with FRELIMO in 1972.[12] Perhaps the book hovers a bit uneasily between being a memoir and being an analytical account, but the sense of new societies building institutions responsive, for the first time in many generations, to the needs and desires of the people themselves is nicely communicated.

In addition, as I had occasion to note during my own trip, the continuing confrontation also meant that the leadership as well as the people had a greater opportunity to become aware of the complicated network of external forces which locked Portuguese hegemony into place; the crystallization of a much more meaningful anti-imperialist ideology was a result. This gain, like the others mentioned above, is significant. In these varied ways, in fact, the knot of neocolonialism and underdevelopment was being untied at a very early stage in "Portugal's African colonies." Consequently, it was not merely a fight for independence that was under way there, but a genuine revolution, a revolution full of great promise for post-liberation society in the ex-Portuguese territories.

Such a pattern of development had one tremendously important corollary: the creation of some degree of tension within the African nationalist camp itself. Davidson summarizes this point succinctly in his book: "There is a general rule by which all movements of resistance produce and deepen conflicts within themselves as the reformists draw back from the revolutionaries and, in drawing back, fall victim to the game of the enemy regime." Thus movements like PAIGC, FRELIMO, and MPLA were, in reality, two entities for much of the early period of their existence: a conventional nationalist movement unable to secure an easy transition to power, and a revolutionary movement, struggling to be born. Concretely, this dichotomy found its expression in a struggle within the leadership—with those prepared and those not prepared to make the transition to revolutionary practice increasingly pitted against one another. As the struggle developed, the broader mass of the people also came to be arbiters of this conflict, in defense of their own interests and in the interests of genuine change. It was, in fact, this "logic" of the struggle in Portugal's African colonies which could be seen to be working itself out and making the process of radicalization a cumulative one.

The result of this process in Guinea was the success of the

PAIGC and the crystallization of a revolutionary line of development. Cabral's assassination by Portuguese-sponsored infiltrators of the movement did demonstrate some of the dangers which continue to plague a guerrilla force during the transition period and under pressure from the colonial power. However, it was the smooth transition to a new leadership—Aristide Pereira as secretary-general of PAIGC and, more recently, Luis Cabral as president of the new Council of State—and the continuing strength of the post-Cabral PAIGC which became its most striking feature, a fact confirmed by the aforementioned proclamation of an independent Guinea in September 1973. We have noted the military basis of this proclamation; its political basis is of at least equal importance. Thus, twelve years of patient work by PAIGC in the rural areas of the country organizing village and sector committees to manage local affairs had resulted in the emergence of a viable nationwide system of popularly elected Regional Assemblies, a system which now culminates in a National Assembly. In 1972, PAIGC sector committees registered about 58,000 voters, and the series of elections which followed produced the popular representatives to the National Assembly. It was these representatives, sitting in the Assembly alongside a minority of members nominated directly by PAIGC, who then adopted a constitution, elected a Council of State, and proceeded to declare Guinea-Bissau an independent and sovereign republic. The fact that this republic was soon recognized by over eighty other countries was an indication of the importance of this development, and in retrospect can be seen as a crucial step forward in the further isolation of Portugal.

Guinea-Bissau, independent on this basis and under the leadership of PAIGC, is obviously no ready candidate to partake of a "neocolonial solution." The same is true of FRELIMO in Mozambique, though the latter movement has come to such a position of strength and clarity with somewhat more difficulty. Thus some unsympathetic observers—like Richard Gibson in his tendentious and misleading volume *African Liberation Movements*—saw signs of weakness in the fierce infighting within FRELIMO in the period both before and after Eduardo Mondlane's assassination by the Portuguese (in 1969). In fact, this was precisely the period when the most progressive of the FRELIMO leadership consolidated their position, finding their base in the new reality of the liberated areas and in their ability to move with the radicalizing logic of a genuinely popular struggle. There were opportunist elements in FRELIMO (like the movement's onetime vice-president, Uriah Simango) who harbored elitist or entrepreneurial ambitions, who feared the people and who manipulated regional, tribal, and racial slogans to advance their own interests. But they found themselves isolated, soon to drop away from active struggle or even to pass over to the side of the Portuguese. As a result, subsequent meetings of the movement's central committee and other bodies were able to devote their full attention to the more positive tasks of laying down plans for the future with significance both for the quality of life in the liberated areas and now for the shape of a free Mozambique. It is readily apparent that FRELIMO, under the leadership of its new president Samora Machel, had developed in practice a most revolutionary form of nationalism.[13]

As noted, it was precisely the kinds of tension attendant upon the transition to revolutionary nationalism which Richard Gibson has chosen to concentrate upon in his book—and willfully to misinterpret. For his picture of FRELIMO is an entirely fabricated one, made up of "feuding, restive troops," of "exaggerated war claims," of justifiably "irate students" (Gibson here ignoring Father Gwenjere's crude attempts to manipulate racist and elitist sentiments at the Mozambique Institute during the period of FRELIMO's crisis), and of an "incredible tendency to settle inner-party squabbles in blood" (Gibson here relying almost exclusively for "evidence" on the desperate accusations of that archreactionary Uriah Simango at the time of the latter's expulsion from the movement). One gets little sense of the realities which would eventually find Gwenjere and Simango surfacing in Mozambique to support the abortive white-led counterrevolutionary coup in September 1974, a coup designed to reverse the granting of Mozambican independence. Yet such a denouement for these men's careers was fully predictable from their opportunistic actions at the time of the struggles within FRELIMO, important struggles the significance of which Gibson entirely fails to document or to explain.

In a similar vein, COREMO (a virtually nonexistent Mozambican "liberation movement") is propped up—like other similarly shadowy movements in other territories—for the reader by Gibson as some vague kind of alternative to FRELIMO, while hints are dropped from time to time that the latter movement is, in any case, merely a subservient wing of the African National Congress of South Africa—and hence of Moscow! Worse yet, Gibson's chapter on FRELIMO is of a piece with his misleading accounts of liberation movements elsewhere in Africa. Throughout, a pseudo-Maoist perspective is adopted in order to legitimize the presentation of scurrilous rumor after scurrilous rumor, all serving to *denigrate* the African side of the struggles in Southern Africa. After all, academics might ask, would a "Maoist" purposely attempt to make the liberation movements look bad? *Ergo*, his charges must be true—the more outrageous the better. But why continue? It would be tedious to document the case against Gibson further. One might better query why one bothers at all with such a book—even if it does bear the imprint of Oxford University Press. Perhaps it is because many Africanists—who should know better—continue to treat the volume as a reputable source.

Building his analysis on such flimsy foundations, Gibson could conclude his account of the Mozambican situation at the end of 1971 by stating that "as 1971 passed, COREMO was unable to repeat this success, and with the continuing debility of FRELIMO, it was nevertheless obvious there existed no more constant or immediate threats to the Portuguese than those created by their own contradictions!" No benefit of hindsight is necessary here; any close and honest observer of the Southern African scene would have known, *at the time*, that such a conclusion was laughable. Subsequent events have only made it seem the more so. We have mentioned the fact that FRELIMO's continued and growing strength helped bring about the coup in Portugal. It must also be stressed that the irresistible force of FRELIMO—and of PAIGC in Guinea-Bissau—were equally crucial factors in the post-coup period. For the Spinola faction within the

Portuguese junta worked vigorously to facilitate that "false de-colonization" conceptualized in the general's famous book. Soon various compromise formulae were being offered to the movements—Portuguese-supervised elections, various forms of cooperative coalitions, and the like. Yet the liberation movements never lost sight of the fact that they were now playing from strength, with a base for further military operations, if necessary, in the liberated areas, and with obvious manifestations of popular support breaking out everywhere in the country, including in the larger towns and cities. Their demand: unequivocal recognition of their independence. Their principled position was a particularly crucial challenge to Spinola; he had no real answer to the colonial question. The continued pressure of the liberation movement thus combined with factors mentioned earlier—with the further radicalization of the Armed Forces Movement and with the dramatic release of popular energies in Portugal—to sweep the general aside. The way was then open for genuine negotiations, for Mozambique's political independence—and, eventually, for carrying out the further revolutionary task of reshaping those cruelly twisted socioeconomic structures which are Portugal's chief legacy in Africa.

Unfortunately, as hinted earlier, the Angolan picture has been much more complicated, marred by a degree of factionalism and intrigue on the African side vastly more disruptive than in Mozambique and Guinea. Nor does Gibson, for all his fascination with any hint of divisiveness, shed much light on this phenomenon where, in Angola, it has surfaced significantly; he is much too preoccupied with explaining away MPLA as some mere expression of Moscovite maneuverings and with validating UNITA's slender claim (based, it would seem, on an occasional rhetorical flourish) to Maoist orthodoxy. At the same time, it is precisely here that one must also express certain misgivings about Davidson's own account of Angolan developments. He does, of course, trace in an exemplary manner the early struggles—even more harrowing than those which racked FRELIMO in Mozambique—to forge a revolutionary direction for MPLA, and dates the "Conference of Cadres" held by the movement in 1964 as the point at which President Agostinho Neto began to point the way forward to the consolidation and radicalization of the movement and of the new Angola which has since begun to take shape in the liberated areas.

He is also determined not to gloss over many of the difficulties which have since confronted MPLA, particularly the problem of gaining military access to the economically strategic and populous northern and central regions of Angola, via Zaire; as already noted, Zaire's President Mobutu has chosen to favor Holden Roberto's FNLA, a conservative and militarily passive movement which has often played upon ethnic tensions to retain even a semblance of support. This much is clear. However, the ground is less adequately prepared by Davidson for understanding the divisions which *reemerged* to disrupt MPLA itself in 1973 and 1974 when, most notably, Daniel Chipenda, military leader and second-in-command, made a damaging bid for power, attempting in his turn to manipulate tribal (Ovimbundu) consciousness as a building block for his own aggrandizement. It is apparent, at least in retrospect, that MPLA—operating, admittedly, in a harsher geographical and socioeconomic setting than its counterparts in Guinea-Bissau and Mozambique—had not altogether succeeded in finding the political keys to revolutionary success.

Davidson's overall emphasis is sound, nonetheless. MPLA, having fended off Chipenda's challenge and continuing under the leadership of Dr. Neto, remains the only real vector for comprehensive and meaningful change in Angola. Certainly General Spinola was under no misapprehensions in this regard, and as long as he remained a significant factor in the post-coup decolonization equation, he worked to isolate MPLA and advance its rival movements. This was a reality presented clearly by no less respectable a source than London's *Sunday Times* when it summarized Angolan developments—including an important secret meeting between Mobutu and Spinola, held on the island of Sal shortly before the latter's fall from office—as follows:

> When Roberto announced his ceasefire on Tuesday from Kinshasa . . . the Portuguese governor's offices in Luanda applauded the news. . . . He added that everything now favoured the opening of

official missions by the various liberation movements in Luanda—
with the exception of the MPLA and "in particular its Agostinho
Neto faction."

Nobody will be more pleased by this outcome than the Western
oil executives who are beginning to see the prospects of huge profits
from Angola. So long as MPLA had a chance of becoming the
dominant liberation movement, the oil companies had good reason
to be worried. In February MPLA had warned them that when
Angola became independent "all these companies will be chased
from our national territory and all their equipment and assets
seized."

Spinola's elaborate courtship with Mobutu, Roberto and Savimbi
has made Angola safe for capitalism—for the moment. And the new
Lisbon junta has not allowed its more left-wing domestic policies to
stand in the way of the "spirit of Sal."[14]

In any event, further radicalization in Portugal did work, ultimately, to change the Portuguese input. With the temporary
appointment of Admiral Rosa Coutinho—the "Red Admiral"—to
replace the abovementioned governor in Angola, MPLA was
brought firmly back into the picture, if only as one movement
among three coequals. Interestingly, Coutinho in a recent interview has presented a particularly clear picture of what is at stake
in the inevitable jockeying for position which must follow from
such a situation.[15] For him, FNLA can be seen to be a movement
of the right and the one with the closest ties to large-scale international capital. UNITA, closer to the center of the spectrum, is the
movement with closest ties to local, especially Portuguese-settler,
capital (a very large and politically active settler population being
another distortion in the social structure left behind by the Portuguese). And MPLA, with its progressive ideas and working-class
base, Coutinho sees to be very much the party of the left. Note
the emphasis: Here factionalism is interpreted without illusion—
as being in large measure the manifestation of external interests
introduced by colonialism and now anxious to divide and rule in
order to reduce the lowest common denominator of postcolonial
politics to a very manageable minimum.

Reinforcing this general pattern are other closely related and
cumulatively damaging effects which spring from the existence of

FNLA and UNITA—the politicization of ethnicity, for example. Thus FNLA will certainly continue to fan the flames of Bakongo ethnic consciousness, while Savimbi seems already to have made great headway in post-coup politics by presenting himself as the champion of the Ovimbundu.[16] Of course, it remains true that these and other problems have not forestalled the recent forging of an alliance between the three movements, an alliance which has proven sufficient to facilitate negotiations with the Portuguese and to guarantee the creation of a transitional government united at least until the time of elections immediately prior to independence day (November 11). Yet the fact remains that not far beneath the surface of this alliance lurk many of the features of a classic neocolonial syndrome. In consequence, concerned observers will want to watch the further evolution of the Angolan situation with great care. It remains to be seen whether MPLA—in a political context very different from the forcing-house of guerrilla struggle—can move to reactivate the Angolan revolution and thus fulfill the broader promise of its anticolonial struggle. In Angola, especially, *a luta continua*—the struggle continues.

This, then, is the essential backdrop to the current conjuncture in Portugal's former colonies: A revolutionary nationalism which has broken through the barrier of Portuguese "ultra-colonialism" now stands poised to confront the more subtle dangers of a threatened neocolonialism. In Guinea-Bissau and Mozambique the strength and sense of direction of PAIGC and FRELIMO greatly enhance the prospects of those countries' carrying the struggle forward with success into the postcolonial era, while in Angola the situation is much more hazardous, the continued "negation of the historical process of the dominated peoples" by imperialism (in Cabral's phrase) representing a very real danger which cannot be ignored. To attempt any more precise predictions at this point would, of course, be foolhardy. But something of the drama of the continuing stuggles in soon-to-be-independent "Portuguese Africa" may be grasped by so posing the issues involved.

Very specific predictions are unlikely to be much more rewarding with reference to the rest of white-ruled Southern Africa. Nonetheless, here too a few general comments may be in order. Lenin once remarked that these are places and periods where history seems to move forward with seven-league boots. Clearly, the breakthrough in Portuguese Africa exemplifies the existence of just such a period in Southern Africa. First to feel the true magnitude of the change is Zimbabwe/Rhodesia. Having faced, over the past few years, its first really damaging military challenge from the African population, and now much more uncategorically vulnerable with a free and unfriendly Mozambique along its flank, the illegal Smith regime has come to seem an increasingly bad bet even to its South African supporters. Recent events suggest that the latter are prepared to pull the rug out from under Smith and company—to attempt to buy time by making a deal with black Africa at the expense of the Rhodesian settlers. Yet it will be difficult for the South Africans to draw the line there. Its own illegal hold upon Namibia is also coming under increasingly effective fire from within that territory and in the international arena. And even at home there have been more signs of ferment in the past few years—among workers, among students, in the bantustans—than for some time previously. A revolution has come not merely to Portuguese Africa but to all of Southern Africa.

Let us return by this route to our introductory paragraph. Perhaps, in the wake of the dramatic developments which have been traced in the essay, it will be more difficult for Canadian "Africanists" to patronize and to ignore the Davidsons, the Minters, and the Cornwalls who will continue to chronicle this ongoing revolution. Perhaps we will see fewer reviews like that by one significantly misinformed Canadian Africanist who once praised Gibson's volume (in *African Affairs*) as a "timely and lucid monograph" and who then proceeded to take at face value such Gibsonesque propositions as the "fact" that conflicts within the movements "explain the protracted nature of the liberation struggle" or that movements like GRAE and COREMO (by name) are to be considered "more radical and self-reliant transnational groupings" than MPLA and FRELIMO! At the same time, it should not be considered adequate merely to *understand* the situation more clearly. The struggles in Southern Africa deserve *active support* in their own right. Moreover, Canada's record in that part of the world leaves much to be desired, our occasional pious pronouncements being completely undercut by our economic, military, and diplomatic links to the side of the white regime; such a situation calls for *active resistance*.[17] But how many Africanists—all of whom, the present writer included, have carved lucrative careers for themselves out of Africa like so many latter-day Henry Morton Stanleys—can be expected to so engage themselves in significant action in support of African freedom? Past experience suggests that, initially, their number will be small. Even in Canada, however, the struggle continues.

Notes

1. Perry Anderson, "Portugal and the End of Ultra-Colonialism," *New Left Review*, nos. 15–17 (1962), Part II, p. 92.
2. Ruth First, *Portugal's Wars in Africa* (London: International Defense and Aid, 1971), p. 2.
3. Anderson, "Portugal and the End of Ultra-Colonialism," p. 97.
4. Amilcar Cabral, "The Weapon of Theory," in *Revolution in Guinea* (London, 1969 and New York, 1972).
5. First, *Portugal's Wars in Africa*, p. 26.
6. Richard Barnett, "Nixon's Plan to Save the World," *New York Review of Books*, November 16, 1972.
7. Of course, there have been other, even more immediate, costs of the Portuguese presence in Mozambique which bear noting. Thus, at the time of writing, the transitional government is faced with something approximating a famine in parts of Cabo Delgado province—precisely where Portugal's retaliatory raids and strategic-hamlet programs had been most intense during the war years!
8. Significantly, these realities are not lost on Portugal's new leaders. In an interview in December 1974, Portugal's minister of foreign affairs, Mário Soares, noted that "in small countries like ours, which are still in the beginning of development, the multinationals tend to be a model of economic colonialism. We have dissociated ourselves from colonialism; we absolutely do not want to contribute in any way to the creation of other forms of colonialism and abuse. In fact we were a colonial power that in turn was colonized by the multinationals, operating predominantly in the Portuguese overseas territories. The fruits of the immense riches of Angola and Mozambique were not for Portugal, but served to enlarge the profits of the multinationals,

which had an interest in the existence of colonial rule." See *La Stampa*, December 3, 1974, translated in *Facts and Reports*, 4, no. 26 (December 21, 1974).

9. Basil Davidson, "Angola," in *The Spokesman* (London), December 1970, p. 17.

10. The following argument draws upon the more detailed presentation in my essay, "FRELIMO and the Mozambique Revolution," *Monthly Review* (March 1973) and reprinted as ch. 8 in Giovanni Arrighi and John S. Saul, *Essays on the Political Economy of Africa* (New York, 1973).

11. Julius Nyerere, "Introduction" to his *Freedom and Socialism* (London, New York, and Dar es Salaam, 1968), p. 29. Of related interest is the distinction between "revolutionary nationalism" and conventional nationalism developed by FRELIMO vice-president Marcellino dos Santos in an interview entitled "FRELIMO Faces the Future," *The African Communist*, no. 55 (1973); see also the speeches of Samora Machel, FRELIMO's president, collected in Samora Machel, *Mozambique: Sowing the Seeds of Liberation* (London, 1974).

12. An account of my trip was published in *Monthly Review* (September 1974) and reprinted as essay 2 below.

13. My own detailed account of this period of FRELIMO's development, written, it would seem, only shortly after Gibson's, appears in the article cited in note 10.

14. "Angola: The Carve-up of Africa's El Dorado," *Sunday Times* (London), October 20, 1974.

15. Interview with Rosa Coutinho in *El Moudjahid* (Algiers), December 17, 1974.

16. There are even some additional "movements" which have surfaced in the post-coup period in Angola and which may yet cause damage—FLEC, a seperatist movement in the oil-rich Cabinda enclave, for example. Rumored to be working in collusion with Gulf Oil and possibly General Mobutu, this group has been demobilized, at least for the time being, by MPLA and the Portuguese. And Chipenda himself has surfaced with a handful of followers, first in Zaire, under the protection of Mobutu, and more recently in Luanda. See also essay 4 in this volume.

17. For an introduction to the theme of Canadian complicity in Southern Africa see my *Canada and Mozambique* (Toronto, 1974), or contact the Toronto Committee for the Liberation of Southern Africa (TCLSAC), 121 Avenue Road, Toronto. See also Cranford Pratt, "Canadian Attitudes Towards Southern Africa: A Commentary," *International Perspectives* (November–December 1974), p. 38, and essay 6 in this volume.

2

INSIDE MOZAMBIQUE

Bourgeois commentators have taken to writing smugly of "the myth of the guerrilla."[1] Yet guerrillas in Mozambique (together with their counterparts in Angola and the independent Republic of Guinea-Bissau) have now brought down the Portuguese government! President Kaunda welcomed Samora Machel, president of the Front for the Liberation of Mozambique (FRELIMO), to Zambia (where the latter had come in June to commence talks with Mário Soares, the new Portuguese foreign minister) by stating: "Without the FRELIMO fighters led by Comrade Samora on this continent, Portugal herself would still be under a dictatorship. Freedom fighters on this continent have also freed the people of Portugal."

This was no overstatement. General (now President) António de Spinola's own book, *Portugal and the Future*, first placed the fact that Portugal had no hope of winning a military victory in its colonial wars firmly on the public record. A strong assertion, coming from a man who had won his considerable fame as a ruthless and efficient (though not markedly successful) commander in Africa. Moreover, the spectre of military defeat was a major theme which underlay the coup itself and which continues to underlie the actions of the Armed Forces Movement in Portugal to the present.

Not that the struggle for the independence of "Portuguese

This essay was first published as "Portugal and the Mozambican Revolution," *Monthly Review*, September 1974.

Africa" is now neatly concluded. Certainly a major step forward has been taken, but it is difficult to assert more with any kind of confidence. There are a considerable number of unknowns in the current equation and, concomitantly, a wide range of possible scenarios for the future. At this point, it seems wise merely to identify a few of the most important variables which are likely to affect developments in Mozambique, as I shall do in Section I. Some variables, however, are less "unknown" than others— much the most important of these being FRELIMO itself, its strength and its clear sense of direction. In fact, it is this reality above all others which permits us to have confidence in the future of the continuing struggle for Mozambique. I have analyzed the consolidation of the movement in an earlier article ("FRELIMO and the Mozambique Revolution," *Monthly Review*, March 1973). Here, in Section II, I hope to reinforce that argument by drawing on the experience of my own trip to the liberated areas of Mozambique in late 1972. All evidence suggests that the positive trends which I witnessed then have been further strengthened in subsequent months.

I

Five aspects of the post-coup situation and its implications for Mozambique give rise to speculation, and these can be briefly summarized as follows:

(1) *The Portuguese Metropolis.* The coup in Portugal was the product of a number of contradictions, some being very deep-cutting indeed. The changing economic base was particularly important, for within the cocoon of an agrarian-based, oligarchical fascism there has emerged a small but growing industrial sector, one closely linked in its turn to international capitalism. For the Portuguese trusts (and their transnational corporate partners)—CUF, Champalimaud—the closed and backward structures of Salazarist Portugal, as well as the futile colonial wars which they spawned, had become costly irrationalities, driving away vital labor supplies to other parts of Europe, for example, and providing a source of embarrassment in the negotiations to enter the Common Market (EEC). Something more akin to the

"liberal democracy" of Western Europe—involving, among other things, the prospect of a "responsible" trade-union movement—better suited many of the bourgeoisie, especially the businessmen and technocrats, of Portugal. Even Caetano himself, Salazar's successor, was said to be concerned to shift things in this general direction, though in the end he found himself strung out helplessly between the forces of the past and the forces of the future.

Such a trend was an important permissive condition, but not the whole story. The liberal ethos which such developments encouraged has not always been quite so calculated a phenomenon. Evidently many members of the Armed Forces Movement (the military group which made the coup and then summoned General Spinola to the presidency) believe much more straightforwardly, after so many years of overt authoritarianism, in the promise of open elections and freedom of expression, of independent trade unions and of decolonization.[2] Other AFM partners in the new government—the Communists and the Socialists, for example—are of a similar left-liberal bent. Moreover, the coup has also unleashed popular pressures of an even more unequivocal kind: to an astonishing degree, workers' actions and demands have outrun the efforts of the Communist Party and other reformers to insert themselves as their spokesmen. Obviously, these various "progressive" tendencies have also been crucial to the coup itself and to the post-coup situation, their demands for change being reinforced, particularly for the military men, by the attendant fact of grinding military defeat, by the cruel and wasting operation in Africa. In fact, it was the latter reality—the further elaboration of the contradiction *within the empire* between the national liberation movements and the Portuguese state—which triggered the various contradictions within Portugal itself and which finally and decisively tilted the balance there—motivating, as we have seen, even General Spinola to drop his literary bombshell.

It is too early to strike a balance sheet concerning Portugal, but it is clear that tensions have already begun to surface over the direction of domestic development—differences of opinion between those who favor a more controlled and manipulative liberalization (Spinola and the trusts, for example) and those committed to a rather stronger dose of reform (sections of the Armed Forces Movement apparently being the most important in this regard). Meanwhile, at the edges of this debate hovers the right—the legatees of the Salazarist system, up until now strangely silent—and the various forces on the left. Obviously, this is not the kind of conflict situation that even the promised election in a year's time can hope to settle, and many twists and turns are likely before a new balance of class forces can be struck.

Continuing struggle within Portugal necessarily results in equivocation in Africa. Thus Spinola's book merely painted the prospect of a new kind of federation, with Portugal to retain many controls and to work through congenial African lieutenants, now provided with a few more of the trappings of formal independence. These and subtler variations on the neocolonial theme undoubtedly still motivate many of the liberalizing elements which now rule Portugal; for them, the pursuit of a means by which to retain a stake in Africa while defusing international opprobrium continues. Even prominent actors who may prefer a cleaner, clearer settlement with the liberation movements (including, perhaps, Mário Soares, the Socialist foreign minister in the provisional government and up to now the chief negotiator with the liberation movements) are hamstrung by the realities of Portugal's cross-purposes. This much was clear from the London/Algiers talks held with the PAIGC of Guinea-Bissau and the Lusaka talks with FRELIMO (in May and June). As a result, and of necessity, *a luta continua*. Yet there is one immediate weakness of Portugal's position which bears emphasizing. Whatever the calculations that ultimately emerge from the struggle within Portugal concerning the terms of negotiations with FRELIMO, time is not standing still for the Portuguese in Mozambique. Numerous reports in late July make it clear that their soldiery now sees less reason than ever to engage a formidable enemy. Even as forces jockey for position in Portugal over this and other issues, in Mozambique soldiers are refusing to fight.

(2) *Portugal's Allies.* Portugal's indecision and weakness must surely alarm the South Africans, for their stake in Mozambique is high. Not only is Mozambique an important labor pool for the

republic, a site of strategic investment (Cabora Bassa), and a vital entrepôt; equally crucial is the fact that a free Mozambique will bring the tide of liberation merely "a few days march from the Transvaal." However, the South African response is less easy to predict. Needless to say, South Africa is already active beyond its borders—directly in Rhodesia (Rhodesian forces in turn operating deep inside Mozambique's Tete province), in a less overt supporting role in Portugal's colonies—and armed intervention is certainly not beyond the realm of possibility. Still, there are constraints upon South Africa's capacity to so act, most notably the lack of availability of white laborpower. For the moment subversion seems the order of the day, exacerbating tensions, fanning the flames of white terrorism in Mozambique (with Jorge Jardim, businessman and apparently now the pillar of the Mozambican Right, operating out of a Johannesburg hotel room), perhaps even in this way establishing its alibi—the existence of a "deteriorating situation"—for an eventual intervention. It seems likely that South African resources will be similarly available for attempts to promote ethnic and other kinds of factionalism within the black population. Of course, it is also possible that South Africa might ultimately decide to live with a FRELIMO government, hoping, with time, either to intimidate or seduce it into a relatively passive role. Again, speculation abounds, but that the combination of FRELIMO advance and Portuguese coup has posed in a much more dramatic fashion than ever the question of *the whole of Southern Africa* cannot be doubted.

Despite certain risks involved in so opening up the Portuguese system, it seems likely that transnational corporations and Western governments basically approve the coup and the country's subsequent liberalization. It is also true that their interests, somewhat different from those of South Africa, are greater with respect to wealthy Angola (with its oil, iron, and the like) than to Mozambique. Nonetheless, such actors can hardly be expected to remain indifferent to the prospect of an unqualified FRELIMO triumph and its likely radical implications for the shape of postcolonial Mozambique and for the long-term future of Southern Africa; we need have no illusions about the range of subversive options which may therefore be contemplated in the Western camp. Moreover, something of a rationale for such action has already been carefully crafted. Thus, within NATO, much has been heard about "the Soviet maritime threat" in the Indian Ocean and the danger of further coastline falling into "hostile" hands; there seems little doubt that the mythology of the "red menace" will hound FRELIMO at each stage of its continuing struggle. For this reason it is fortunate that the logistics of any proposed Western intervention provide real difficulties for decision makers in the State Department and elsewhere. Nonetheless, the need to be on the alert for subtle variations on all-too-familiar imperial themes cannot be overstated.

(3) *Mozambique Itself.* While the intentions of the Armed Forces Movement are not entirely clear, certainly the interests of other prominent actors in Portugal and beyond would best be served by the establishment of a neocolonial regime in Mozambique.[3] It is therefore important to understand that the possibility of such a neocolonial solution has already been virtually undercut by FRELIMO. Clearly the deep roots which the movement has struck in the liberated areas (to be further examined in Section II) are important in this respect, as is its dramatic capacity for continuing military advance. It was, after all, actions in Manica and Sofala province which sapped the will of the Portuguese, and each day now brings news of fresh successes: the recent launching of armed struggle in Zambezia province (where more than two thousand new recruits sprang almost immediately to FRELIMO's side, often bringing Portuguese-supplied arms with them), sustained assaults on communications arteries (seventy-four attacks *in one day* in July on the Tete railway, for example), and so on.

But these continuing realities are merely the most familiar signs of FRELIMO's undoubted hegemony. Equally crucial currently is the nature of the popular response in the nonliberated parts of the country—where FRELIMO has heretofore worked only clandestinely—to the movement's promise of revolution. In the new, somewhat more liberal atmosphere prevailing there, large rallies supporting FRELIMO have taken place (in Beira and Lourenço Marques, for example) and almost all journalists have noted that the strength of the tide of popular opinion is running toward the liberation movement. GUMO (the Mozambique United Group, an organization originally established in the last stages of Caetano's regime and with the latter's blessing as a neocolonial hole-card to be played if and when it should become necessary to do so) has gained virtually no positive response in Mozambique, and has had increasingly to attempt to sound just like FRELIMO in order to keep from disappearing altogether.[4] Even within the white community itself some elements have begun to yield to the inevitability of a FRELIMO-based regime, making a unified settler response, à la Rhodesia, somewhat less likely.

This is not to say that potential puppet elements among the black population (particularly in the bureaucracy) are absent, nor is it to insist that the settler problem has been solved. As one leading white Mozambican liberal recently phrased it:

> Submerged in the old machinery and still-existing old-boy nets of the Salazar era, the well-meaning Army officers just cannot cope. They haven't even been able to look into DGS files. If FRELIMO gave up the war and came back here in a political free-for-all, they'd find this place set for them like a mouse-trap.

The London *Observer* correspondent, reporting this statement, concludes with good reason that "here is the unanswerable argument that keeps FRELIMO insisting: 'the only thing to negotiate is the details of a transfer of power to the Mozambique nationalists.'"[5] The main point, then, is not that such a transfer as yet seems likely to be a smooth one; it is merely to reemphasize the fact that FRELIMO—and its insistence upon a full and genuine independence—is now more than ever at the very center of the struggle for Mozambique.

(4) *Independent Africa.* How countries in independent Africa will relate to the new post-coup situation is also important. Mozambique has at least been spared the sinister presence along its borders of a General Mobutu, whose support from Zaire of Holden Roberto's FNLA has so muddied the waters of the Angolan situation. Furthermore, the overwhelming preeminence of FRELIMO within the Mozambican struggle has meant that

Zambian authorities have had less temptation to dabble dangerously in liberation-movement politics—as they too appear to have done in the Angolan case. There was an initial flurry of rumors after the coup that Kaunda and President Nyerere of Tanzania (whose territories still provide an important staging ground for FRELIMO activity) were pressing FRELIMO to be "reasonable" and to seek a "political solution"—i.e., to accept a cease-fire and enter the electoral-cum-referendum arena proposed (and presumably supervised) by the Portuguese. However, there is no real evidence of this having been the case; and, given the difficulties for Portugal of easily establishing a neocolonial, non-FRELIMO regime (one which might then blur the situation and tempt the less committed amongst those classes which rule in the rest of neocolonial Africa to come to terms with Portugal), the support of independent Africa for whatever strategy FRE-LIMO might choose to pursue seems relatively secure for the time being.

(5) *Supporters.* Military and political support from both China and the Soviet bloc are important to FRELIMO, and whether such developments as the fresh establishment of diplomatic relations between Russia and the "new" Portugal will eventually undermine any part of that support remains to be seen. Much more immediately problematic (if less crucial) is the support which has come from sympathetic Western circles. Unfortunately, a few overseas friends of the liberation movements in Portugal's African colonies have already been tempted to act as if the struggle were virtually over. Nor is this surprising: certainly many liberals who find it easy to condemn the crude and un-equivocal colonialism of an overtly fascist regime will have greater difficulty in carrying their commitment to the fight for independence over into the more complex contest which has now begun to present itself. A measure of liberalization within Portugal, an effort to streamline subordination in the colonies (including various neocolonial ploys)—these may indeed reduce much external support, in a way that Spinola and others have presumably had in mind. If, on the other hand, escalation is to be the name of the game (as, for example, with the intervention of South Africa) there may be those who—despite the seamy and

graphic lessons of Vietnam—will draw back from the brink of committing themselves to a genuinely revolutionary alternative. As I have argued elsewhere,[6] it thus becomes all the more important to rally people to the cause of liberation for a country like Mozambique on the basis of an understanding of and commitment to an anti-imperialist perspective. The work of those who wish to support the liberation movements in Portugal's African colonies will be doubly difficult—though doubly important—in the months ahead.

II

We had spent sixteen days with Jose Moyane, FRELIMO chief of defense (and acting regional secretary) for Tete province and had marched with him over seventy miles into the interior of Mozambique—across the main Fingoe-Zumbo road, by then abandoned by the Portuguese, and two-thirds of the way to the Zambezi. Now, as our stay drew to a close, we met with him for the last time. He began by summarizing, for more than an hour, the current state of the struggle in Tete and in Mozambique as a whole, helping us to pull together our myriad impressions from the trip. He explored with us, as well, the implications of FRELIMO's military advance into the crucial provinces of Manica and Sofala, an advance which had only just been confirmed by reports reaching our column (this was in August-September 1972) but which can now be seen, as noted above, to have become the major determinant of the recent overthrow of the Portuguese government itself.[7] The clarity of analysis and the impressive dedication which we had come to recognize as being typical of FRELIMO "responsibles" were again apparent as we talked with him. But it was when we turned to more personal matters that we reached what I now see to have been an even deeper level of understanding of the meaning of the Mozambique revolution.

We had asked almost all of the many Mozambicans we interviewed inside the liberated areas to supplement their analysis of the current situation with some autobiographical remarks. We did so more reluctantly in Moyane's case, given his position and the many claims upon his time. But once asked he warmed to the theme, and in sketching at length his autobiography he gave us a particularly vivid picture of the realities of Southern Africa and of the grisly nature of Portuguese oppression. Older (at thirty-six) than most of the other cadres we met during our stay, he had also experienced at first hand even more than they the day-to-day humiliation and brutalities of the Portuguese presence. He was able therefore to trace in detail the many menial jobs he had been forced to take (including one in the South African mines, where his father, working there before him, had died), the discrimination and abuse which he had experienced, and his hard struggle over the years to piece together the rudiments of a primary education. He also spoke of his slowly growing political consciousness, sparked in part by events elsewhere—Nkrumah in Ghana, Nyerere in Tanzania, the fight against the Federation, Congolese independence, the outbreak of fighting in Angola— and by the dramatic visit of Eduardo Mondlane to Mozambique (at a time when the latter was still with the United Nations) in 1961. Moyane began to see the way out of his isolation; in 1963 he escaped from Mozambique to Tanzania and, in his own words, then "entered into the collective life of FRELIMO." With this phrase he abruptly brought the account of his "autobiography" to a close. Quite unconsciously, it seemed, he was thus making the point that his history was now the history of FRELIMO and of the Mozambican people as a whole.

The key to the future of Mozambique can be discerned in this anecdote. For Moyane's conclusion reflects a spirit—difficult to present in terms other than those which sound clichéd and romanticized—which is nonetheless discernible everywhere in the liberated areas. I was continually meeting cadres, very often in their early twenties, at various levels of the FRELIMO structure, who astonished me with their sure grasp of the essentials of the struggle and with their obvious dedication. I was tempted to contrast them, perhaps unfairly, with too many of the conservative students (of the same age group) I had known well during seven years at the University of Dar es Salaam. After drawing such a comparison, the fields of practice and of struggle appeared even more obviously to be the ideal terrain for leadership training—

better, certainly, than most of the formal education system which has been inherited from colonialism elsewhere in Africa.

There were some closely related aspects of life in free Mozambique which also struck me. Traveling with armed combatants and occasionally staying at military bases deep inside Mozambique, it was impossible not to consider the dangers of militarism—all the more so in light of the past decade of continental developments. Significantly, FRELIMO seemed equally preoccupied with such problems, and with any future danger to the nature of postliberation Mozambican society which might arise from this quarter. Sebastiao Mabote, FRELIMO's chief of military operations, with whom we also traveled throughout our stay in the liberated areas, raised the question on a number of occasions, discussing frankly both the Algerian case and the grotesque situation in much of army-dominated black Africa. Too often elsewhere, he felt, "they don't explain to the soldiers why they have these arms"; in contrast, "politics commands the army in our case."

Thus all militants, including those most clearly assigned to administrative posts, had military training and, as we saw for ourselves, ordinary villagers were everywhere actively engaged in local militia units. Moreover, those involved directly in military work were constantly reminded of, and instructed in, the basically political nature of the overall struggle for Mozambican independence of which they form a part;[8] we were even fortunate enough to meet several of the political commissars who were undertaking precisely this kind of educational work within the army and at the movement's "Centers of Preparation." After obtaining independence, Mabote assured us, the campaign will continue against the establishment of any form of caste system premised on what he dismissively termed "military professionalism." Many of the military personnel we interviewed echoed, in one form or another, Mabote's statement that "we are making a revolution, not a war of conquest."

The latter statement is particularly crucial. For, ultimately, the main check upon militarism and other forms of bureaucratic involution of the liberation struggle in Mozambique was seen, by

Mabote and others, to be the existence of an active popular base for that struggle. Equally important, the existence of such a base is also the key to the military success which has thus far been achieved against the Portuguese; in Mabote's words, "the atomic bomb in this war is the people's consciousness." There is of course a strong popular sentiment upon which to build in Mozambique; the Portuguese have seen to that. At a large public gathering which we attended inside the country, the proper mood was established at the outset by requesting an indication from the crowd of all those who had been abused or stolen from by the Portuguese, all those pressed into labor on the roads or in the South African mines, all those who had carried a white man's sedan chair (as several of the very old men evidently had done in their time), and the like. Yet spontaneity has not been the whole story either. Beyond this, we witnessed the importance of the *institutions* which give a new form to the hostility felt by peasants toward the Portuguese, and of the *methods of political work* which provide that vague sentiment with a new content, revitalizing and further radicalizing it.[9]

Thus, in institutional terms, we found an ongoing political system, spawned by FRELIMO, which reached right up from the village level, and we learned, from those involved, of the active political life at village, circle, district, and regional levels where the work of elected representatives meshed remarkably smoothly with that of FRELIMO-appointed officials. Obviously there are possible contradictions here, but all the evidence indicated that these were being effectively resolved. Certainly, the most important guarantee of this was that the point was constantly being made to FRELIMO cadres, in all the movement forums in which we participated, that they take great pains to premise their political activity and mobilizational responsibilities upon respect for and confidence in the people. Nor was it at all unusual to find even ordinary soldiers saying, as one did in the course of our interviews, that "without the people we cannot do anything."

One incident in particular suggests itself to me as a measure of this reality. In visiting a village of about three hundred people at a few hours' march from the district headquarters where we were staying, we were accompanied by a group of forty or more armed men and women. Yet when we arrived in the village we were warmly welcomed; more important, the soldiers mixed freely with the villagers, helping with chores or sitting casually with old women by the fire as the latter cooked supper. There are not many countries in the world where the arrival of a group of soldiers (or even a single policeman!) could be the signal for life to continue normally. Yet in liberated Mozambique this is the order of the day.

At one level, the immediate advantages of using methods of work which can produce this kind of link between guerrilla and peasant are self-evident. We saw, for example, the extent to which the active involvement of ordinary villagers in the transportation of war matériel and other essentials is basic to the ongoing confrontation with the Portuguese; and we learned of the importance of agricultural supplies provided by villagers to FRELIMO forces. The existence of such a milieu also guarantees greater security for FRELIMO movements and the more ready recruitment of new full-time militants. And the long-term implications are no less important: the discouragement of any drift toward elitist preconceptions and/or self-defeating authoritarian methods on the part of the cadres certainly, but, equally impressive, the growing self-confidence of the villagers themselves. This was evidenced for us by their active participation in public meetings and in the quality of their discussions with us at the village level. But perhaps it was epitomized most pointedly by one of a village's elected officials who, in an exchange with the FRELIMO district commissar traveling with us, stated that he and his fellow villagers now felt FRELIMO to be really concerned to serve the interests of the people. But if things didn't change basically after independence? Then we would have to think again, and act accordingly, he said. A firm basis, one might suspect, for the sustaining of FRELIMO's revolutionary trajectory!

"Revolution" was a word we heard often inside Mozambique. In fact, one of the first points which Comrade Mabote made to us as we set out from the Zambian border for the interior was that the imperatives of mobilizing against a recalcitrant colonialism like that of Portugal gave Mozambicans a chance most other African states had missed. Here nationalist self-assertion could not remain a surface phenomenon, but inevitably involved a basic reordering of social relationships inherited from traditional society and from colonialism—in short it meant, in Mabote's words, "the opportunity to have a revolution." For Mabote, "It is not sufficient merely to defeat the enemy; we must also be prepared to remake things afterwards. We conquer, but this is not the main point. Rather, we are 'conquering' the consciousness of the people with the concept of a society worked out by the people." And he specifically echoed an idea I had first heard expressed by Eduardo Mondlane himself shortly before his assassination: that it would be almost a pity if Mozambicans were to defeat the Portuguese too quickly since so much is being learned in the course of the struggle. In so arguing, it is evident that both Mondlane and Mabote were only half joking.

The checks upon elitism and the stimulus to the people's own self-confidence, discussed above, are examples of the lessons being learned, as are the strenuous efforts devoted in the liberated areas to developing educational and health systems tailored to the people's needs. We saw clear evidence of the latter accomplishments when we visited schools and clinics—profoundly impressive, however underequipped they might be—in a part of Fingoe district where such facilities had been unknown throughout the long years of Portuguese control.

Other evidence was the conscious concern to transform the substance of women's roles in the new Mozambique. This will be a long process which has only just begun, but it could be measured, modestly, in the statement of one very young woman cadre in FRELIMO who told us that the biggest change which the movement had brought to her life was that now when she spoke men listened to her. Certainly, FRELIMO's concern with this issue was most apparent. At one public meeting we attended, much the largest proportion of the discussion was devoted to exploring with the villagers the importance of affirming women's basic equality. And, significantly, three recent deserters from the Portuguese side spontaneously pinpointed the treatment of women as comrades within the movement as the most striking of many differences which they had noted since joining FRELIMO. It was this, one said, which had suggested to them most forcefully that "something new is being created." Moreover, the challenge to preexisting orthodoxies regarding the question of women was merely one part of a much broader cultural revolution. Just as impressive were the efforts, described by a young teacher (and exemplified for us by the students at his school), to play subtly upon the prevailing art forms of the area, encouraging the local people to rework their songs and dances so that, without denaturing them, they could be given a political or social shading relevant to contemporary imperatives. Indeed, something of the breadth of the revolutionary concept which was at work in free Mozambique could be glimpsed in another of Mabote's half-joking remarks when he insisted good-humoredly to a gathering of FRELIMO militants that "not to sing well is a political error."

Finally and centrally, there were changes to be seen in the economic life of the liberated areas. "We know that the basis of the struggle is economic," Mabote observed, "that there are two classes: the exploited and the exploiters. Colonialism and capitalism develop from this point." FRELIMO's emphasis is to be a different one: "Our population produces individually, but we are working towards collective production—that is the general goal." One example of this collective emphasis was provided by the two hard-working "responsibles" from FRELIMO's Department of Production and Commerce who accompanied us on our trip and whose current task was the establishment of a number of "people's stores" in that part of Tete province which we were visiting. But it was the changing relations of production in one of the villages which particularly caught my attention—perhaps because of my own studies of efforts at collective rural development in neighboring Tanzania. In this village, to quote a previously cited article, "I discovered a division of labor which incorporated a significant proportion of collectively farmed fields, work on these being recorded in a logbook against eventual distribution of the proceeds. I found metalworkers and basketmakers, who had originally worked as mini-entrepreneurs in the village, now working as part of this collective division of labor, their time spent also being recorded in the village book." The community spirit thus engendered seemed also to make it easier for the village to shoulder those broader responsibilities noted above—helping to feed the fighting forces by providing produce and joining periodically in the carrying of vital materials from the frontier. In short, this was an experiment which compared favorably with most of the "*ujamaa* villages" that one knew in Tanzania. Here, too, the evidence begins to suggest "that in such a peasantry, increasingly well organized and now working self-consciously against various forms of exploitation, there can be seen some guarantee of the continued forward momentum of the Mozambican revolution, even after independence has been won."[10]

Slowly, then, during our stay inside the liberated areas a picture of the new Mozambique took shape for us, a picture of a revolutionary society *in the making*. It remained true that the achievements visible on the ground had not yet been formulated into a fully coherent ideology. In fact, the thrust of FRELIMO's accomplishment remains profoundly populist in some respects, and certainly Mabote himself, in our conversations, eschewed the use of an unambiguously socialist vocabulary. Yet the direction of development emerged clearly enough in the movement's practice, and it is this very *process* of radicalization which is increasingly being codified by FRELIMO responsibles, and increasingly being grasped by ordinary Mozambicans.[11] Discussion of the dangers of "exploitation" and of elitism and entrepreneurship, continual emphasis upon the need for the most basic sorts of democratization, knowing comparisons between the various development choices made by Russia, Korea, China, Scandinavia—such topics were the stuff of our dinner-table conversation inside Mozambique. To be sure, some left sectarians—secure within the cocoons of their own theoretical abstractions—will recoil from the loose ends which a real revolution thus evidences. Nonetheless, we may be certain that the guardians of the status quo in Southern Africa are well aware that such a process has all too great a promise, that from their point of view it presents all too pressing a threat.

It is important to note, therefore, that about the latter—those guardians of the status quo—FRELIMO has no illusions, for the most theoretically developed aspect of the movement's ideology is undoubtedly its anti-imperialism. How often we heard it reiterated inside Mozambique that the enemy is not the Portuguese people but the Portuguese state and its colonial apparatus, not the white race but the imperialist system. Opportunist brands of racism and "ultra-nationalism" were constantly being condemned and the dangers of neocolonialism widely discussed. The reverse side of this coin was also much in evidence—a profound and deeply moving internationalism. The welcome afforded us throughout the liberated areas was proof of this, of course. It was gratifying for me, as a white and a Canadian, to be warmly accepted as a comrade by such people, despite the graphic realities on a world scale of racial oppression and North American imperialism. But such a reception also heightened my own awareness of how much more progressives in the metropolitan countries must do about Southern Africa in order to be worthy of such trust and friendship.

III

In January of this year (1974) I was in Tanzania, and had the opportunity to speak with Samora Machel, the president of FRELIMO, who was passing through on his way back to the liberated areas of Mozambique after a successful visit to Somalia. I knew of the dramatic military advances which had been made in the sixteen months since my own visit to Mozambique— advances such as the successful attacks on critical communications arteries linking Rhodesia, through Manica and Sofala, to the sea—which were now being widely reported in the South African press, and which had already sown the seeds of the subsequent coup in Portugal. I expected Samora to speak primarily of these developments and was surprised when he chose instead to emphasize the continuing social and political consolidation of free Mozambique. Thus, throughout 1973, a number of conferences of FRELIMO personnel had been held, devoted to exploring crucial questions of national reconstruction— education, health, production, the question of women (the latter conference being attended by some eighty women cadres of FRELIMO). Samora Machel also spoke of an August meeting in Cabo Delgado where key militants from all over the country had assembled to assist the movement in a broader effort at "ideological clarification." There, in particular, methods of political work had been a key theme, and Samora concluded his description of that meeting to me by stressing the three key phrases which had come to summarize the deliberations there: "Popularize the political line, democratize the methods of work, collectivize the leadership." Clearly, the practices which I had observed in 1972 were now being even more clearly theorized and generalized by FRELIMO.

There was of course no reason to be surprised at such an ordering of priorities. As argued above, one of the great strengths of FRELIMO has been the fact that, quite literally, politics is in command; central to the movement's success remains the realization that popular involvement and responsive and committed leadership go hand in hand, and that these, in turn, *premise* military accomplishment. Moreover, this reality continues to make FRELIMO the formidable protagonist it is—a movement now playing from strength in its bargaining with the Portuguese. Nor is it surprising that Mozambicans beyond the bounds of liberated areas are responding so unequivocally to the movement's promise of a genuine revolution in their country. These are the positive signs, though we have seen in Section I above other factors which counsel caution in predicting the short-run ramifications for Africa of the Portuguese coup. Indeed, in such an unresolved situation, it is obvious that the need to sustain the struggle against Portuguese colonialism continues to be a pressing one. Furthermore, the various aspects of the broader Southern African picture which are ominously reminiscent of the build-up of the Vietnam conflagration make the urgency of a growing concern on the left for the struggles there especially clear. Here it remains only to reaffirm the main point of this article: that amidst all the uncertainties of the Southern African situation we can at least be certain of our responsibility to support FRELIMO in its exemplary and genuinely revolutionary efforts.

Postscript, August 1

In the two weeks since this article was completed (in mid-July) the situation in Portugal and in Mozambique seems already to have shifted somewhat. In a confrontation between the two wings of the junta—that led by General Spinola on the one hand and that led by the AFM on the other—it is the latter which has carried the day, at least for the time being. Spinola's bid to promote a new right-of-center cabinet fell short, and instead a left-of-center group has consolidated its hold upon the government, under the leadership of Colonel Vasco dos Santos Gonçalves, the new prime minister. [12] Apparently yielding to the logic of this development (and, without doubt, to the attendant fact of Portugal's complete inability to tame FRELIMO militarily or politically[13]), Spinola spoke to the nation on July 7, and in doing so presented a guarantee of the colonies' unequivocal *right to independence*, a formulation which went far beyond anything heretofore proposed by the Portuguese. Certainly, this does seem to be another significant step forward. Yet once again the details of the kind of transitional process toward independence which Spinola and others now have in mind remain all too ominously unspecified. In addition, many of the other dangers discussed above remain. It is true, of course, that these dangers may be especially menacing in Angola—where international capitalism presents even more of a threat *and* where the liberation forces have been cruelly fragmented—but for FRELIMO, too, great caution will be the order of the day. Fortunately, as we have seen, FRELIMO seems more than equal to even the complex and delicate challenges which the coming weeks and months may bring.

Notes

1. See for example, J. Bowyer Bell's book with this title, *The Myth of the Guerrilla* (New York, 1971), and subtitled "Revolutionary Theory and Malpractice"; Bell's volume contains a particularly ugly and misleading chapter on Southern Africa.
2. Some of the officers in the Armed Forces Movement are rumored to be even further to the left than this—socialists, even Marxists.
3. Of course, opinions might vary somewhat among those actors as to the nature of the neocolonial links preferred—Portuguese interests being more concerned to sustain as many ties as possible directly with Portugal, international capital much less concerned with such requirements.

4. FRELIMO seems to have had similar success in preempting the manipulation of tribal encounters by GUMO and others. Thus, an attempt to simulate Macua hostility to the movement (in part by making use of corrupted chiefs as agents) broke down when Macua demonstrated vociferously in Nampula to state their strong support for FRELIMO.

5. Gavin Young, "Spinola Will Find FRELIMO Holding All the Best Cards," *Observer*, June 30, 1974. Unfortunately, even Soares and others of his persuasion seem, thus far, to have been unduly preoccupied with electoral procedures and the like, rather than with a more straightforward transfer of power to the liberation movement.

6. In my "Neo-Colonialism vs. Liberation Struggle: Some Lessons from Portugal's African Colonies," in R. Miliband and J. Saville, eds., *The Socialist Register 1973* (London, 1974).

7. I went to Tete with three comrades from the Committee for Freedom in Mozambique, Angola, and Guinea (CFMAG) of the UK. FRELIMO had been fighting fiercely to claim the area we visited less than two years previously, a fact which made the level of social and political infrastructure we found there all the more impressive. By the time of our arrival, the Portuguese could penetrate the area only rarely, and then only by jet plane and helicopter, in order to destroy crops or to make short-lived raids.

8. For Mabote, "a soldier who has not been mobilized politically is like a dismantled weapon." Or, as one soldier (who had once served as a draftee in the Portuguese army before deserting) put it when contrasting his work there with his FRELIMO activities: "Then I was able to see only straight in front, but not to the sides."

9. For a more analytical approach to the dialectic established between peasant and cadre in building a base for revolution in Mozambique, see my "African Peasantries and Revolution," essay 11 below, especially Section IV.

10. Ibid., where the question of the collectivist components of peasant-based revolution in Africa is another of the themes discussed.

11. In particular, it is being codified in the speeches of Samora Machel. See, for example, his *Mozambique: Sowing the Seeds of Revolution* (London, 1974) with an introduction by John Saul.

12. An interesting analysis of these developments is contained in Marcel Niedergang, "Portugal—A Breathing Space for 'Democratization,' " *Le Monde*, translated in *The Guardian Weekly*, July 26, 1974.

13. The same could be said for the PAIGC in the Republic of Guinea-Bissau. The complicated picture in Angola clearly requires the sort of separate and detailed analysis which is not possible here.

3

FREE MOZAMBIQUE

June 24, 1975. On the main road to Machava Stadium, Lourenço Marques, Mozambique. Soon to be *free* Mozambique—the People's Republic of Mozambique. But now, a driving rainstorm, heavy traffic. Will we make it by midnight to see the Portuguese flag come down and the new Mozambican flag replace it? Out of our minibus and a wild dash for the stadium, joined by hundreds of others caught up in the spirit and drama of the occasion, afraid, amidst the mounting excitement, to miss even a moment of the events.

Just in time. Samora Machel, president of the Front for the Liberation of Mozambique (FRELIMO), and soon to be the first president of Mozambique, has also been delayed by traffic. Now, in the early minutes of June 25, the flag-raising ceremony proceeds, the vast crowd cheering as Comrade Samora, briefly but eloquently, proclaims the country's independence. We're together, representatives of various Western support groups, and we embrace one another enthusiastically. Embrace, too, Mozambicans, strangers and old friends. I greet Janet Mondlane, wife of Eduardo, FRELIMO's first president, assassinated by the Portuguese in 1969, greet Felisberto, a FRELIMO comrade from the days when the movement's headquarters was a dingy office on Nkrumah Street in Dar es Salaam, greet two militants with whom I traveled to the liberated areas of Tete province in 1972.

This essay was first published in *This Magazine* (Toronto), November–December 1975, and in *Monthly Review*, December 1975.

Was that really only three years ago? Enthusiastic guerrillas fill
the sky with tracer bullets. Too much like the real thing for my
taste, but who can blame them? Independence Day.

I

No one knows better than the FRELIMO leadership that the
changing of a flag marks merely the beginning of a new phase of
their struggle. Nonetheless, Mozambicans weren't about to underestimate the significance of their accomplishment—the military defeat of a ruthless colonial power, one with full imperialist
backing—nor deny themselves the opportunity of celebrating
their victory. And the first ten days I spent in Lourenço Marques
were just that, a celebration—a celebration in which the ceremony at Machava Stadium was merely one highlight among so
many others.

It began for us the Friday John Saxby and I—the "Canadian
delegation"—reached Lourenço Marques by plane from Lusaka.
On the flight was Oliver Tambo, president of the African National Congress of South Africa, and the airport was packed to
overflowing with cheering people for his arrival—here, in
Lourenço Marques, less than a hundred miles from the South
African border! Of course the crowd was even larger and more
enthusiastic a few days later when Samora himself arrived in the
city for the first time in well over a decade of self-imposed and
active exile. Then even the streets—already festooned with in-
numerable banners, signs, and window displays—were lined with
people every inch of the way along the route of his entry into the
city, and we joined with thousands of others in welcoming him.

Follows the flag-raising, and early the next morning (after only a
couple of hours' sleep) the formal investiture of Samora Machel
as president. It took place in a small room in the city hall, but I
was fortunate enough to be invited—sitting, as it happened, in
the same row as Alvaro Cunhal and Mário Soares, come from
Portugal. Here, at close range, I experienced most fully the
meaning which these days must have held for the direct participants in them. Marcellino dos Santos, vice-president of FRE-
LIMO and one of the first militants enlisted to the cause of

Mozambique's national liberation, read a brief statement, proclaiming the choice of Samora Machel as president, and Machel made an even briefer statement of acceptance. They then turned to each other and embraced—a conventional enough gesture among Mozambicans. But this was an embrace with a difference—slow, measured, deeply felt, as they looked at each other, their eyes filming over with tears. Two comrades of long years in the struggle, firmly united in their pride and in their accomplishment.

Words fail me here—I have never been so moved. I watched as the new president next went onto the balcony and proceeded to address the huge crowd gathered in the civic square. Characteristically, his speech, one of the most important ever delivered by an African leader,[1] now dealt not so much with what had been accomplished as with what remains to be done. For FRELIMO, and for Mozambique, the struggle, as they have affirmed so often, continues.

But the celebrations continued, too. That afternoon, an amazing parade—floats dramatizing, often with high good humor, the evils of colonialism, the realities of the struggle, and the possible areas of future social and economic advance. And thousands upon thousands of people marching past under the banners of workers' groups, the women's organization, the military. Afterwards, the chanting crowd surging around the reviewing stand to greet the president, who mixed with the people freely. But how would he ever get away? Joaquim Chissano, FRELIMO's prime minister during the transitional-government period, took the mike. "Comrades, the president is not visiting among you, he has come to stay. But now he must go. Please clear a way." Little response. Then: "Comrades, are we an organized people?" A huge roar: "We are." Chissano: "Then organize yourselves. You don't need police to do it for you. You are your own police. Please let the president through." And slowly, but surely, they did!

The next day, an impressive youth festival at the stadium, and at night, a banquet for all the guests. Speeches by Siad Barre of Somalia, chairman of the Organization of African Unity, and by President Samora, who made a point of singling out for thanks those support committees who, he said, had worked "on the difficult front of the Western countries." A frank and friendly exchange of speeches between Samora and Vasco Gonçalves, then prime minister of Portugal. Yet another chance to see old friends and make new ones, FRELIMO militants from all levels of the organization and comrades from around the world. That night, for example, we ate dinner with Shafrudine Khan, FRE-LIMO's New York representative for many years and guest of honor at a 1974 session of TCLSAC's (Toronto Committee for the Liberation of Southern Africa) "Cinema of Solidarity" in Toronto which was attacked by white-power thugs. And the next evening a brief meeting with the president himself. At a reception for the various delegations, he received with enthusiasm the greetings we conveyed from the many Canadians who had gathered in Toronto on June 25 to celebrate Mozambican independence. "International solidarity," "proletarian internationalism," call it what you will—such phrases inevitably seemed less abstract for me, more real and urgent, in such a setting.

Nor was this all. Throughout these ten days, woven around the various formal ceremonies, there was also a rich array of cultural events—plays, singing, dancing, poetry readings, marionettes—taking place throughout the city (and, as I later learned, throughout the country). The cultural sphere has always been an arena of major FRELIMO accomplishment—something which I had seen for myself in the liberated areas in 1972—and so it proved to be again in Lourenço Marques. Two plays in particular stood out: one on the history of Mozambican women from traditional society through colonialism to the revolutionary present; another on the broader development of the liberation struggle itself, with its many deep-seated contradictions and its impressive resolutions of those contradictions. As John Saxby has written of one of these plays:

> In a dramatic sense it was splendid stuff: warmth, humor, passion, and dignity, as well as political sophistication; first-rate acting, with subtlety of expression and manner and obvious enjoyment on the part of the actors; and the language itself a delight to hear, musical lilts and great rolling phrases all intermixed. One can

usually excuse a bit of amateurishness for good intentions and political awareness, but this gave away nothing to anyone.[2]

Once again, a phrase from the revolutionary chapbook was leaping off the page. "Liberation as the release of creative popular energies": the real thing was all around me.

II

The celebrations over, I stayed on in Mozambique to look behind the scenes—talking with leaders in the capital about their plans and visiting Zambezia province in the agricultural heartland of the country, in order to see FRELIMO at work closer to the ground. The experience was instructive, reinforcing impressions already gleaned during the celebration period. For if the coming of formal independence has not altered substantially anything in many other African territories, this is unlikely to be the case in Mozambique. Here was a movement come to power with a clear sense of purpose, a firm popular base, and a cadre of leaders of the very highest caliber.[3] In consequence, a process of profound and revolutionary change, already underway in the liberated areas well before independence, seems certain to continue, despite the greater problems which Mozambique now faces.

Such problems are, needless to say, the main legacy of Portugal's five-hundred-year colonial record in Mozambique. Though finally defeated militarily by FRELIMO, the Portuguese left behind the devastation caused by their brutal military tactics and, even more importantly, the structure of an economy warped to service the needs of Western commodity markets, of South Africa, and of Portugal itself, rather than the needs of the African population. It will require considerable skill to reconstruct the economy along alternative, more self-reliant and productive lines.

It was too early, at the time of my trip, to confirm what this would mean substantively in every sector. But it was immediately clear from talks with Marcellino dos Santos (the vice-president, who was appointed minister of development and economic plan-

ning in the first days after independence) that existing links with
multinational companies and agribusiness conglomerates will
be severely scrutinized, with nationalizations sure to follow.
Moreover, some of the crucial keys to control already lie with the
new government. The Banco Nacional Ultramarino (the Overseas National Bank) played a ubiquitous role in the private sector
of the economy in both pre-coup Portugal and Mozambique.
Nationalized by Lisbon in 1974, the bank now passes to FRE-
LIMO as part of the independence settlement. And this appears
to be only the beginning. There can be little doubt that a full-
fledged socialist solution to the problem of Mozambique's underdevelopment is on the agenda.

Ultimately, this will also involve a complete economic break
with South Africa, although the extreme dependence of the
Mozambican economy on that country means that it will not
come precipitously or at the expense of the wholesale disruption
of the economy. For example, dos Santos confirmed that in the
short run workers will continue to go to South Africa—though
Mozambique will press for better conditions and wages. Meanwhile, the new government will work as rapidly as possible to
restructure the economy along self-reliant lines so that these
workers can soon be absorbed at home. The same strategy will
hold for creating alternatives to dependence on earnings from
South Africa's traffic through Mozambican ports and its use of
Cabora Bassa hydroelectric power.[4] There are clearly dangers in
such a strategy of phased disengagement, but I found that no one
understands this better than FRELIMO's own leaders. There are
good reasons to have confidence in their skills and commitment
during this difficult transitional period.

Of course FRELIMO's idea of the proper terrain for national
reconstruction is a broad one, and in the service sector, where
the opportunities for significant transformation are most readily
available, the substance of change has been even more immediately apparent. Talks with Helder Martens, the minister of
health, with Graça Simbine, the minister of education, or with
Fernando Ganhão, new rector of the university, documented the
dramatic shift of priorities in an egalitarian, rural-oriented direction. Not merely talk, but action. Within the first few weeks,

private medical and legal practice and private funeral services were nationalized. It was made clear that in free Mozambique no one was to make a profit from the personal discomfiture of his or her compatriots. Private schools met a similar fate. And positive efforts to forge a new educational format and a nationwide program of cultural revitalization, efforts which had given rise to important conferences and planning sessions even before independence, are to be reinforced. Hard to miss the fact that the future seemed vibrantly open-ended in so many spheres. Hard not to feel, somewhat enviously, how exciting it must be to be a teacher or a culture worker in such a setting.

As always with FRELIMO, the underlying basis of success is political. Here continuity is crucial. I had first witnessed the impressive methods of political work—the building of grass-roots participation and village-level democracy which has been so important to the movement's success—when I visited the liberated areas with FRELIMO guerrillas. Now, in independent Mozambique, I found an impressive attempt to generalize these methods to the rest of the country, to places where only clandestine political work had been possible prior to liberation. In fact, this task was FRELIMO's central preoccupation during the period of the Transitional Government (those months from September 1974 to June 25, during which FRELIMO shared power with the Portuguese). Now the coming of independence can only serve to intensify such an effort.

In the sprawling city of Lourenço Marques, as in Zambezia province, the key has been the *grupos dynamizadores* (dynamization groups). FRELIMO's most impressive peacetime innovation, these *grupos* are committees established in every sector of the society—in school and workplace, in urban neighborhood and rural village—which, from my observation, are now providing Mozambicans with impressive new opportunities for self-government and political education.

We had seen the *grupos* at work in Lourenço Marques, but it was on the trip to Zambezia province that I felt able fully to grasp their vitality. We visited a number of them, including the regular weekly meeting of the chairpersons of the area's *grupos*, and were as excited to hear of their work—literacy training, the facilitation of women's participation, construction of schools and local community centers, political struggle sessions, and the like—as we were moved by the warm reception for the "comrades from abroad" which we received everywhere. Of particular interest was a visit to a "pre-cooperative," a large collective rice farm which represented the joint activity of three or four different *grupos* in the area. Here, in embryo, was FRELIMO's long-run plan for the rural areas, a move toward collectivization, the establishment of rural "communes," premised on an avoidance of the bureaucratization and coercion all too characteristic of neighboring Tanzania's related attempts at *ujamaa*-villagization. And the safeguard against any such denouement is to be precisely the political self-management of a self-conscious peasantry, acting through agencies like the *grupos dynamizadores*.

Leadership is also crucial to this process, and it was therefore encouraging to meet the full range of FRELIMO cadres at the provincial and district levels in Zambezia. I was able to confirm, in particular, that a high caliber of personnel is not merely a feature of the very top of the organization. To be sure, recruitment of skilled cadres remains important, and FRELIMO has made the establishment of a party training school an urgent priority. But many outstanding people have begun to come out of the ranks of the guerrilla movement, adapting to the new tasks at hand. Fortunately so, for the need is great. A visit to the British-owned Sena sugar estate and a morning spent with the European manager—a man of predictable views and demeanor—touring the locations which housed the migrant workers in desperate conditions, confirmed that much. That same afternoon, a long talk with the recently arrived, FRELIMO-appointed political commissar on the estate provided a sharp contrast in viewpoint and a sense of the work already begun (even prior to any nationalization which might eventually be forthcoming) in mobilizing the workers on the new economic battlefront.[5]

Politicization is an equally pressing priority in the urban areas, especially in a city as large and as corrupt as Lourenço Marques. Seeing it for the first time, I could not but feel some sympathy with the Cambodians in their haste to evacuate their own capital after liberation! Still, it is here that the working class is to be found, a potential pillar of the revolution despite the fact that an effective urban police network had made clandestine political work tremendously difficult in the cities under the Portuguese. Now the integration of the workers into the FRELIMO scheme of things presents some real challenges. Nonetheless, *grupos* in the workplace are providing a stepping stone—to all appearances an effective and democratic one—toward the new trade unions which are coming into being; indeed, in several cases they have even become the nucleus of real workers' self-management (in a cashew-processing factory abandoned by its Portuguese owners, for example).

Even at the university—most hierarchical and deeply colonized of inherited institutions—the *grupos'* initiative was in train, throwing up, in addition, a new kind of structure for the faculty boards. From now on the latter are to be constituted by three representatives from the teaching faculty, three from the students, and three from the staff (typists, cleaners, etc.)—the dean to be chosen, in turn, from that number. Seven years spent teaching in an African university helped me to realize how startling a beginning this was.[6]

There was one final question that preoccupied me during my visit, and that concerned the links of a free Mozambique with the ongoing struggle for the liberation of the rest of Southern Africa. In this regard, the reception accorded Oliver Tambo was a significant event. And a similar reception greeted Agostinho Neto, president of Angola's MPLA, when he arrived in Lourenço Marques. The latter movement is engaged in a life-or-death struggle against two other movements with unequivocally neocolonial credentials; indeed, one of them, Holden Roberto's FNLA, has the firm and aggressive backing of Zaire's sinister General Mobutu and the Americans (as well as, for no good reason, the Chinese). FRELIMO's several strong statements on MPLA's behalf during the week of ceremonies could be seen as serving notice on the rest of Africa—and on the very large Chinese delegation in attendance—as to where their true responsibilities lie in Angola. It was evident that the liberation of Mozambique has added a strong, fresh, and progressive voice to African councils.

Of even more direct concern is Rhodesia/Zimbabwe, now exposed along an extended frontier to a fully liberated Mozambique. FRELIMO has said it will shoulder the burden of sanctions against Rhodesia despite the dislocations in Mozambique's domestic economy which are sure to follow. At the same time there is probably some despair at the reluctance of Zimbabwean Africans to break off their internecine struggles long enough to focus their armed attention on the Smith gang, still in power. Here, backing the African National Congress is deemed the best bet: a vehicle for at least the preliminary merging of Zimbabwe's factions and a possible forum within which a process of renewal and radicalization might eventually emerge. In the meantime, though they don't talk about it, it is likely that well-trained FRELIMO personnel will be at work to pass on some of their expertise to ANC forces regrouping along the Zimbabwean border.

And diplomatic pressure on South Africa over the Zimbabwe question will also continue. Indeed, something of a domino theory seems to be at play: to up the ante for South Africa in its involvements beyond its borders—in Zimbabwe and Namibia—sufficiently to peel off these territories from the white *laager*, with the much tougher nut of the republic itself waiting to be cracked at a later stage. Obviously, this broad struggle will not be an easy one. But in talks with Marcellino dos Santos, Jorge Rebelo (minister of information), and others, there was little doubt that free Mozambique has enlisted for the duration in the battle for Southern Africa.

Coolheaded and committed appraisals of their economic and social problems, of the challenges of continuing political mobilization, of the broader Southern African context in which they find themselves. And, increasingly, firm action springing from such appraisals. This is what I found in Mozambique during the first weeks of freedom. Perhaps Joaquim Chissano, now Mozambique's minister of foreign affairs, put it best. When we met for the first time in several years and joyfully embraced at a reception early in the week of celebrations, he said, quite simply, "So, we did it. . . . Let us continue."[7]

III

For Canadians there was an additional message in the ceremonies that marked Mozambique's celebrations of the winning
of independence, a graphic significance in the fact that FRE-
LIMO, quite consciously, had chosen *not* to invite the Canadian
government to participate. This was in spite of Canadian representations to FRELIMO requesting such an invitation, and, as
one senior Zambian official in attendance in Lourenço Marques
explained to me, in spite of our attempts to persuade Zambia to
intervene with FRELIMO on official Canada's behalf.

Instead, the "Canadian delegation" consisted of myself and
John Saxby, a fellow member of TCLSAC. We were invited, we
were informed in Mozambique, to represent the many people in
Canada whom FRELIMO knew to have been sympathetic to its
cause during the ten long years of war. In contrast, the Canadian
government was seen as having lent its firmest support to the side
of continuing Portuguese colonial hegemony.[8]

FRELIMO was quick to point out that reluctance to invite the
Canadian government should not be seen to prejudice future
diplomatic relations between the two countries. It was meant
primarily to underscore the fact that the celebrations were a
gathering of friends, of those who had supported the Mozambican people's lengthy struggle. On that basis Canada was not
invited, although the guest list ranged all the way from the
representatives of many Western churches through officials of a
number of the Scandinavian countries to a delegation from the
People's Republic of China.

One should not underestimate the importance of this action by
FRELIMO. Those of us who have, over the years, argued the
case that Canada's economic, military, and diplomatic support
for the white-minority regimes of Southern Africa far outweighs
the formal lip service that we sometimes pay to the cause of
African freedom, have been met by the charge that this is an
intemperate view, that Africans see these things quite differently,
that they recognize the "positive role" which this country plays.

Marcellino dos Santos himself gave the lie to this argument
several years ago when he told a CBC radio interviewer:

> Really, Canada has made many statements but . . . I must say
> frankly that, knowing and having heard what Canada [has] said
> several times . . . but knowing that Canada is doing nothing real to
> help the liberation movements, one should at least ask: Is . . . the
> government of Canada sincere? We don't believe it, and we hope
> that Canada will try to show that it really is sincere.

To what would dos Santos attribute "this ambiguity in the attitude of Canada," then? "I'm forced to accept that Canada
continues to think it preferable to have relations with colonialist
and fascist regimes than with people who are fighting for their
freedom and dignity." The vice-president was equally frank when
I spoke with him in Lourenço Marques.

To be sure, we need have no illusions that significant change in
Canadian policy is in the offing merely as a result of our government's failure to be invited to Mozambique. Canada's stance in
Southern Africa is not some arbitrary *jeu d'esprit*, but reflects
instead deeper imperatives which are built into the very structure
of our society and economy. Nonetheless, FRELIMO's rebuff is
a hard and undeniable *fact*, one which helps refute the government's publicly stated case for its policies. Perhaps, in consequence, official Canada will be somewhat less prone in future to
fob off its domestic critics with shallow arguments.

For many Canadians, however, this is pretty small solace. To
us, it is as obvious as it is to FRELIMO that Canada, acting in its
official capacity within the international state system, presents
itself at virtually every opportunity as the firm ally of imperialism.
Of course, it is equally obvious that dos Santos' "explanation,"
quoted above, of the roots of Canadian policy does not represent
anything like a fully theorized statement concerning Canada's
external role. Indeed, it is doubtful whether FRELIMO has had
either the time or the occasion to address itself to a careful
appraisal of Canadian political economy. Clearly, we are the ones
who must do more of the spadework which is required: to specify
the extent to which our acting in concert with imperial designs is
merely the external expression of our dependent subordination to
the United States, to reveal the important domestic classes and
interests which have a stake in our playing this role.

In this, we will not be wasting our time. For there is no reason
to think that resistance to our negative role abroad will be any less

important than resistance to other manifestations of the contradictions within our society in building, over a broad front, an effective movement of the Left in Canada. Enough, in this regard, that FRELIMO has made a firm and absolutely crucial distinction between the Canadian state on the one hand and the Canadian people on the other. Especially since, in doing so, the movement has provided us with something else of importance: an opportunity to exemplify, on the occasion of Mozambique's independence, *a genuine internationalism*, this being an opportunity which is generally denied to Canadians by the actions and intercessions of our official spokespersons in the international arena!

Home thoughts from abroad. Triggered, perhaps, by a remark of Comrade Chauke when he introduced Polly Gaster (of the U.K. Solidarity Committee) and myself to a meeting of the chairpersons of the *grupos dynamizadores* in the town of Quelimane, Zambezia province. We had told the meeting something of our own countries and of the conditions under which we had been carrying out our support work. Chauke then reminded the audience of the ways in which Tanzania and Zambia had, in years past, provided FRELIMO with a base area from which to launch its successful struggle. Turning to us, he told the others: "Mozambique is now their base."

It was a *bon mot*, of course, obviously more metaphor than reality. Even as a metaphor, however, it did have resonance, at least for me. It is important, no doubt, to avoid the temptation of merely getting off on other people's revolutions, thereby evading the more difficult task of bringing about necessary changes in one's own society. Yet it would be equally mistaken to forget that progressives in Canada (and, of course, in the United States) are participants in a worldwide struggle, or to downplay the significance of the kind of unofficial "people's diplomacy" in which we engaged in Mozambique. To be in Mozambique this summer was certainly to sense more deeply than ever before the rewards of genuine freedom, the drama of a people making its own history. But it was also to feel, tangibly, the importance of our reinforcing each other, around the world, in our efforts to attain such goals.

Notes

1. The speech is reprinted in its entirety in *Review of African Political Economy*, no. 4 (1975).
2. John Saxby's own illuminating account of the Mozambique celebrations, from which this quote is taken, is available in mimeographed form from TCLSAC, 121 Avenue Rd., Toronto.
3. For an account of the revolutionary process which has given rise to such a movement in Mozambique, see my two previous articles in *Monthly Review* (March 1973 and September 1974); the latter is reprinted as essay 2 of this volume.
4. The Cabora Bassa arrangement seems to represent, as well, a gesture of solidarity toward the new Portuguese government, which would be placed in a difficult financial position by outright nationalization. Instead, the Portuguese will continue to control the dam, retiring their debts by selling power to South Africa, and passing the dam to Mozambique at term—by which time it is intended that Mozambicans will themselves be ready to use the power domestically.
5. One additional, rather chilling, feature of our trip to Zambezia was a visit to the FRELIMO office in Quelimane, formerly the PIDE (secret police) headquarters. It had been called the "house of death" in colonial times—i.e., only a few months previously—and we saw some of the torture apparatus and propaganda material found in the building. Its choice as an office by FRELIMO was as much symbolic as practical, of course; the occupation was a tangible exemplification, for local people, of the reality of liberation. For us, it served as a reminder that, for all our preoccupation with FRELIMO's future plans, we should not underestimate the importance of what has already been accomplished.
6. My chance to talk with the rector, Fernando Ganhão, was relatively brief. The university having been shut down for a month for the purpose, well over half the faculty, students, and staff, the rector included, were leaving the next day to join workers' brigades in the countryside.
7. A current issue of the *Guardian* (New York), October 15, 1975, also quotes Chissano: "In a recent visit to the United Nations to address the General Assembly, Mozambique Foreign Minister, Joaquim Chissano, was introduced to Henry Kissinger. . . . 'I hear you people in Mozambique are revolutionaries,' Kissinger greeted Chissano, pumping his hand. 'Yes, we are,' Chissano quietly replied. 'And we mean it.'"
8. In a related manner, "nonofficial" delegations from the United States were welcomed in lieu of an invitation to the U.S. government.

4

ANGOLA AND AFTER

The Angolan situation has been widely misinterpreted (often quite willfully, it would seem) not only in conventional liberal/conservative circles in Canada but also in some radical ones. Rather surprisingly, the essence of such misinterpretations has been similar. It stems from a temptation to ignore the concrete history of the struggle in Angola and the specific social and political characteristics of the territory itself. The result: the reduction of the full complexity of the situation there to some mere manifestation of "great-power politics."

Thus, in the Canadian mainstream, concern about the role of the Soviet Union and its assistance to MPLA (Popular Movement for the Liberation of Angola) holds interpretative sway, with the hoariest old Cold War mythologies of the 1950s having been dusted off to distort the claim of the MPLA to primacy. In the process, that movement's twenty years of political and military struggle are consigned to limbo, its long-term historical thrust reduced to some mere manipulation from Moscow (whether this be interpreted as direct manipulation or as being orchestrated via Havana). From this perspective, the "pro-Western" FNLA and UNITA are viewed as nobly battling the "Soviet-backed" MPLA, and even South Africa—the very heart of brutal white hegemony in Southern Africa—has been allowed to appropriate the halo of

This essay was first published in *This Magazine* (Toronto), April–May 1976, and, in a somewhat modified form, in *Monthly Review*, May 1976.

resistance to "Communist aggression." This in spite of the fact that the latter country has actually *invaded* Angola in order to challenge MPLA's attempts to consolidate independence!

Left of center, there has been the curiously parallel tendency to emphasize, in quasi-Maoist fashion, the dangers of "superpower rivalry" and "Soviet social imperialism" and on this basis to deny support to the MPLA, in spite of the latter movement's indisputable claim to represent the most vibrant and praiseworthy forces thrown up by the Angolan revolution. This, in turn, has led either to an irrelevant call to support "the Angolan people" (somehow miraculously freed of internal turmoil) or, at worst, to actual backing for UNITA and/or FNLA over and against MPLA. Even the fact that any such posture places Canadian militants firmly in concert with South African and American designs in the area seems not to have dissuaded some of them (e.g., CPC-ML) from their foolhardy course.

A Distorted Picture

Both these sets of distortions are of interest, the "Maoist" variant because of what it reveals about the pathology of the left in Canada, the conventional variant because of what it reveals about the strength of a phalanx of news media which is profoundly hostile to revolutionary change and a political consensus which is blandly and unreflectively "liberal."[1] To the pathology of the left we shall return. As for the heavy weight of "conventional wisdom," we need only consider the terrifying ease with which Canadian "public opinion" could move, in a matter of a few weeks, from a point where almost no one in the country had even the most minimal awareness of Angola to a point where virtually everyone did have an opinion—albeit the same opinion and a grievously erroneous one. Once again, the true character of the African challenge to the racist and imperialist status quo in Southern Africa had been denatured for public consumption by press and politicians. Equally unsettling is the likelihood that such distortion will increase as the battle for Southern Africa draws closer to the core of racist oppression and Western involvement in the area—South Africa itself. The Angolan case demonstrates clearly the difficult work ahead for all those who would seek to advance the cause of the African liberation struggle in this country.

The key to a more realistic analysis of what has transpired in Angola lies precisely in turning the above viewpoints inside out, starting not with a global formula but with an historical analysis of the Angolan liberation movements which have now laid claim to world attention. A statement made at the time of the Portuguese departure from Angola (November 1975) by Samora Machel, president of FRELIMO, provides the best starting point:

> Let me speak to you about how Mozambicans regard the events in Angola. For us, the problem is posed in the following way: Who has led and is leading the struggle in Angola? And against whom? Who is the enemy? Who is responsible for the destruction of both human life and villages? Who shoots, who kills the people? We have analyzed the Angolan situation throughout the many years of its evolution. We have asked ourselves: Who has really struggled against colonialism? Who has really fought?
>
> There is no doubt that it is the Popular Movement for the Liberation of Angola, which has directed and continues to direct the struggle in Angola. And today, just as the Portuguese colonialists are departing, when the Angolan people, who identify strongly with the MPLA, prepare to celebrate their victory, just as they are about to enjoy the fruits of their liberty, various groups guided by imperialism try to impede the process of liberation in order to delay independence and leave the way open for foreign military intervention.
>
> What one must understand, the whole of Africa must realize, is that the outcome of the revolution in Africa is being determined right now in Angola. As in the past, we have always supported the MPLA with whom we are allied. We are continuing and will continue our support. This act is neither spontaneous nor impulsive. Our relations of concrete and effective solidarity have been forged in the course of a long struggle against the same enemies. Because for a long time we have defined the common enemy according to common principles and with common objectives in mind. . . .

The Angolan Movements

A brief consideration of the two movements which have been advanced as alternatives to MPLA confirms the strength of such a perspective. Certainly, as regards Holden Roberto's Front for the National Liberation of Angola (FNLA), there is no room for even the slightest misunderstanding. Militarily active only very briefly in the early 1960s, it quickly retired to Congo-Kinshasa (now Zaire) where, under the patronage of the sinister President Mobutu, it passively awaited an invitation to participate in any neocolonial solution which might be forthcoming in Angola. As recent American disclosures have documented, the movement was ultimately deactivated, with Holden for some years being granted only a $10,000-a-year retainer as "information gatherer" by the CIA.

"Reactivated," in the pungent phrase of one American official, after the Portuguese coup of 1974 and soon enjoying material assistance from China[2] as well as from Zaire and the United States, FNLA played the only card it could in the Angolan power game. Lacking any such vigorous popular base as might have been nurtured through years of guerrilla activity, it fell back upon the desperate use of brute military force—in Luanda, the capital of Angola, and throughout the north—in an attempt to block MPLA. Fortunately, the judgment of Nathaniel Davis proved sound. Kissinger's man-in-Africa (as he had once been his man-in-Chile), Davis resigned from the State Department in opposition to the American policy of backing FNLA and UNITA and striving to isolate MPLA. His reason: the former two movements couldn't fight their way out of a paper bag (as he put it)! In fact, much of the fighting in northern Angola, while it lasted, was carried out by Zairian troops and white mercenaries.

The National Union for the Total Independence of Angola (UNITA) also was insignificant militarily during the colonial period. Al J. Venter's *The Terror-Fighters*, a first-hand and knowledgeable early-1970s appraisal of Portugal's wars in Africa written from the South African side, scarcely mentions that movement, emphasizing that the Portuguese attached importance only to the threat from MPLA. Basil Davidson's magisterial *In the Eye of the Storm: Angola's People*, also written at first hand but from the side of liberation, came to a parallel conclusion. More recently, Davidson's suspicion that UNITA—small and ineffectual—existed mainly on sufferance from the Portuguese has been given weight by letters, released in Portugal after the coup, which show Savimbi to have been in close touch with the Portuguese during the "war years," exchanging arms and information. Add to this a telling statement from former Portuguese dictator Marcelo Caetano's autobiography, *Depoimento*, to the effect that the strategy of Costa Gomes and Betancourt Rodriguez on Angola's Eastern Front in the early 1970s "included negotiations with UNITA, a group of rebels which, under the leadership of Savimbi, was operating there against MPLA" and you soon have a picture of no movement at all during the long years of struggle.

Small wonder that Savimbi was first to announce a cease-fire in Angola—in June 1974, even as PAIGC in Guinea-Bissau, FRELIMO in Mozambique, and MPLA were intensifying the military struggle against the intrigues of General Spinola, still president of Portugal. Or that Savimbi could show up on the Isle of Sal in September 1974, to plot with Mobutu, Roberto, and Spinola as to how best to sidetrack MPLA—a meeting whose immediate outcome the *Sunday Times* (London) could summarize by saying that "Spinola's elaborate courtship with Mobutu, Roberto and Savimbi has made Angola safe for capitalism—for the moment" ("Angola: The Carve-up of Africa's El Dorado," October 20, 1974). To reinforce this possibility Savimbi soon found himself bankrolled by right-wing Portuguese business interests in Angola, then allied with well-heeled American agents, with European mercenaries, and, ultimately, with the South African army itself. As Samora Machel concluded in the statement cited above: "In Angola, two forces are confronting each other: on the one hand, imperialism and its allies and its puppets; on the other, the progressive popular forces which support MPLA. *There is nothing else.*"

MPLA's Achievement

Against this dismal record, we can set that of MPLA. Media coverage—and some left debate—might lead one to think that this movement had emerged only in recent months, despite the fact of its having been founded in the mid-1950s and having engaged in fifteen years of armed struggle. Hampered by lack of access, via Zaire, to the most populous regions of Angola, MPLA first built an effective military presence in the Cabinda enclave and then, operating from Zambia after 1964, in eastern Angola, slowly but surely pushing westward during subsequent years. Equally important, it began to develop the social infrastructure of a new Angola in the liberated areas (see Davidson).

Perhaps MPLA was somewhat behind FRELIMO militarily and politically when the Portuguese coup came in 1974. The scattered population of the east made that a difficult terrain for triggering off the same "logic of protracted struggle" which had served to radicalize FRELIMO.[3] Moreover, internal tensions—orchestrated by opportunistic and conservative elements within the movement (the Chipenda faction) and by Portuguese intrigues—continued to rack the movement right up until the time of the coup. Nonetheless, a process of radicalization had begun and a direction been set, and it was this increasing clarity of purpose, forged in the struggle, against which "the West" reacted. Clearly, outside interests—Zaire, South Africa, the United States, and Western European countries—have felt threatened in Angola not so much by the presence of Soviet arms and Cuban troops as by the promise of a genuine and radical decolonization which MPLA represents. For any such decolonization could be seen to involve, sooner or later, a stiff challenge to corporate access to Angola's riches, a tantalizing and attractive counter-example to faltering neocolonial projects in the area (e.g., Zaire, Zambia), and a firm base for the escalating struggle, spearheaded by SWAPO, in bordering Namibia, a territory now occupied illegally by South Africa.

Indeed, the shift of the center of MPLA's activities after the coup to the crowded capital city of Luanda—MPLA's original spawning ground in the 1950s and a long-time source of underground support—served to reinforce the movement's radicalization. In the wake of General Spinola's ouster from power in post-coup Portugal, MPLA, alone of the three movements, tried to make the short-lived, power-sharing Angolan transitional government work; it then moved, under siege, to the establishment of the independent People's Republic of Angola in November 1975.

But during both phases the movement was increasingly premising its activity upon *poder popular*, people's power, a program which involved the establishment of vital organs of popular participation everywhere at the base of the new system. Spurned from the outset as a dangerously democratic departure by FNLA and UNITA, but real enough in its practice to have impressed even some of the most jaded of Western correspondents, *poder popular* has been one of the crucial features distinguishing MPLA's positive plans for a transformed Angola from those of its rivals. Moreover, this program has begun to be a springboard for distinctive departures in the direction of workers' control in industry and for a move toward collective productive activity in the rural sphere (to the extent that the logistics of war have permitted). And it contains the promise of even more radical undertakings to come. Certainly, the popular identification with MPLA which *poder popular* has facilitated has been one key to the military success of the new People's Republic.

Equally impressive, and quite important in present-day Angola, have been MPLA's efforts, once again rooted in its long history, to transcend tribalism and to forge a genuinely national policy. Again this contrasts sharply with the activities of FNLA and UNITA. First and foremost the cat's-paws of outside interests, these movements (and especially UNITA in Ovimbundu areas) have managed to strike some indigenous roots by the demagogic manipulation of ethnic fears. Though this is a common enough tactic among the more opportunistic of petty-bourgeois politicians in Africa, it is always difficult to know how deep the resultant kind of ethnic ideology and identification really cuts. What can be said with more confidence, however, is that MPLA has begun working to redress this kind of negative "learning experience" in such areas even as the war has begun to wind down. Particularly encouraging in this respect is the fact that MPLA has heretofore demonstrated, in Luanda and elsewhere, precisely the methods of political work which can be expected to displace such difficulties and bring all Angolans to a higher level of consciousness. But this is merely to repeat the same point from another angle: that MPLA is a revolutionary movement, whereas its so-called rivals are not and never have been.

Such a judgment provides the proper touchstone for evaluating external involvement in Angola. The imperial linkages of FNLA and UNITA are patent, their domestic counter-revolutionary credentials impeccable. Yet Soviet arms and Cuban soldiers have also been important to MPLA's success. What is one to make of these realities? There will be some, of course, who have no difficulty here and who will see this merely as a laudable manifestation of proletarian internationalism and revolutionary solidarity. As noted, others, of right and left, will have greater misgivings about Soviet intentions. However, the crucial point is that whatever one's interpretations of these intentions, there is absolutely no reason to think that MPLA, having struggled for its freedom for twenty years, is about to deliver up that freedom again, even to its friends. As we have seen, the whole thrust of MPLA's development demonstrates the movement's autonomy and drive, as well as distinguishing it clearly from its rivals. In the words of Agostinho Neto, independent Angola's first president, "Just because the Soviet Union supplies us with weapons, it doesn't mean that we have become a satellite. We've never been one. We've never asked Moscow for advice on how to set up our state. All the major decisions in our country are taken by our movement, our government and our people."

Moreover, MPLA has over the years accepted concrete assistance from a wide range of sources in addition to the Eastern bloc—the World Council of Churches, the governments of the Scandinavian countries and Holland, Oxfam-Canada and SUCO, and the like—without feeling its autonomy or its policies to have been compromised; it will probably continue to do so. Similarly, the movement has been firm about keeping the door open to China—not the normal practice for a "Soviet puppet," to say the least. Again, Neto's own words are worth quoting at length:

> One must recognize the People's Republic of China has played an important role in southern Africa in sustaining the liberation

movements of many countries. However, China has erred in certain cases, perhaps for lack of correct analysis. Thus we have seen China support reactionary secessions and coups d'etats. Also in Angola, we see China supporting the reactionary forces created, armed and financed by the Americans with the aim of impeding Africa's revolutionary path. Thus we see China at the side of the Americans fighting against the only forces of national liberation. We hope wholeheartedly that a new analysis of the situation will lead the Chinese to modify their attitude and to support the only progressive forces in Angola. But, on our part, there is no hostility with regard to China. On the contrary, we desire good relations. After independence, we are going to establish relations with the People's Republic of China.[4]

Here spoke the leader of a genuine national liberation struggle, radical and robustly independent—a leader and a movement fully deserving of its prize after twenty years of struggle against a cancerous colonialism and that colonialism's imperial allies.

Why have these realities been ignored in Canada? It is not difficult to understand the reasons for distortion on the part of media and politicians. How much more palatable is opposition to a process of profound social transformation if it can be packaged as resistance to Soviet or Cuban "aggression." Just why some sections of the left should also play this game is more problematic. Perhaps this reveals, first and foremost, the tendency of a left, foiled of significant practice, to permit abstract formulae ("Marxism-Leninism" and the like) and favored centers of revealed revolutionary truth to dictate thinking and strategizing, rather than to undertake the more arduous work of concrete analysis. Certainly, for anyone who has, like the present author, spent more than a decade analyzing the liberation struggles in Southern Africa, the mushrooming of ill-informed instant expertise on the subject of Angola has been particularly distressing. But is it merely the exotic which has been so deformed? In fact, awareness of the difficulties of the Canadian left in dealing with Angola may help sharpen awareness of the extent to which a failure to concretize Marxism in Canada itself has also led to sloganeering and distortion in the discussion of Canadian political economy!

Whatever the case in this regard, it is clearly fortunate that the accumulating victories of MPLA have rendered the vicious distortions of that movement's position a matter of merely academic, not practical, concern. History seems to have left at the starting gate those Canadian parliamentarians of all parties who piously and unanimously agreed, as late as February 9 of this year, to call on "the three major Angolan political groups—the MPLA, FNLA and UNITA—to desist from armed combat and proceed towards a mutually agreed upon peace settlement." So, too, those denizens of the Canadian left who were busy hosting a UNITA representative in Canada at about the same time.

Canada Drags Its Feet

Even "official Canada" now has been forced to keep pace with events. To be sure, for many months delegations requesting that Canada recognize the People's Republic of Angola met a stone wall in Ottawa, the government's refusal sometimes phrased in ironic counterpoint to its earlier and parallel refusal to recognize Guinea-Bissau for long months after that country's winning of independence. Then one of the Canadian government's primary arguments was that PAIGC did not hold the capital city, Bissau. In the Angola case, MPLA's holding of Luanda was seen as being unimportant. *Plus ça change* . . . Similarly, Prime Minister Trudeau, far from using the opportunity of his Cuban visit to enlighten Canadian opinion about Angola, chose to further mystify it, the Canadian government adopting a position on the issue worthy of Henry Kissinger and tacitly accepting the latter's "threat to NATO"–"red menace"–ignore South Africa bluster. Nonetheless, by the end of February, Canada had followed other Western countries—though not yet the United States—in recognizing the People's Republic of Angola as the country's legitimate government.

That much seems settled, then. The fact remains that the continuing confusion over what really happened in Angola—the victory of the popular forces—has obscured the broader significance of the confrontation there. The reference here is to the overt involvement of South Africa in the Angolan struggle, its defeat by a combined MPLA–Cuban force, and the ramifications of this involvement and defeat. To be sure, as of this writing, South Africa is still a military presence in Angola (blandly reported in the press to be defending "its" dam—fifty miles inside another country!) and the Angolan drama may not yet have been played out completely. But what is evident is that the question of South Africa itself has now been placed on the historical agenda more forcefully than at any previous time, and the myth of the white *laager's* invincibility tarnished, perhaps irrevocably. Revolutionary forces within South Africa can only be the beneficiaries.

Of course, South Africa has used the opportunity of military action in "the North" to buttress itself in Namibia (see Roger Murray's article, "South Africa Grabs Opportunity to Bash SWAPO," *African Development*, January 1976). But internally, African advances in Mozambique already have had their impact, as the trial of the SASO Nine in Pretoria for last year's pro-FRELIMO demonstrations is currently demonstrating. Now, not only have Vorster's catastrophic Angolan adventures thrown the South African white community off its stride, but they have also made a further contribution to growing black militancy, *viz.*, the fourth annual Congress of the Black People's Convention, meeting amidst war hysteria in South Africa in December, which came out in direct support of MPLA. Internationally, the republic's illegal hammerlock on Namibia must be even more open to question, and SWAPO will now have its Angolan base, as MPLA has promised. In addition, the military situation in Zimbabwe has begun to heat up again, with African action resting this time on a much firmer foundation. And then there are the hopeful signs that the Soviet Union, having reaped propaganda gains in Africa from its assistance for MPLA, will seek similar gains by backing more effectively liberation groups elsewhere. Perhaps China too will have learned something from its disastrous Angolan policies and begin again to play the positive role in supporting genuine popular forces in other Southern African locales that it once did in Mozambique. In short, it is a heady time indeed in Southern Africa.

The Struggle Continues

At the same time, it would be foolish to underestimate South Africa's continuing strength; it remains a very tough nut to crack. There is also the possibility that Western influence will now consolidate even more forcefully behind South Africa; certainly, this will be the case if saber-rattlers like Kissinger and Ford have their way, the legitimate claims of the liberation movements continuing to be boiled away in a frenzy of anticommunism. Fortunately, the legacy of Vietnam is sufficiently strong that, as the refusal to bankroll heightened American intervention in Angola has recently demonstrated, there is a limit to how far the American Congress will go in backing adventurism in the area. Moreover, on the African continent itself there is considerable solace to be drawn from difficulties experienced by the Organization of African Unity (OAU) in dealing with the Angolan question. The OAU has finally recognized the People's Republic of Angola, but in the months of politicking which preceded that denouement the sheep were firmly separated from the goats in Africa—the Mozambiques, Guineas, and Tanzanias from the Zaires, Kenyas, and Zambias. A more realistic debate within Africa may be the result, one less obscured by the political pursuit of an impossible continental unity on these matters. Less talk, more action—with regard to Zimbabwe, to Namibia, and to South Africa itself. Certainly the seductive South African policy of "detente" and "dialogue" with black Africa—so disastrous in its implications for African hopes—seems to have been the chief casualty in Angola. Clearly, in Southern Africa, now more than ever, *a luta continua*—the struggle continues.

For Canadians concerned about African liberation, the further escalation of the struggle in Southern Africa is likely to be at once an inspiring and a frustrating experience—inspiring at a distance, frustrating closer to home. What, ultimately, are we to do about a situation in this country which finds Ivan Head, the prime minister's foreign policy advisor, surfacing in London (Toronto *Globe and Mail*, February 14, 1976) more concerned about the dangers of the Cubans "going on a rampage" in Southern Africa than about the presence of South African "defence" lines inside Angola. Or about a Toronto *Star* article which crudely summarizes the decades-old struggle for independence in Zimbabwe under the headline "Rhodesia next target for Soviet bloc in Africa"! Obviously only a very different Canada could give rise to a markedly different kind of debate—in fact, only a socialist Canada. At present, we must do what we can to enlighten Canadian discussion and reshape Canada's actions on the difficult terrain available to us.

Notes

1. On this subject see "Liberals and Liberation" by the Toronto Committee for Liberation of Southern Africa (TCLSAC) in *This Magazine*, May–June 1975; that essay now comprises a chapter of TCLSAC's longer book, *Words and Deeds: Canada, Portugal, and Africa*, available from the Committee at 121 Avenue Rd., Toronto.
2. Chinese backing for such a movement—weaponry until June–July 1975, advisors until at least November—can only be explained in terms of that country's misapplication of its stance of global hostility toward the USSR to the Angolan situation—as if Soviet support for MPLA exhausted the meaning and significance of the latter. Similarly, China's continued, and irrelevant, post-November calls for "unity," combined with the shrill invective against "Soviet social imperialism," which has led, in practice, to a downgrading of MPLA's claims in Angola, must have similar roots. At best, this policy has represented a grievous mistake on the part of the Chinese.
3. A study of the "logic of protracted struggle" in the Mozambican case and its effect upon FRELIMO and its policies can be found in ch. 8 of Giovanni Arrighi and John S. Saul, *Essays on the Political Economy of Africa* (New York, 1973).
4. Paulo Jorge, the MPLA representative responsible for external affairs, made a similar remark when addressing a TCLSAC-sponsored meeting in Toronto in late October 1975. Asked about China's role, he stated that "we think the only people who can really explain this position are the Chinese themselves. As for MPLA we find it difficult—very difficult—to understand why a revolutionary government and a revolutionary people should supply arms to a movement like FNLA which in no way represents the aspirations of our people for a genuine independence." Significantly, Jorge's public meeting

was not well attended by members of the Toronto left, many of whom seem to prefer the firm smack of theoretical principle to hard data; moreover, his press conference the next day was virtually ignored by members of the press, many of whom seem to prefer the comfortable certainties of American wire service reports to first-hand international news!

5

TRANSFORMING THE STRUGGLE
IN ZIMBABWE

In 1972, writing about FRELIMO's growing success, military and political, in Mozambique and about the escalation of the struggle in Southern Africa attendant upon such a development, I underscored a problem which this situation was likely to present to those engaged in support work in the metropolitan centers.[1] Events in Mozambique were making clear the extent to which a successful liberation struggle gives rise "to a social revolution and to an anti-imperialist" denouement. In consequence, it was possible to anticipate some of the difficulties that many North Americans would have in "facing squarely the necessity of backing socialist and revolutionary solutions to liberation struggles" and in making the unavoidably "subtle discriminations" between diverse claimants to the nationalist mantle in Southern Africa. Clearly, one felt, our work would become much more difficult as the whole question of the kind of "independence" likely to follow from liberation became as important to support work as the much more straightforward question of resisting white minority domination itself.

The Angolan experience proved the seriousness of the problem. Not surprisingly, many liberals embraced the media-sponsored image of Soviet aggrandizement in that country, sparing themselves the necessity of exploring MPLA's long history of struggle and the indigenous roots of its revolutionary vocation.

This essay was originally published, in substantially the same form, in *Southern Africa*, February 1977.

Unfortunately, many further to the left were similarly confused. Abandoning concrete analysis for the *a priori* approach of pseudoradicalism or for the dictate of some preferred center of revealed revolutionary truth, such people were, at best, reduced to calling irrelevantly for a strategy of "unity" in Angola. At worst, they moved positively to support such grotesque creatures of ethnic manipulation and U.S. and South African design as FNLA or UNITA. Either way, all those who refused to support MPLA's revolutionary project found themselves acting in concert with State Department designs to facilitate a neocolonial solution in Angola and acting against the interests of the Angolan people.[2]

The Lessons of Angola

There are important lessons to be learned from the experience of Angola. However, it seems that Kissinger and Co. began to learn these lessons even more rapidly than those who oppose U.S. imperial designs in Southern Africa. How else to explain Kissinger's dramatic initiatives of this past autumn (1976), as he sought to intervene in the situation in Zimbabwe and Namibia. In Angola, as he apparently felt, the attempt to advance a neocolonial replacement for Portuguese colonial overrule had been left too late. Despite the fact that FNLA and UNITA were willing to play the puppet's role, their bids were viable only to the extent that South Africa itself was prepared to intervene militarily and the United States willing to be fairly open about its participation on the counterrevolutionary side of the equation. Obviously such a direct imperial role had its costs. It helped legitimize Soviet and Cuban assistance to the besieged MPLA. It also aroused the opposition of Congress, still smarting from the precedent of U.S. defeat in Vietnam. Kissinger obviously felt there had to be a better way. And in Rhodesia/Zimbabwe there was—at least in theory.

There was opportunity—but also urgency. For a process of radicalization was under way in Zimbabwe which began to parallel the kind of developments which had led to the emergence of revolutionary projects out of national-liberation struggles in Mozambique and Angola. The independence of Mozambique had opened a much longer and more accessible border to Zimbabweans eager to fight for their freedom. Equally important, FRELIMO was prepared to help Zimbabwean militants learn the lessons Mozambicans had already learned—the necessity to clarify their goals and genuinely to mobilize their people—so that they could overcome their chronic disunity and toughen themselves for effective struggle. The result was signs of the emergence of a new kind of Zimbabwean leadership with a new sense of direction and new methods of working with the people inside the country. Not coincidentally, it also became possible now, for the first time, to pose a serious military threat to Smith. Clearly, the handwriting was on the wall for "Rhodesia."

Kissinger read it. Left to run its course, the Zimbabwean struggle would produce not merely "independence," but a social revolution. Where, then, was Kissinger's opportunity? It lay in the fact that the process of radicalization had only just begun. Fortunately for the secretary of state, there were still many of the old-guard African leaders left over from earlier phases of Zimbabwean politics. Although some had suffered severe hardship—imprisonment and the like—they had passed the years since Smith's Unilateral Declaration of Independence in 1965 engaged primarily in making demands that Britain pull their chestnuts from the fire for them (remove Smith, impose majority rule, bring about change in Zimbabwe). There had also been much jockeying for political advantage in "soon-to-be-liberated" Zimbabwe. Such elements were much more reluctant to embrace the imperatives of guerrilla struggle.

These men, perhaps unbeknownst even to themselves, were Kissinger's secret weapon. Still maintaining considerable credibility with the African population inside the territory, they might be brought to the bargaining table—and to formal political power. Moreover, a shrewd old political chess player like John Vorster of South Africa—holding landlocked Rhodesia's thin economic lifeline in his hands—could also be persuaded to see the elegance of such a gambit. Smith became a pawn to be sacrificed, with a "stable" black regime a consummation more devoutly to be wished.

As subsequent events have made clear, there were flaws in this

Kissinger "game plan," and it seems also to have been mounted rather carelessly. But however sloppy the execution, there can be no doubt about the intention of the operation. It was designed to guarantee "false decolonization." Kissinger had spelled out the premises of this approach quite unequivocally, testifying before the Senate Foreign Relations Committee in May 1976 that "we have a stake . . . in not having the whole continent become radical and move in a direction that is incompatible with Western interests. That is the issue." It was left to Britain's Foreign Secretary Anthony Crosland, addressing the NATO foreign ministers in Brussels during December's Geneva meetings between Ian Smith and the old-guard nationalist leaders, to make the application of this approach to Zimbabwe perfectly clear. Stating that "he had not abandoned hope of success for the [Geneva] conference" he went on to say that

> if the British government gave up hope, there would be no doubt over who would eventually win on the battlefield. But if the issue were settled on the battlefield it would seriously lessen the chance of bringing about a moderate African regime in Rhodesia and would open the way for more radical solutions and external intervention on the part of others. . . .[3]

Note, in particular, the order in which these dangers are presented. It is not the spectre of Soviet aggrandizement which is first and foremost in the minds of such plotters. Rather it is social revolution that they fear.

Zimbabwean Nationalism

Let us set aside, for the moment, one range of questions concerning the Kissinger/Crosland scenario—such questions as: How easily can Smith be cowed into cooperation? How far is Vorster really willing, and able, to go in applying pressure to Smith to so cooperate? And so on. Here it is more important to elaborate upon the apparent premises of Kissinger and Crosland regarding the African side of the Zimbabwe equation. If, from the point of view of imperial interests, neocolonialism is the name of the game, who, more specifically, are the prime Zimbabwean candidates for the role of "intermediary" (to borrow Frantz Fanon's pungent term)?

This is one crucial question. There is a second: Where within the Zimbabwean struggle is the more genuinely revolutionary impulse (an impulse so obviously feared by "the West") to be found? As noted at the outset of this article, these are precisely the kinds of questions to which those who support the cause of Southern African liberation must increasingly address themselves. What has been said subsequently about imperialism's designs in Zimbabwe can only have served to reinforce this point. A thumbnail sketch of the recent history of Zimbabwean nationalism may help to provide more precise answers to these crucial questions.

Zimbabwean nationalism crystallized organizationally in the 1950s when the previously rather tame African National Congress was taken over by more radically populist elements from such groups as the City Youth League and the trade unions; Joshua Nkomo was elected president of the "new" ANC in 1957. This basic thrust survived into the 1960s even though the form of its expression changed—from ANC to National Democratic Party (NDP) to Zimbabwe African People's Union (ZAPU)—as each preceding organization was banned, in turn, by the Rhodesian government. Even more serious for the future than such changes, however, was the split within ZAPU in 1963. This split gave rise to a second, parallel claimant to nationalist primacy, the Zimbabwean African National Union (ZANU). As the struggle between these two movements still scars the nationalist landscape of Zimbabwe, the story of this original split continues to be rewritten to service their latter-day jockeying for political advantage.

Recently, for example, some ZANU-inspired accounts have presented the founders of ZANU as being distinguished by their articulation, in those early days, of a strategy of armed resistance to white minority rule far in advance of the conventional nationalist approach of Joshua Nkomo and his colleagues, left behind in ZAPU. Yet the analysis presented some years ago by Giovanni Arrighi seems closer to the mark. Employing a class analysis, he gives ZAPU the better of the argument, stressing that this was a confrontation between a faction of educated, middle-class, rather elitist elements who had joined the nationalist movement in the early sixties (these men now becoming the core of ZANU under Ndabaningi Sithole) and those populists from the mid-1950s (he mentions Nyandoro and Chikerema) who had much firmer roots among the migrant workers and the peasantry itself.[4]

But even if there is some truth in the latter emphasis, what seems even more obvious, in retrospect, is that *neither* group readily found the key to mobilizing and focusing popular energies in ways which could be effective under the circumstances presented to them. Symbolic actions and mass protests worked politically in situations where Britain was eager, after initial African assertions, to strike a neocolonial bargain. In Rhodesia such actions merely pushed the dominant settler caste further to the right, on a course which led ultimately to the unilateral declaration of independence. To be sure, ZAPU had already begun to take some steps toward launching a more effective (and necessarily violent) form of resistance even before the 1963 split, and both movements were to undertake military and quasi-military actions in subsequent years. Yet in both cases the political clarity necessary to underwrite effective guerrilla struggle was apparently lacking. At the same time, the absence of that meaningful revolutionary practice which effective guerrilla struggle provides forestalled much real political growth for Zimbabwean nationalism! The dynamic process which had become a self-reinforcing pattern of development in the case of Mozambican revolutionary nationalism—political clarity facilitating guerrilla activity, this in turn encouraging greater clarity[5]—remained for Zimbabweans a negative vicious circle out of which they found it difficult to break.

Instead, Zimbabwean exile politics, both inside and between the liberation movements, came to manifest many of the most negative features characteristic of petty-bourgeois politics in already independent, neocolonial Africa. There is, to be sure, a certain irony in this since it is the phantom of power rather than its reality which has provided the focus for such activity. As Kenneth Good has described it: "Settler colonialism in Rhodesia has taken full advantage from the existence of a constitutional mystification over the location of ultimate political power. . . . Britain has cooperated with Rhodesia in the maintenance of an important illusion, which has misdirected African nationalism away from Salisbury and towards London."[6] But however unreal such shadow-boxing, the upshot has been the same: In the absence of revolutionary politics, intra-elite factionalism has filled the political vacuum, one temptation for such factions being the use of any existing ethnic tensions to build their own constituencies. Thus, in Rhodesia, conflicts between Shona and Ndebele, or among Shona subgroups, have been heightened, instead of ended, in the years of nationalist infighting.

In independent Africa such a pattern of petty-bourgeois politics serves to preempt the kind of radical politics which might eventually lead to the launching of development strategies genuinely designed to meet popular needs. In Zimbabwe it has served to forestall the day when Smith might be put under significant pressure by the force of African nationalism!

Internal Conflicts

Such, then, has been the politics of charge and countercharge between ZAPU and ZANU over the years. Such was the politics of ZAPU's desperate collapse into internecine squabbling in 1969–70, one upshot of which was the addition of yet a third (though, happily, marginal) "liberation movement" to the kaleidoscope of Zimbabwean petty-bourgeois politics (ZAPU and ZANU dissidents forming the Front for the Liberation of Zimbabwe—FROLIZI). More unfortunate was the fact that this infighting came hard on the heels of ZAPU's most dramatic military undertakings, the bold strikes, launched jointly with South Africa's ANC, into the Zambezi valley at Wankie, Kariba, and Victoria Falls between 1968 and 1970. Unfortunate because these actions, despite their boldness, had revealed profound weaknesses in ZAPU's whole approach to liberation, especially in the movement's relative disregard for those methods of political work which might have served to provide the popular basis for effective guerrilla struggle. Yet the movement's further internal difficulties dictated that there was little opportunity for the lessons of Wankie to be learned or for ZAPU to then develop a more revolutionary practice.

Rather more militarily promising, and duly celebrated in the recent literature on Zimbabwe, was the ZANU-sponsored guerrilla activity mounted in the northeast of the country from December 1972. This, plus the fact that ZANU enjoyed Chinese backing, has given rise, in some circles on the left, to the view that ZANU had here emerged as the cutting edge of the Zimbabwean revolution. However, this interpretation demands careful scrutiny—particularly since any such judgment has important implications for the evaluation of the current balance of forces in Zimbabwe.

Certainly the "Chinese factor" can be more or less discounted. China's dismal record in Angola would, in and of itself, suggest this. The fact is, however, that Angola provides merely the most extreme example of a generally disturbing pattern. Whatever China's distinctive merits on other grounds, its policy in Southern Africa has been quite appalling, reduced to the backing of almost any movement which did not already enjoy Soviet support—quite without regard to the objective merits of the various movements involved. But if the fact of Chinese backing is no ready index of revolutionary merit, what of ZANU's guerrilla activities themselves?

These have been impressive in many ways—particularly relative to previous Zimbabwean military undertakings—although it is nonetheless difficult to avoid the impression that accounts by Maxey and others have somewhat romanticized them.[7] As is well known, ZANU's incursions from 1972 on were facilitated by FRELIMO, who had, at this point, liberated enough of Tete province to permit passage of the guerrillas into Zimbabwe. FRELIMO has been well placed, therefore, to witness and evaluate the progress being made. Yet when I visited Tete in late 1972, at a time when the groundwork for ZANU activity was being laid, it seemed to me that FRELIMO then entertained few illusions that ZANU had yet defined a political line capable of sustaining a genuinely transforming process of popular struggle. I was to get the same impression three years later, in June

1975, in discussing Zimbabwean developments with officials of the new Mozambican government in Maputo. My impression was that to FRELIMO the fighting of 1972–75 in the northeast of Zimbabwe, while of obvious importance, had remained too exclusively militarist in its orientation, ZANU's methods of work being still far removed from those which characterize a people's war. In fact, FRELIMO was most unwilling to differentiate between ZANU and ZAPU as regards their military or political capabilities at that point, seeming instead to be rather discouraged by the performance of both movements.

It is significant that it was toward the end of this period that ZANU came apart at the seams, much as had ZAPU several years previously—the assassination of Herbert Chitepo, ZANU's acting chairman, being the most dramatic outcome of such a pattern of development. Some attempt has been made to portray these events as reflecting a contestation between right-wing opportunists on the one hand and all those within the organization who were prepared to move with the radicalizing logic of protracted struggle on the other. Supporters of this view draw an analogy with the Simango crisis, which had signaled a critical turning point in the progressive transformation of FRELIMO itself in the late 1960s. On such an interpretation, the process of the emergence of a genuinely revolutionary nationalism in Zimbabwe is seen as playing itself out *within* ZANU, that movement then having a claim to priority with respect to support from all those who wish the Zimbabwean struggle well.

Yet, again, this is not a parallel which FRELIMO personnel have found to be an illuminating one when it has been put to them. A much stronger case can be made for the view that such internal problems as ZANU experienced in 1974–75 smacked more of the same old wasting kind of petty-bourgeois political infighting—centered upon personalities, intrigues, and the mobilization of constituencies around ethnic identifications (in this case, various Shona subgroups), all long-time features of a Zimbabwean exile politics untransformed by effective struggle. Small wonder that FRELIMO officials with whom I talked in mid-1975 saw the military and political struggle in Zimbabwe at this time as more or less starting from scratch. Indeed, Mozambique stated at this juncture that it would not cut the vital Beira rail link to Rhodesia nor act to reinforce sanctions until Zimbabweans were ready to take advantage of such moves and present a real challenge to the Smith regime. Significantly, Mozambique did not act until fully nine months later, in March 1976. Explaining Mozambique's actions that month, President Machel said:

> In Zimbabwe, it will be a people's struggle and it will be protracted. It will allow Zimbabweans to transform the present nationalist struggle into a revolutionary struggle that implies profound changes in the society. . . . So we would like the struggle to be a long one in order to liberate the mentality of Zimbabweans.[8]

ZIPA the Key

Thus neither ZANU nor ZAPU were seen to hold the key. No more did the African National Congress. The ANC had sprung into life to give focus to African rejection of the 1971 compromise constitutional proposals put forward by Britain. The British sent the Pearce Commission to Rhodesia to test African feeling. The answer, often expressed through the ANC, was a resounding NO. The commission went home to England, but the ANC continued to exist, adding another quasi-movement to Zimbabwe's nationalist sweepstakes (alongside ZANU, ZAPU, and, much more marginally, FROLIZI). The ANC's success also added Bishop Abel Muzorewa to the corps of senior political notables who have become well known to the Zimbabwean populace. In 1974–75 the ANC became the umbrella organization under which the leaders of the front-line states encouraged the old political notables (Muzorewa, Nkomo, and Sithole in particular) to establish a common front and to begin negotiations with Smith and Vorster. Very soon, however, this new umbrella ANC simply reverted to the old pattern of Zimbabwean politics with the revival of intense fragmentation among the old-guard leadership and the old-line organizations.

Small wonder that FRELIMO—mindful of its own experience—chose to give its firmest support to the new military-cum-political leadership which it felt *could* emerge from the camps within Mozambique and Tanzania as the guerrilla struggle gathered new impetus along the extended frontier provided by a free Mozambique. Moreover, it seems that FRE-LIMO's assessment has proved to be at least partially correct. The Zimbabwe People's Army (ZIPA) which has now emerged has drawn on the energies and dedication which existed below the top leadership level, in the military wings of both ZANU (ZANLA) and ZAPU (ZIPRA), and it has begun to focus these and build upon them. Dzinashe Machingura, ZIPA's deputy political commissar, recently epitomized the founding of ZIPA as follows:

> After the fighters had realized the incompetence of the ANC leadership they took it upon themselves to reconstitute themselves into an army that would fight for the independence of the Zimbabwe people. The combatants from both former ZANU and former ZAPU agreed to form a joint military command that would lead the armed struggle. . . . The joint military command was formed on the understanding that the liberation of Zimbabwe could only be realized through an arduous armed struggle; secondly, on the understanding that the traditional leadership of Zimbabwe had divided the people of Zimbabwe.[9]

Such were the origins of ZIPA. The interview from which these statements are taken (see *Southern Africa*, November 1976) also has a great deal to say about the conceptions currently guiding ZIPA's practice:

> ZIPA is an army in the traditional sense of the word. But ZIPA is a unique and revolutionary army in the sense that it has a strategic role in transforming itself into a political movement. The ZIPA structure accommodates the shouldering of both the military and political tasks of the revolution. We have, within the ZIPA structure, a political department exclusively charged with the responsibility of shouldering the political tasks that are normally shouldered by a revolutionary political organization.
> . . . we have to establish a formal political structure in order to give better direction to the armed body that is now fighting inside Zimbabwe. And moves to do this are already underway, moves to transform this organization into a revolutionary vanguard for the people's struggle.

This formulation, and others like it from ZIPA's cadre of guerrilla leaders, represents something fresh and promising within Zimbabwean nationalism. Certainly these are not the familiar formulations of ZANU or ZAPU.

The actual practice of ZIPA has also differed from that of the old organizations. There has been a distinctive measure of military success, which has been linked to other signs that, within ZIPA, Zimbabweans have at last begun to break out of the vicious circle alluded to earlier, just as did the Mozambicans before them. New methods of political work in the field are one such sign; another is the beginnings of a capacity to *transcend* (and not merely temporarily to paper over in the name of "unity") earlier organizational loyalties and subnational identifications. Of course, in this and other areas we must guard against overstatement. As Samora Machel's observation, cited above, might warn us, it is still early days in the transition to revolutionary nationalism in Zimbabwe. There seems little doubt that ZANU/ZAPU infighting, and even ethnic tensions, have continued to make themselves felt from time to time within this "Third Force"; in fact, some "ZAPU commanders" of ZIPA are said to have withdrawn their cooperation in recent months and relocated their activity inside ZAPU and within Zambia.

Even if this is the case, however, it would still be a great mistake to see the ZIPA initiative as having collapsed to the point where it is merely ZANU/ZANLA operating under another name. Yet this is the interpretation which much of the press, both left and right, has tended to present. Thus, in the context of the Geneva talks, Robert Mugabe, a long-time ZANU activist who has replaced Sithole as the dominant figure among those claiming the mantle of ZANU leadership, is being packaged by the media as spokesman for both ZANU and ZIPA. This in spite of the fact that Mugabe's recent base of political operations—in Quelimane on the Mozambican coast—has been well away from the centers of guerrilla activity, that his position on the Geneva talks has not been the same as that of the public pronouncements of the ZIPA leadership, and that ZIPA spokesmen have shown themselves to be quite loath to identify themselves politically with Mugabe in any straightforward manner. It seems clear, in other words, that the distinctive process which has been shaping the promise of ZIPA's future development has not been Mugabe's, or ZANU's, handiwork; nor has it been the handiwork of any other of the old-guard leadership sitting across from Smith in Geneva.

The Future

Will Kissinger's adventures, and the Geneva charade, serve to forestall the radicalizing process which we have been discussing? An important query, to be sure, but with it we enter more deeply into the realm of journalistic scenario-building than this article can or should hope to venture. Suffice to say here that Geneva has, for the moment, brought the old guard back more firmly into the game—this being precisely the intention of Western strategists, as we have seen. Obviously this creates the danger that the revolutionary process will be short-circuited by the old guard (by virtue of their striking a neocolonial bargain), as well as the concomitant possibility that the renewed jockeying for position among these notables will serve further to activate old-style fragmentation along party, ethnic, and other lines even within the Zimbabwean revolutionary camp itself.

At the same time, there are also hints that an alternative, more revolutionary kind of logic may be at work. It is difficult, for example, to escape the conclusion that part of the reason the old guard (Nkomo and Mugabe in particular) have been as united as they have been at Geneva (the "Patriotic Front"), and so little prone to compromise away the essence of African demands, is because they realize that they are no longer exclusive arbiters of the nature of Zimbabwean nationalism.[10] Perhaps the revolutionary process which ZIPA represents has gone far enough that the guerrillas, with their promise to the Zimbabwean people of a more meaningful independence than that which neocolonialism can offer, have become crucial participants in the negotiations almost in spite of themselves. They thus force the entire spectrum of Zimbabwean nationalism further to the left. And meanwhile, in Zimbabwe itself the guerrillas' struggle is continuing, with further radicalizing implications.

Which tendency within Zimbabwean nationalism will prevail?

Unfortunately, there are far too many relevant variables to allow any very meaningful speculation. In any case, the precise timing of developments will obviously be delicate and of crucial importance. Many of these variables will lie on the side of entrenched power—the intentions and capabilities of Smith and the settlers, of Vorster and South Africa, of Jimmy Carter—about which we have said little here. Yet what this article may at least have suggested is that supporters of the struggle for the liberation of Zimbabwe cannot avoid carefully scrutinizing the revolutionary capacities of various nationalist claimants, however much we may wish to avoid the appearance of "sitting in judgment."

For the Kissingers and the Croslands are making and acting upon such judgments. The implication is clear: We shall find ourselves disarmed if we are not prepared to operate on the same terrain as they. It is in this spirit that I have made, somewhat controversially, the case for taking the novel initiative which ZIPA has represented very seriously, and for differentiating it sharply from other institutionalized expressions of Zimbabwean nationalism. I see this as a premise for support work, not merely a disembodied analytical judgment.

Postscript 1978

More than any of the other essays in this book, the present one has been outpaced by events—albeit by events consistent with the possibilities foreshadowed in the essay's final paragraphs. The positive initiative exemplified by ZIPA did collapse in the face of Kissinger's ploy and under the weight of the past; it was not long, for example, before one heard of ZANU members who had participated in the ZIPA experiment (including, apparently, Dzinashe Machingura, quoted above) being "disciplined" by a resurgent ZANU leadership. At the same time, it seems clear that I did overestimate—as even FRELIMO may have done—the possibility of ZIPA's project meeting with success under existing Zimbabwean circumstances. Yet the essay remains something more than a mere requiem for ZIPA. It does cast real light on the kinds of difficulties Zimbabweans have had in consolidating their liberation struggle; moreover, by bringing into focus the vicious circle created by the pattern of petty-bourgeois politics in the Zimbabwean liberation camp and by highlighting the processes which have periodically held some promise of breaking that circle, the analysis makes for illuminating comparisons with the cases of Angola and Mozambique, studied earlier in this book. For these reasons I have allowed it to stand as originally written.

Not that the brief moment represented by ZIPA has been entirely without its positive legacy. The Patriotic Front, mentioned at the conclusion of the essay, has continued to provide some kind of framework for a loose alliance of ZAPU and ZANU, and even if Mugabe and, more especially, Nkomo are still wooed assiduously by imperialist strategists, such is the legacy of Geneva that they have not been inclined to countenance many of the latter's more obvious ploys and enticements. Indeed Smith, when he has occasionally contemplated, at Western and South African encouragement, a "false decolonization," now looks to safer leaders like Muzorewa and Sithole. Meanwhile in both ZAPU and ZANU genuine militants have continued to surface out of the ongoing struggle and to have some positive effect on the character of these movements' activities. Enough has been achieved, for example, to allow the military-cum-political undertakings of both movements inside Rhodesia significantly to escalate the pressure against the Smith regime. Of course, the situation remains one of obvious complexity and is in constant motion, defying easy prediction. Under such circumstances it seems likely that the evolving situation will continue to teach us a great deal about the forces which facilitate or impede a revolutionary denouement to the struggle for liberation in Africa. But it is equally clear that such a situation will not render any more straightforward the task, in Western countries, of liberation support work around the Zimbabwean issue.

Notes

1. See "FRELIMO and the Mozambique Revolution," in Giovanni Arrighi and John Saul, *Essays on the Political Economy of Africa* (New York, 1973); preceding essays in this volume are also relevant to the argument presented here.

2. There are grounds, certainly, for querying the Soviet Union's global intentions. The point here is that MPLA was, and is, in no way to be reduced to a mere manifestation of these intentions, as anyone with the slightest acquaintance with developments in Angola over the years should know. The subject is explored further in an extended exchange in *Monthly Review*, June 1976, of which essay 4, above, formed a part.

3. As paraphrased in a Reuters account in the *Globe and Mail* (Toronto), December 10, 1976.

4. Giovanni Arrighi, "Black and White Populism in Rhodesia," unpublished ms., 1967.

5. The Mozambican case is examined in my "FRELIMO and the Mozambique Revolution"; the argument there also provides a more general model in terms of which one can evaluate the Zimbabwean case, as does essay 1 of this volume.

6. Kenneth Good, as quoted in A. R. Wilkinson, "From Rhodesia to Zimbabwe," in Davidson, Slovo, and Wilkinson, *Southern Africa: The New Politics of Revolution* (Harmondsworth, 1976).

7. See Kees Maxey, *The Fight for Zimbabwe* (London, 1975), which is nonetheless a gold mine of carefully collected information.

8. Interview with Samora Machel in *The Observer* (London), March 28, 1976.

9. Interview with Dzinashe Machingura by the Mozambique Information Agency, September 22, 1976, first published in English in the *Daily News* (Dar es Salaam) and now available from the Liberation Support Movement as *Zimbabwe People's Army*.

10. It is, of course, also true that Smith's outrageous demands and calculated intransigence have made it very difficult for such leaders to go very far in the direction of compromise.

6

CANADA AND SOUTHERN AFRICA

In a recently published book, *Words and Deeds: Canada, Portugal, and Africa*, the Toronto Committee for the Liberation of Southern Africa (TCLSAC) analyzed the nature of Canada's links to the liberation struggles that were waged for over a decade in Portugal's former African colonies—Angola, Mozambique, and Guinea-Bissau. The pattern that emerged: "Rhetorical commitment to the cause of popular freedom on the one hand and 'business as usual' with the oppressive white-minority regimes on the other." As demonstrated in detail in that volume, Canada's support for Portuguese rule "took three inter-related forms: economic, military, and diplomatic":

> Economically, our bodies corporate and governmental partook readily, and greedily, of the spoils available from the super-exploitation which Portuguese hegemony guaranteed in its African holdings. In doing so, we chose to ignore that such economic activity also helped bankroll an otherwise shaky Portuguese economy in its feckless military endeavours. Militarily, through uncritical acceptance of the NATO connection which married the arsenal of the West to Portuguese colonial purposes, Canada made itself, willy-nilly, a partner of the Portuguese. Perhaps most galling of all, on the diplomatic front our spokespersons also served the cause of Portuguese oppression and Western imperialism well by undermining, systematically, the claims of the liberation

This essay was first published in *Canadian Dimension* (Winnipeg), February 1977.

movements—and of the African people—to their rightful primacy in arbitrating the fate of their own countries.

In short, the evidence came overwhelmingly to support the proposition that "official Canada's record with respect to Portugal's African colonies was a bleak one indeed."

Of course, the military phase of these struggles is over, and Angola, Mozambique, and Guinea-Bissau are now politically independent. Not that this signals their retirement to the sidelines in the ongoing struggle for the liberation of Southern Africa. Angola has moved, for example, to provide the SWAPO guerrillas fighting in Namibia with a more effective springboard for action than they have ever had before. And the crucial role of Mozambique, both in underwriting the increased success of Zimbabwean guerrillas within their own country and in turning the screw of sanctions ever more firmly upon Smith, cannot be doubted. The fact that each of the former Portuguese colonies has chosen to embark upon ambitious and genuinely radical paths toward development in the wake of winning independence is also important. Certainly Mozambique's example—its radicalization part and parcel of the waging of a successful guerrilla campaign—has been an instructive one for others in Southern Africa (e.g., for a new generation of Zimbabwean leaders, eager to transcend the chronic disunity and lack of firm purpose which has haunted their struggle) and beyond. Moreover, the willful distortion of the undertakings of these regimes—the highly misleading rumor-mongering about internal discord or Soviet control—which fills the North American press must be seen for what it is, part of a counteroffensive against the prospect of a genuinely revolutionary change throughout Southern Africa. There are good reasons, then, why Canadians concerned about Southern Africa must not forget the fact that in ex-Portuguese Africa *a luta continua*—the struggle continues.

At the same time, there can be no mistaking the significance of the fact that the front line of contestation in the area has now shifted farther south. In the past year Zimbabwean guerrillas have for the first time evidenced a clear capacity to confront successfully the settler regime in their country, and in Namibia, too, the pace of liberation has begun to quicken. Most dramatically of all, the beleaguered populations of Johannesburg, Capetown, and other South African centers have demonstrated to the world that apartheid is not quite the closed and stable engine of oppression that it has sometimes appeared to be. Even in South Africa, then, and in spite of the fact that the process will undoubtedly prove to be a long and bitter one, significant transformation of the status quo has been placed on the agenda more unequivocally than ever. Indeed, it is precisely with the struggle escalating so rapidly throughout the area that one now asks the further question: What is Canada's role likely to be on the fronts which are thus being brought into renewed prominence?

TCLSAC's prognosis in this regard is worth noting. *Words and Deeds* concludes that:

> Canada's role is likely to become an even less savoury one as the struggle escalates beyond "Portugal's African colonies," in Zimbabwe/Rhodesia, in Namibia/South-West Africa, and in South Africa itself. In these areas, and particularly in the Republic of South Africa, official Canada is likely to feel it has a much more substantial economic stake than ever it had in Angola and Mozambique. Since this is also the calculation of American corporations and of the United States and other NATO-involved Western governments, it is difficult to see Canada breaking with the latter interests or countering any drift toward intensified Western sponsorship of the white minority regimes.

In fact, a closer look indicates that this was already the pattern which characterized Canadian policy further south even before the recent escalation. The dichotomy between "words" and "deeds" was by no means confined to the case of "Portuguese Africa."

The irony of the situation is perhaps best captured by Prime Minister Trudeau's own pithy remark of several years back on the subject of trade with the white minority regimes in Southern Africa: "It's not consistent . . . We should either stop trading or stop condemning"! In practice, of course, Canada has done neither. Take, in the first instance, Rhodesia (Zimbabwe) and

South-West Africa (Namibia). Here we have two pariah states—
illegal regimes—which Canada has never tired of condemning in
the course of supporting various international resolutions. Yet
the limits which hedge in such condemnation are very real.

In the Rhodesian case, to be sure, many more of the forms of
resistance to white domination have been observed than is true
elsewhere; most prominent in this respect has been our partial
adherence to the policy of sanctions against the Smith gang in
power. Yet this is not difficult to explain. After all, the enactment
of sanctions was seen by Britain and its allies as being a much less
explosive way of dealing with the 1965 Unilateral Declaration of
Independence (UDI) than other more tough-minded solutions
being pressed for by African and other Third World countries at
the time. In consequence, Canada actually enacted into Canadian law certain provisions of the UN's mandatory-sanctions
regulations, the result being the decline of our direct trade with
Rhodesia to a trickle and the rendering of many other economic
operations of Canadian-based companies there much more complex and difficult. Of course, the recent interception in London
of Rhodesian tobacco, lightly disguised, bound for MacDonald
Tobacco of Tillsonburg, Ontario, may be merely the tip of the
iceberg with respect to the scope of any continuing illicit trade as
may be the recent exposé of the Canadian Imperial Bank of
Commerce's role in bankrolling expansion of the Rhodesian cop-
per industry through its Nassau office. It seems equally clear that
some firms (Massey-Ferguson, for example) merely continue to
trade with Rhodesia via their South African subsidiaries.

Moreover, the narrow limits which the government has set on
action in this sphere are at least as revealing as the action which
has been forthcoming. To begin with, Canadian law enacts only
very limited aspects of the relevant UN sanctions, and one could
make a very convincing case for the proposition that those terms
which do exist in our law have been selected with care so as not to
impinge on the functioning of such important corporations as
Bata and Falconbridge—whether one considers the matter of
paying taxes in Rhodesia or of dealing with the illegal regime via
South Africa or (as in the case of Falconbridge) of entering into
joint development ventures with the Rhodesian government. In

addition, even our enforcement of those sanctions which do exist in Canadian law has been slack. One could note here such relatively minor peccadilloes as the failure to restrict the operations of Canadian travel agents vis-à-vis Rhodesia, but more sinister, once again, has been the kind of kid-gloves treatment afforded a corporation like Falconbridge.

One kind of answer to embarrassing questions on this subject was the astounding response in Parliament of Mr. Breau, then parliamentary secretary to the minister of industry, trade, and commerce, to the effect that "Our records reveal no evidence that there are direct corporate ties between Falconbridge Nickel Co. Ltd. and Blanket Mines [in Rhodesia]," this in spite of the fact that Falconbridge's annual report normally discusses in detail its Blanket Mines operations and the profits earned therefrom. Other pressures, from the Task Force on the Churches and Corporate Responsibility, for example, have brought more subtly evasive responses from government spokesmen. Apparently Falconbridge feels itself to be under so little pressure from either government or citizenry, however, that it need be neither subtle nor even particularly evasive. Asked at the 1976 shareholders meeting why the 1975 annual report this time contained no report on Blanket Mines, the chairman of Falconbridge blandly replied that most senior employees of Blanket Mines were now enlisted in the Rhodesian army and had therefore had not had time to send in their report![1]

Namibia provides an even more startling example. South Africa's hold upon Namibia has been clearly identified as an illegal one both by the World Court and the United Nations, a fact freely admitted to by Canadian spokespersons both in various international forums and in the House of Commons. Yet in this case Canada has not bothered to enact into Canadian law any of the relevant UN resolutions that would serve to choke off economic interchange with the regime there. Indeed, no limits whatsoever have been placed upon Canadian-based corporations operating in Namibia, and such important firms as Falconbridge and the Hudson's Bay Company have been very prominent on the scene, operating upon the most exploitative terms imaginable.[2] Not surprisingly, the business community has stood foursquare for "business as usual" under these circumstances. Such was the case, for example, after Bishop Richard Wood, in exile from Namibia, had patiently explained the facts of life in that country to an annual general meeting of the Bay in Winnipeg in early 1976. After gracelessly defending the company in the meeting itself, George Richardson, governor of the Hudson's Bay Company, returned to the charge the next day at a press conference, reiterating the most misleading of pieties:

> George Richardson believes Canada should review its pledged support of the United Nations ruling that member countries abstain from any business dealings with Namibia, formerly South-West Africa. . . . Mr. Richardson said that "maybe" the Bay's trading with Namibia was illegal but he still considered what the company was doing was morally right. . . . "The Namibians and the United Nations and all this is after the fact. We were there long before it came up [*sic*]. We actually ran a sorting station for them down there employing native people. If it weren't for this sorting station they wouldn't have the competency to get the pelts out of the country and market them. I may be prejudiced but I view what we're doing as a service."
>
> Mr. Richardson said he spent some time in Namibia. . . . "I saw the administrator of Namibia and heard what he was trying to accomplish. I saw the prime minister of South Africa and heard what he said. And if you can believe them—and I think you have to—and when you see what they're doing, the kind of thing we [Canada] can do is leave them alone." (*Winnipeg Free Press*, May 28, 1976)

In fact, the Canadian government has not been as far out of step with Bay policy as Mr. Richardson might like to suggest. Indeed, so quiescent has it been—quiescent even in comparison with the American government, which has gone so far as to caution its bodies corporate about operating in Namibia—that at least one U.S. corporation (Brilund Mines) is said to have established a small Canadian subsidiary precisely to exploit Namibian business opportunities from a Canadian rather than a U.S. base! The Canadian government remains unflappable about such anomalies. Indeed, quite apart from its predictable failure to challenge the actual legitimacy of any Canadian corporate presence in Namibia, the government has also chosen to ignore the invitation to pursue even so moderate and eminently "liberal" a course as a questioning of the brutal character (in terms of wage levels and working conditions) of the operations of Falconbridge and others on the ground.[3]

Or consider the several challenges mounted in the House of Commons over the fact that Falconbridge receives credits against Canadian taxation for monies paid to an illegal authority—recognized as such by Canada—in Namibia. Most often, again, the official response to any such inquiries has been merely evasive, as in Allan McEachen's "answer" to this tax-concession question when it was put to him quite concretely and specifically:

> Of course, there is no way under Canadian law by which the government can force any mode of conduct on business operations of Canadian subsidiaries in other countries. Furthermore . . . it is a principle of government policy not to interfere in the operations of Canadian companies abroad.

Namibia? "In a more general way the Canadian government, of course, does not recognize the authority of South Africa over Namibia. We have recognized the authority of the United Nations Commissioner and we regard the present situation as illegal." Of course. But what of tax concessions? That part of the question, the guts of it, is, quite simply, ignored!

Sometimes the answer has been more forthright, however. Here is the excuse of Maurice Foster, parliamentary secretary to the minister of energy, mines, and resources, when confronted with a similar query: "However, we must recognize that South Africa does de facto remain in control of Namibia." It need hardly be emphasized that neither response, neither McEachen's nor Foster's, to the charge of government inaction is particularly palatable. And little more need be added to them here. Little, that is, but to contrast this kind of sluggish myopia with the warm welcome received by SWAPO delegations (SWAPO being Namibia's liberation movement) from workers in Sudbury (principal Falconbridge base in Canada) on the two occasions when

SWAPO visited that city. Here, perhaps, we can glimpse the seeds of a different kind of relationship between Namibia and Canada than the one to which we are accustomed.

Obviously, the South African regime is not "illegal" in the same sense that those in Rhodesia and South-West Africa are. But this is not the point at issue; "official Canada" has had no difficulty in recognizing, verbally, the outrageous nature of the system in South Africa and the affront to "morality" which apartheid represents. The most public arena for expressing official indignation has been, of course, in the realm of sports. The Canadian government has consistently and aggressively sought to stem Canadian sporting links with South Africa, often going against the grain of prominent opinion-makers in so doing and thereby demonstrating some willingness to shoulder the resultant political costs. The denying of federal funds to the Olympiad for the Disabled in the summer of 1976 and the righteous indignation—from *Sun, Star,* and *Globe and Mail* in Toronto—which this act called down upon the government's head provide a case in point. Moreover, it would be churlish to suggest that the government's action was occasioned entirely by the fear of African boycott of Olympic and Commonwealth games in Canada. Certainly Marc Lalonde's various public statements on the issue have had the firm smack of sincerity.

However, such gestures mark the outer limits of the liberal imagination and the liberal possibility in fighting apartheid. Move beyond such an arena—an arena in which words can spill over into modest deeds without representing any real challenge to the broad economic and strategic parameters which hedge in this country's policy—and the story quickly becomes the more familiar one. Thus, Canada's economic links to the status quo in South Africa range from bizarre anomaly (South Africa's sugar and certain other commodities still enjoy Commonwealth preference in this country more than fifteen years after South Africa's expulsion from the Commonwealth) to systematic exploition by a range of Canadian corporations of what come close to being slave-labor conditions (see "The Nangle Report"). Place in the latter category, among others, Alcan, Massey-Ferguson, Ford of

Canada (and note that Ford South Africa is a subsidiary of Ford of Canada, not Ford U.S.!). Place alongside them a Canadian government that works overtime to press the claims of South Africa's investment and commercial opportunities upon the Canadian business community. A reading of any of the numerous glowing articles on the subject which have appeared in *Commerce Canada* in recent years would serve to make this by now familiar point. Related evidence of the government's sense of the economic main chance in contemporary Africa can also be gathered from the fact that Canada has had, for many years, more ministry of trade and commerce personnel on assignment in South Africa than in all the remaining countries of the African continent combined.

Such a list could be extended indefinitely. All in all, it is small wonder that the level of Canada's economic interchange with South Africa has continued to rise dramatically, with the complementary flow *into* Canada of an increasingly large amount of South African capital (Anglo-American, Rothmans) merely serving to cement such a partnership.[4] Small wonder, too, that Canadian banks should be partners to the powerful, semi-secretive banking consortium which has stepped forward in the 1970s to help stabilize a faltering South African economy; so far four Canadian banks have been implicated in these activities. A similar consortium was crucial in helping the badly shaken white regime to reconsolidate its control over a freshly mobilized populace in the wake of the Sharpville massacre of the early 1960s. Canadian bankers—generally considered to be the cutting edge of any independent imperial project which Canada might be thought to possess—have become active participants in a similar endeavor.

Beyond this kind of evidence, it can also be emphasized that its vital economic stake in apartheid has meant for imperialism generally a growing preoccupation with the defense of such a stake. Under the cover of concern about the growing Soviet "threat" to sea lanes in the Indian Ocean and the South Atlantic, this has dictated a slow but certain convergence between NATO and South African defense activities. Recent years have brought revelations concerning NATO's having undertaken (through

SACLANT, the Supreme Allied Command Atlantic) contingency planning for Southern Africa in conjunction with the South African government, and of South Africa's having been brought into the NATO defense-code area as part of the alliance's extensive cooperation in developing Project Advocaat, a grandiose naval-surveillance system established at Silvermine, new headquarters for the South African navy.

Moreover, such NATO activity is of a piece with what we know (from the exposure of U.S. National Security Study Memorandum No. 39 and from other sources) of U.S. designs to vigorously support South Africa in the event of any sustained contestation in the area. And while it is true that there has been some rather muted protest within NATO against the drift of such developments, this protest has never come from Canada. Instead, we have found ourselves—just as in the case of Portugal in Africa—tacitly supporting escalation. To be sure, Canada has demonstrated some facility in fending off the most overt military entanglements which might otherwise seem to be part and parcel of our government's sustained commitment to defense of the "free world." Perhaps this will also prove to be the case in Southern Africa. What does seem unlikely is that any escalation which evokes a continuing NATO preoccupation with the area will leave us with very clean hands.

As noted earlier, *Words and Deeds* pinpointed a third aspect, beyond the economic and the military, of our negative record in "Portuguese Africa." For, even as we participated through NATO in the arming of Portugal, we also chose, through our efforts in the diplomatic arena, to help *disarm* those who fought against the Portuguese—by preaching peace when conflict was both necessary (because of Portuguese intransigence and state-sponsored terror) and progressive, and by generally denying meaningful assistance, and even legitimacy, to the liberation movements engaged in armed conflict. A similar pattern has marked our approach to struggles elsewhere in Southern Africa, and this is an aspect of policy which, in light of recent developments in imperial strategies in the area, could become much more prominent in the future.

This latter reference is to the recent Kissinger initiatives, designed, apparently, to bring a "peaceful" denouement to the struggles in Zimbabwe and Namibia. The rationale underlying these initiatives is all too clear. Protracted struggle in Mozambique and Angola gave rise to regimes there with a revolutionary vocation, regimes which have not so readily accepted the neocolonial terms dictated to newly "independent" nations elsewhere in Africa. In Angola, Kissinger and Vorster made a last minute attempt to stem MPLA's consolidation in power by backing pliant puppets (FNLA and UNITA) and ultimately by sponsoring South Africa's direct military intervention. Having failed in this attempt, they clearly resolved that they would never again leave it to the last minute to counter the logic of revolution in Southern Africa. Not that "false decolonization" is an entirely novel ploy for South Africa. The bantustan policy (dramatized in late 1976 by the granting of "independence" to the Transkei) reflects that country's conviction that the emergence of dependent black-ruled states on (and within!) its borders can help apartheid to buy time for itself. Currently, however, this has meant a Kissinger/Vorster agreement to force Smith to the bargaining table in an attempt to negotiate a neocolonial solution with pliant old-guard leaders, before the more revolutionary cadre of leaders which is being forged through intensified guerrilla struggle in Zimbabwe becomes the dominant African voice there. This has also meant some greater pressure on South Africa to hasten its pace in reaching a "settlement" in Namibia, a settlement which, however, is obviously geared to providing a mere quasi-autonomy satisfactory to neither SWAPO nor the United Nations.

Of course, it is not clear that either of these neocolonial ploys can be made to work as smoothly as Kissinger must hope they will. Here it is important to note, merely, that they represent "solutions" tailor-made for eliciting "official Canada's" enthusiastic support. The Canadian government has invariably been ahead of the United States in speaking out in support of the minimal demands for self-determination made by African peoples. At the same time, we have been not much less reluctant than the United States about supporting revolutionary regimes (as, for example, was the case in Angola, when we backed off from support of MPLA and dragged our feet about recognizing the new government there—once it seemed possible, for a brief moment, that there were other, much more neocolonially minded African forces in the field). Who is better suited, then, to help facilitate the legitimization of moves toward quasi-independence in Southern Africa than ourselves? Don Jamieson's uncritical and almost instantaneous public embrace of Kissinger's initial Rhodesian package (including the apparent promise that Canada will assume a part of its financial burden) gives some indication of what may be in store in this respect.

There are limits. To give them their due, Canadian policy makers have shown no signs of falling for the crudest of such tricks; we firmly avoided participation in the recent charade of Transkeian "independence," for example. But there can be little doubt that much more subtle imperial gambits are in the works, and it is in respect to these that the trajectory of Canadian policies is so unpromising.[5] Moreover—a point to which we will return—where such ploys have some chance of success, at least in the short run, the realities of the situation will be ever more difficult to communicate, against the drift of media bias and government presentation, to Canadians, namely the fact that not all blacks look alike politically and that meaningful issues, transcending Cold War categories, are at stake in the confrontation between, say, MPLA on the one hand and UNITA on the other, or between any equivalents of these movements and their conflicts which recur farther south.

It is possible, therefore, that *both* escalation *and* "false decolonization" could be in the cards across Southern Africa's diverse terrain, but despite these new complexities, the broad outline of Canada's policy in the area is clear. So, surely, is the responsibility of Canadian radicals to expose and to resist the negative activities of our own government and corporations, while simultaneously giving support to those Africans actively engaged in genuine liberation struggles on the ground. Nor need the mere reiteration of the pieties of internationalism provide the exclusive rationale for such activity, valid though these sentiments are. It should be equally emphasized that such support work can make a very real contribution to developing a progressive movement in Canada itself. Not that the nature of this contribution is entirely straightforward. The whole question of the "Southern Africa connection" (like other international questions) has been gravely twisted by the false dichotomies which all too often characterize left debate in this country. Thus, some left nationalists have seemed to argue that any focus on such questions as that of Canada in Southern Africa is something of a diversion—directing attention away from the central aspect of Canada's political economy, the powerful control exercised by American imperialism over our own country. Alternatively, other activists have seized upon the realities of Canada's less-than-admirable role abroad—in South Africa and elsewhere—to pinpoint Canada's own imperialist attributes, and to downplay any suggestion that we are ourselves dependent or "colonized" in any very fundamental way. Yet the fact remains that both of these positions are misleading, as the Southern Africa case reveals. Clearly, Canada's role abroad sheds considerable light on the way in which American hegemony, institutionalized by branch plants and global defense imperatives (e.g., NATO) and legitimized by the world view of global liberalism, imposes its logic. Just as clearly, domestic classes—clustered around the state and around Canadian corporations—are seen to be enthusiastic partisans of such global activity as is exemplified by Canadian policy in Southern Africa. In consequence, those engaged in liberation support work seem well placed to question the necessity of structuring debate in such a way as to blur either dimension of Canada's political economy. Instead, they are forced to affirm the proposition that so tight is the weave between American hegemony and the dominant interests of domestic classes in Canada that the thrusts of anti-imperialism (left nationalism) and of class struggle coincide.

This fact should also help to lay to rest the fear expressed by some radicals that liberation support work provides in any case a merely quasi-progressive escape hatch for conscience-stricken dropouts from the bourgeoisie, a "Third-Worldist" diversion from the necessities of articulating a radical theory and practice even more directly focused on Canada itself. For any sphere of political work which carries one quite so quickly into the central complexities of Canadian political economy, and reveals so clearly the structural constraints upon more humane policies, cannot help but be an arena for radicalization. Nor, quite obviously, would very many of those engaged in such support work advocate that their degree of involvement in this field be paralleled by all those active on the left. Rather, they see their contribution as the small but far from negligible one of blazing forward one important path on behalf of the much broader left movement in this country.

Nonetheless, as noted, the fragmented nature of that left movement has its cost with reference to support for Southern African liberation, the unnecessarily schematic polarization of nationalist and internationalist positions in this regard being a case in point. Moreover, there are other divisions on the left, overlapping the nationalist-internationalist dichotomy, which have begun to push themselves forward more stridently as Southern Africa has become a more prominent terrain of struggle. One consequence has been the mushrooming of instant expertise on Southern Africa questions, with such "expertise" too often premised upon treasured abstractions or upon a line derived from some center of revealed revolutionary truth, rather than upon genuine knowledge as to the nature of the African struggles themselves.

This was demonstrated at its most grotesque in the reaction on the Canadian left to the complexities of the Angolan struggle in late 1975. Here, for example, "Maoists" of various stripe, suspicious (not unjustifiably) of Soviet intentions, found it all too easy to caricature MPLA as a mere extension of Soviet scheming, in so doing willfully peeling away the concrete history of MPLA's autonomous revolutionary development in Angola over several decades. Indeed, some such denizens of the Canadian left carried the profound confusions which characterized Chinese policy in Southern Africa much further than even the Chinese themselves were prepared to do. They then found themselves fulsomely supporting in Angola so rank a creature of American and South African intrigue as UNITA! Simultaneously, many left liberals and social democrats, cowed by the shrill anticommunism of the media and faced with the reality of the revolutionary denouement to liberation exemplified in Mozambique and Angola, also began to get cold feet, with the result that they too manifested a growing taste for "reasonable" compromise in Angola and real hesitancy about supporting MPLA.[6]

But this may be only the beginning of such difficulties. There is a very real danger that, as the struggle against neocolonialism comes much nearer to the surface of the unfolding situation in Southern Africa and as imperial strategy becomes more subtle amidst these new complexities, this kind of confusion on the left will be intensified. Then the situation may continue merely to be blurred by a cacaphony of left sloganeering of various kinds. Then, too, the fact that many more Canadians are becoming increasingly vocal about Southern Africa will not necessarily make for a more united and efficacious political thrust against established Canadian policy. It follows that a great deal of self-education about Southern Africa will be necessary if the Canadian left is to realize the latter goal and succeed in staying the Canadian government from doing the worst that it might otherwise do in Southern Africa in the continued service of "Western interests." Yet surely the example of the growing resistance to such interests on the part of the African people themselves makes it especially imperative that Canadian activists do what is necessary—and do it quickly—in order to complement them in their struggle.

Notes

1. For information on this and other fronts of questionable corporate activity, see Task Force on the Churches and Corporate Responsibility, *Annual Report*, 1975–76.
2. On this subject see Susan Hurlich, "Up Against the Bay: Resource Imperialism and Native Resistance," *This Magazine*, September–October 1975; and John Deverall and the Latin American Working Group, *Falconbridge*.
3. These grisly facts, as well as much else of interest concerning the operation of Canadian corporations in Southern Africa, can be

found in Hugh Nangle, *Canadian Business in Southern Africa* ("The Nangle Report"), this being a compilation of a series of articles which appeared in the *Montreal Gazette* and *Ottawa Citizen* in 1973.

4. Some of these backward linkages—South African investment in Canada—have been traced in the useful publication *Millions and Millions*, published in late 1976 by the Free Southern Africa Committee (Edmonton).

5. It is important to note, simultaneously, that no parallel "compromise" with black aspirations is even remotely considered for South Africa itself. In all his recent interventions into the Southern African situation, Kissinger has had virtually nothing to say about the tumultuous situation inside South Africa. In fact, it seems all too likely that even if the neocolonial ploy is now the preferred American strategy in Zimbabwe and Namibia, the *quid pro quo* for South African cooperation in mounting such a strategy increased guarantees of support for Vorster and Co. at home—military, economic (U.S. promises to help hold up the price of gold have been mentioned), and diplomatic. Under such circumstances, Canada's entanglement in the escalation syndrome remains the dominant feature of our link to South Africa itself. Moreover, military support from the West to back, when it falters, any neocolonial regime which might be established in Zimbabwe or Namibia is also a possibility, one which would be ominously reminiscent of the Vietnam situation.

6. Several meetings held recently in Toronto also have witnessed the possibility that polarization in South Africa itself will merely give rise here to conflicting and highly schematic claims as to who represents South Africa's "genuine proletarian core"—once again very much at the expense of a concrete examination of the development of the struggle in that country and at the expense of any very effective solidarity with that struggle.

PART II

TANZANIA
AND THE RESISTANCE
TO NEOCOLONIALISM

The second section of this volume extends the analysis of socialism in Tanzania previously synthesized in my chapter "African Socialism in One Country: Tanzania" in *Essays on the Political Economy of Africa*. Here the primary thrust is further to theorize those findings and, in addition, to contest other interpretations of the Tanzanian experience that have appeared in recent years. The abovementioned essay noted the clear risks of economic stagnation and bureaucratization attendant upon the halfheartedness of many of that country's efforts, concluding that "it is difficult to be sanguine about the fate of a socialism which defies in so many evident ways the pull of objective conditions and whose weaknesses in organization and ideology are at the same time being only slowly overcome." This basic evaluation is confirmed in the present section (as well as in essay 11 of the following section, which discusses Tanzania's rural sector within a comparative framework); indeed, several of the essays suggest that forces hostile to a more solidly (and popularly) based socialist endeavor—the fierce but subtle grip of imperialism and the crystallization of a defensive petty-bourgeois class around the state machinery—have, if anything, become much stronger in the period since that original chapter was written. Thus the substantive study of the parastatal sector in essay 9 pinpoints the weakness of initiatives there, underscoring both the costly compromises made with Western capitalism and the actions undertaken to suppress such positive expressions of working-class energy as began to surface in the industrial sphere in the early 1970s. Some of the parallel shortfalls in the *ujamaa*-village/rural-socialism program are touched upon in other essays (numbers 10 and 11). The picture which emerges is not a particularly encouraging one, and casts grave doubt upon the other conclusion of my earlier chapter: that, despite the difficulties, "the struggle in Tanzania remains a qualitatively different one from [that of] most of the rest of independent Africa" and its experiment therefore "deserves the solidarity . . . of every international socialist."

All the more reason, then, to be skeptical concerning views that are relatively uncritical in their interpretation of Tanzania's socialist project, whether such views conceive of the latter as the logical and ineluctable extrapolation of the country's nationalist impulse (the approach of the Dar es Salaam historians, discussed in essay 7) or as the relatively straightforward and uncontested working-out of the admirable insights and commitments of President Nyerere and most other prominent Tanzanians (the thrust of Cranford Pratt's well-known approach, criticized in essay 10). Moreover, in both these essays there are larger theoretical stakes, centering on the necessary importance of class analysis (and the drawing of a firm bead upon the machinations of imperialism) to any study which would take "nationalism" or "socialism" or "democracy" seriously in Africa. In this respect Pratt's approach to the question of democracy is seen to be particularly weak, becoming (as Claudín has characterized Kautsky's social-democratic approach to the same issue) a "fetishization," a "manipulation of the concept of 'democracy' beyond any class content." However, my essay is also intended to demonstrate that the kind of interplay which is established between leadership and populace (read: popular classes) is indeed a crucially important, if complex, issue and, further, that the degree of genuine democracy which exists is a crucial variable in assessing the substance of any claimed "transition to socialism" in Africa. Since Tanzania falls so short here, this becomes—ironically and quite contrary to Pratt's emphasis—a particularly revealing standard against which to measure the gap between Tanzania's protestations and its practice!

Not that a wholly negative judgment of Tanzania's undertakings is even then in order. The other side of the coin in this section of the book is a strong criticism of the view—primarily associated with the work of Issa Shivji and synthesized in his widely read volume, *Class Struggles in Tanzania*—that "Tanzanian socialism" was from the outset a self-aggrandizing swindle perpetrated by that country's "bureaucratic bourgeoisie." The counterargument advanced in essay 8 is that rather more subtle processes have been at work in Tanzania, processes which permitted one fraction of the petty bourgeoisie to spearhead some progressive developments internally—in part, paradoxically, by raising the class consciousness of various subordinate classes, even if ultimately to resist the further political (and democratizing) logic of such increased consciousness—and externally (with respect, in particular, to the struggles in Mozambique and elsewhere in Southern Africa). More generally, a thesis concerning the strategic importance of the postcolonial state in Eastern Africa is spelled out here, and a discussion launched as to the range of possible projects open to the petty bourgeoisie in postcolonial Africa. This is a subject which is further theorized in the next section (essay 13), but such a perspective does help explain why some positive achievements have been possible for the Tanzanian leadership. Of course, the cumulative impact of the essays in the present section also suggests the severe constraints upon any such "petty-bourgeois socialism," constraints which have made it difficult, in Tanzania and elsewhere, to move forward from this starting point toward a more meaningful revolutionary-socialist project.

7

NATIONALISM, SOCIALISM, AND TANZANIAN HISTORY

This article is, in the first instance, a review of *A History of Tanzania*, edited by Isariah Kimambo and Arnold Temu and published in 1969 by East African Publishing House.[1] However, I have used this occasion to present a number of broader arguments about Tanzanian historiography, and its relation to the needs of contemporary Tanzania as well. I am conscious that in so doing I cannot hope to do full justice to many of the positive features of the book; nonetheless, I hope that the urgency of the larger problems of method and approach which are discussed will be seen to provide sufficient warrant for a somewhat one-sided emphasis.

The Problem

A History of Tanzania is an important book, a milestone in Tanzanian historiography. With chapters written by four Tanzanians and by six expatriates (whose experience in the country and commitment to many of its aspirations are readily apparent), it is designed to cover certain major aspects of the historical development of the area which comprises present-day Tanzania during the period "from Olduvai to the Arusha Declaration" (as

---

This essay was first published in Lionel Cliffe and John Saul, eds., *Socialism in Tanzania* (Nairobi, 1972), and reprinted in Peter Gutkind and Peter Waterman, eds., *African Social Studies: A Radical Reader* (New York and London, 1977).

the editors put it in their introduction). Moreover, it seeks quite explicitly to break with the dominant themes of "imperial" history and to write Tanzanian history more from the "inside," i.e., from the standpoint of the African population itself.

The latter is, of course, a particularly laudable aim—identified by the former professor of history at the University College, Dar es Salaam, Terence Ranger (in his remarkable Inaugural Lecture[2]), as "the attempt to recover African initiative in Tanzanian history"—and it has characterized much of the other work emerging from the history department at the college (now university) besides that which appears in the book under review. Such an emphasis does involve certain dangers, however, some of which have been mentioned by Professor Ranger in his lecture, but not all of which have been avoided in the preparation of the present volume. As these can be expected to have important implications, beyond the academic community, for Tanzania's current efforts to construct a socialist society, it will be useful to refer specifically to the most important of them at the outset.

The main dangers inherent in too straightforward a focus "on the African himself" (to use the editors' phrase) are (1) that this can shift attention too far away from the overall imperialist framework within which African initiatives are taken, and (2) that it can encourage a blurring of relevant distinctions and differentiations within the African community itself, (3) with the result that the full *meaning and significance* of African initiatives is lost and, moreover, that (4) the accomplishments of Africans (unity, nationalism, and political independence) are, therefore, overvalued, at the expense of a frank discussion of the very real challenges which remain (the realization of socialism and self-reliance, and the fulfillment of the country's productive potential).

In short, what must be critically scruntinized are the very questions scholars ask when examining the historical record. The contention of this essay is that the questions which underlie the Kimambo-Temu volume are too exclusively those relevant to a nationalist perspective on Tanzanian history, at a moment when a socialist perspective and a set of socialist questions are increasingly imperative.[3] Obviously it will be necessary to elaborate upon the four points listed above, and to examine some aspects of the book itself in greater detail, before accepting this assertion and commenting upon its possible implications.

We shall see that the selection of an outspokenly nationalist emphasis can subtly distort discussion even of the earliest periods of "Tanzanian" history, but its weaknesses are the more graphic the closer the historian moves to the present day. This is so chiefly because the major outside force impinging upon the people of what is now Tanzania during the last century or more has been the international capitalist system, and it has affected developments here in a wide variety of complex ways. So pervasive has been its impact that economic initiatives taken by Africans, either because of external force (including many forms of compulsory tax) or in response to various incentives, generally conform to terms dictated by the logic of this worldwide economic system. This means that, as economic growth takes place, its cumulative effect will be the further subordination of the colony to the requirements of metropolitan Europe and the creation of an increasingly *dependent* economy. Some economists have defined this process as "the development of underdevelopment,"[4] and certainly the economic relationships with the outside world which result remain the major constraint upon genuine development in Africa. Moreover, formal education (mission and government schools) is part and parcel of this larger environment and inevitably reflects and inculcates its values— those of the "possessive individualism" characteristic of advanced capitalist societies—even while communicating skills, technical capacity, and/or the key to salvation.

Paradoxically, these economic and educational forces are those which, at one and the same time, both tie an emerging country like Tanzania more tightly into the international capitalist system *and* create the conditions for a nationalist challenge to formal colonial rule. Numbers of Africans, freed by economic activity and/or education from a narrow focus upon their own locality and the subsistence economy, increasingly act on a territorial scale, and realize the frustrations to their own advancement characteristic of colonialism.[5] Moreover, in confronting the latter system, they can often expect to enlist mass support, itself the by-product of disruption of traditional ways inherent in the colonial-cum-capitalist impact.[6]

But it should be apparent that a challenge to formal colonial rule is not necessarily a full-fledged challenge to imperialism. Given both the fact that the economies of the "colonies" have developed into dependencies of the worldwide system and that the new African leaders (politicians and bureaucrats) are themselves often active participants in such economies (while having, in any case, absorbed its values through the educational system), the imperial powers have had little to fear from decolonization.[7] Once having sensed the initial stirrings of discontent, the colonial government characteristically has begun to evolve a *strategy of decolonization* on the basis of which it can bargain with an African group eager to agree to marriages of convenience all along the line. The resultant successor-state, as Fanon has stressed, could represent merely a change in the color of those in positions of authority, while maintaining its internal socioeconomic structure and major links with the outside world more or less intact.

It will already be apparent that an understanding of the full complexity of these links with imperialism, their historic roots and present implications, must go hand in hand with a concern to identify the growing differentiations in African society. This is a process of historical evolution which begins even before colonialism, as we shall have occasion to mention later, but it is particularly graphic in the later period when indigenous classes can become more obviously the domestic guarantors of continued international subordination as well as exploiters in their own right. One dimension of the preindependence political activism of "leaders" will generally have been a desire for advancement as individuals and as a group or class in any case. Once in power, they soon come to realize all the more clearly that any attempt to challenge the imperial status quo in a more fundamentally threatening manner could involve both short-term disruption within the existing system and the necessity to arouse popular energies more powerfully. This in turn might unleash forces prejudicial to the retention of their own relatively privileged positions, however, and, therefore, could not be a realistic option for them. It is clear, in short, that whatever may be the popular mythology encouraged by contemporary leaders, Africa has moved some way from the communalism of the traditional past, and serious historians must look for the first seeds of class formation as assiduously as they trace the initial sparks of nationalist consciousness! Nor should this concern with inequality be seen merely as an exercise in moralizing—far from it. Historically, patterns of inequality and class formation have been related in crucial ways to the process of economic development, sometimes facilitating, sometimes hindering the expansion of the productive forces in a society. By focusing upon classes we are, in fact, carried to the very heart of the development problem.

Of course, such an emphasis should not be allowed to boil away the idealism and the vigor which often characterized the nationalist impetus in Africa. If one dimension was inevitably more narrow and self-interested than is sometimes admitted, another undoubtedly consisted of an identification with larger goals and more popular aspirations. Nor need other African achievements be downgraded by virtue of hindsight, even if it is now apparent that their accomplishments did serve, in time, to define a fresh set of problems for Tanzanians. What *is* necessary is to insist upon the reality of those deeper currents of socioeconomic change which give a fullness of meaning to events; otherwise the latter, taken in isolation, would remain obscure in its significance or, more dangerously, further mystify the understanding of the current generation.

In this context we can return to the theme of nationalism—a significant accomplishment, but also a potent myth with great potentiality for good and evil in contemporary Africa. Unity, an achieved national identity, such as has characterized the emergence of Tanzania, can minimize and displace the dangers of internecine ethnic conflict. Control of the state by indigenous personnel is an important precondition for future action along various lines, including socialist ones, if other factors permit this. For these reasons, among others, a clarification of the processes through which these ends were achieved, as well as an emphasis upon them, are important. But to the extent that a "united" society benefits one or several classes at the expense of others, and to the extent that "self-determination" ultimately confirms rather than challenges the hegemony of imperialism, then one may suspect that to such an extent nationalist slogans have succeeded only in rationalizing the socioeconomic status quo and anesthetizing the mass of the population. And under such circumstances an extreme form of patriotic, nationalist historical writing can, even with the best of intentions, come primarily to service a bankrupt balance of forces.

It may help to place this problem of method in comparative perspective; fortunately an instructive parallel with recent trends in American radical historiography offers itself. One school, led by Staughton Lynd and others, has tried to demonstrate the importance of viewing American history "from the bottom up" (compare the use of the phrase "the African initiative"), and in so doing has seized upon the impressive wave of labor activity in the 1930s in the United States as a powerful testimony to the vitality of radicalism. Yet, as James Weinstein has observed of this emphasis,

the possibility that the workers were . . . militant in behalf of a trade unionism that tied them closer to the system, that integrated their lives more tightly with that of the corporation, never occurred to Lynd. To him it was sufficient that the workers, those at the bottom, were engaged in militant activity.[8]

The overarching structures of capitalist (read, in Africa, "imperialist") dominance remained unperceived and unchallenged; union leaders could be absorbed into the system, gradually transforming their relationship with the mass base which had given substance to their challenge to the establishment.

This illustrates the fault of Lynd's concept of history from the bottom up: it cannot explain or understand the *meaning* of actions taken by those at the bottom because it does not examine their relationship to the actions and consciousness of those at the top. For just as the meaning of ruling class thought and action cannot be understood without knowing what was going on in the under classes, neither can the activity of the under classes be understood except in the context of the actions and consciousness of the upper classes.

American trade unionism, like African nationalism, was an accomplishment, but not one that cut down to the deeper currents of capitalist development, be it domestic or worldwide. To the extent that it failed to do so, "the ruling class [was] left in a position to steer militancy (and radicalism) in the direction advantageous to itself. . . ." Then the very accomplishments of the movement can serve merely to deposit institutions and social relationships—bureaucratized unions and leadership with vested interests (compare, in Africa, "states" and "parties")—whose major role is to defend the status quo, which stand, in fact, in the way of further advance.[9] For American radical historians of the period there is a temptation similar to that which presents itself to the "patriotic" historian in Africa:

> [Such history] is too busy celebrating successful tactics and militant actions, too busy attempting to give "radicals" "their own history"—which is to say a false sense of accomplishment, and therefore a pious satisfaction with the past. . . . [There is] a one-dimensional glorification of motion.

Weinstein concludes by questioning "the usefulness of the concept of radicalism, now that a socialist consciousness is widespread in the new left." Both in history and in the movement, radicalism "has no content. It is purely formal." Again there is a parallel, though it is by no means exact. It would be too much to say that "nationalism" in Africa has no content, nor is it purely formal. Nonetheless, it is *too formal*, and it certainly lacks sufficient content, to be adequate to the task of ordering historical investigation. Moreover, the solution to many of the weaknesses of such a perspective lies in a program of historical inquiry premised upon "a socialist consciousness"!

The Book Itself

The fact that the Tanzanian leadership has itself taken cognizance of these deeper currents and, with the Arusha Declaration and other attendant initiatives, moved some way to challenge the realities of economic and cultural dependency and internal class formation, distinguishes this country from much of the rest of

the continent. It also means that there is every reason for the
concerns stressed in the preceding section to be less profane
knowledge here than is the case elsewhere. Yet this is precisely
where the book under review is to be found most wanting. For,
on one level, a generally undiluted ethos of nationalism pervades
the book, so that even its earlier chapters contribute to an uncritical celebration of political achievement. Possible complementary themes concerning hierarchy and exploitation are muffled
and the multifaceted nature of growing dependency is blurred.
The mind of the reader is encouraged, in short, to follow a single
track.

But it is not only this general ethos that discourages a crystallization of socialist consciousness and concern. Specific issues of
immediate relevance to policy making, which cry out for the
addition of an historical dimension in order to illuminate them,
also fail to surface. What is the exact character of dependency as
it has emerged over time? Only in such a context can one
evaluate the strengths and weaknesses of recent nationalizations
and other steps taken to define new directions. What is the
precise texture of differentiation in Tanzania? This is important
at the national level, where the quality of instruments available
for socialist construction needs continuous discussion. It is even
more the case at the local level, where the distinctions of rank
characteristic of a number of different epochs overlap each other
and must be understood if meaningful strategies for implementing rural socialism are to be developed. But enough of generalization: let us now give some specific examples.

Kimambo deals with a period which long antedates colonialism
and the rise of nationalism (chapter 2). He presents what is, in
many of its particulars, an exemplary account of developments in
the region now comprising Tanzania prior to 1800. In stressing
the growth of more centralized political systems during the
period, he finds this to be clear evidence of "the efforts, initiative
and even success achieved by the people of Tanzania even in the
distant past"—citing, for example, "the efforts *of the people of
Ugweno* in evolving a system which achieved centralization and
unification" (emphasis added). This is merely one instance of
"the Tanzanians of that period" being "able to create political

ideologies which suited their own environments and needs."
Kimambo concludes that "it is from the realization of such
achievements that the Tanzanians of today must draw inspiration
and courage as they strive in developing a modern nation
founded on their own culture."

It would seem, however, to be of at least equal importance to
suggest that this political "creativity" was in part a reflex of the
establishment of more hierarchical, quasi-feudal socioeconomic
systems that weakened the simpler forms of egalitarianism characteristic of prefeudal systems. Not that this would necessarily be
a wholly negative occurrence; presumably many emergent patterns of exploitation were linked with the growth of the productive forces in Tanzanian society, and it is upon such a base that
even higher forms of economy and society could be constructed
in the future. Unfortunately, Kimambo's account does not help
us much with this sort of query. Moreover, as with other, more
recent periods, it may be safer to characterize such changes as
the work of groups and classes within societies, rather than overemphasizing the role of that mystical entity, "the people." It will
already be apparent that these are not mere academic points. An
identification of such changes may cast a searching light on any
too-simple generalization about the collective, "socialist" nature
of "traditional" African society, for example, and thereby sharpen
socialist debate. As suggested above, a clarification of the legacy
of structures from this period may also be of some help to contemporary socialist planners in identifying likely points of support
and resistance in particular localities. But, more generally, once
it is emphasized that an interest in the "chiefdoms" of this period
is linked not merely to investigating processes of state formation
but also to questions of hierarchy and equality, exploitation,
productive capacity, and the like, then we may feel certain that
these issues are becoming a central preoccupation of every Tanzanian concerning all periods.

Andrew Roberts (chapter 4) is, perhaps, a little less sanguine
about the results of the processes of political centralization as it
continued into his period of reference—the nineteenth century.
"Increasing external contacts multiplied the opportunities for
leaders to obtain men and weapons with which to enforce their

authority" and this process was "[not] necessarily progressive." For example, "often it involved a great deal of fighting, raiding and brutality." But even his subtle account of political changes seems to call out for further complementary analyses of the various modes of production of the peoples concerned (as well as any shifts in productive capacity which might be involved). This could help save the investigation from becoming too exclusively preoccupied with undifferentiated "peoples," on the one hand and heroic individuals, on the other, as is sometimes the danger in this chapter.

As for the expansion of trade, which both Roberts and Edward Alpers, in another valuable chapter (chapter 3), take to be a key variable during the period, one senses that something more is required than to see this (as Roberts does) as involving simply "greater access to the material and intellectual resources of the world outside" or to conceptualize it, straightforwardly, as "a world of expanding horizons." To be sure, Alpers is more concerned with the external links of this trade, but even he sees the most important effect of the caravan trade to be "the germ of unity which it planted in the middle of those who were involved in it." Again the nonspecialist senses that the theoretical framework is not adequate to the task, for even at this early date it seems probable that the economic development of Tanzania is being distorted by the manner of its insertion into the world economy. The long-term result is dependency; what questions must be asked to find its seeds in this period?[10]

Gilbert Gwassa deals with the German period (chapter 5) and, significantly, deals with it almost exclusively from the angle of African resistance to the imposition of colonial rule. His is a dramatic and inspiring story, to be sure, and does not require the somewhat strained definition of resistance he is prepared to adopt ("adaptive resistance") in order, for example, to absorb Merere, in fighting with the Germans against Mkwawa, into the pantheon of national heroes. It does not make imperialism any less reprehensible to say that indigenous individuals, groups, and classes can ally with it for their own gain. Indeed, this is a common pattern on the continent to the present day, and might better be identified at the outset as such. Other moments might appear more ambiguous if greater attention were paid to distinctive aspects of the overarching process of absorption into the world economy introduced during the period. It is easier to present Abushiri and Bwana Heri simply as patriots if their complex links to the declining slave trade are not mentioned, and the statement that "German occupation threatened the existence of their power politically but especially economically" could well be enlarged upon to capture more clearly the essence of the German colonial presence and the socioeconomic changes it introduced.

Moreover, only a brief concluding reference is made to the emergence of inequalities during the period; thus, the practice of education for the civil service of a limited number of Africans is seen to have "created privileged groups in a society that had in the past stressed egalitarianism in communities." Nothing is said to document the degree of egalitarianism in, say, Mkwawa's armed camp. Nor is the scope of the new inequality (as between regions, individuals, or classes) introduced by educational and economic change identified clearly or evaluated in terms of its implications for future Tanzanian socioeconomic development. The focus upon the legacy of resistance and the seeds of unity, visible, in particular, in *Maji Maji*, virtually crowds out all other concerns.

Iliffe's chapter on "The Age of Improvement and Differentiation (1907–45)" (chapter 6) is probably the strongest in the book, for it brings together more of the components necessary to clarifying the movement of Tanzanian society than any other. As befits the general tone of the book, the main motif remains that of identifying the roots of unity, national consciousness, and political achievement. But Iliffe is careful to trace other significant aspects of the life of the period, most notably that of novel and emerging differentiation and division, the latter including, as he notes, "divisions of education and wealth, divisions of culture and belief." In particular, "looking backward, signs of economic class formation can be seen," and he provides a rich store of observation about this process in both urban and rural areas.

Even with Iliffe, however, the full logic of imperialism is consistently blurred, so that there is little sign of that deepening dependency upon the economies of the metropolitan centers

which now seems so striking a characteristic of colonial development. Yet a recognition of dependency would render those efforts at "improvement," which Iliffe emphasizes as being the
characteristic feature of the period, more ambiguous than they
can ever appear in the absence of such an overarching
framework. For Iliffe "education, economic development, and
the modernization of local government" are the instruments of
"improvement" which Tanzanians are using at this time to prepare their challenge to external control. But what if the kind of
economic development that is taking place serves the needs of
the imperial power in such a way as to make Tanzania's realization of self-sustained growth and genuine independence at a later
stage more difficult.[11] Iliffe also attributes to his "men of improvement" a "deep commitment to education, Christianity and
the Western variety of civilization." But what if such values,
absorbed while achieving education, in fact define the terms of
continued subservience and create a hegemonic culture which
narrows the range of alternative development strategies likely to
be contemplated. Such results would indeed be ironic; yet something of the sort was occurring in Tanzania.

Thus, Iliffe's "modernizers" were "modernizers" perhaps, but
almost inevitably this meant being "capitalist modernizers," the
qualifier being of very great importance. Of course they are not,
therefore, to be seen as "just the stooges of an alien Government," as Ranger correctly observes in a related chapter on the
movement of ideas during the period (chapter 7); indeed, "many
of them had to fight hard to get the opportunity to improve."[12]
But, more subtly, they were increasingly part of the same underlying system as that "alien government," and there was, therefore, a growing tendency for the interests of such "capitalist
modernizers" (and for the character of the society and economy
which they were, in effect, constructing by their efforts) to become complementary to those of the alien economy and culture.
Not conspiracy, but a particular pattern of uneven and combined
development, is the key![13]

This is the irony of "improvement," then, that Iliffe fails to
catch, though his chapter brilliantly, but in the last analysis
uneasily, combines a portrait of the modernizers as both

nationalists *and* as class-in-formation. The reason for this is a familiar one: Iliffe is too committed to writing "nationalist" history to follow unflinchingly the logic of his own evidence. What is of central importance to him is that such efforts are "heroic" in their own way—they are a valued component of the tradition of resistance. Improving within the framework of colonial rule, overcoming "the problem of ignorance," is necessary for the time being in order for "Tanzanians" to gather strength for a future confrontation; "they had to sacrifice their own freedom for that of their children."

That imperialism might be consolidating its position even while the seeds of challenge to formal colonialism were being sown is a possibility unlikely to emerge from a framework so singlemindedly in search of resistance. Equally important, the formation of classes takes on a particular texture when viewed from this perspective. As noted, Iliffe is well aware of the latter pattern; he is also aware, with Ranger, that some protests against such developments were manifesting themselves during the period. But it remains, in effect, the accidental by-product of unevenly distributed resistance to European rule and/or nationalist strivings, rather than the inevitable result of capitalist development which, therefore, manifests the spirit of entrepreneurial aggrandizement and possessive individualism attendant upon such a process.

In reality it is perhaps something of both, but it is difficult not to feel that in this case nationalist consciousness has been ascribed a little too uncritically to all comers in the period, not only as the major clue to the larger significance of their activity, but even as to the content of their intention. One may feel as well that such an emphasis has the effect of blunting and softening contradictions which can then be admitted without being brought center stage; praise displaces a perception of process and subtly denatures the kind of challenge to future generations which is involved. Iliffe stresses, of course, that nationalism is still in embryo here, but having subtly elided resistance and improvement, he is quite prepared to assimilate the latter to nationalism. He does so by emphasizing strongly (and probably overemphasizing) the centrality of "the dream of unity" which he sees to be an increasingly potent force in the period and, moreover, a further guarantee that "improvers" of various sorts are, first and foremost, to be considered "nationalists" working for the common good.

As usual with Iliffe, the evidence is carefully marshaled and impressively synthesized. And, in the last paragraph, the reality of class formation (if not dependency) *is* passed on intact to a later chapter as one of several crucial problems which face the emergent nationalist movement. To the extent that Iliffe's chapter is missing certain crucial nuances, it at least forces one to recognize the subtle shadings that will eventually be necessary in any definitive history of a socialist Tanzania. Unfortunately, this is not as true for Arnold Temu's chapter on "The Rise and Triumph of Nationalism." Here the dangers which one struggles to isolate and label in Iliffe's complex argument appear much more starkly, though they are in certain important respects identical.

The litany of resistance is duly recited by Temu, with continuity all the more heavily emphasized. There is throughout the book a tendency to discuss "Tanzania" prematurely, assuming the entity even while it is in the process of formation. This tendency underwrites a second and even more important one, that of making "the Tanzanian people" (once again a somewhat amorphous and mystical entity) the crucial motor of change. With Iliffe, for example, the idea that "Tanzanians" were overcoming the problem of ignorance was the essential key to the "improvers' " educational advancement, thereby subtly distorting other important features (class formation, cultural transformation, dependency, and so on) of that occurrence. Temu seems to take his cue from this and is even less hesitant to interpret historical patterns in Tanzania as being primarily a product of the corporate activity of "Tanzanians." *Maji Maji* is one early effort at resistance undertaken by Tanzanians. "Self-improvement" (Temu's phrase) is another, for *"implicit* in this was that self-improvement in education and economic self-sufficiency would place them in a better position to fight against the British who had replaced the Germans in Tanzania" (emphasis added).

The emergence of the nationalist movement, and the interpretation of its implications, poses no problems for such a model. It is merely the culmination of the corporate activity previously traced, for Tanzanians have learned from their past mistakes and laid the groundwork well. Temu actually argues that "it was largely these early failures that determined the way in which the people of Tanzania were to be mobilized for *uhuru* later on"! As compared with Iliffe, even less is heard of emergent groups and novel classes among the Tanzanian populace whose varied interests might be expected to "determine," in some part, the nature of the colonial political process at its various stages of development. And as little is said about the character of the imperial power's relationship to the colony, or about any possible changes in its own calculations as a factor affecting the activities of the nationalists. Tanzanians are merely trying a new tactic against a familiar enemy, a tactic that this time is supremely successful.

This is not satisfactory. For one thing, such a formulation provides no room for the bargaining role of the colonial government mentioned much earlier in our analysis. The Germans in 1905 and the British in 1960 become interchangeable terms with, apparently, a similar and single-minded ambition: political oppression of the African people. Temu notes, for example, "that the associations kept African politics alive through discussion and dialogue at a time when the colonial administration did the best it could to stifle any political activities aimed at opposing either central or local administration." But why was a more concerted effort not made to stifle TANU? The British were prepared to use military force in Malaya, Kenya, Guyana, and South Arabia to safeguard their position or to guarantee a palatable successor; the Portuguese resist even armed assault upon their direct colonial hegemony to the present day, just as the Americans continue the work of the French in Indochina. The British would not have left without a push, but had their interests so dictated they would have been a more active antagonist. What does this tell us of dependency and of British (and international capitalist) views concerning the degree of menace manifested by their successors? What interests, what linkages, really were at stake? The nationalist movement was important then, but it did not merely drive the British out in a straightforward and unambiguous manner, as Temu seems to imply for much of his paper. That version is stirring stuff, but, as argued previously, one result may be to overemphasize the accomplishment of nationalism and deemphasize the continuing challenge.

A second point is equally important in this regard. Nyerere has written that for TANU "the aim was *Uhuru*, pure and simple. . . . It made everything simple. We deliberately refused to answer the question as to what we would do after *Uhuru*, because the moment we had started to do that we would have got our forces divided about future plans and that would have been wrong. Instead, from 1954 onwards, we were absolutely clear in our singleness of purpose."[14] For a nationalist leader like Nyerere this may have been both a legitimate and a necessary tactic at the time, but such an agnosticism about the detailed motives and long-term goals of participants in the nationalist movement is not something that historians of the period can permit themselves. In fact, Nyerere himself has forged subsequently some of the alternative questions which are of relevance. He writes that[15]

> many of the leaders of the independence struggle saw things in these terms. They were not against capitalism; they simply wanted its fruits, and saw independence as the means to that end. Indeed, many of the most active fighters in the independence movement were motivated—consciously or unconsciously—by the belief that only with independence could they attain that ideal of individual wealth which their education or their experience in the modern sector had established as a worthwhile goal.[16]

The mass of the population partake of this general ethos and "simply [demand] the replacement of white and brown faces by black ones. . . . Capitalism was the system which the masses knew in the modern sector, and what they had been fighting against was that this modern sector should be in alien hands."

For Nyerere the denouement to such a process comes as no surprise:

> Once in power, some of the leaders whom the people have learned to know and trust will think their nationalism demands expropriation of non-Africans in favour of African citizens; the more sophisticated may deny this but think of economic development in terms of expanding capitalism with the participation of Africans.

> Such leaders as these may well identify the progress they have
> promised the people with the increasing wealth of the few; they will
> point to African-owned large cars and luxurious houses and so on,
> as evidence of growing prosperity and of their own devotion to the
> cause of national independence.[17]

In fact, "the most active, and, therefore, the most popular, of the
nationalist leaders may have been people without a socialist conviction. They may either have never had an opportunity to study
the problems and possibilities of social and economic organization, or they may have been people who were motivated by a
personal desire for the fruits of capitalism." To such people
"exploitation was only wrong when carried out upon the masses
by people of a different race."

As for the masses, the carryover of nationalist enthusiasm,
complemented by defections from their ranks to those of the
privileged, may lead to a short-run acceptance of this emergent
status quo:

> The perpetuation of capitalism, and its expansion to include Afri-
> cans, will be accepted by the masses who took part in the indepen-
> dence struggle. They may take the new wealth of their leaders as
> natural and even good—for a time they may even take reflected
> pride in it. . . . This public acceptance of African capitalism will be
> obtained because the people have learned to trust their nationalist
> leaders, and wish to honour them. Also there will inevitably be new
> jobs and opportunities for a good number of the most active, vocal
> and intelligent of those who might otherwise have led criticism.[18]

In sum:

> Everyone wants to be free, and the task of the nationalist is simply
> to rouse the people to a confidence in their own power of protest.
> But to build the real freedom which socialism represents is a very
> different thing. It demands a positive understanding and positive
> actions, not simply a rejection of colonialism and a willingness to
> co-operate in non-co-operation.

Yet, as Nyerere stresses, by escalating racialism, apotheosizing
opportunistic politicians, and single-mindedly emphasizing the
significance of the achievement of formal independence, *"the*

*anti-colonial struggle will almost certainly have intensified the
difficulties"* of building "this real freedom which socialism represents" (emphasis added).[19]

Unfortunately, there is more wisdom about the paradoxes and
ambiguities of nationalism in these few pages by Nyerere than in
the bulk of the book under review. Temu celebrates the political
leadership, rather than situating its strengths and weaknesses
within a complex and multidimensional analysis of the overall
decolonization process. Nor is anything heard of the character
and significance of rising African bureaucrats and entrepreneurs
outside the immediate circle of political activists, though these
are as much the inheritors of the fruits of independence as the
"leaders," more narrowly defined. The contribution of the workers to nationalist resistance is identified, though a deeper analysis, both of their relationship to the socioeconomic transformations of the period and of the actual basis of their protest, might
have revealed the roots of the conflict between government and
trade union which was to emerge in the postcolonial period.
Similarly drawing upon the earlier investigations of Cliffe, Temu
stresses the peasant contribution to successful nationalism, but
neither is this analyzed in such a way as to explore the quality and
diversity of peasant consciousness.[20] In short, all "opposition" is
reduced to its lowest common denominator, and a relatively
undifferentiated effort by all Tanzanians to reclaim their liberty
becomes the sum total of relevant occurrence during the
period.[21]

The possibility of contradiction having been more or less
banned from the preceding discussion, one is startled to learn, in
Temu's final paragraph, that "the replacing of the colonial administration did not mean a complete break with the British or
with their institutions. . . . It was at first more a change of
personnel in the top echelons of government and the civil service
than a change in our institutions, attitudes and thinking." However unexceptionable, this conclusion seems arbitrary in context;
what has preceded has not prepared the ground for such a dilemma so baldly stated.[22] A "nationalist" history of nationalism
has failed, in other words, to aid in the identification of those
barriers to "real freedom" which are being erected by class forma-

tion, dependency, and the like during the very period of nationalist achievement. Whether some form of internal class struggle may be necessary to advance such a situation, on what novel fronts and with what degree of urgency imperialism is now to be confronted, such questions acquire little currency from such an investigation.

But if the historical genesis of barriers to further advance is slighted here as elsewhere in the book, a second and more novel danger becomes apparent in this particular chapter. For the characteristic method of the book tends to encourage oversimplification concerning the emergence of the socialist initiative itself! A careful reading of Temu's final paragraph, quoted above, suggests that socialism has become merely the next historic task for the corporate Tanzanian. Socialism is, in its turn, assimilated (even reduced) to nationalism, becoming for Temu, and perhaps for other participants in the book, merely an inevitable stage in the great tradition of resistance. Tanzanians learn, in effect, that formal independence is not enough, that socialism is, logically, the next tactic. Again, subtly, one is encouraged to think that such a transition can be smoother, more straightforward, more unanimous, than it is ever likely to be.

This is not to deny the possible existence of genuinely positive links between nationalism and socialism; it is merely to insist, among other things, upon the centrality of such ambiguities as Nyerere's paradigm of decolonization helps to underscore. For it must be emphasized that nationalism has not tended to have this denouement elsewhere on the continent. What combination of historical forces and historical phasing can have led to the somewhat unlikely development of a serious socialist impulse here?[23] And, in light of such factors, how strong is it likely to be? Thus, despite the many merits of Temu's chapter and of the book as a whole, both the positive and negative sides of the current situation—and the tense contradiction between constructive socialist effort and hostile objective conditions which is the drama of contemporary Tanzania—remains blunted and mystified. The situation continues to cry out for further scientific illumination and the application of a fully effective historical perspective.

The Challenge

Several remarks might be made by way of conclusion. The first is more narrowly methodological. For part of the problem of Tanzanian historiography, as exemplified in this book, may arise quite simply from too narrow a focus upon the purely political dimensions of Tanzanian history. It is significant that the editors, in stating their determination in the introduction to focus on "the African himself," further note that "there has been no attempt to deal with colonial administrative structures." Perhaps if they had been more self-conscious about the fact that imperialism involves economic and sociocultural dimensions of even greater importance than "colonial administrative structures" they would not have been so eager to discard the imperial factor from their African-centered history or to make more difficult an identification of the subtle dialectic between external and internal factors by removing one of its terms. The early development of a school of economic historians in Tanzania is one major imperative which suggests itself from this. But even this may be misleading, for it has been apparent throughout our essay that institutions and culture, social structure and productive capacity, must all be understood to interpenetrate. More important, therefore, is the development of an increasingly sophisticated methodology, specifically tailored to Tanzanian needs (and preferably by Tanzanians) but drawing upon worldwide canons of left debate (in particular, one may suggest, the Marxist tradition), which stresses the complex and inseparable interplay of political, economic, and sociocultural variables.

It is worth repeating that there are strengths in this book, nonetheless—a less illuminating book would not be worth discussing at this length. We have already noted that in Africa an achieved nationalism like that of Tanzania is of great importance and that African seizure of state power is also of great potential significance. Another more complicated factor is at stake: In a world where white dominance and white racism have worked for centuries to degrade and humiliate black people, it is no small thing to write history which emphasizes African accomplishment and thus makes available a sense of pride and self-confidence to black people in general and Tanzanians in particular. This is probably a more valid excuse for some slight tilting of the scale of the historical record than one could find for the sort of oversimplified radical history which we have seen Weinstein to be denouncing. But clearly a balance must be struck between the burden of the past and the stark imperatives of the future. On officially accepting a copy of the book under review, President Nyerere himself "called on African historians to refrain from exaggerating facts about Africa simply because their alien counterparts played them down or excluded them from the annals of history in the pre-independence era."[24] In the last analysis problems and contradictions do not disappear by ignoring them and the most responsible and progressive nationalism may be that which is most conscious of this fact.

The positive contributions of a historiography which raises questions of pressing importance to socialist Tanzania in its examination of the past will not bear extended recapitulation here; continued mention of these has been made throughout the text. In fostering a general spirit of critical inquiry (alive, in particular, to the realities of exploitation and dependency), and in further clarifying both the obstacles which contemporary socialist planners must face and the forces to which they may look for support, there lies a clear challenge. Nor should historians mistake their role. Honesty and rigor are essential, but the past does not interpret itself; it springs to life in the present only in relation to the questions it is asked. And there is evidently enough life in socialist questions about the past to engage the energies of several generations of Tanzanian historians. Those who accept this challenge can expect to play a vital role in raising the level of consciousness of their countrymen and contributing to "the Tanzanian revolution."

Notes

1. I. N. Kimambo and A. J. Temu, *A History of Tanzania* (Nairobi, 1969).
2. T. O. Ranger, *The Recovery of African Initiative in Tanzanian History*, The University College, Dar es Salaam, Inaugural Lecture Series No. 2, March 1969.
3. Alternative perspectives or combinations of perspectives could be

imagined, but one such alternative is not that positivist will-o'-the-wisp "objective history," which imagines that data interpret themselves in the absence of evaluation and commitment. On this subject, see Hugh Stretton, *The Political Sciences* (London, 1969).

4. The phrase is that of Andre Gunder Frank; see his *Capitalism and Underdevelopment in Latin America* (New York, 1967) and *Latin America: Underdevelopment or Revolution?* (New York, 1970). For a more detailed elaboration of this and other aspects of the present author's choice of emphases see G. Arrighi and J. S. Saul, "Socialism and Economic Development in Tropical Africa," *Journal of Modern African Studies* 6, no. 2 (August 1968) and Arrighi and Saul, "Nationalism and Revolution in Sub-Saharan Africa," in *Essays on the Political Economy of Africa* (New York, 1973).

5. Liberalism, in itself a by-product of capitalist development, becomes a tool in their hands at this point—at once stimulating and rationalizing the drive for self-determination.

6. For a case study of this and other aspects of decolonization see Martin Kilson's valuable *Political Change in a West African State* (Cambridge, Mass., 1968). But see also my review of Kilson in *Journal of Modern African Studies* 6, no. 3 (October 1968).

7. The rise of the United States to a position of hegemony within the international capitalist system is also of importance here, for it had little, if anything, to gain from the perpetuation of formal colonialism with its accompanying barriers to economic penetration.

8. This and the succeeding quotations are from James Weinstein, "Can an Historian Be a Socialist Revolutionary?" *Socialist Revolution* 1, no. 3 (May–June 1970).

9. Significantly, Nyerere himself has recently written to the effect that "the anti-colonial struggle will almost certainly have intensified the difficulties" of building socialism. This may seem to many readers a startling statement, particularly coming from Nyerere; it is one to which we shall return in due course.

10. More could also be done by both these writers to link the growth of trade and the creation of a new territorially defined (though externally dependent) mode of production with changes in the mode of production at the local (regional, ethnic-group, village) level.

11. More recently Iliffe has made certain of these questions more central to his concern; see his suggestive paper "Agricultural Change in Modern Tanzania: An Outline History," mimeo. (Dar es Salaam, 1970).

12. As Iliffe phrases this point, "Improvement was not something Euro-

peans did for Africans. It was something Africans did for themselves."

13. Unfortunately, in this chapter, as in others, there is relatively little
said about the pattern of penetration of European companies and
banks and of the Asian trading community, or about the overall
pattern of overseas trade, though these would be necessary to the
more rounded picture which we have in mind. For the beginnings of
such a discussion see A. Seidman, "The Dual Economies of East
Africa," in Lionel Cliffe and John Saul, eds., Socialism in Tanzania
(Nairobi, 1972).

14. J. K. Nyerere, "Introduction" to Kathleen Stahl, Sail in the Wilder-
ness (London, 1961).

15. This and succeeding quotations are from Nyerere's introduction to
his Freedom and Socialism—Uhuru na Ujamaa (Dar es Salaam,
1968), the section of the introduction entitled "The Problems of
Building Socialism in an Ex-Colonial Country," pp. 26–32. It is
reprinted in J. K. Nyerere, Nyerere on Socialism (D. S. M., 1969),
pp. 52–58.

16. It is worth noting the president's parenthesis here to the effect that
"it was not always selfishness which made leaders think only in terms
of Africanizing the capitalist economy of the colonialists; often they
had no knowledge of any alternative." This may remind us of the
need to see these developments not as a conspiracy but as a process,
a particular process of capitalist development.

17. As he further notes, "it was on this basis, for example, that some
Tanzanian leaders criticized the Arusha Declaration."

18. He continues ominously: "But, sooner or later, the people will lose
their enthusiasm and will look upon the independence government
as simply another ruler which they should avoid as much as possible!"

19. Cf. note 9, above.

20. The reference is to Cliffe, "Nationalism and the Reaction to Enforced Agricultural Change During the Colonial Period," paper
presented to the EAISR Conference, December 1964. This has
recently been published with a brief postscript by the author in
Taamuli (Dar es Salaam) 1, no. 1 (July 1970). I have briefly discussed
the issue of "the quality and diversity of peasant consciousness" in
my "On African Populism" in G. Ionescu and E. Gellner, eds.,
Populism (London, 1968), and the somewhat ambiguous role of the
cooperative movement in "Marketing Co-operatives in Tanzania,"
in Peter Worsley, ed., Two Blades of Grass (Manchester, 1971), and

in Lionel Cliffe and John Saul, eds., *Socialism in Tanzania*, vol. 2 (Nairobi, 1973).

21. The institutions of nationalism would make another interesting focus; in exploring the character of TANU, for example, with an eye to evaluating its likely strengths and weaknesses with relevance to subsequent tasks, points about its historical character would be likely to emerge which might otherwise be missed.

22. It is worth noting that Cliffe's concluding chapter, more an exercise in contemporary analysis than an historical contribution, does raise a number of basic issues which parallel the concerns of this paper. But most of his emphases are not anticipated or illuminated in the historical sections, and that is the major point of the argument here.

23. An attempt to explore this subject further will be found in the present author's paper "African Socialism in One Country: Tanzania," in Arrighi and Saul, *Essays on the Political Economy of Africa*.

24. From a report (under the headline "Be Honest, Nyerere Tells Historians") in *The Standard* (Tanzania), November 11, 1969.

8

THE STATE
IN POSTCOLONIAL SOCIETIES:
TANZANIA

With the recent work of Samir Amin and others, Marxist understanding of African economies has begun to progress; political analysis has lagged far behind, however. For too long the ground has been ceded, by default, to the ideologues of establishment political science and to their various permutations on the themes of "political modernization" and "one-party states." This comment applies not merely to "radical Africana" of course. A similar shortfall in radicalism's scientific understanding of the political can be noted with reference to Asia and Latin America as well. The problem of "the state" as it presents itself in the context of "underdevelopment" has been undertheorized and little researched. The present essay seeks to contribute to a further discussion of this issue.

Needless to say, it does not do so in a complete vacuum. Most notably, Hamza Alavi has recently provided an important starting

---

This paper was originally presented in the "Views from the Left" Lecture Series, Toronto, Canada, February 1974, and was published in Ralph Miliband and John Saville, eds., *The Socialist Register 1974* (New York: Monthly Review Press, 1974; London: The Merlin Press, 1974). For an overview of the Tanzanian situation which spells out both the country's achievements and its continuing contradictions in much more detail than has been possible here, the interested reader may wish to refer to the author's "African Socialism in One Country: Tanzania," in Giovanni Arrighi and John S. Saul, *Essays on the Political Economy of Africa* (New York and London, 1973), ch. 6. The present paper is, in effect, a theoretical extension of that earlier essay. There are also the various materials collected in Lionel Cliffe and John S. Saul, eds., *Socialism in Tanzania: Politics and Policies*, 2 vols. (Nairobi, 1972 and 1973).

point for analysis of "the state in post-colonial societies," premising his argument

> on the historical specificity of post-colonial societies, a specificity
> which arises from structural changes brought about by the colonial
> experience and alignment of classes and by the superstructures of
> political and administrative institutions which were established in
> that context, and secondly from radical re-alignments of class
> forces which have been brought about in the post-colonial situation.[1]

In general, the propositions developed by Alavi in his analysis of Pakistan and Bangladesh prove most illuminating when applied to the Tanzanian experience—as will be seen in the following pages. At the same time, such a comparison suggests certain qualifications and extensions of his argument which are here discussed tentatively as well as fully in the spirit of Alavi's conclusion that "comparative and critical studies are needed before we can hope to arrive at a general theory of the state in post-colonial societies."

There are certain dangers in focusing upon Tanzania to make such points—a possible confusion of the particular for the general, for example, a danger which may be intensified with respect to Tanzania because of that country's somewhat atypical postcolonial pattern of development. But there is a compensating advantage of some significance: discussion of the Tanzanian case provides the opportunity to work with an analytical literature of a very high order, a literature which is not widely enough known outside East Africa. Specifically, the past few years have seen the emergence, around the journal *Maji Maji*, of an important school of Tanzanian critics of that country's "socialism."[2] The body of work which these writers have begun to produce is rooted in the Marxist tradition, and it has provided a stimulating domestic counterweight to the formulations of President Nyerere, in terms of whose approach to Tanzania much previous analysis has been conducted. As a result, a discussion of "the state" with reference to Tanzanian experience can serve not only as an invitation to others to undertake similar inquiries in a variety of African settings, but also as an opportunity to discuss critically this *Maji Maji* school of socialist theorists.

The State in Postcolonial Societies

There are three points which define the crucial significance of the state in postcolonial societies—two of which can be drawn directly from Alavi. For the first, we quote at length:

> The bourgeois revolution in the colony, in so far as that consists of the establishment of a bourgeois state and the attendant legal and institutional framework, is an event which takes place with the imposition of colonial rule by the metropolitan bourgeoisie. In carrying out the tasks of the bourgeois revolution in the colony, however, the metropolitan bourgeoisie has to accomplish an additional task which was specific to the colonial situation. Its task in the colony is not merely to replicate the superstructure of the state which it had established in the metropolitan country itself. Additionally, it had to create a state apparatus through which it can exercise dominion over *all* the indigenous social classes in the colony. It might be said that the "superstructure" in the colony is, therefore, "over-developed" in relation to the "structure" in the colony, for its basis lies in the metropolitan structure itself, from which it is later separated at the time of independence. The colonial state is therefore equipped with a powerful bureaucratic-military apparatus and mechanisms of government which enable them through its routine operations to subordinate the native social classes. The post-colonial society inherits that over-developed apparatus of state and its institutionalized practices through which the operations of indigenous social classes are regulated and controlled.[3]

Much about this formulation is exemplary—and immediately illuminates the historical basis of the situation in East Africa.

A second, complementary, point also can be drawn from Alavi, for the state's prominent place in postcolonial society is rooted not only in the colonial legacy, but also in the contemporary production process. "The apparatus of the state, furthermore assume[s] also a new and relatively autonomous *economic* role, which is not paralleled in the classical bourgeois state. The state in the post-colonial society directly appropriates a very large part of the economic surplus and deploys it in bureaucratically directed economic activity in the name of promoting economic development." Since these two features characterize the East African situation, they also serve there, in Alavi's words, to "differentiate the post-colonial state fundamentally from the state as analysed in classical marxist theory."[4]

There is a third feature, about which Alavi says little. In advanced capitalist countries the state is the "dominant classes' political power centre" and in this respect comes to have an important ideological function. For in fact it symbolizes the unity of the social formation, seeming to transcend any narrow class or sectional interest and thus helping to legitimize the status quo. It is for this reason that Poulantzas has conceived the state as being "not a class construct but rather the state of a society divided into classes," a fact which does not negate the further reality that such a capitalist state "aims precisely at the political disorganization of the dominated classes."[5] But the state's function of providing an ideological cement for the capitalist system is one which has evolved slowly and surely in the imperial centers, in step with the latter's economic transformation. In postcolonial societies, on the other hand, and particularly in Africa, this hegemonic position *must be created*, and created within territorial boundaries which often appear as quite artificial entities once the powerful force of direct colonial fiat has been removed. Peripheral capitalism, like advanced capitalism, requires territorial unity and legitimacy, and the postcolonial state's centrality to the process of *creating* these conditions (like its centrality in "promoting economic development") further reinforces Alavi's point about that state's importance. Indeed, when viewed from a Marxist perspective, this is what all the fashionable discussion of "nation-building" in development literature is all about![6]

These three points, taken together, help define the centrality of the state in the postcolonial social formation. And this centrality, in turn, is sufficient to suggest the importance of *those who staff the state apparatus* within such a formation. In Alavi's terms, the latter are members of "the military-bureaucratic oligarchy," who thus come to play a semiautonomous role in the situation created by the lifting of direct metropolitan control. The nature and extent of this autonomy—of the state and of those who staff it—from the determinations of other classes more directly rooted in the production process (Alavi identifies these as "the indigenous bourgeoisie, the metropolitan neo-colonialist bourgeoisie, and the landed classes") is more controversial. And it must be admitted that Alavi's answer to this question is not entirely clear. He does suggest that the "oligarchy" acts "on behalf of [all three propertied classes] to preserve the social order in which their interests are embedded, namely the institution of private property and the capitalist mode as the dominant mode of production." Moreover, this would seem to be the premise which underpins one of his explanations of the oligarchy's position:

> . . . a new convergence of interests of the three competing propertied classes, under metropolitan patronage, allows a burcaucratic-military oligarchy to mediate their competing but no longer contradictory interests and demands. By that token it acquires a relatively autonomous role and is not simply the instrument of any one of the three classes.

But what is being claimed here? Does this autonomy arise because these classes balance each other off, thus providing openings for the exercise of leverage by the "oligarchy" in their own interests, or is some different concept at play? In fact, other of Alavi's observations cast doubt on his own use of the term "convergence." Thus he notes on the one hand that "such a relatively autonomous role of the state apparatus is of special importance to the neo-colonialist bourgeoisies because it is by virtue of this fact that they are able to pursue their class interests in the post-colonial societies." Compare this subservient status with the oligarchy's relationship to the "weak indigenous bourgeoisies": here it is the latter who "find themselves enmeshed in bureaucratic controls by which those at the top of the hierarchy of the bureaucratic-military apparatus of the state are able to maintain and even extend their dominant power in society. . . ." Nor is it merely the notion of "convergence" which is called into question by the existence of such gross imbalances between the three classes. What of Alavi's other explanation of the oligarchy's autonomy: its ability to "mediate . . . between competing interests"? "Mediation" scarcely summarizes the oligarchy's drive to "extend their dominant power in society" at the expense of the indigenous bourgeoisie, though this is the situation just described by Alavi. And what, in any case, is the nature of the oligarchy's distinctive interest, which any "autonomy" it may win permits it to advance and defend?

East African experience reinforces the importance of these and related questions, in part because the imbalances between the three classes are even more striking there than in South Asia. In fact, the two indigenous classes to which Alavi refers—"the landed classes" and "the indigenous bourgeoisie"—are very much less prominent. This is true, in part, because of the nature of precolonial African society. Historically, the colonial state in East Africa became "overdeveloped" not so much in response to a need to "subordinate the native social classes" as from a need to subordinate precapitalist, generally nonfeudal, social formations to the imperatives of colonial capitalism. As a result, there is no equivalent, even today, to the "landed class"; rather, we find a precapitalist agriculture which is moving, under the pressures of commercialization, directly toward capitalist relations of production with scarcely any quasi-feudal stopovers along the way.[7] Nor has the "indigenous bourgeoisie" developed even to the degree described by Alavi for Pakistan and Bangladesh. Primarily confined to retail trade and services, it has been mainly comprised of "Asians" (Indians) rather than Africans, and this fact too has weakened such a class's ability to defend its stake in the system.

At one level, this greater weakness of the indigenous classes might seem to strengthen the positions of those who directly control the state apparatus—Alavi's oligarchy. But, as we have seen, Alavi also emphasized the importance to the latter's power of its ability to mediate *competing* interests. It has therefore appeared to some observers that, under East African circumstances (with weak indigenous classes), the oligarchy falls much more directly under the thumb of the "metropolitan neo-colonialist bourgeoisie"—the transnational corporations—whose influence may now seem even more imbalanced and unalloyed there than in the case studied by Alavi. In consequence, certain theorists (like Fanon) have presented the new oligarchies as mere transmission belts for these transnationals: "the national middle-class discovers its historic mission: that of intermediary."[8] And Issa Shivji, of whom we shall say more later, was similarly tempted in his first essay on Tanzania to conclude that the real "socioeconomic base" of those elements who directly control the state lies "in the international bourgeoisie"![9]

There is, of course, much truth in such an emphasis, but it remains an overstatement. True, Alavi's attempt to premise an explanation of the relative "autonomy" of those elements which cluster around the state upon the nature of the interplay of other classes in postcolonial society is not entirely convincing, particularly with reference to East Africa. But some measure of autonomy does remain to those elements nonetheless—an autonomy rooted in the centrality of the state in these societies which Alavi's other arguments, cited earlier, do in fact help to illuminate. Indeed, some analysts would strengthen the point by extending the argument concerning the nature of the state's stake in the production process beyond Alavi's rather bland statement that it deploys surpluses "in the name of promoting economic development." Rather, they suggest that the strategic position which the state occupies vis-à-vis the economy, including the privileged access to the surplus which is thus available to the oligarchy, defines the latter's interest as being that of a *class*. Perhaps this is what Poulantzas has in mind when he cites "the case of the *state bourgeoisie* in certain developing countries: the bureaucracy may, through the state, establish a specific place for itself in the existing relations of production. But in that case it does not constitute a class by virtue of being the bureaucracy, but by virtue of being an effective class."[10]

Indeed, in East Africa, where other indigenous classes are so relatively weak, the position articulated by Debray in his discussion of the Latin American "petty bourgeoisie" may seem to such analysts to be quite apropos: "It does not possess an infrastructure of economic power before it wins political power. Hence it transforms the state not only into an instrument of political domination, but also into a source of economic power. The state, culmination of social relations of exploitation in capitalist Europe, becomes in a certain sense the instrument of their installation in these countries."[11] Thus the use of the state—through special financing arrangements, training programs, manipulation of licenses and the like—by newly powerful elements in postcolonial

Kenya to parachute themselves into the private sector at the expense of the Asians is instructive in this respect.[12] Moreover, Shivji suggests that *a very similar logic* leads to a somewhat different result in Tanzania merely because of certain features distinctive to the political economy of the latter country. But on the essential similarity of the process he is quite outspoken.[13] At the same time it must be emphasized that there are others, equally convinced of the relative autonomy of the state in many postcolonial African settings, who would draw rather different conclusions. In doing so, such observers have extended the notion of autonomy far beyond anything conceived by Alavi, arguing that it can actually provide the initial lever for mounting *socialist development strategies* in parts of Africa—including Tanzania! We must now turn directly to these various formulations.

Models for Africa

Implicitly, some crude notion of the "autonomy" of the state lies at the root of modernization theory, for example. Much the least interesting of the three broad formulations we shall mention in this section, it is a model which conceives of those who inherit the postcolonial state as "benign elites"—the "new middle class" or the "modernizers." Their role, within the trickle-down process of enlightenment from advanced countries to backward countries, is naturally to facilitate the "development," the "modernization," of their "new nation." In addition, there is a left variant of this essentially benign interpretation—an interpretation which, quite uncritically, sees this new stratum as a force for socialism! Of course, this has been the stuff of much political rhetoric in many centers of "African Socialism," but Green has recently given this argument an academic formulation (albeit with primary reference to Tanzania). Quite aware that "the elite" in many parts of Africa may, in the service of its own self-interest, abuse both its opportunity for service and the trust of the mass of the people, Green nonetheless concludes that, for some unexplained reason, this does not occur in a country like Tanzania. Thus, in the case of Tanzania, it would be fair to say that virtually every general and specific issue raised by university critics had been posed (sometimes in even harsher terms) at least six months (and in certain cases up to two years) earlier by members of the "neo-bourgeois bureaucratic elite" and that almost all were under active study aimed at evaluating alternative operational solutions both at official and political level. There is no reason to suppose this is a totally unique record even if it may well be atypical in degree. Further, the public sector elite has accepted material rewards substantially lower than those in neighbouring states, and than those prevailing in Tanzania five years ago, with no evident general loss of morale or loyalty. To say that shortcomings can be cited and that the elite is still far above average material standards is fair comment; to argue that it has on any broad scale deliberately obstructed or been unable because unwilling to move ahead on the implementation of the Arusha Declaration is much more dubious. There is no logical reason to assume that because technical competence need not be positively related to political commitment it must always be negatively related. [14]

It is interesting that so close an observer of the Tanzanian scene as Green could come to such a conclusion, but it must also be asserted categorically that his remarks—so sweepingly stated—cannot be squared with the findings of most other students of Tanzanian realities. [15]

At the opposite end of the spectrum from the "benign" school are those who perceive in parts of Africa the crystallization of a fully formed class around the apparatus of the state—a class with an interest quite distinct from and antagonistic to the interests of the mass of the population. Fanon hints at some such formulation, but it has been given its most vigorous scientific statement by Claude Meillassoux in his important "class analysis of the bureaucratic process in Mali." [16] He focuses on "the bureaucrats," defining them as "a body generated by the colonizers to carry out the tasks which could not (or would not) be undertaken by the Europeans themselves." In this capacity they were entrusted with some of the instruments of power, notably with expertise. In other words, education and government (and business) *employment* are the crucial features. [17] He then argues that in Mali, having been the instrument of the colonial power, and having turned against it to become the mouthpiece of the exploited Malian peasantry, the bureaucracy was gaining (with its access to power) some of the characteristics of a social class: control of the economic infrastructure and use of it as a means of exploitation, control of the means of repression involving a resort to various devices to maintain dominance. Some of its features are original: its opposite class is not yet socially well defined; it does not own the means of production on a private judicial basis, but controls them on a constitutional basis. There is no room here for a parliamentary system, regulating conflicts between a great number of private owners or corporations. The situation is better controlled through the single-party machine, within which open conflicts can be reduced to inner struggles between hidden factions. Appropriation of the economic bases of power cannot come from individual endeavour or entrepreneurship, nor from inheritance. It can come through co-operation by the people in position, or as the bargain lot of a *coup d'état*.

Meillassoux's findings parallel those of Alavi in several respects. There is, for example, the subordination to imperialism of this "class":

> Given the economic dependence of the country, the bureaucracy is itself a dependent group, and its origin as an instrument of Western interests continues to influence its development. Instead of striving towards a real independence after winning the right to assert itself as political intermediaries with the outside world, the bureaucrats are content to return (with a higher international rank) under the rule of the old master.

Furthermore, their position is consolidated in contestation with (weak) indigenous classes: in the Mali case, an aristocracy (formerly slaveholders—a class for which there is no equivalent in East Africa) and a fairly well-developed trading class.[18] However, having gone so far, Meillassoux remains reluctant in the end to call this group a class outright: "It is also crucial that a distinction be made between the class proper and the dependent social elements which are the out-growth of classes, but which may, in specific historical circumstances, assume important historical functions." Others, as we shall see, are prepared to go further in this direction, but for the moment another of Meillas-soux's points may be cited. In noting the bureaucracy's attempt "to gain certain positions of control in the modern economy and to eliminate opposition spreading from the Malian historical classes," he comments on their moves "to infiltrate the national economy through the creation of a nationalized economic sector" as follows:

> This was done under the label of "socialism" which provided them with a convenient ideology to bring the economy under their control, supposedly of course on behalf of the entire population. "Socialism" permitted them to put the bureaucracy into the position of a managerial board of a kind of State corporation.

This is striking; it is almost identically the analysis that Shivji seeks to document with respect to "Tanzanian socialism"![19]

It also bears a remarkable resemblance to the analysis by Fitch and Oppenheimer of Ghanaian developments under Nkrumah.[20] It is therefore interesting to note that a third model of the role of the oligarchy—he does not, of course, use that term—was articulated by Roger Murray precisely in the context of a brilliant critique of Fitch and Oppenheimer's position.[21] Murray's is a model which falls somewhere between the polar opposites of the "benign" and the "class" models sketched above, and, like Meillassoux's argument, is of particular interest because it too foreshadows an approach to Tanzanian developments, in this case an approach very different from Shivji's. Murray is well aware of "the sedimenting of new and gross class and power dispositions centering upon the state" in Ghana. Yet he is uneasy with Fitch and Oppenheimer's reduction of the socialist impulse there to the status of "*mere* manipulation," suggesting that in so arguing the authors lapse into "pseudo-Marxist determinism." A richer, more complex picture of those who inherit the over-developed state in the postcolonial period is needed.

What he sees instead is "the accession to *state power* of unformed classes." Concentrating on the CPP leadership and cadres,[22] he notes that

> they were drawn from the *petty bourgeois salariat* (clerks, primary schoolteachers, PWD storekeepers, messengers, etc.)—a mixed

stratum which concentrated many of the political and cultural tensions of colonial society. It is precisely the socially ambiguous and unstable character of this stratum which helps us to understand its *relative autonomy and volatility* in the political arena. The CPP "political" class did not express or reflect a determinate economic class.

Murray is trapped, almost inevitably, by the concreteness, the static and undialectical nature, of terminology here, for even categories like "unformed class" or "class-in-formation" remain essentially teleological.[23] Thus the "political class" to which he refers might really be best considered a "political *x*" since any other formulation (including the term "oligarchy") will mean that the relative social autonomy and plasticity of the political class-in-formation is lost to view. Yet this is a result Murray obviously wishes to avoid, as his further conclusion demonstrates:

> The essence of the matter is that the post-colonial state (the "political kingdom") has simultaneously to be perceived as the actual instrument of mediation and negotiation with external capitalism, and as the possible instrument of a continuing anti-imperialist and socialist revolution. In this setting, the "relative autonomy" of the ruling "petty bourgeois" (we can see how unilluminating the category is at this point) stratum becomes a critical issue, whose import has to be examined in its *modus operandi* of state power.[24]

In other words, the autonomy of this *x* is real, very real; in this "uncertain historical moment," its members can attempt to opt for different historical alternatives, alternatives which would actually affect in *different* ways their own positions in the production process.

This is not to abandon class analysis. It is merely to highlight the "social *uncertainty* and susceptibility to multiple determinations and influences which make the dimension of *consciousness* so crucial to the analysis—a dimension consistently underestimated by Fitch and Oppenheimer. The contradictory situation and experience of these typically transitional and partial post-colonial ruling groups is mediated through the transformations, incoherences, oscillations, 'false' and illusory representations and reconciliation at *the level of ideology*." Thus, in discussing the

CPP's left turn in the early 1960s—a "new articulation of ideology and organization . . . which made socialist Ghana something of a model type in possible postcolonial African development"— Murray mentions as crucial factors not only the economic crisis of the late 1950s but also "the whole *trajectory* of ideological evolution since the 1940s."[25] Nor is this to underestimate the determinations which encourage such elements—harassed by a "frustrated national bourgeoisie," seduced by the easy lure of "bureaucratic consolidation" and alternately tempted and tormented by imperialism—to entrench themselves as an "oligarchy" or dominant "class." Murray states clearly that there are real limits upon what is "historically possible" under such conditions. But he does at least affirm the possibility, in the realm of *praxis*, of a real struggle over the direction which development should take.

It follows that if such a struggle is possible, it may take place precisely *within* this unformed *x*, between those of its members who seek to consolidate the neocolonial setup and those who are moved, increasingly, to challenge it.[26] Furthermore, such a model can then be interpreted as providing a scientific basis for one of Amilcar Cabral's most suggestive metaphors. For Cabral, in identifying the "revolutionary" wing of a crucial class-in-formation which he dubs the "petty bourgeoisie" (and which is strikingly similar in many of its characteristics to that "political class" discussed by Murray), states that "this revolutionary petty bourgeoisie is honest; i.e., in spite of all the hostile conditions it remains identified with the fundamental interests of the popular masses. To do this it may have to commit suicide, but it will not lose; by sacrificing itself it can reincarnate itself, but in the condition of workers and peasants."[27] As Murray demonstrates, there were no significant sections of the Ghanaian leadership who could bring themselves, ultimately, to "commit suicide" in this sense. Nor did the CPP, the political expression of that leadership, realize any such possibility, failing as it did even to attempt the effective mobilization of that active popular base which could alone have guaranteed forward momentum in the longer run.[28] What of Tanzania? Clearly, Walter Rodney's application of Cabral to the Tanzanian situation is of interest in this respect:

[Cabral] considers the petty bourgeoisie not as a decadent stereo-
type but as a stratum with various possibilities, and he includes
himself. Cabral was concerned with evaluating the "nationalist
capacity" of the petty bourgeoisie as well as their "revolutionary
capacity" in the post-independence phase. He speaks about a "revolutionary petty bourgeoisie," meaning that section which has joined
the Liberation Struggle and is already carrying it forward in the
direction of socialist reconstruction in the liberated zones. In other
words, the African petty-bourgeois stratum includes Shivji, the
other TANU Youth League comrades at the University (of Dar es
Salaam) and most of the national leadership in Tanzania—
irrespective of political convictions. Sections of the petty
bourgeoisie have broken with their mentors, and individuals within
the group have at various times wholly or partially opposed the
external or local capitalists.[29]

Socialism and the State in Tanzania

Turning to Tanzania, we may note at the outset that each of the
models sketched in the second section has found its echo in the
wide-ranging debate about the nature of Tanzania's "socialism."
Thus, the "right-benign" interpretation is seen at its most
sophisticated in the writings of Cranford Pratt, who eventually
gives most bureaucrats and politicians in Tanzania high marks as
"developers," despite what to him appear as the unnerving hi-
jinks of some few "political ministers" and the occasional dangers
of a "doctrinaire determination of policies."[30] We have already
taken note of Green's "left-benign" variant. Both wings of this
approach present much too oversimplified an account to warrant
their further discussion here. Rather, the really significant differences of scientific opinion lie between what are, in effect and
broadly speaking, the protagonists of the Meillassoux and of the
Murray/Cabral models.

On the one hand, and closer to Meillassoux, are the *Maji Maji*
socialists, most notably Issa Shivji, author of two of the most
important papers to have emerged from the Tanzanian debate.[31]
It is in point to recapitulate his argument concerning the nature
of class struggle in postcolonial Tanzania, for it is also a significant statement concerning the nature of the state there. As

noted earlier, Shivji's skepticism about the socialist vocation of wielders of state power in Tanzania first found theoretical expression in his attempt to view these elements as quite straightforward agents of the international bourgeoisie. His second paper continues to stress the extent to which such elements service the interests of international capitalism, but he has gone on to develop a much more sophisticated analysis of their own stake in the system.

The class which takes power is, once again, the "petty bourgeoisie," particularly its "upper level" ("the intelligentsia") identified, rather eclectically, as comprised of "intellectuals, teachers, higher civil servants, prosperous traders, farmers, professionals, higher military and police officers." The inclusion of the (African) "traders" and "farmers" in this class and in the nationalist coalition is not crucial, however:[32] "One of the outstanding features of the petty bourgeoisie was that they overwhelmingly came from the urban-based occupations, with some education and some knowledge of the outside world."[33] This class spearheads the struggle against the colonial state. In doing so, their interests merely "coincide with those of the broad masses." The same is true, Shivji states, for the next stage of development—the struggle with the Indian "commercial bourgeoisie." The role of the latter class-cum-ethnic group—which has controlled the intermediate sectors of the economy—is analyzed by Shivji with great subtlety; in fact, he has provided the first really convincing class analysis of the Asian community in East Africa to date. On the African side he extends his analysis in a manner which is much more controversial.

For the confrontation which Shivji sees to be taking place between petty bourgeoisie and commercial bourgeoisie for economic power is complicated by a further development, one which emerges precisely with the accession to state power (at independence) of this petty bourgeoisie:

> In an underdeveloped African country with a *weak petty bourgeoisie*, its ruling section, which comes to possess the instrument of the state on the morrow of independence, relatively commands enormous power and is therefore very strong. This was precisely the case in Tanzania. . . . The Tanzanian scene . . .

comes closer to the "Bonapartist" type of situation where the contending classes have weakened themselves, thus allowing the "ruling clique" to cut itself off from its class base and *appear* to raise the
state above the class struggle. Of course, it is not that the contending classes had weakened themselves in the independence struggle.
But a somewhat similar situation resulted from the fact that the
petty bourgeoisie was weak and had not developed deep economic
roots. This allowed the "ruling group" a much freer hand. In other
words the control of the state became the single decisive factor. For
these and other reasons . . . it is proposed to identify the "ruling
group" as the "bureaucratic bourgeoisie." Before the Arusha Declaration, this would comprise mainly those at the top levels of the
state apparatus—ministers, high civil servants, high military and
police officers and such like. One may also include the high level
bureaucrats of the Party and the cooperative movement, because of
the important role the latter played in the pre-Arusha class struggles.[34]

Shivji does note that the weakness of the petty bourgeoisie referred to here "is due to the fact that it is still 'embryonic'; the
whole class structure is in *the process of* formation." The same
caveat is introduced with reference to the bureaucratic bourgeoisie. Is it "a class *as distinct* from the petty bourgeoisie"?
Not quite. "Suffice to say that the post-independence class
struggles (including the Arusha Declaration) were themselves a
process leading to the emergence of the 'bureaucratic bourgeoisie.' The process may not be complete." But having noted this,
Shivji, unlike Murray, does not draw back from his terms. He is
unconcerned with the weight of teleology which they bear. As he
proceeds with his analysis, classes-in-formation behave, unambiguously, like fully formed classes. And this is the chief weakness
of his argument.

For Shivji, in sum, the "historical moment" is by no means
"uncertain." On the contrary, he now uses this conception of
Tanzania's class structure—straightforwardly and however much
the "structure" may be "in the process of formation"—to explain
the history of postcolonial Tanzania: it is the case of "a *non-
proletarian class* after coming to political power . . . now trying
to wrest an economic base" from the commercial bourgeoisie.
Half-measures, like the encouragement of the cooperatives, having failed, "the only alternative, both for further struggle against

the commercial bourgeoisie and for further penetration of the economy, was state intervention": "it was thus that the Arusha Declaration was born in 1967." With it, and with the attendant nationalizations, a new stage in the class struggle, à la Shivji, is reached:

> Up until the Arusha Declaration the "bureaucratic bourgeoisie" was essentially of the politico-administrative type. Although the state played an important role in the economy it was mostly a regulatory one. With the Arusha Declaration the state and state institutions (including parastatals) became the dominant actors in the economy. Thus a new and more important wing of the bureaucratic bourgeoisie was created. Political power and control over property had now come to rest in the same class.

Socialism as "*mere* manipulation"—Shivji comes very close to such a position. Nevertheless, he does recognize that there is some difficulty in reconciling this with the Arusha Declaration Leadership Code—a code designed to prevent leaders from involving themselves—profitably—in the private sector. Here Shivji's explanation, in order to save his hypothesis, is that "the ideology had gained the upper hand, for even a rhetoric has its own momentum and can have important effects on concrete measures." This would also appear to be his "explanation" for the very real constraints (certainly as compared with other parts of Africa) on elite income and consumption which have been a part of Tanzania's "socialism." In addition, Shivji states, as if to reinforce his general argument, that the code has often been flouted since its inception. This, in turn, suggests (quite accurately) that there was a "spontaneous" tendency for "leaders" to overlap into the private sector—as in neighboring Kenya. Yet such a reality seems to contradict Shivji's emphasis. Why didn't the petty bourgeoisie use the state to facilitate their own movement in upon the Asians on a private basis—again, as in Kenya—rather than publicly and collectively?

Shivji is aware of this problem, of course, and his explanation is of considerable interest:

> In Kenya, there were important sections of the petty bourgeoisie— yeoman farmers and traders, for example—besides the urban-based

intelligentsia, who had already developed significant "independent" roots in the colonial economy. Thus the petty bourgeoisie itself as a class was strong and different sections within it were more or less at par. This considerably reduced the power of the "ruling clique" irrespective of its immediate possession of the state apparatus and kept it "tied" to its class base—the petty bourgeoisie.

But this does not convince. Even if the entrepreneurial elements were stronger in transitional Kenya, the difference from Tanzania was not so striking as Shivji suggests, and in any case these Kenyan Africans' commerical opponents (European and Asian) were themselves much stronger than any counterparts in Tanzania; thus the *relative* economic weight of the African entrepreneurs cannot have been that much different. Moreover, it is quite unnecessary to make such subtle distinctions. As noted, it seems obvious that large sections of Shivji's bureaucratic bourgeoisie continue to cast envious glances at their civil-servant and political counterparts in Kenya and at the gross (and rewarding) "conflicts of interest" which serve to characterize Kenyan economic and political life. And, being disproportionately drawn from commercialized, cash-cropping rural areas like Kilimanjaro and Bukoba, they do in fact have intimate (familial) connections with a "yeomanry." Unless contested, such a group would have had Tanzania gravitate in the Kenyan direction, a point made by Nyerere himself on more than one occasion.[35] It is difficult, in fact, to avoid the conclusion that the Arusha Declaration package of policies—the opting for collective solutions to the Tanzanian development problem—represented, first and foremost, an *initial victory* for a *progressive wing* of the petty bourgeoisie (and the announcement of its continuing commitment to the interests of the workers and peasants), rather than some cold-blooded fulfillment of the class interests of that stratum's bureaucratic core.[36]

This difference of opinion requires detailed exploration of a kind that is beyond the scope of the present paper. Suffice to say that for Shivji this kind of "manipulation" also tends to characterize each of the specific arenas of post-Arusha policy making, while for each such arena it can be shown that this is an oversimplification. Take, for example, the *"ujamaa* village" program (designed to promote a Tanzanian brand of agricultural collective), in Shivji's eyes merely a calculated and perfunctory gesture—an expression of "intermittent ideological hostility" to "kulaks"— designed to maintain for the petty bourgeoisie its "popular peasant base." But this was not an immediately popular policy even among much of the peasantry; support for it would have to be *created*, sometimes in a manner (as in Ismani) which challenged the local dignitaries of the party itself. Nor is it entirely true that this policy was "not basically against the interests of the petty bourgeoisie." The fact that in practice bureaucrats often worked hard to defuse the policy by directing it away from the "advanced" areas (Kilimanjaro and Bukoba mentioned above) and toward more defenseless, backward regions (with many fewer kulaks) testifies to their uneasiness. Nor were the extensive nationalizations of 1967 merely a charade. International capitalism was stung and the conventional wisdom of most civil servants visibly affronted. In other words, these and other initiatives represented real achievements in a transition toward socialism.[37] That the full potential of these policies' possible contribution to such a transition has not been realized is, of course, also true, a point to which we shall return.

However, there is one crucial area of inquiry which cannot be passed over here, and which also sheds considerable light on the issue under discussion. Thus, Shivji argues that the main contradiction in Tanzania is now between the working class and the bureaucratic bourgeoisie, and cites the dramatic assertions of Tanzania's working class in recent years. Indeed, the further investigation of this subject by Shivji's colleague, Henry Mapolu, reveals a level of proletarian action in Tanzania which is virtually unparalleled elsewhere in Africa.[38] As Mapolu writes:

> By any standards the progress made by the working population in Tanzania in the last few years as far as political consciousness is concerned is astounding. To begin with, at no other time in the whole history of this country have strikes and industrial disputes generally been so much a day-to-day affair as has become since 1970. But more important, at no other time have such strikes and disputes been of such a political nature! . . . It has indeed been a veritable revolution for the Tanzanian workers; within a period of

three years they have moved from a state of docility, timidness, and above all disunity to one of tremendous bravery, initiative and class solidarity.

Beginning with the downing of tools and with lock-outs, some Tanzanian workers had moved, by 1973, to the stage of actually occupying factories (both state-owned and private) and continuing production on their own. And the issues were not, by and large, of a conventionally consumptionist nature. Disputes concerned, firstly, "the question of humiliation and oppression on their person by managements" and, ultimately, "issues of general mismanagement and sabotage of the country's economy." Predictably, such initiatives began to earn reprisals from the bureaucracy (including police intervention and arrests), thus polarizing the Tanzanian situation to an unprecedented degree.

But where did such a high level of consciousness come from? This too must be explained, especially when one compares this development with experience elsewhere in Africa. Moreover, the Tanzanian working class is small, even by continental standards, and, in the past, not marked by notably radical leanings.[39] Once again, the conclusion suggests itself that initiatives taken by a certain sector of the leadership—notably by Nyerere and his supporters—played an important role in bringing about this development and in facilitating the emergence of what Shivji calls "the proletarian line." Unlike their Ghanaian counterparts, such a leadership did sense, albeit haltingly, that "the oppressed" could "alone have provided the conscious support for a socialist path of development"[40] and they therefore sought to create such a base. Initiatives designed to facilitate "workers' participation" (workers' councils) and peasant participation (*ujamaa* and decentralization) reflected this concern, despite the distortion in practice of these programs by the dead hand of the bureaucracy.[41] However, most significant in this respect has been *Mwongozo*, the TANU Guidelines of 1971—a crucial document in crystallizing worker consciousness and in legitimizing, *even demanding*, the unleashing of popular pressures against oligarchical tendencies on the part of wielders of state power ("leaders"). Yet the drive for these measures did not come from below. Even Shivji must come part way to meet that reality.

In the international situation where capitalism has become a global system and socialism has been established in a large area of the world: where both internally and externally physical and intellectual wars are raging between the capitalist and socialist lines, the world-wide circulation of progressive ideas has become commonplace. It is not surprising therefore that even capitalism and neo-colonialism have to be wrapped up in socialist rhetoric and vocabulary. But more important is the fact that though material *class* forces may not immediately warrant it, a few progressive and revolutionary leaders manage to push through (officially) radical ideas and policies. The adoption of the Mwongozo by TANU, with its progressive features, was such an event.

But who are these "few progressive and revolutionary leaders"? As Shivji suggests, they do shape and crystallize, rather than merely reflect, popular consciousness; moreover, they seem to be cutting sharply against the interests of the bureaucratic bourgeoisie. It is precisely because Shivji's approach cannot fully illuminate such matters that other analysts have felt some other formulation than his to be necessary in order to explain, in class terms, the "socialist" dimensions of Tanzania's experiment.

Indeed, it is only because it is much too evocative and dismissive a phrase that one avoids applying to Shivji's analysis Murray's epithet, "pseudo-Marxist determinism." Nonetheless, Murray's critique of Fitch and Oppenheimer is in many respects the best approach to Shivji. And Murray's positive formulations can also serve to promise much the most effective alternative approach to Tanzanian reality. In this respect it is worth noting that even the definitional problem (which Murray himself approached somewhat too obliquely) has been faced, quite straightforwardly, by Micheala von Freyhold—working from what is in effect a closely related viewpoint to that of Murray. Her solution, in a recent paper, is to use the term "nizers" for the x in our sociopolitical equation. As she explains it:

"Nizers" or "nizations" (from Africanization) is a term applied by Tanzanians to refer to that stratum or class which social scientists have called "educated elite," "labour aristocracy," or "petty bourgeoisie"—those who took over important administrative and economic positions when colonialism was defeated.

"Educated elite" is an ideological term bound up with the elitist theories of dubious origin. "Labour aristocracy" suggests a link between workers and "nizers" which . . . does not exist. "Petty bourgeoisie" has a double meaning: it refers to small capitalists on the one hand and all those who look to the bourgeoisie as their model on the other. As long as the educated stratum to which we refer is directly employed by colonialists or a national bourgeoisie it is necessarily a petty bourgeoisie in the second sense. In the absence of such direct employers the educated stratum can choose whether it wants to remain subservient to those by whom it has been created. Since the stratum in question may decide to become a petit bourgeoisie in both senses we would prefer to reserve the term for that particular situation.

"Nizers" is a precise and dialectical term. It refers firstly to the progressive aspect of Africanization, to the promise that those who take over the power would return this power to the people on whose behalf they took it away from the colonialists.

It refers secondly to the fact that the "nizers" have not created the existing economic and social structure but have taken it over, either adapting to it or changing the built-in dependency on imperialism.

It refers thirdly to the negative possibility that the original promises are not held, that the structure is not changed, that those who have taken the power will usurp it for themselves.

Which of the connotations of the term "nizers" will emerge as the decisive one is subject to the still on-going struggle among the nizers and the kind of support the different factions can mobilize among other classes—the workers and the peasants.[42]

It is precisely to this "still on-going struggle among the nizers" that von Freyhold traces the socialist impulse in Tanzania: "In 1967 an enlightened political leadership had decided that Tanzania should not turn into a neo-colonial society. The Leadership Code was to cut the links between public office-holders and petty capitalism and nationalisations were to bring foreign capital under control. . . . Both measures were . . . a vital first step." And the direction of further steps also remains, in her eyes, a contested matter:

While the transformation of the nizers is an obvious prerequisite for the promised creation of a socialist society it is obvious that it will not proceed without a protracted struggle within that educated stratum itself. What the progressive parts of Tanzania's nizers envisage as their future is not yet reality. As long as the future is undecided there are still two ways in which one can look at the present educated stratum: as a nascent petty bourgeoisie which will not only be a faithful agent of international capital but which will eventually solidify into a class with petty capitalist connections and orientations or as the precursors of a socialist avantgarde.

Of course, the general definitional problem has probably not been laid to rest by von Freyhold's coinage, suggestive though it is; nor does she directly address herself to Shivji's prognosis of bureaucratic consolidation *without* "petty capitalist connections." But the emphasis seems to me to be basically correct.[43]

To argue so is not to ignore the contradictions which mitigate, and even undermine, the achievements of Tanzania's progressive "nizers." Quite the reverse. In the essay cited above (note 43), I have stressed the extent to which various pressures—international and domestic—do play upon the system in such a way as to strengthen the least progressive elements in the "present educated stratum" and to "solidify" that stratum into a privileged class. It is quite true, as Shivji has demonstrated in another of his papers, that international capitalism can make adjustments and begin to shape to its own purposes the fact of nationalization. Corporations join with aid agencies and international economic institutions in reactivating "conventional wisdom" and co-opting those "oligarchs" who are inclined to be so tempted. In addition, the expansion of the state sector has had the *result* (but, to repeat, not the primary purpose) of expanding the number who are prepared merely to feed off it, in the absence of countervailing tendencies.[44] If, unlike Ghana, some more real effort has been made to create a new base for the state among the workers and peasants, the pace of bureaucratic consolidation seems to be outstripping that attempt. In consequence, demobilization of the peasantry becomes the more likely result, while workers find themselves set not merely against the most conservative of managers but against the state itself and the increasingly homogeneous class which defends it.

The negative weight of "objective conditions" has been reinforced by subjective conditions. As Murray's analysis would suggest, ideological contestation in Tanzania has been a creative factor of great importance, with Nyerere's formulations in particular being crucial to facilitating a move to the left. But this ideology of the progressive "nizers" has also been marked by inadequacies which some might like to term "petty bourgeois" in nature: a hostility to Marxism, for example, and the consequent lack of a fully scientific analysis of imperialism and class struggle.[45] And this problem has been compounded by a much too sanguine reliance on existing institutions of the inherited state (ministries and cabinets, an untransformed party) which cannot easily be turned to purposes of socialist construction.[46] As demonstrated in my earlier essay, these factors too have made it difficult for Nyerere and others to consolidate their original initiatives. The results are paradoxical (and not preordained, à la Shivji). The conservative wing of the nizers now threatens to inherit a socialist initiative (and an even more "overdeveloped" state than existed at the moment of independence) in the creation of which it had little hand but which it has sought to warp to its own purposes from the moment of the policy's first being announced. All of which is to approach Shivji's conclusion, though not by Shivji's route:

> This marks the beginning of the political struggle and the rise of the proletarian line. There is bound to be increasing opposition to bureaucratic methods of work and "management's" dominance, themselves a reflection of the neo-colonial structure of the economy and the corresponding class structure. The struggles of the workers and peasants against internal and external vested class interests will characterize the subsequent class struggles in Tanzania.[47]

For it is necessary to reaffirm that much about this continuing class struggle has been shaped by the reality of struggle within the stratum of the "nizers"—within the "oligarchy-in-the-making," if you like—during the first postcolonial decade.

The critique of Shivji is also a qualification of Alavi's approach. Apart from points made earlier concerning the important differences in context which East Africa presents, and some of the implications of these differences, it can now be argued that Alavi's approach is too rigid to fully comprehend the uncertainties which define the historical process in the immediate postcolonial period. In Tanzania, his "oligarchies" become such only more slowly and with much more ambiguous results than his model would lead one to expect. At the same time it can be firmly stated that the pressures which move the situation toward such an unsavory result as he seeks to theorize are indeed powerful. And, as noted, there is no doubt that these pressures have been, and are continually, making themselves felt upon Tanzania. As a result, "oligarchical" tendencies—the consolidation of Shivji's "bureaucratic bourgeoisie" (self-interested and ever more subservient to imperialism)—seem to have been the increasingly obvious result.

Has the further development of this trend altered perspectives on practice in Tanzania? Writing two years ago, I felt confident to conclude a survey of Tanzania's efforts at socialist construction in the following terms: "Indigenous radicals will decide their own fates. Yet the fact that almost all have chosen to work within the established structures and upon the régime is no accident."[48] And there is still some significant contestation within the "petty bourgeoisie" and within the established institutions.[49] But where, for example, one could then argue with some confidence that the control of working-class organization by party and state had played, despite the costs, a positive role in curbing consumptionism and raising worker consciousness, there is now reason to be more skeptical about the logic of continuing control. Faced with "nizers" more bent than ever upon consolidating their power, independent organization of the working class may seem an increasingly important goal.[50] Similarly, the time may be approaching when the independent political organization of progressive elements, already a (difficult) priority in most other one-party and military/administrative regimes in Africa, becomes a priority for Tanzania as well. Smash the postcolonial state, or use it? But this is really a question which can only be asked, and answered, by those engaged in significant *praxis* within Tanzania itself.

Notes

1. Hamza Alavi, "The State in Post-Colonial Societies—Pakistan and Bangladesh" in *New Left Review*, no. 74 (July–August 1972), pp. 59–81.

2. The most prominent of these is Issa Shivji, author of "Tanzania: The Silent Class Struggle" in *Cheche*, Special Issue (Dar es Salaam), September 1970, reprinted in L. Cliffe and J. S. Saul, eds., *Socialism in Tanzania*, vol. 2 (Nairobi, 1973), pp. 304–30; and "Tanzania: The Class Struggle Continues" (mimeo, Department of Development Studies, University of Dar es Salaam, 1973). See also his *Class Struggles in Tanzania* (New York: Monthly Review Press, 1976; London: Heinemann, 1976). The interesting work of Henry Mapolu (see notes 38 and 41 below) and Karim Hirji (note 37), among others, can also be cited in this connection.

3. This quotation and others in this section are from Alavi, "The State in Post-Colonial Societies," unless otherwise indicated.

4. Alavi may overstate this particular point. Ralph Miliband has recently paraphrased Poulantzas approvingly to the effect that "the political realm is not, in classical Marxism, the mere reflection of the economic realm, and that in relation to the state, the notion of the latter's 'relative autonomy' is central, not only in regard to 'exceptional circumstances,' but in *all* circumstances." And Miliband concludes that "in fact, this notion may be taken as the starting point of Marxist political theory." Nonetheless, Alavi's formulation of the concept of autonomy with specific reference to the postcolonial state—his focus on the "overdevelopment" of the inherited colonial state, for example—is a crucial and distinctive one. See Ralph Miliband, "Poulantzas and the Capitalist State," *New Left Review*, no. 82 (November–December 1973), p. 85.

5. Nicos Poulantzas, *Political Power and Social Classes* (London, 1973), p. 191.

6. It must also be noted, though only in passing, that other attributes of the postcolonial state, and of the elements which control it, can work simultaneously to undermine this very kind of unity. See Richard Sklar, "Political Science and National Integration," *Journal of Modern African Studies* 5, no. 2 (1967) and John S. Saul, "The Dialectic of Class and Tribe," in this volume.

7. The movement is "direct" but it can also be very slow, with the possibility of many of the newly created "peasantry" being caught, under African conditions and in the absence of genuine mobilization, in a kind of limbo of underdevelopment. See, generally, John

S. Saul and Roger Woods, "African Peasantries" in T. Shanin, ed., *Peasants and Peasant Societies* (London, 1971), pp. 103–13, and for a striking, if controversial, East African case study, Colin Leys, "Politics in Kenya: The Development of Peasant Society" in *British Journal of Political Science*, no. 1, pp. 307–37.

8. Frantz Fanon, *The Wretched of the Earth* (London, 1967), p. 122.
9. Issa Shivji, "Tanzania: The Silent Class Struggle."
10. Poulantzas, *Political Power and Social Classes*, p. 334.
11. Régis Debray, "Problems of Revolutionary Strategy in Latin America," *New Left Review*, no. 45 (September–October 1967), p. 35.
12. This does, of course, raise some questions—for East Africa—about Alavi's juxtaposition of oligarchy and indigenous bourgeoisie. In Kenya, these two elements—among the Africans—interpenetrate to a significant degree, rather than compete with one another, though the strategic position of the *Asian* "commercial bourgeoisie" might be argued to have affected this pattern on the African side. This is, in any case, an area of inquiry to which we will return in subsequent sections.
13. Shivji, "Tanzania: The Class Struggle Continues."
14. R. H. Green, "Economic Independence and Economic Cooperation," in D. P. Ghai, ed., *Economic Independence in Africa* (Nairobi, 1973), p. 85. In fact, Green's error lies in vastly *overestimating* the progressive attributes of the Tanzanian situation—even as Shivji, in his turn, underestimates them (see below).
15. For summaries of such findings, see John S. Saul. "African Socialism in One Country: Tanzania," in G. Arrighi and J. S. Saul, *Essays on the Political Economy of Africa* (New York, 1973), ch. 6, and Uchumi Editorial Board, *Towards Socialist Planning*, Tanzanian Studies No. 1 (Dar es Salaam, 1972).
16. C. Meillassoux, "A Class Analysis of the Bureaucratic Process in Mali," *Journal of Development Studies* (January 1970).
17. Interestingly, Meillassoux makes no distinction between party and administration in his analysis: "In this situation the only people able to take responsibility and power upon themselves were those with literate, administrative and managerial capabilities, equally necessary to handle a political party or to govern a State."
18. Thus, "if the conflict with local business was a consequence of the necessity of the bureaucracy to provide itself with an economic base, the fight against the aristocratic class was a more direct competition for political power" (ibid., p. 106).
19. It is worth noting that these extensions of the argument differ from

Fanon's conclusion to what is otherwise a somewhat similar analysis, for Fanon seems to imply that such elements will infiltrate the national economy by moving in on the trading sector as entrepreneurs—viz., the very definition of this class as "an intellectual élite engaged in trade." Here is a very significant difference of opinion, as we shall see in examining Shivji's work more closely in the next section.

20. R. Fitch and M. Oppenheimer, *Ghana: End of an Illusion* (New York, 1966).

21. Roger Murray, "Second Thoughts on Ghana," *New Left Review*, no. 42 (March–April 1967).

22. It should be noted that Murray tends to talk only of the members of the ruling political party when he discusses those who inherit the state; he does not really deal with the bureaucracy's role in all of this, despite his recognizing the need for "an appraisal of the politico-administrative role and weight of the *civil service* within the state apparatus." However, his characterization of the "autonomy and plasticity" of "the political class" would seem also to apply to the bureaucracy; under such circumstances they seem equally to be elements whose "partial and 'transitional' character . . . expresses itself in its absence of a determinate class standpoint grounded upon its site in the process of production." Interestingly, Meillassoux, from his different perspective, makes little distinction between bureaucrat and politician in identifying the state-based dominants in Mali (see note 17, above). This is also Shivji's approach; in Tanzania the civil service and political hierarchies interpenetrate and he is prepared to view members of both as candidates for his categories of "petty bourgeoisie" and "bureaucratic bourgeoisie."

23. On the problem of developing terms adequate to the task of dialectical analysis of real historical processes, see Bertell Ollman, *Alienation: Marx's Conception of Man in Capitalist Society* (Cambridge, 1971), especially Part I.

24. As Murray continues: "Socially, then, the picture we have is of a petty-bourgeois group projected into the power vacuum caused by the lack of objective maturation of a nationalist capitalist class and the subjective errors of aspirant bourgeois politicians."

25. Thus, "the whole Nkrumahist ideological complex was undergoing profound mutation in the 1960s. This process has two particularly striking features: the attempt to transcend the 'African Socialism' current of thought in favour of a more universal and scientific theory; and the related effort to institutionalize and accelerate the formation of an *ideological vanguard* of cadres who might then strive to make

ideology a mass force (*Winneba*). This development, marked as it was by bizarre juxtapositions and unresolved contradictions, nevertheless acquires considerable significance. . . ." All of which is not to deny that it was a "misconceived contradictory 'socialism' " which emerged, characterized by (among other things) "the loss of any *integral commanding strategy*."

26. Actually, this struggle can even be seen to take place *within* the individual members of this unformed *x* as they struggle with the "bizarre juxtapositions and unresolved contradictions" in their own lives, a reality which was dramatized for me during seven years of work with young recruits to the "petty bourgeoisie" at the University of Dar es Salaam.

27. Amilcar Cabral, "Brief Analysis of the Social Structure in Guinea" in his *Revolution in Guinea* (London, 1969 and New York, 1972), p. 59; the point is elaborated upon in his excellent essay "The Weapon of Theory" in the same volume.

28. Thus Murray states that the "implicit positive model" offered by Fitch and Oppenheimer is "that of a political party which made the situation and demands of the most oppressed classes (urban and rural proletariat, sharecroppers, indebted tenant farmers) the absolute 'moral imperative' of its organization and action. This class-based party, acting for and through the oppressed but potentially revolutionary strata of society, could alone have provided the conscious support for a socialist path of development—with all its costs and risks." But he concludes of Ghana that "instead, the CPP demobilized these 'potential' forces."

29. Walter Rodney, "Some Implications of the Question of Disengagement from Imperialism" in *Maji Maji* (Dar es Salaam, 1971), and reprinted in Cliffe and Saul, *Socialism in Tanzania*, vol. II. The explicit reference to Shivji arises from the fact that Rodney is here reviewing the first of Shivji's two papers cited in note 2, above.

30. See, among other of his articles, Pratt's "The Cabinet and Presidential Leadership in Tanzania: 1960–66" in M. Lofchie, ed., *The State of the Nations* (Berkeley and Los Angeles, 1971) and reprinted in Cliffe and Saul, *Socialism in Tanzania*, vol. II. See also essay 10 below.

31. See note 2, above; succeeding quotations are from the second of Shivji's two papers, unless otherwise indicated.

32. Not crucial, but there is an ambiguity in the term "petty bourgeoisie" which is revealed here, one to which we will return in discussing Freyhold's attempt to conceptualize Tanzania's class structure. ·

33. Shivji gives no numerical basis to his argument, but I have elsewhere

cited Resnick's argument that "out of 350,000 persons employed in wage and salaried jobs in 1968, only 44,000 fall into the 'privileged' class, . . . that is, are in occupations classified as 'high- and middle-level' by manpower definitions." See I. N. Resnick, "Class, Foreign Trade and Socialist Transformation in Tanzania," paper presented to the Economics Research Bureau Seminar, University of Dar es Salaam, 1972.

34. As noted above (note 22), Shivji makes little distinction between party and civil service; nor do his critics who adhere, in effect, to the Murray line of analysis— although the latter might argue that rather more representatives of this progressive petty bourgeoisie are to be found in the party (which has, however, a tendency to become itself bureaucratized).

35. Thus Nyerere has argued that "some Tanzanian leaders criticized the Arusha Declaration" because "they wished to use positions of power for private gain" and "almost the only way in which Africans could get capital to become landlords or capitalists was by virtue of their office or their seniority in the public service"; see his "Introduction" to J. K. Nyerere, *Freedom and Socialism* (Nairobi, London, New York, 1968).

36. Such a conclusion with reference to the Tanzanian case, paralleling Murray's critique of Fitch and Oppenheimer's handling of Ghanaian developments, also raises some retrospective doubts about Meillassoux's discussion of Mali. Was the socialist assertion there as straightforwardly manipulative as Meillassoux suggests?

37. Shivji's model has been applied, with interesting results, to the educational sphere by Karim Hirji in his essay "School Education and Underdevelopment in Tanzania," *Maji Maji*, no. 12 (September 1973). More alert to the ideological dimensions of Tanzanian development and very insightful, Hirji's analysis suffers, nonetheless, from some of the same rigidities as Shivji's. I intend to discuss his argument in more detail in a monograph on the University of Dar es Salaam, now in preparation.

38. Henry Mapolu, "The Workers' Movement in Tanzania," *Maji Maji*, no. 12 (September 1973). See also Mapolu's "Labour Unrest: Irresponsibility or Worker Revolution," *Jenga* (Dar es Salaam), no. 12 (1972) and Nick Asili, "Strikes in Tanzania," *Maji Maji*, no. 4 (September 1971).

39. For a subtle account which highlights the dialectic established in Tanzania between a committed section of the leadership and a working class with steadily rising consciousness, see M. A. Bienefeld, "Workers, Unions, and Development in Tanzania,"

paper delivered to a conference on "Trade Unions and the Working Class in Africa," Toronto, 1973. Even NUTA, the official trade union ("that moribund organization," in Bienefeld's words) is seen to have played a role in this respect: "For its creation did forestall the creation of the self-centred, competitive unions, whose function and mentality is so well suited to the kind of interest group politics which the most powerful interests in an open economy find congenial, and who are so easily moulded into the business unions whose existence is defined by the capitalist economy. . . . [T]he worker was freed from the mesmerising spectacle of the perpetual competition for leadership by men who fight with promises for the spoils of office, while . . . the very bureaucratic nature of NUTA made it possible for the workers' allegiance to be transferred to the government more permanently."

40. See note 28. Nyerere very early sounded the themes which were later to find expression in *Mwongozo*; thus, in 1967, he "called on the people of Tanzania to have great confidence in themselves and safeguard the nation's hard-won freedom. He warned the people against pinning all their hopes on the leadership, who are apt to sell the people's freedom to meet their lusts. Mwalimu (i.e., Nyerere) warned that the people should not allow their freedom to be pawned as most of the leaders were purchasable" (*The Nationalist*, September 5, 1967).

41. On the very real and disturbing distortions in practice, however, see the striking analyses of Henry Mapolu, "The Organization and Participation of Workers in Tanzania," Economics Research Bureau Paper 72.1 (Dar es Salaam, 1972) and Phil Raikes, "Ujamaa Vijijini and Rural Socialist Development," paper delivered to the East African Universities Social Science Conference, Dar es Salaam, December 1973.

42. M. von Freyhold, "The Workers and the Nizers," mimeo. (University of Dar es Salaam, 1973). At the same time, it is also worth noting (as I am reminded by John Loxley) that in its popular usage the term "nizers" is generally applied by workers and peasants in a pejorative sense!

43. Indeed, it is quite close, in certain respects, to my account of the emergence of Tanzanian socialism in "African Socialism in One Country: Tanzania." There, however, the prognosis of bureaucratic consolidation without petty capitalist connections *is* explored and one all too possible post-"socialist" system characterized as "the creation of a vicious circle within which a petty bourgeoisie, on

balance still relatively untransformed, demobilizes and instrumentalizes the mass of the population and guarantees, at best, a stagnant quasi-state capitalism, thereby checking further progress" (p. 298).

44. This is all the more likely to be the case precisely because this expansion of state activities into the economic sphere does expand the contact of the nizers with international corporations, through management contracts, etc., and with international economic agencies, which are among the most co-optative of imperialism's many mechanisms.

45. Unfortunately, this tends (as again argued in my earlier paper) toward the same result as Murray noted in Ghana: "the loss of any *integral commanding strategy.*"

46. This is the strongest point made in Haroub Othman, "The State in Tanzania: Who Controls It and Whose Interests Does It Serve," mimeo. (Institute of Development Studies, University of Dar es Salaam, Tanzania, n.d.).

47. Shivji, "Tanzania: The Class Struggle Continues," p. 107. Furthermore, if such a polarization of classes is indeed taking place in Tanzania, it can be predicted that an increased emphasis upon the *repressive* functions of the state will also serve to enhance that state's prominence in postcolonial Tanzania!

48. Saul, "African Socialism in One Country," p. 312.

49. An example is the passage of a quite progressive income-tax bill in late 1973. Originally rejected by Parliament, it was passed without dissent by the same Parliament when it was reconvened for the purpose by an irate President Nyerere. The latter stated that "I am not prepared to accept that a Bill beneficial to the majority, should be rejected simply because it is not liked by a minority. If we agree to this, we will be setting a dangerous precedent whereby an entrenched minority can prevent measures aimed at promoting *ujamaa* from being taken. I reject this vehemently in the name of Tanu" (*The Daily News* [Tanzania], November 29, 1973). Paradoxically, this incident reveals both some of the strength and some of the weakness of the president's role in trying to lead a socialist transition. Moreover, the president's response to worker unrest has been rather more equivocal.

50. The place of popular forces in the Tanzanian socialist equation, although it has been somewhat slighted in this essay, has been discussed further in "African Socialism in One Country: Tanzania." Moreover, the possible role of the "peasants" in defining Tanzania's future raises even more complex questions than does the case of the

workers. The range of variation of "peasantries" across so large and diverse a country is vast in any case, and expressions of peasant consciousness have not been so dramatic as those of the workers. But it seems likely that the experience of "nizer-socialism" has had some positive impact upon consciousness—and upon the future (despite the fact that bureaucratization, and World Bank "assistance," has undermined many officially sponsored programs). For a suggestive case study see Adhu Awiti, "Class Struggle in Rural Society in Tanzania," *Maji Maji*, no. 7 (October 1972) and, for a broader overview, my "African Peasantries and Revolutionary Change," in this volume, especially the section on Tanzania.

9

MULTINATIONALS, WORKERS, AND THE PARASTATALS IN TANZANIA

The multinational corporations cast a giant shadow across Africa. Moreover, as the official statement submitted by the Tanzanian government to the Lusaka Non-Aligned Summit of 1970 concluded its analysis of the multinationals' role in the world economy, their "investments will not normally make the economy of the Third World nation concerned any more self-reliant as long as the multinational retains its control. The satellite relationship will continue to exist while questions of output, markets, technology, research and management are determined by corporations which are basically North American, West European, Japanese, and South African. From all this it becomes obvious that Third World countries need to consider very carefully the potentialities and the dangers of multinational corporations."[1] At the most general level, Tanzania's own response to this reality has been equally clear. In discussing the nationalizations which were attendant upon the promulgation of the Arusha Declaration in 1967, President Julius Nyerere put the relevant point succinctly:

> The real ideological choice is between controlling the economy through domestic private enterprise, or doing so through some state or other collective institution. But although this is an ideological

This essay was originally published in *Review of African Political Economy* 2 (1975). It was coauthored with John Loxley, for whose permission to reprint it here I am grateful.

choice, it is extremely doubtful whether it is a practical choice for an African nationalist. . . . He will find that the real choice is between foreign private ownership on the one hand and local collective ownership on the other. . . . Private investment in Africa means overwhelming foreign private investment. A capitalistic economy means a foreign-dominated economy. These are the facts of the African situation. The only way in which national control of the economy can be achieved is through the economic institutions of socialism.[2]

Nonetheless, as a wide range of experience in Third World countries has amply demonstrated, mere "nationalization" is not, in and of itself, any guarantee of an effective check upon the multinationals, nor is state ownership or control a synonym for socialism. It is necessary to examine critically the *real* impact of any attempt at direct state involvement in the economy. For Tanzania this concern dictates, in turn, an exploration of *the parastatal sector*, since that sector provides the arena of such involvement by the Tanzanian state. The burden of this paper thus becomes the presentation of a "political economy of the parastatals" in Tanzania.

The Parastatals

The term "parastatals" is generally used to refer to those governmental organizations which fall outside the main lines of the departmental and ministerial hierarchies and which have, in consequence, some measure of quasi-autonomy in their day-to-day activities (though of course all are ultimately tied into the centralized decision-making process). Moreover, all of them function primarily in spheres of active economic endeavor—production, commerce, and service—and most of them have been established since the Arusha Declaration and the accompanying nationalization measures of 1967. Initially most of the companies nationalized, with the exception of finance, trading, and sisal concerns, were placed under the umbrella of the National Development Corporation (NDC) which acted as a holding company and which rapidly developed into an unwieldy conglomerate with interests in such diverse fields as beer, cement, timber, textiles, cashew nuts, leather, curios, painting, tourism, livestock, diamonds, publishing, meat packing, construction, and estate agriculture. At the peak of its activities the NDC was controlling about forty subsidiaries and twenty-five associate companies.

All commercial banking in Tanzania was placed under the control of the National Bank of Commerce, insurance under the National Insurance Corporation, and import-export and wholesale business was gradually, but never entirely, centralized under the State Trading Corporation (STC). The Tanzania Sisal Corporation took charge of the nationalized sisal estates, and canning and milling was placed under the control of the National Milling Corporation. Parastatals were also established in such service areas as audit, legal work, housing, building design, shipping, and road transport.

An important characteristic of all these corporations was their highly centralized bureaucratic organization. It could be argued that this was necessary in their formative years, and, indeed, the more successful organizations like the National Bank of Commerce and the Sisal Corporation have, over the years, progressively decentralized decision-taking to branch/plant level with corresponding increases in efficiency. But the NDC and the STC failed to do this and became increasingly less capable of handling the huge volume of business with which they had been entrusted. As a result of their growing inefficiency and the sheer impossibility of their providing creative and dynamic initiatives in their broad areas of "specialization," the government has, since 1972, gradually broken up these organizations and formed a number of small, more highly specialized, parastatals. Thus the NDC has spawned the Tanzania Tourist Corporation, the Tanzania Wood Industries Corporation, the National Agricultural and Food Corporation, the National Textile Corporation, the Tanzania Cashewnut Authority, the Tanzania Livestock Authority, etc. Most of these have been established as holding companies with shares in subsidiary or associate companies, i.e., as smaller, more specialized NDCs.

The STC, whose performance was much worse than that of NDC, and which, at one time, was making huge losses, has been broken down into independent Regional Trading Companies, serviced by nine specialized import-export firms such as the Domestic Appliances and Bicycles Company, the National Pharmaceutical Company, and the General Agricultural Products Export Company, etc. All these companies are planned, monitored, and controlled from above by a new Board of Internal Trade.

It is too early yet to assess the impact of these decentralization measures on the performance of the parastatals. Certainly the new companies seem to be more successful than their predecessors in terms of carrying out the important day-to-day functions of ordering, producing, and selling. Nevertheless we see little in the new structure to warrant reassessing the views expressed below, which were formed primarily with reference to the predecentralization system.

What of the economic significance of these institutions? Official statistics leave much to be desired, but it appears that parastatals are extremely important in certain key growth sectors of the economy, though of only moderate importance in terms of contribution to total gross domestic product and as employers of labor. They are, above all else, important as generators—and more especially as users—of the national surplus, and in that way, of course, they are also crucial to the process of defining the long-run shape and structure of the economy.

In 1972 the contribution of the parastatal sector to monetary gross domestic product was less than 12 percent (Table 1). This low proportion is largely because agriculture and commerce, the biggest sectors of the economy, are still in private hands. Nevertheless the parastatal sector has been growing steadily since 1967, when it accounted for less than 10 percent of a much smaller gross domestic product, and it is extremely important in the mining, electricity, finance, and manufacturing sectors and in estate agriculture. In 1972 it was responsible for employing 80,000 workers, or about 20 percent of officially recorded noncasual employment, and accounted for about 25 percent of the nation's wage bill.

It is, however, in their contribution to national fixed-capital formation that the real significance of parastatals lies. In the years

Table 1
Tanzania (Mainland) 1972: Value Added by Parastatal Sector

	Shs (millions)	Percent of total monetary GDP
Agriculture	79	4.3
Mining	91	76.5
Manufacturing	320	29.0
Electricity and water	81	79.8
Construction	20	4.0
Commerce	143	11.4
Transport	109	12.3
Finance, real estate, and services	212*	57.0
Total	903**	12.7

*Includes imputed service charges of banks.
**Excludes imputed service charges of banks.
Source: Computed from *National Accounts of Tanzania*, 1964 to 1972, Bureau of Statistics, Dar es Salaam, February 1974.

immediately following the Arusha Declaration, parastatal investment activities were confined mainly to the building up of the pipeline and road-transport links with Zambia, most of the newly formed parastatals being preoccupied with the task of establishing workable operating systems. As the Zambia transport links were completed, the share of parastatal interests in the total declined, reaching a trough in 1969. Since then this sector's capacity to initiate and implement investment projects has grown rapidly. It now accounts for 45 to 50 pecent of total national fixed-capital formation and dominates the more dynamic sectors of the economy (Table 2).

In general, parastatals invest much more than they save, and rely heavily on foreign finance. For the financial year 1974/5 it is planned that 45 percent of all parastatal investment (Shs 450 million out of Shs 1,000 million) will be financed directly from overseas, while a further 15 percent will come from local investment banks which receive most of their finance from abroad. Reinvested surpluses will account for 24 percent and transfers from the Central Government Development Budget for about 16 per-

Table 2
Parastatals and Gross Fixed-Capital Formation, 1966 to 1973

	Investment by parastatals (Shs M)	Total national investment (Shs M)	Parastatal investment as percent total (%)
1966	91	910	10.0
1967	283	1086	26.1
1968	241	1182	20.4
1969	165	1101	15.0
1970	659	1879	35.1
1971	1084	2387	45.4
1972	1186	2308	51.4
1973	1170	2686	43.6

Source: National Accounts of Tanzania, 1964 to 1972, and Annual Economic Survey 1974.

cent. Dividend payments to government (about Shs 100 million) are approximately equal to 6 percent of planned parastatal investments. So in effect the central government is contributing, net, about 10 percent and the parastatals themselves about 30 percent of total parastatal finance.

Finally, the parastatals are now the largest borrowing customers of the commercial bank, accounting for over 60 percent of total credit outstanding (or for Shs 900 million out of a total of Shs 1,380 million in June 1973). This pattern of investment financing has several important implications, both for the way in which parastatals conduct their business and for the possibility of their being effectively controlled.

One-half of our subject—"the parastatals"—being thus clarified, it can also be stressed at the outset that the notion introduced above of a "political economy of the parastatals" is somewhat misleading. For in order to investigate such institutions meaningfully we must really confront the larger reality of the Tanzanian system as a whole. There are some who would prefer, nonetheless, to discuss the parastatals "in their own terms," but it is an underlying premise of this article that any such attempt is almost invariably misleading. The elements which comprise the totality of Tanzania's socioeconomic system are in fact the major determinants of how the parastatals function. What is really at stake, therefore, is a "political economy of Tanzania."

Obviously, we cannot attempt to present a full analysis of the political economy of Tanzania in this article. Our focus will remain centered on the parastatals themselves. But the crucial relationships which link the parastatals to their wider social, political, and economic context will remain as important to our concern as any characteristics of the group of parastatals taken as a whole or of individual parastatals viewed separately. Moreover, it will be apparent that this broader emphasis refers not merely to the relationships which exist between the parastatals and the formal governmental planning system. This is important, of course, and will certainly claim our attention: indeed, the costs and benefits of relative parastatal autonomy within the established framework of bureaucratic decision making is a live question and a currently changing feature in the Tanzanian situation. But it is still primarily a question of the division of labor within the conventional bureaucratic structures. There is a broader context beyond this to which we must also refer the student of progress and performance in the parastatal sector—to the realities of imperialism and dependence, to the nature of the domestic class structure, and to the characteristics of Tanzania's ideological and political accomplishments, all of which impinge upon the functioning of the institutions immediately under review.

Aspects of a Political Economy of Tanzania

In the sections which immediately follow the present one, we shall look directly at the functioning of the parastatals *per se*; in the next section, investigating the ways in which they both coordinate among themselves and relate their activities to the broader apparatus of bureaucratic decision making and control; in the following section, exploring the ways in which individual parastatals order and institutionalize their own activities within the specific spheres assigned to them. Naturally, in these two sections, we will pinpoint those efforts which are being made to streamline operations, train badly needed personnel, and guarantee increased efficiency. But in both cases we will also return to a similar and essential point: shortfalls in performance are still to be understood more as a reflection of the major contradictions which continue to characterize the overall Tanzanian system than as failures of organization, narrowly defined, at either the sectoral or the enterprise level. Indeed, it is precisely as weaknesses in the fields of bureaucratic coordination and control, structural reorganization, and training begin to be overcome that the deeper contradictions which bedevil Tanzanian socialism come more clearly to the fore. It will be the task of the present section, therefore, to identify the nature of these contradictions as briefly, even as baldly, as possible, trusting that their importance will be further clarified by the analysis of subsequent sections.

The first relevant feature is Tanzania's continuing dependence on the international capitalist system. The movement toward "socialism and self-reliance" characteristic of policy making in the post-Arusha period has redefined this relationship in certain important respects. Indeed, the attendant sweeping nationalizations gave the parastatal sector its central importance in the present Tanzanian economy.

It is difficult to affirm unequivocally that this expanded state control over economic surplus and over centers of economic decision making has always been used in ways most effective to restructuring the economy. Too often the rhetoric of self-reliance has not become the reality of a "self-centered" economy, an economy which would be based upon production for mass needs, upon the movement toward indigenous manufacture of capital goods, and upon the development of a locally based and wholly relevant technological capacity. Too often "the tyranny of the demand concept" has carried the day[3]—the investment of surplus often being directed first toward such immediately profitable domestic spheres as luxury consumption goods and toward such immediately effective earners of foreign exchange as tourism, rather than toward structural transformation. These kinds of choices (made almost by default, it would seem) characterize most centrally the workings of the National Development

Corporation, but the lack of a root-and-branch challenge to dependence must inevitably shape the activities of most of the parastatals.

One must be circumspect about this: for example, some industries are being established which do forge close links with agriculture, and the need for a growing capital-goods sector is recognized in the Second Five-Year Plan. But significant accomplishment in such spheres is still much more randomly than systematically achieved. The government seems, in fact, increasingly aware of this weakness—the need for an "industrial strategy" is also stressed in the Five-Year Plan, and the phrase has been trotted out on a number of subsequent occasions. And yet *almost nothing has been done to remedy such a defect and to spell out such a strategy.* As a result, decision making in the field of industrial development remains premised on the shopping-list approach: 385 "possible" projects for the second-year plan period! Under such circumstances, even if care is taken to safeguard "internal economies" on a project-by-project basis, the choice *between* projects will almost inevitably be dictated as much by short-term opportunity and accident as by more relevant criteria. Moreover, as we shall see, even when increasingly successful efforts (on the part of the treasury, the planning ministry, or financial institutions) are made to coordinate activity and plug project planning into a broader framework, these efforts also break on the reef of lack of principle and strategy; fully effective criteria for the exercise of such critical control are, quite simply, lacking.

Moreover, it is into such a strategic vacuum that there rush the various purveyors of "soft options" which cumulatively forestall radical structural transformation: those multinational-corporate wielders of "management agreement" and "partnership" proposals about which Shivji has correctly urged suspicion, those donors of what is, measured against any broader criteria, very costly "aid" (the Canadian bakery, for example, and the Danish-funded Mount Meru Hotel), those "advisors" of caution and convention, of which Harvard's Development Advisory Service (recently called in to help in the "industrial strategy" field) is only the most odious. And, of course, there are the home-grown guarantors of this pattern: the national elite which controls, formally, the commanding heights of the bureaucratic decision-making apparatus, for inevitably Tanzania's class structure vitally affects parastatal performance.

The elite's situation is somewhat more equivocal in Tanzania than it is elsewhere in Africa. A real struggle has begun to be waged for the commitment to socialist goals of a growing proportion of this "petty bourgeoisie," and in the course of this struggle some real sacrifices—in *amour-propre*, in privileged access to surpluses, and in private-sector economic aggrandizement—have been extracted from them. Obviously some of these changes can only serve to facilitate socialist economic development: thus income redistribution begins to undermine some of the logic of luxury-goods production, for example. Moreover, it might be hoped that the Tanzanian emphasis on activating "workers and peasants" to underpin and push forward progressive demands and policies will ultimately transform even more of the texture of the inherited system. Yet in the short run it can hardly be said that most members of the elite have fully and actively engaged themselves in the task of socialist construction. Their continuing lack of a fully realized capacity for socialist creativity remains a major weakness.

Partly this is a matter of self-interest, partly of cultural set. Thus, further, more genuine sacrifice is not readily elicited, nor is further, more radical transformation easily sanctioned. From the standpoint of bureaucratic incumbents (including those in the parastatal sector), whose paternalistic and hierarchical styles of work have not altered much since independence, the latter process is particularly unpredictable and worrisome. Reference to the Chinese experience and the insights of "Maoist economics," for example, conjures up for them images of a release of human energies which may not be easily channeled along established grooves—much safer to ride the existing system unadventurously. And a variety of inherited theoretical constructs are ready to hand which can serve to rationalize these tendencies. Conventional wisdom about development, albeit bent by the impact of the Arusha Declaration and by "socialism and self-reliance," reasserts itself more subtly in the bowels of the policy-making process: the "necessity" of aid, the (unequivocal and neutral) "superiority" of Western technology and management systems, the priority of "efficiency," narrowly and technocratically conceived, over radical risk and the release of human energies referred to as a possibility above. Concrete socialist programs, of necessity the end-point of creative but laborious day-to-day planning and implementation, only spring with difficulty from such infertile soil.

The creative terms of the Tanzanian socialist equation have most often lain elsewhere, in any case—in certain features of the country's political and ideological development which seem almost to defy the logic of the objective conditions within which they have emerged. A political leadership has surfaced—the party (TANU), the president (Nyerere)—which has managed both to exemplify unity and to link its destinies to the needs of the masses in ways almost unknown elsewhere on the continent. And a distinctive ideology—extrapolating and consolidating the most progressive tendencies of the nationalist moment, suspicious of imperialism in at least some of its guises and caustic toward many of the pretensions of Africa's new elites, confident of the creative potential of the mass of the African population—also came to power with this leadership.

These factors have been crucial. It is Tanzania's progressive constellation of "organization and ideology" which has pushed imperialism and the locally privileged as far as they have had to go in order to accommodate to the imperatives of Tanzanian socialism. But, as we have been noting, the latter goal has not yet been reached, and indeed many of the most subtle barriers to socialist reconstruction remain to be smashed. It is when confronted with such tasks that the more equivocal aspects of organizational and ideological factors in Tanzania have become apparent. These features have begun to present themselves as weaknesses which remain to be overcome. Thus an ideology which is merely "suspicious" of imperialism (in a manner sometimes little more than the obverse of its parallel suspicions of the socialist camp!) is probably not a wholly adequate key to understanding the present-day ramifications of the historically defined relationship of dependence. Tanzania lacks, in effect, a theory of imperialism. Similarly, it has been argued by some observers that an insufficiently forceful emphasis on the contradictions which continue to characterize the relationship between privileged domestic classes and the "workers and peasants" has also blurred the possibilities for progressive advance; such observers have therefore pinpointed the leadership's failure to confront adequately the realities of class struggle as another crucial ideological weakness.[4]

For our purposes it is important to note a vital corollary to such a set of arguments: that these very weaknesses at the ideological level help to forestall the definition of a coherent radical strategy for development and industrialization. A "major roadblock to progress still appears to lie precisely at the point where technical calculation begins to shade over into *divergent ideological perceptions*, into fundamentally different problematics, as to the very nature of underdevelopment and the strategic imperatives which that reality suggests."[5] Moreover, this discussion carried us into the organizational sphere. For, as noted above, the party has been the bearer of the positive ideological impetus in Tanzania. Necessarily it also exemplifies many of the weaknesses we are now discussing. In addition, it has remained an institution capable of directing the system only on the most general plane. TANU has never developed the capacity continuously to concretize goals and in that way both guide the bureaucracy and hold it effectively to account. Similarly, while it has certainly embodied many of the best instincts and most genuine interests of the masses, the party has been less successful in developing the organizational capacity and methods of political work which would guarantee the mobilization and self-expression of an active, highly conscious and militant mass base for Tanzanian socialism. However, it is also eminently clear that any progress which Tanzania makes in these spheres of ideological elaboration and organizational creativity can be expected to affect the functioning of the parastatals in dramatic ways.

There will be differences of opinion about how much of this kind of progress is really possible. Thus, for instance, Shivji has subjected the dominant elements in Tanzania to root-and-branch kinds of criticism and has interpreted even the "socialist" impulse itself as a startlingly self-interested expression of petty-bourgeois hegemony. We are more prone to grant credence to the reality of a struggle within the petty-bourgeois stratum over the direction of development and over the kind of role which popular forces will be encouraged to play in the society, but would nonetheless raise doubts about the capacity of the state which has crystallized in Tanzania to remain a progressive instrument in the longer run, whatever the positive implications of some of its involvements in the economy to date. Needless to say, we cannot hope to exhaust such a vital and comprehensive debate about the nature of Tanzanian socialism and its future prospects in this paper. Nonetheless, we will return briefly to some of these questions in the final section, after a closer look, in the next two sections, at the parastatals themselves.

The Planning and Control of Parastatals

We have seen that the importance of the parastatals lies not so much in their share of total national production as in the generation and, more especially, in the use of investable surpluses. As noted earlier, their current activities will therefore be crucial in shaping the future economic structure of Tanzania, and in determining the speed and nature of the development of the whole economy. For that reason their activities must be carefully planned and controlled to ensure their maximum contribution to the socialist transformation of the economy. But while some progress has been made, the integration of the parastatals into the planning system has not proved an easy task. There are several reasons for this. To begin with, the planning system itself was not set up to deal with a large publicly owned modern sector, and has experienced difficulty in accommodating it. Secondly, the parastatals themselves have not found it easy to plan and have often both resented and resisted the discipline that effective planning and control entail. Thirdly, there has so far been a failure to chart out a long-term national development strategy into which parastatal activities should fit and against which their policies and performances could, in consequence, be judged. These difficulties are to some extent technical and mechanical ones and are slowly being tackled, but in addition, they also reflect basic ideological problems of a more intractable character. Before the Arusha Declaration, planning in Tanzania was of a loose, indicative nature. Planning of the directly productive sector was virtually nonexistent because this sector was almost entirely privately owned. What passed for planning was therefore simply the "guesstimation" of how much the government thought this sector might produce, save, invest, and import. At the same time, central government activities which were carefully *budgeted for* were almost equally *unplanned*, for there was little detailed scrutiny of projects at the appraisal, implementation, or follow-up stages, and no clear investment criteria by which to rank and select projects. The budget and the financial process therefore dominated the so-called planning process. As a result, the planning ministry was most ineffective, especially since it did not control the purse strings.

There was insufficient time after the Arusha Declaration to achieve any fundamental improvements in public-sector planning which could be embodied in the Second Five-Year Plan. The result was that parastatal plans consisted of lists of projects—unappraised, uncoordinated, and with no indication of detailed sources of finance. Even where more information was forthcoming, there was for many years a reluctance on the part of parastatals to make this available to the planning ministry, and there was no machinery for ensuring that such information would flow to the center. The reluctance stemmed partly from a lack of clarity in the delineation of responsibilities between parastatal boards of directors and the other planning bodies—the sectoral ministries, Devplan and Treasury—and partly from a failure on the part of parastatal management to appreciate the importance of planning. Until recently the management of parastatals often resented outside "interference" in the running of their firms, and since they had no clear-cut national plans to follow, nor any serious shortages of finance, they were able for some time to withstand pressures from the planning machinery. The inadequate coverage of the parastatals in the Second Five-Year Plan provided the justification for parastatals to resist later attempts to incorporate their activities into the planning machinery itself.

It should also be pointed out that neither Devplan nor the sectoral ministries have had sufficient skilled laborpower to allow careful scrutiny of parastatal activities, so that parastatals have complained, with some justification, of bureaucratic delays in their dealings with them. Sectoral ministries in particular have failed to build up cadres of competent staff and have as a result been ineffective in their dealings with the more dynamic and efficient parastatals.

In addition, parastatals themselves have been loath to plan. The very idea of planning has been and still is alien to the managements of most enterprises, who, as is shown below, are hired from Western firms, and in some cases from the very firms that were nationalized. It is not easy to change work systems that have for so long been geared to anarchic "laissez-faire" business principles. It is even more difficult to change one's approach—in effect, the ideology—upon which such systems rest. As we shall see, it was a minor financial crisis at the national level which strengthened the hand of the planners and forced parastatals, reluctantly and so far with only moderate success, to plan their activities.

Even now there is still some confusion over the function of enterprise plans. Some parastatals view the preparation of annual plans and budgets as pure *management* control tools for internal consumption rather than as essential components of *national planning*. Thus, enterprise plans for the NDC subsidiaries are sent to NDC headquarters, where they are reviewed "for completeness, accuracy, internal consistency, format, adherence to policies, procedures, etc. When the review is completed, the plans are sent back to individual companies accompanied by comments. Then the final plans are presented to the company board of directors for approval and to NDC headquarters for information. When approved, the plans are ready to be integrated into one overall NDC plan which is presented to the NDC Board of Directors for approval." But this plan appears to be drawn up after the Annual Plan rather than forming, as we would expect, an integral part of the national plan. Indeed, NDC gives the impression that once its overall plan is approved by the board, that is the end of the process, and it speaks of planning solely in terms of being "a major management tool in the NDC."[6] While this is an important function of enterprise plans, it must not be allowed to remain the sole one. The real difference between economic anarchy under capitalism and economic order under socialism lies not in the fact that enterprises plan in the latter but not in the former, for capitalist enterprises have been planning for years. Rather it lies in the coordination of enterprise plans and the subservience of the individual plan to the nationally determined performance targets. That this is not the case so far in Tanzania seems to be a reflection of the "capital budget" orientation of annual planning and a failure to extend planning to production or even recurrent spending in the modern sector. This deficiency is, however, widely recognized. The minister for finance has observed that "parastatal budgets—recurrent as well as capital, cash flow as well as profit and loss—must come to be at the central core of national planning. To date this is only partly true of their capital budgets, and almost not at all of their recurrent. Yet until it is true we are not really planning for production nor for overall efficiency in resource use very much better than we were prior to 1966, when we tried to run a national capital budgetary and planning exercise which took no serious account of recurrent revenue and expenditure of their cost-benefit efficiency."[7]

Underlying the technical problems of learning how to plan operations, and the mechanical problem of building up the planning system and defining relations within it, has been the much more serious problem of the lack of a clear-cut national-development strategy, which, in turn, has made the technical and mechanical problems that much more insurmountable. Such a strategy requires a consensus of opinion as to the nature and causes of underdevelopment and on the type of society that Tanzania wishes to create, for only when there is agreement on these fundamentals will it be possible to identify development paths which are both feasible and desirable. These are therefore very much ideological questions over which there appears to be significant disagreement. In 1971, for instance, there were two quite conflicting statements from ministers about the desirable future role of the external sector in Tanzania's development—one calling for an inward-looking strategy, the other for expanded exports of primary commodities. Clearly, until such issues are resolved, including the time span over which changes are to take place, there can be no unambiguous guidelines for parastatals—or any other public-sector investor—to follow. This then opens the way for considerable dispute between the government planners and the parastatals, for, as the general manager of the NDC has complained:

> If Party policy is defined in broad terms and if responsibility lines between the civil service and parastatals are indistinctly drawn, serious clashes over interpretation of Party policy will develop when practical cases are examined in the light of that policy . . . In several cases in the past, we have been blamed for misinterpreting Government and Party policies.[8]

What is worse, in the absence of a clearly defined strategy for the socialist transformation of Tanzania there have been no rational criteria by which public-sector investment and other spending decisions could be assessed. Parastatals have therefore either behaved in exactly the same manner as their private-enterprise forerunners or have attempted to draw up their own criteria. Recently the planning ministry itself confessed that parastatals "remain so far largely outside attempts at socialist planning of the economy; investment decisions are made in essentially the same way as in the private sector of an unplanned economy."[9] At the end of 1971 NDC made the following revealing statement: ". . . as the government develops an industrial strategy to ensure that industrialization follows a socialist pattern, and as NDC and other institutions implement this strategy . . ."[10] This simultaneously raises the question of, and provides the answer to, how parastatal decisions have been taken since the Arusha Declaration. The need for strategy is most seriously felt in the industrial sphere, where the dilemma has been summed up in the following terms:

> If you put together all the industrial investment figures of the plan where NDC's name is mentioned, you will come up with an

astonishing figure of Shs. 1,300 million. You may say that these 93 industrial projects contained in the plan constitute a marvellous action programme for the NDC. Unfortunately, apparently no one was seriously aware of the critical deficiencies in the plan which made it manifestly inadequate as an action programme . . . the plan as a whole is overestimated by about 30 per cent as far as financial resources are concerned and also overestimated by about 30 per cent as far as market capacity is concerned. Without details as to which projects are affected by these overestimations of financial resources and market capacity, the individual industrial projects listed become surrounded by a veil of uncertainty. . . . What should be taken now, therefore, as an official guideline in the formulation of our industrialization policies?[11]

In fact, strictly speaking, and as Mramba and Mwansasu have pointed out, an industrial strategy for the Second Five-Year Plan was actually announced in 1969 by the minister responsible. This aimed to achieve:

(a) an increase in per capita income;
(b) an increase in the rate of industrial income;
(c) an increase in the rate of growth of industrial development;
(d) an increase in technical knowledge;
(e) an increase in capital investment in the rural areas and in *ujamaa* villages;
(f) an increase in import substitution;
(g) an increase in export of our manufactured goods;
(h) an increase in employment;
(i) an increase in the quality of labor force;
(j) an increase in industrial contribution to regional development and a decrease in disparity between income in different regions;
(k) an increase in the efficiency of firms;
(l) an increase in utilization of domestic raw materials;
(m) laying the foundation of heavy industry—especially coal, iron and steel.

A similar list of aims was published in 1971–72, but this time with the addition of the need for large-scale manufacturing plants to take advantage of economies of scale. It is clear that such a crude but comprehensive listing of objectives could be used to justify almost any conceivable project but is useless in terms of specifying, in concrete terms, what the Tanzanian industrial sector should look like in several years' time and what its contribution to the economy and to socialist aspirations generally should be. It is therefore not surprising that a shopping-list approach to planning ensued and it says little for NDC that it "has attempted to formulate its investment strategy within the framework of the plan and the (above) Ministerial policies."[12]

The same problem is encountered in other sectors. Criticism has been leveled at NAFCO projects in the Second Five-Year Plan, most of which were entered there with little background preparation or justification in terms of overall socialist strategy. NAFCO therefore operates with no clear-cut guidelines on such important issues as what its producer prices are designed to achieve vis-à-vis its own surpluses and peasant income levels, what choice of technique it should adopt, and what value it should place on saving or earning foreign exchange. Lack of strategy has further resulted in questionable investments by state financial institutions.

In fact, as the above government statement claims, most parastatals have used commercial profitability—discontinued cash flow[13]—as their investment yardstick. Little thought seems to have been given to the appropriateness of this technique in the Tanzanian context. It is, however, apparent that in a situation of high protective tariffs or hidden subsidies and monopolistic market structures in which many small disorganized buyers or sellers must deal with large parastatal firms, often on a contractual basis, the use of DCF will almost inevitably give results which have little meaning in social terms and can be used to justify almost any project. In addition, this measure of desirability favors "building on the best" to use Gurley's expression, which summarizes the way in which the logic of internal and external economies[14] perpetuates and magnifies inequalities of wealth and opportunity at the personal, regional, or national level.[15]

Tanzania's urban policy is a recognition of this danger and an attempt to restore regional balance to the economy. But even this is a partial attempt, since the moving of industry away from Dar es Salaam to upcountry towns does not in itself constitute regional planning but simply one small aspect of it. There is still a need for comprehensive regional plans, but again these presuppose the existence of a national development strategy.

Public investment decisions should therefore be based on criteria which put social considerations very much to the fore and not simply on DCF, which, while having serious social and political implications, does not explicitly recognize any objectives other than profit maximization. Such criteria can only be derived once the government has decided precisely how best the economy should develop in future if socialist goals are to be achieved. Attempts by parastatals to develop their own criteria, however well intentioned, can be no substitute for nationally agreed ends and means.

Mramba and Mwansasu claim that the NDC does in fact consider a number of different criteria before investing. These are broken down into primary criteria which must be *satisfied* by all projects and secondary criteria which must be *considered* for all projects. The primary criteria are (a) profitability, (b) national cost/benefit, and (c) foreign-exchange effects, while the secondary criteria are ranked in the following order of importance: (a) employment, (b) location, (c) industrial linkage, (d) budgetary impact, (e) investable surplus. It is immediately apparent that as operational guidelines these criteria are of little value. In what way can primary criterion (a) be said to differ from secondary criterion (e), assuming the NDC's prime objective is *not* to maximize profit outflow overseas? What meaning can be attached to national cost/benefit if it is not commercial profitability adjusted for the social valuation of foreign-exchange effects, employment, linkage, location, and budgetary effects? The secondary criteria are therefore implicit in primary criterion (b). Furthermore, how much weight is to be attached, in money terms, to the "social" considerations? As Penrose has put it: "In weighing these criteria in any given case the difficulty of course lies in the nature of the 'trade-off'; how much to sacrifice employment to improve industrial linkages, or location to increase investible surplus, etc."[16] But this is not a difficulty which can be resolved at the level of the individual parastatal; the weight to be attached to each criterion must be determined nationally and applied uniformly to all investment decisions in the economy. The real power of such criteria in the planning process lies in their being used to rank alternative projects in a consistent manner, and this cannot be done if the weights are not specified or if each investing body is applying a different set of weights.

So far the planning ministry and the sectoral ministries have failed to produce investment, or more generally, spending criteria of any sort. Parastatals have therefore been left to analyze projects as best they could. As a result there has been little if any ranking of projects within parastatals, and almost no ranking of projects between parastatals and government. The allocation of resources has therefore been extremely arbitrary, and if any criterion has been used at all, it has been that of commercial profitability. The situation is, however, changing, and the recent budget and balance-of-payments problems have been instrumental in bringing about a greater concern for the way in which investment allocations are made. But even now this concern has not gone as far as the formulation of national investment criteria. Indeed, since such criteria must be derived from national development strategies, their formulation awaits the tackling of this much larger problem.

What makes the lack of national investment strategies and criteria doubly serious is the manner in which many projects seem to originate in Tanzania. Often the initiative comes not from the parastatal itself, but from foreign machinery salesmen. The persuasiveness of these characters in pushing dubious projects on parastatal managements, which, in addition to having no clear investment guidelines, often suffer from a lack of competent staff, necessitates extremely careful control over parastatal affairs by ministerial planning bodies. The irony is, however, that in the present situation the scope of "control" is limited to avoidance of the worst abuses, for effective control presupposes meaningful planning of activities, and without this, control operates in a vacuum. Until the parastatals are effectively integrated into the planning system and until the fundamental problems of strategy and criteria have been resolved there will be severe limitations on the meaningfulness of the formal control system. This formal system is described elsewhere by Carvalho. He neglects the growth in the importance of the state, and of central, commercial, and investment banks since 1967 in the control of parastatals, but otherwise presents a reasonably comprehensive picture. The major weakness in his presentation is, however, a failure to differentiate between the *formal* legal and administrative controls, and the *effectiveness* of such controls in practice. For instance, Carvalho argues that the activities of foreign management agents are controlled by the boards of directors of parastatals. "It is through the budgetary control that the *main* control lies. Any deviation from the approved budget warrants an explanation from the managing agent."[17] The formal mechanism is clear, but the financial year 1971/72 was the first one in which NDC companies were required to draw up budgets, and only 30 out of 39 attempted it. Acute shortages of skilled accountants and finance staff are common in NDC group companies and other parastatals, so that even where budgets are prepared they are often incomplete, late, or inadequate, and the reporting on the progress of implementing a budget and follow up action to rectify deviations from the budget leave even more to be desired. But even if efficient budgeting existed, as it most certainly will in the near future, there is still a large question mark over the ability of boards effectively to control foreign management. Packard, for instance, argues that

> for the most part, the members of boards are civil servants. Their experience, together with their attitudes, militates against too detailed questioning or understanding of management . . . The most likely result is that review of management actions by the board of directors will be perfunctory, so that the board in effect abdicates any responsibility for shaping the operations and development of the enterprise.[18]

True, the decision-taking powers of boards of directors or, if one accepts Packard's arguments, of parastatal management, have in fact been severely curtailed in recent years. Uniform terms and conditions of employment and a national incomes policy have limited their ability to fix wages and salaries and to compete for staff; the products of several parastatals are subject to national price control; and the investment and day-to-day expenditure decisions of parastatals are being scrutinized increasingly by the banks, which also dictate overseas profit-remittance rates. Management agreements are now carefully screened by Devplan and the banking system.

In addition, the recent credit squeeze was accompanied by a growing concern over the lack of the control over parastatal decisions. In 1970 the planning ministry complained that "there are serious data deficiencies that limit the forward planning, particularly financial planning, of several parastatals . . . we have inadequate knowledge of sources of finance for that sector, such as the need for borrowing from banking institutions. Parastatal external borrowing also remains partly autonomous and very little is known in the aggregate about the generation and uses of funds by parastatals including their subsidiaries."[19] With the growing sophistication of the finance and credit plan, this problem is less acute than it used to be, but it still remains. In the last budget the minister for finance argued that, "In a situation where there are conflicting claims for available resources, the retention of surpluses by parastatals does not necessarily ensure that resources are channelled to the priority areas according to national requirements . . . The object should be to ensure that each operational unit must justify its demands for retention of surpluses on the basis of its operating and capital programme and in the context of national requirements."[20] He then went on to announce that in future all parastatal surpluses would be compulsorily paid into a centrally administered common pool "out of which allocations will be made according to concrete approved programmes." This measure would have given the treasury complete control over declared parastatal surpluses, but, in fact, the pool idea has never been fully implemented, most of the surplus being retained for reinvestment by the parastatals. It has now been superseded by the establishment of special production-development funds to be financed by taxes on the commodities in question and by surpluses from the parastatals involved. Permission to draw on the fund is required from treasury, but the revenues and the expenditures involved will no longer find reflection in the central government budget. It is difficult to see just what extra bureaucratic efficiency or control this measure is likely to achieve, although clearly if the annual financial plan were operating as it should, such separate funds, which have the undesirable feature of introducing rigidity into public-sector financing by earmarking specific sources of tax revenue for specific commodity development, would not be required.

Despite this, it is apparent that the financial plan and the special funds both reflect the concern of the government to improve investment planning—though, in future, such efforts will also need to be accompanied by a tightening of controls over recurrent spending in order to ensure that declared surpluses are, as nearly as possible, at the optimal level. Yet the fact remains that, even if the formal machinery of control is to be improved in these and related ways, the need for a careful definition of strategies will merely be felt that much more acutely. Until the development policies and goals of government are spelled out more clearly, there will always be ambiguity over what parastatals are supposed to be doing, and therefore doubts as to what the control mechanism is designed to achieve.

Management and Management Systems

The nationalization of the major modern-sector means of production in Tanzania was not accompanied by a complete break with Western capitalism. On the contrary, "full and fair" compensation was offered to all former owners, specifically to avoid such a break, and only in a few isolated instances was deadlock reached in compensation negotiations. New parastatal investments continue to rely heavily on foreign borrowing and/or foreign minority-share participation, and foreign companies aggressively sell "projects" in the form of machinery and equipment to parastatals. But it is in the field of management—in terms of both personnel and systems—that the influence of Western capitalism is still all-pervasive. In many instances the former foreign owners of enterprises have entered into management agreements with the government or the parastatal holding companies; in other cases new management partners have been found, almost without exception from Western capitalist countries. In addition, extensive use has been made of foreign management consultants for the introduction of new management control systems in the parastatal sector, and finally, parastatals turn almost exclusively to Western business schools and companies for the training of management personnel.

There is therefore a firm belief in the "neutrality" of management—that management systems are capable of universal application regardless of the sociopolitical and the ideological basis of the economic system. Even the recent provision for more effective workers' participation, a bold move which has its roots in a genuine concern by TANU to eradicate the obvious alienation of labor in the parastatal sector, and which we shall examine in much more detail in the next section, is not regarded as posing any fundamental threat to the inherited management systems.

It is generally felt that this new policy can be accommodated with only marginal adjustments by management, and yet, as we shall see in the next section, there are already clear indications that effective workers' participation and orthodox Western management systems are incompatible. Western management systems are unquestionably elitist and extremely hierarchical. Management tends to be remote from the workers and to rule by decree. Workers' participation is rigidly circumscribed and, outside of negotiations concerning material rewards (conceived of in very narrow terms), is limited in such a way that it does not interfere seriously with management's discretion over all major decisions. The Western management style would also seem to be at odds with Tanzania's socialist aspirations in a myriad of other ways. High salaries, fringe benefits, and expense account living; heavy reliance on advertising, frequently with appeals to sexism and the superiority of "bourgeois" life styles and consumption patterns; liberal use of "public relations" personnel as protective cocoons to hide the truth from the public; maintenance of rigid specialization so that workers gain proficiency in only one or two monotonous repetitive activities; an acute sensitivity to matters of profit and loss and an acute insensitivity to the implication of their activities for society at large—these are but a few obvious examples; there are many other, perhaps not so obvious, ways in which Western management systems and practices might be open to question.

Management systems are not, therefore, ideologically neutral, and hence the wholesale importation of Western capitalist management systems into Tanzania should be viewed with concern. The extensive use of the purveyors of these systems—Western management consultants, and in particular the American company, Mckinsey—is an even more bewildering aspect of Tanzania's policy in the public sector. Mckinsey has been given contracts to set up management and control systems for NDC, STC, and East African Harbours Corporation (as well as being given the much more important responsibility of setting up the new machinery for the decentralization of government activities). Other Western consultants have been active in parastatals, and they have come in for heavy criticism in Tanzania. They are extremely expensive, stay for very short periods of time, and frequently use Tanzania as a training ground for young staff fresh out of business school. They have obtained access to information denied even to many senior Tanzanians, and their views tend to be given much more weight than those of people who have worked for years in the local situation—indeed it is often asserted that they charge high fees in part so that their advice *will* be regarded as preeminent.

No one has seriously questioned the appropriateness of the experience and training of such consultants as Mckinsey and hence of the particular type of advice that they have given. Indeed their work would have to be analyzed in detail for this to be possible, and, for the most part, their manuals and recommendations are confidential. There are, however, sufficient grounds for doubts about their possible long-run contribution to socialist development, given the nature of their training, their extensive involvement in helping organize such pillars of Western capitalism as the Bank of England, ICI, Shell, and Dunlop, their conception of what constitutes efficient management, and the political conservatism of their staff. Mckinsey has, for instance, been severely criticized in Britain and America for its "known distaste for any kind of committee work and [its] tendency to see individuals as little more than statistics in a balance sheet."[21] It is pertinent to ask, therefore, how useful it could possibly be in drawing up systems designed to break down worker alienation and to build up worker participation in management.

Even more telling is the fact that Mckinsey's staff are judged to be politically conservative by the very business circle that they serve—"Their style of dress is strictly on the conservative side. So are the politics of Mckinsey consultants, most of them in their early 30s, many with business school degrees and all frighteningly intelligent. The Company could never conceive of a super management whizz-kid with strong left-wing views . . . It just could not think of the two going together." But it is not the reactionary politics of the Mckinsey staff that worries some elements of the business community in Britain and America (although it should be a cause for grave concern in Tanzania); rather it is that Mckinsey and other consultants have a great deal of power with little or no responsibility, and that it is almost impossible, in practice, to gauge the impact of their advice on a company's subsequent performance. This is of great relevance in Tanzania, where the State Trading Corporation proved to be a costly failure after Mckinsey had been heavily involved in setting up management and control systems.

This corporation has now been completely reorganized and decentralized, and one is left wondering whether this was necessary *because* of or *in spite* of Mckinsey's involvement. The very least we can say is that the centralized accounting and stock-control systems, both with a heavy emphasis on computerization, that Mckinsey advocated proved to be totally inappropriate to the situation and broke down.

In defense of consultants against some of the above criticisms and doubts, Mramba and Mwansasu argue that "anyone who has had experience with [consultants] would know that their recommendations are not imposed on their principal and that their job is only to offer a possible solution to the organization." This is true in theory, but in reality one wonders how much detailed scrutiny of proposals one can expect from part-time, overworked, and frequently nontechnocratic boards of directors, what alternatives they can be expected to perceive, and how critical they are likely to be, having taken the decision to spend so much on consultancy services.

It is, therefore, our belief that too much confidence is placed in overseas consultants and far too little confidence in the ability of parastatal management and workers to set up their own systems and to solve their own problems. Several of the more successful parastatals, such as the banks, the Sisal Corporation, and the Milling Corporation, have managed very well without the services of foreign consultants and have made only minimal use of foreign management personnel. The TSC has significantly increased efficiency in the production of sisal since 1967, has cut back expatriate staff to a mere handful, has been extremely successful in developing Tanzanian talent from within the corporation, and has excellent worker-manager relations. It also managed to earn a cash surplus between 1970 and 1973 in spite of very low world sisal prices. If any form of foreign-exchange shadow pricing were in operation, it would undoubtedly have been seen as one of the most "profitable" companies (as it is now that sisal prices are at record levels) although it has always maintained a low-key approach to publicity and hence is regarded as a "poor relation" compared with the more "glamorous" publicity oriented (but much less successful) parastatals. Apart from giving security of employment to its workers when world prices slumped (it employs about a fifth of all parastatal employees) the corporation also prudently invested both in sisal, to give Tanzania a reduced but nevertheless still dominant share of world production of this crop in future, and in a variety of diversification programs, mainly in food production.

The banks and the NMC are also generally well organized, their senior posts are Tanzanianized, they have forward-looking manpower development programs and, on the whole, have been very innovative in extending and diversifying their activities. In short, these parastatals have set up their own systems, have good worker-manager relations, and, even if this is no sure guarantee of their having a clearer ideological perspective than other institutions, they have at least succeeded in reducing significantly their dependence on foreign manpower.[22]

Foreign management is usually part and parcel of package deals involving machinery and raw-material supplies, product purchases, and loan or equity participation by foreign manufacturers. The terms on which foreign participation takes place are usually specified in a management agreement—a legal contract between the parties involved. These agreements have attracted a good deal of hostile criticism in recent years, largely because parastatal managers insist on keeping them secret and because the ones that have leaked out have done so only after it had become clear that something was drastically wrong in the way the projects were being managed. There is therefore an unhealthy suspicion that parastatals have something to hide in not publishing details of the agreements. Such suspicions are not, of course, allayed by the almost pathological insistence by those involved that bygones be bygones, that old agreements should not be reexamined lest, curiously enough, this should cost Tanzania "millions of shillings."[23] One would have thought, on the basis of published information about two such agreements, Kilimanjaro Hotel and MECCO Construction Company, that there were possibilities of substantial savings from the reexamination of old management agreements.

Furthermore, the experience in these two cases indicates that the training of Tanzanians is not treated as a priority by the foreign partners, so there is a real danger that what was intended as short-term assistance might easily become a permanent arrangement. In spite of what was stated in the formal agreements to which they were party, the training obligation was almost ignored by the foreign managing agents of Kilimanjaro Hotel and MECCO. What little has been revealed to the public does not, therefore, inspire confidence in the bargaining abilities of those responsible locally, or in the integrity or usefulness of foreign partners. The adverse publicity surrounding the two published agreements did, however, have some beneficial effects. There has since been a considerable tightening up of control over the terms of new agreements by Devplan and the Bank of Tanzania so that the worst excesses of the past are not likely to be repeated. Nonetheless, while this is yet one more instance of improvement in the mechanics of parastatal control, there is still the failure to confront the basic ideological problem underlying all such agreements—that of how far socialism can be built with Western management personnel and systems.

All too often the justification for reliance on Western management is couched in terms of simple technological determinism. It is argued that Tanzania is dependent upon Western companies for the supply of modern technology and does not have the personnel with sufficient technical skills to run the machinery purchased; therefore Tanzania must also seek managers from the company supplying the technology. This argument, which is advocated by Carvalho in the article cited above, is frequently part of a broader argument which treats the problem of underdevelopment in similar deterministic fashion, claiming that the predominance of modern technology in the developed world and its relative absence in underdeveloped countries is the real causal factor underlying the disparity in the level of productive forces between rich and poor. This more general argument, still popular in conservative Western circles, has been convincingly refuted by some Marxist economists who argue that it was the exploitative character of imperialism and of neocolonialism which created and continues to consolidate "underdevelopment," and that the technology gap is itself a product of this exploitation, so that simple technological transfers will not close the gap until these more fundamental exploitative ties have been severed. Related to this theme is Shivji's argument that nationalization is, by itself, insufficient to eradicate exploitation when foreign management ties remain intact. What then is the justification for the use of foreign managers and how far is their presence due to the technology gap?

It is our belief that there has been an overemphasis on the technical aspect of management, in part because the broader technological-determinism theory of underdevelopment is accepted by large sections of the Tanzanian elite and in part because Western firms have a vested interest in providing complete management services and not just technical advice and expertise, for the simple reason that complete control of the managerial function qualifies them for the management fee and a share of profits (even of turnover in some cases) and also gives them access to any number of ways of making money for themselves. The worst abuses in the Kilimanjaro and MECCO cases took place precisely because the foreign involvement covered the whole management field instead of being confined to the more complex technical aspects of the business. This led one observer to state that MECCO "developed the law of . . . everything for big Dutch business and nothing for Tanzania. This they applied to the letter where personnel, profits and building materials were concerned."[24] This separation of the broader management function, which is of course partly technical but which is also concerned with social relations at the workplace, from the more narrowly technical operation has in fact been achieved with a good deal of success in the Chinese-built factories in Tanzania.

Here the management has always been entirely in the hands of Tanzanians, and Chinese technical experts have confined their attention to training personnel and to keeping the machines going. After four years they had fully trained Tanzanians to do this technical work at Friendship Textiles, so that the whole factory is now in local hands. Meanwhile Mwatex, a capital-intensive mill with the same production capacity as that of Friendship and established at about the same time, still employs about forty expatriates, and the management is largely foreign. The extent to which the distinction between the broader management and the narrower technical function can be made will of course vary with the industry in question, but it does seem that the rate of Tanzanianization could be speeded up if the distinction was at least recognized by the planners.

There are, of course, dangers inherent in even this more narrow definition of the technical input, as another area of recent Tanzanian experience neatly illustrates. In a move designed to compensate at least partially for the disadvantageous position in which it finds itself in dealing with foreign management at the technical level, Tanzania has appointed the General Superintendance Company of Geneva to act on its behalf in assessing the price, quality, and quantity of imported goods. This is an expensive service, but apparently the results achieved so far have more than justified the expense. On a number of occasions this company has exposed transfer-pricing rackets in which the foreign management manipulated machinery or imported-raw-material prices in order to transfer profits, untaxed and uncleared by exchange control, out of the country. One classic example of this found a company to be purchasing supplies in bulk for the whole of its world operations and obtaining thereby a 10 percent discount. None of this was ever passed on to Tanzania, and instead a 5 percent handling commission was charged to the Tanzanian plant. In another case the foreign management wanted to order machinery at a price of Shs 9.4 million. It was found that a reasonable price for this machinery (which, in any case, was inadequate for the output it was supposed to meet) was only Shs 3.2 million. Thus, even if foreign management is concentrated in the technical field, it will need to be observed very closely! Short of even more fundamental changes and given the almost complete absence of trained engineers and technicians in Tanzania (itself a reflection of the absence of basic industries and until recently of high-level training facilities—the first engineers trained in Tanzania are not to graduate until 1977), resort to costly but reasonably independent expertise is essential in dealing with foreign managers who put Tanzania's interests well below those of their parent company, where, after all, their future careers lie.

Even more importantly, it must be emphasized that the replacement of foreign managers by Tanzanians and the confinement of foreign participation to technical advisory posts will not, in and of itself, guarantee any positive move toward the introduction of socialist production relations at the workplace and the broader benefits (discussed in the following section) which can be expected to follow from such relations. Tanzanian managers will still need to be trained in the techniques of management itself (as distinct from the engineering aspects of machine technology), and hence the nature of that training will be crucial in determining whether or not there will be any qualitative difference between Tanzanian management and the Western management that it replaces. At the moment this is unlikely to be the case, since the task of training Tanzanian managers is left to Western managers or to Western business schools, and hence there is a danger of perpetuating the management values and outlooks that we have criticized above. This danger could be averted if the new management-training institutions recently established in Tanzania pay serious attention to the problem of reorienting management training and hence local management systems along lines which are consistent with Tanzania's declared socialist objectives. The creation of these institutions opens the way for the critical evaluation of management tools currently employed in Tanzania and for the production of more politically aware Tanzanian managers. Until these are produced in sufficient numbers, it would pay Tanzania to seek out individual foreign managers with progressive outlooks who can at least appreciate why orthodox management systems have limitations in the Tanzanian context. But this can only be a second-best short-run expedient, and in the final analysis a committed cadre of Tanzanian socialist managers must be one crucial component of a solution to the management problems of parastatals.

Workers' Participation and the Party

Training committed managers is only part of the solution. Planning is too important—and, inevitably, too impregnated with ideological considerations—to be left to the "experts" narrowly defined; this is one of the most important implications of preceding sections. The more radical perceptions concerning the imperatives of development which are available to progressive members of the petty bourgeoisie must override the views of the conservative members of that class, while pressures from an ever more conscious mass of peasants and workers must, simultaneously, impose their *objective interest* in the structural transformation of the economy upon a bureaucratic group tempted by self-interest toward caution and convention. In short, the generation of *concrete* socialist strategies cannot be simply regarded as the responsibility of the civil-service technocracy; clearly other inputs into the planning process are necessary.

One major means by which the ideological underpinnings for such strategies, and for detailed socialist planning more broadly conceived, have been guaranteed elsewhere is by the mechanism of unequivocal (and effective) party hegemony. Similarly, in

Tanzania, TANU could well play the essential role both of focusing the energies and insights of the most progressive members of the petty bourgeoisie (those who have, in Cabral's suggestive phrase, decided to "commit suicide" as members of that class "in order to be reborn as revolutionary workers, completely identified with the deepest aspirations of the people to which they belong"), while also acting as a conduit for the novel assertions of the mass of the population.

As observed in the first section, this is, in certain respects, the role TANU has always played. The dramatic expansion of the parastatal sector by means of the nationalizations of 1967 sprang precisely from an initiative of the party designed to alter much of the inherited economic structure, for example, and not from any conceptions first developed by the civil service. More recently *Mwongozo*, the TANU Guidelines of 1971, suggests that the party's net is to be cast even more widely, and the comforting assumption that, very general socialist guidelines having been laid down, "neutral" technocrats, foreign and domestic, can be left to get on with the job of implementation, is beginning to be discarded:

> The responsibility of the party is to lead the masses with their institutions in the efforts to safeguard national independence and to advance the liberation of the African. The duty of a socialist party is to guide all activities of the masses. The Government, parastatals, national organizations, etcetera are instruments for implementing the party's policies. Our short independence history reveals problems that might arise when a party does not guide its instruments. The time has now come for the party to take the reins and lead all mass activities.[25]

More specifically,

> the conduct and activities of the parastatals must be looked into to ensure that they help further our policy of socialism and self-reliance. The activities of the parastatals should be a source of satisfaction and not discontent. The party must ensure that the parastatals do not spend money extravagantly on items which do not contribute to the development of the national economy as a whole.

And, finally, we might take note of an item which appeared in the Tanzanian press later in the same year, which concluded that "TANU is to extend its grip on the economic affairs and running of the various government institutions and other organizations, now that the economic affairs sub-committee of the TANU Central Committee has vigorously begun the task it was charged with when it was established in 1969."[26]

Here might seem to be emerging precisely that input which we have seen to be lacking in the parastatal sector—a *concretization* of the socialist ideology into *specific strategic directives* (or, at the very least, an informed and constant political pressure upon the bureaucrats to come up with such directives themselves). Under such circumstances one might expect the parameters of parastatal choice to be meaningfully narrowed and defined and the new network of checks and controls upon the parastatals within the overall bureaucratic system (which we have seen to be emerging) to be at last provided with its strategic *raison d'être*. Yet the weaknesses of the party, noted above, also remain a crucial reality; *Mwongozo*, for all its vigor and insight, has not conjured them away.

Thus, all party functionaries are *not* drawn exclusively from the progressive wing of the petty bourgeoisie; in their day-to-day activities many party people are no more "red" than their civil-service counterparts. And, equally important, the party is almost certainly much less "expert" than the bureaucracy. In fact, TANU has been systematically starved of high-level manpower of its own who might be expected to help close such a gap and facilitate the necessary marriage of "redness" and "expertise" within the party itself. Add to this the fact that Tanzanian ideological formulations, even at their most militant and most political, leave something to be desired as guides to radical economic strategy—in their conceptualization of imperialism, for example, and of the sort of fundamental economic transformation necessary to realize effective "self-reliance"—and one begins to realize how much more remains to be done to put into practice the rhetorical assertions of *Mwongozo*. Perhaps the president's avowed aim, in handing over day-to-day governmental authority to Rashidi Kawawa (as prime minister) in early 1972, of devoting "more attention to questions of party and national leadership" carried with it some promise in this regard, though it has been difficult, subsequently, to see any dramatic change in this aspect of the situation. In any case, we are here again moving into the broadest kinds of questions concerning Tanzania's overall trajectory, and we have not the space to pursue them further. It is enough, for the moment, to reiterate that the outcome of these developments—of Tanzania's class struggle in both its ideological and political manifestations—could affect the functioning of the parastatals even more fundamentally than it has already done, and that such developments are therefore absolutely crucial dimensions of the political economy of the parastatals, properly defined.

As noted earlier, the party is most likely to play its essential role fully, to the extent that it comes to focus the energies of an aroused mass of peasants and workers. Again, we have not the opportunity here to discuss the exact nature of the dialectic which is being established between party leadership and mass assertions and the extent to which an effective popular base for socialism is emerging—even though the results of such a long-term process can also be expected to impinge in important ways upon the functioning of the parastatals. One aspect of this overall process is of more immediate and crucial significance to the parastatals, however, and we cannot avoid discussion of it here. Thus, while it is important that more highly conscious workers, allied with more highly conscious peasants, may begin to feed into TANU with increasing effect, thereby producing cadres and strengthening the party's hand vis-à-vis the bureaucracy, the *direct involvement* of workers in parastatal enterprises is already a factor to be reckoned with. For certain important innovations during recent years have also seen workers' participation placed on the agenda of Tanzanian socialism.

In much socialist theory, the contribution of the workers has been seen as the most vitally important ingredient in socialist construction; they are the class in whose interest it is to push through socialist solutions to the economic development problem. Similarly, in summing up his recent critique of Tanzanian socialist experience, Shivji has quite specifically concluded (echo-

ing Issac Deutscher) that "building socialism is the workers' and
not the bureaucrats' business." In Tanzania, of course, the situation is more ambiguous than within the model of advanced
capitalism which has underlain some of this theorizing. While
the workers are less favorably placed than the elites, the best
organized and most articulate are still privileged as compared
with much of the peasantry, and a successful assertion of their
demands for an increased share of national surpluses could be at
the expense of the peasant group. Nonetheless, they do, as a
class, have an objective interest in the sort of coherent, mass
based economic-development strategies which we have seen to
be vital to progress, for these strategies could be expected to
guarantee the stabilization and even betterment of their own
employment opportunities. Moreover, such workers have good
and immediate reasons to be resentful of the authoritarian
"methods of work" which characterize bureaucratic structures in
Tanzania and which, from the point of view of the society as a
whole, can cumulatively choke off the full release of human
energies necessary for socialist development. Tanzanian workers,
properly plugged into the national development effort, thus remain a potentially important building block for socialist construction.

The Tanzanian government's initial postindependence moves
vis-à-vis the workers were more by way of disciplining and controlling them than realizing any release of their energies, however; the results of establishing NUTA (the official, government-
controlled trade union), and of attendant legislation in the
industrial-relations field (however well justified by short-run considerations), was in many ways to demobilize the workers. More
recently the tide has seemed to turn and, as already hinted, two
substantial initiatives have together begun to alter the workers'
role within the system; these are, first, the program of workers'
participation itself, which has been already mentioned, and second, the implications of certain closely related sections of *Mwongozo*.

The signal for workers' participation in Tanzania was given in
Presidential Circular No. 1 of 1970, entitled "The Establishment
of Workers' Councils, Executive Committees, and Boards of Directors." In the president's words:

Given a proper work environment, and proper co-operation and support from their leaders and fellows, the majority of Tanzanian workers are capable of accepting more responsibility, and would like to do so; they can become more creative and can accomplish more. Easy communication of ideas and information between workers and all levels of management, can have the effect of improving the quantity and quality of goods produced, provided that an atmosphere of common endeavour and common responsibility is created. In particular, the top management have an attitude which regards the workers and the lower levels of management as partners in a common enterprise, and not just as tools like the machines they work with.

Moreover, "true industrial discipline does not exclude the workers in an industry from participation in the enterprise, or from a responsibility for its improvement. Indeed, true discipline in a workplace should be easier when the workers understand what they are doing, what their objective is, and when they know that they have contributed to the final result as fully respected partners." Therefore, "there must be provision for the workers to be represented on bodies which consider matters of production, sales, and the general organization of the enterprise. It has therefore been decided that all parastatal organizations shall, as soon as possible and in any case not later than the end of 1970, establish workers' councils, and shall establish or re-establish their Executive Committees and Boards of Directors so as to give practical effect to workers' representation and participation in planning, productivity, quality, and marketing matters." And *Mwongozo* in 1971 gave added ideological backing to the more positive features of the workers' participation initiative—particularly in the oft-quoted Clause 15 of the document:

> Together with the issue of involving the people in solving their problems, there is also the question of the habits of leaders in their work and in day-to-day life. There must be a deliberate effort to build equality between the leaders and those they lead. For a Tanzanian leader it must be forbidden to be arrogant, extravagant, contemptuous and oppressive. . . .

Together these items have threatened to constitute a potent combination, as managers of all kinds in Tanzania have been the first to realize.

Yet it has also been strongly argued that crucial weaknesses continued to underlie this initiative, weaknesses both in conceptualization and in implementation. Thus, Mapolu has carefully examined the ideological formulations central to "workers' participation," emphasizing that the program is in no real way designed to resolve the continuing contradiction between workers on the one hand and the petty bourgeoisie on the other in a progressive manner:

> As a consequence of the absence of political strategy due to the lack of a class ideological position, there has also been no conception of bureaucracy as a structural phenomenon. The tendency has been to view workers' participation not as a structural mechanism for the control of certain strata by the class that should be the pillar of socialist construction but principally as a wrong attitude which leads to wrong methods of work. It follows therefore that when one reaches the factory-level, participation can only be minimal in substance. Essentially, the tasks of "management" belong to the managers and the workers can come in only occasionally to "help" in certain fields and to also quench their thirst for information on what is going on in the factory as a whole. This seems to be the only explanation for the preponderance of the managers in the workers' council and the council's mere advisory powers.

Under such circumstances, workers' self-assertion could be too easily co-opted at the enterprise level, on the one hand, and not readily generalized to the system as a whole, on the other. In short, though such workers' participation might occasionally yield some positive results in increased productivity, it is not likely to be converted into a mechanism for fully releasing human energies, for raising class consciousness, or for pressing upon the system those broad strategic concerns which we have seen to be so crucial to socialist advance and in which the workers could begin to take an interest.

Mapolu's suspicions find support in the alacrity with which managers as implementors availed themselves of the program's cautious phrasing. George Kahama, the general manager of NDC, began an important speech to NDC managers in 1971 by noting that industrial relations in the "developed world" manifest "a spiral of escalating irresponsibility" (not any kind of class confrontation—even under capitalism!) and devoted almost all his attention to the need to "educate" the Tanzanian workers to exercise their participation "with discretion."[27] Needless to say, there was almost no mention of possible ambiguities in the managers' role, no mention of a need to check their conservative propensities or to educate *them*. The premises one senses to be lurking beneath the surface of Kahama's speech were much more baldly exposed in a speech to the same Dodoma Conference of Managers by Ferenz Cszogoly, an Eastern European advisor to NDC, who argued, when discussing *Mwongozo* and workers' participation, that "the danger of confusion of rights and duties of management with that of social bodies is very real. I would strongly insist therefore, on the basic principle, that management's responsibility should remain full and intact in any respect without mixing it up with misty excuses."[28] And, as was suggested in the previous section, Mckinsey and Co. has experienced much the same difficulty in integrating genuine participation and control from below into its sophisticated organizational charts. Small wonder that I. J. Maseko could conclude a 1972 case study of workers' participation in two parastatals with the following observation:

> The reason for lack of total acceptance of the circular in both enterprises has always been supported with reasons that the workers are not educated and competent enough to assume the managerial role. Though there is some validity in this argument this is not the main reason. The main reason is that the management is not willing to fully integrate the workers in decision-making. They only want to give piecemeal rights of participation.

Within such a context the panacea of "workers' education" thus became a two-edged sword. Wielded by the elite, the argument that workers must be educated to shoulder their duties "responsibly" could be an excuse for withholding vital information, stacking the councils with officials, and generally delaying the emergence of a real working-class presence within the decision-making process. Not that education is unimportant; we have seen the ambiguities in the workers' socioeconomic position, and it is also true that the workers have not in the past produced, spon-

taneously, much pressure for socialist solutions. But the education which is necessary must be of a certain type, a type which
the elite themselves are generally *least* able to provide—as much
political education, designed to raise consciousness, as "technical" education, designed to provide information about the enterprise itself. Mapolu has criticized the ideological content of the
syllabus laid down for the original crash program in workers'
education which accompanied the setting-up of the workers'
councils in 1970; equally striking has been the absence of that
network of genuine cadres in parastatal enterprises who might be
expected to convert education more broadly conceived into a
full-time preoccupation of the workers. Maseko's observations
concerning the weaknesses of TANU in the enterprises which he
studied were particularly disturbing in this respect.

However, the story did not end there, for a more spontaneous
escalation of the situation was close at hand—both within the
parastatal sector and in the industrial sphere more broadly defined. In fact, the changes which we are discussing had by now
set in motion processes which were not to be so easily controlled
by the elite. In 1972, Peter Lawrence wrote:

> Armed with *Mwongozo*, the workers appear to have gone beyond
> the economism of wage demands (especially since the incomes
> policy makes them redundant) and have been paradoxically "side-
> tracked" into the more difficult but significant pursuit of workers'
> control. Their strikes have been about and against unsympathetic
> management, lack of consultation, "commandism" at the work-
> place, the maltreatment of trade union leaders (or conversely the
> ineffectiveness of the same leaders).[29]

And this remained a continuing trend, summarized thus by
Mapolu:

> By any standards the progress made by the working population in
> Tanzania in the last few years as far as political consciousness is
> concerned is astounding. To begin with, at no other time in the
> whole history of this country have strikes and general disputes
> generally been so much day-to-day affairs as has become true since
> 1970. But more important, at no other time have such strikes and
> disputes been of such a political nature! . . . It has indeed been a

veritable revolution for the Tanzanian workers; within a period of three years they have moved from a state of docility, timidness, and above all disunity to one of tremendous bravery, initiative and class solidarity.

There was a signal development of working-class militancy, going from the straightforward downing of tools through lockouts to a point where, in 1973, some employees had begun actually to occupy factories (both state-owned and private) and on that basis to continue production on their own.

Equally important for our purposes are some of the fruits of the worker initiatives taken in the interests of building their own socialism—most notably, the exposure of a number of the anomalies characteristic of Tanzanian "socialism," especially some of Tanzania's continuing links with imperialism. Thus a confrontation with management in the Robbialac paints firm made clear in the press the extent to which the manager considered himself exclusively responsible to the Nairobi office rather than to any principles laid down by the Tanzanian government. Similar anomalies within the joint-venture world of the parastatal sector have also begun to surface.[30] Secondly, documenting Lawrence's argument, Mapolu has spelled out the manner in which abuses of authority and other forms of nonsocialist activity by management have been a target. Disputes concerned, firstly, "the question of humiliation and oppression of their person by managements" and, ultimately, "issues of general mismanagement and sabotage of the country's economy":

Increasingly, the lock-outs stemmed from managers misusing public funds, squandering resources, failing to uphold national policies and so forth. The clause in *Mwongozo* referred to most often no longer became solely No. 15 which deals with commandism, but No. 33 which says, in part, "The Party must ensure that the parastatals do not spend money extravagantly on items which do not contribute to the development of the national economy as a whole."

Mapolu is thus at pains to demonstrate the broadly political character of the workers' critique. Nevertheless, material inequalities obviously remain in Tanzania, and Mihyo, in his essay, sees no need to apologize for the fact that more narrowly economic demands have also been a dimension of the worker upsurge; their critique on this front is not easily dismissed, as Nyerere, in his response (quoted by Mihyo) to such worker actions, has been the first to concede:

> Strikes for instance; they say that *Mwongozo* makes the worker strike. But we are in an unequal society, how can you expect that workers will not go on strike. They will sit down and we will say, do you understand what going on strike means, and the workers will reply and say do you understand what inequality means? We must have a society where this is accepted, where if you like we experience the birth of socialism. We accept this because we don't pretend we have a socialist society.

Such a response is disarming, though perhaps not surprising given the fact that there *is* a tangible socialist current in Tanzania. Nor is it surprising, for similar reasons, to find in several instances—the "producer democracy" established at the Asian-owned Rubber Industries Ltd., for example—that the government has actually sanctioned the workers' takeover, permitting them to continue their control of such enterprises, now reconstituted as cooperatives! Nonetheless, it must be emphasized that a heavy-handed bureaucratic backlash (often involving police intervention, arrests, and even trials) against assertions of workers' control has been the more common response—directed against a lockout at the National Textile Corporation, for example, or, most dramatically, against the occupation of the Mount Carmel Rubber Factory. Indeed it is the growing prevalence of the latter type of response which has led Issa Shivji to underscore, in his recent writings, what he interprets as being the growing *polarization* of worker and bureaucrat in Tanzania. Nor, from his perspective, is this a negative development. For here lies the seed of what he has termed to be a "proletarian line" for the country, a line, nurtured *in opposition to the present state* and concretized in the activities of the working class, which has more profoundly progressive long-term implications than any other tendency at work in present-day Tanzania.

Conclusion

It is obvious that we are yet again returning to the most basic of questions, those hinted at in concluding the second section. Certainly the overall balance which is struck concerning the general condition of Tanzanian socialism will affect the evaluation of working-class activity just outlined. Some might wish to argue that such activity can still be expected to have a positive effect *within* the established structures, much of it being likely to carry over into the party, into the workers' councils, and into NUTA itself, unleashing creativity, revitalizing institutions, and acting to expose in a fruitful manner the contradictions which beset Tanzania's socialist efforts. Under such pressure, too, many more of the managerial petty-bourgeois class might be forced to examine their own practice and, possibly, to align themselves more unambiguously with popular aspirations. Of course, even those who harbor such hopes cannot pretend that they will be realized easily or without some degree of struggle. And indeed there are others (like Shivji) who argue much more unequivocally that it is already too late—if it were ever possible—to work from within established Tanzanian structures in order to mount a socialist alternative to the syndrome of underdevelopment. Rather, they might say, pressure from *outside* the established state and party system is required—at minimum, perhaps, an *independent worker organization* to replace the moribund NUTA and thus maximize the progressive input of the radicalized proletariat, of which Shivji and Mapolu now write so confidently.

There is not room to extend the discussion of such important issues here. Certainly, the insights of Shivji, Mapolu, and others are important, although, as hinted earlier, there is a measure of uncritical "proletarian messianism" in their work which prompts some uneasiness. This feature of their work may have led not only to some degree of overstatement but, more crucially, seems to have militated against their relating the politics of the *very small* Tanzanian working class entirely convincingly to the range of roles open to the much more numerous peasant masses in Tanzania (e.g., the extent of the congruity of the interests of these two classes, the terms of any class alliances which might be struck between them, etc.). Yet the peasantry must certainly play a significant role in any more fully realized transition to socialism in Tanzania.

By now such questions may seem, superficially, to have carried us away from the parastatals—and from the multinationals. But clearly this is not the case. We are here focusing upon the manner in which the emergence of an appropriate class base for progressive development is beginning to evidence itself and the manner in which the actions of this base are demanding, in turn, the crystalization of more appropriate organizational and ideological expressions. And, as noted earlier, it is precisely in such a broader *context* that many of the most vital keys to an increasingly effective parastatal performance and to an increasingly effective socialist challenge to international capitalism must eventually be seen to lie—not merely in Tanzania but elsewhere as well.

Notes

1. Government of Tanzania, "Cooperation Against Poverty," *The Standard* (Tanzania), September 9, 1970.
2. Julius K. Nyerere, "Economic Nationalism," speech of February 28, 1967, in Nyerere, *Freedom and Socialism* (London, New York, Nairobi, 1968), p. 264.
3. Muhbub ul Haq, "Employment in the Seventies: A New Perspective," *International Development Review* (1971–74).
4. See, for example, Henry Mapolu, "The Organization and Participation of Workers in Tanzania," *Economic Research Bureau Paper 72.1*, mimeo. (University of Dar es Salaam, 1972), pp. 36–37; L. Cliffe, "The Policy of Ujamaa Vijijini and the Class Struggle in Tanzania," in Lionel Cliffe and John S. Saul, eds., *Socialism in Tanzania* (Nairobi, 1973), vol. 1.
5. John S. Saul, "Planning for Socialism in Tanzania: The Socio-Political Context," in Uchumi Editorial Board, *Towards Socialist Planning*, Tanzania Studies No. 1 (Dar es Salaam, 1972).
6. *Jenga* (Dar es Salaam), no. 10 (1971), p. 47.
7. Speech by the Minister for Finance at the opening of diploma courses in the Institute of Finance Management, Dar es Salaam, July 10, 1972.

8. G. Kahama in an interview with "Face the People," *Sunday News*, January 20, 1972.
9. *The Economic Survey and Annual Plan 1970–71* (Dar es Salaam, 1971), p. 90.
10. *Jenga*, no. 10 (1971), p. 19.
11. G. Kahama, *Sunday News*, January 20, 1972.
12. Basil Mramba and Bismarck Mwansasu, "Management for Socialist Development in Tanzania: The Case of the NDC in Tanzania," *The African Review* 1, no. 3 (January 1972), p. 36.
13. Discounted cash flow is widely regarded as a more accurate profit measurement than accountancy measures. It is a cash-flow concept and it weights future cash receipts and expenditure by an interest factor—the time value of money to the capitalist/investor. The decision to invest is taken if discounted cash returns to an investment are large enough to cover discounted cash outlays on fixed assets, working capital, and operating expenses—the discount factor employed being the return on capital available elsewhere.
14. Internal economies of scale refer to the unit-cost reduction and hence profit increases that result from increasing the size of the firm, while external economies are unit-cost reductions resulting from locating firms in areas already well served with infrastructure and other firms. Both these types of economy militate against geographical plant dispersion, the former by raising the minimum plant size, the latter by forming geographical concentration of activities.
15. See John Gurley, "Maoist Economics," *Monthly Review* (February 1971).
16. Edith Penrose, "Some Problems of Policy in the Management of the Parastatal Sector in Tanzania: A Comment," *The African Review* 1, no. 3 (January 1972), p. 50.
17. V. N. Carvalho, "The Control of Managing Agents in Tanzanian Parastatal Organizations, with Special Reference to the NDC," *East African Law Review* 5, nos. 1 and 2 (1972).
18. P. C. Packard, "Corporate Structure and Socialist Development in Tanzania," mimeo. (Dar es Salaam, 1971).
19. *The Economic Survey and Annual Plan 1970–71*, p. 90.
20. Speech by the Minister for Finance introducing the estimates of public revenue and expenditure for 1972–73 to the National Assembly on June 15, 1972, p. 33.
21. "Mckinsey Report," by Christopher Walker, *Business Observer*, August 9, 1970, p. 70.
22. This is not to say that these institutions have been free from the

practices of managerial capitalist orthodoxy. The NMC for instance has been responsible for a bakery project in Dar es Salaam which, when judged by all standards except those of commercial profit for the NMC and more especially for the Canadian supplier of the machinery, is a disaster. It costs Shs 17.4 million, or about Shs 12 million more than the cost of building ten small traditional-type bakeries with the same total production capacity. It has a very high foreign-exchange content and will have the effect of considerably reducing employment in the bakery industry. The capital cost per job in the semi-automated bakery is estimated at Shs 300,000 compared with only Shs 15,000 in the traditional-type bakeries, and the demands upon highly skilled manpower are much greater. The bakery will soon supply half the Dar es Salaam market, but the entire output is processed through only one oven, so that in the event of technical problems there would be tremendous shortages of bread in the capital. The project is financed by Canadian aid and was approved in spite of opposition at several levels of the appraisal procedure. In the case of the banks, the NBC was severely criticized in 1971 for paying the same percentage bonus to all staff regardless of salary grade so that top management received many times the amount paid to the more lowly paid employees. The party directed that those earning Shs 1,000 per month should repay the bonus.

23. See Carvalho, "The Control of Managing Agents," p. 103.
24. For details of the gross mismanagement of these companies, see articles in *The Standard* on December 20, 1970 (Kilimanjaro Hotel) and on January 26, 27, 28, 1971 (MECCO).
25. TANU, *Mwongozo/The TANU Guidelines* (Dar es Salaam, 1971).
26. "TANU Move to Tighten Hold on the Economy," *The Standard*, June 17, 1971.
27. George Kahama, "Town and Country: Partners in Progress," reprinted in *The Standard*, October 28, 1971.
28. Ferenz Cszogoly, "Obstacles to Industrial Development," reprinted in *The Standard*, October 30, 1971.
29. Peter R. Lawrence, "Socialism, Self-Reliance, and Foreign Aid in Tanzania—Some Lessons from the Socialist Countries," paper presented to the UNIDEP Seminar on the "Use of Foreign Funds in the Development of East African Countries," Dar es Salaam, April–May 1971.
30. An excellent example of the conceptualization of workers' participation as a co-optive mechanism and of the manipulative use of the notion of workers' education—an example which also clearly exposes

the ambiguity of Tanzania's continuing links with imperialist penetration—is given in the following statement by the chairman of East African Breweries in the company's 1971 Annual Report:

> In spite of the excellent progress of the trade in Tanzania it is, I believe, my duty to draw attention to certain difficulties which have arisen in the carrying out of our management functions in that country. These have arisen as a result of moves to encourage the involvement of the political party and workers councils in industrial matters. In theory the conception of the party and of workers councils joining hands with NDC and managements to encourage productivity, efficiency and a better understanding between all such organizations is a laudable one, but it is suggested that if such a conception is to be implemented in a constructive and useful sense, it is quite vital, at the outset, to educate workers councils as to the role they are expected to play and as to the true objects behind the exercise.

It is interesting that shortly after this statement was made the manager supplied by this company was retired, after the workers had complained of his abusive and insulting behavior.

Bibliographic Note

A fuller account of the *political economy* of Tanzania is in John S. Saul, "African Socialism in One Country: Tanzania," in G. Arrighi and J. S. Saul, *Essays on the Political Economy of Africa* (New York, 1973).

On the *class struggle* in Tanzania, the work of Shivji is of interest. See Issa G. Shivji, "Tanzania: The Silent Class Struggle," in L. Cliffe and J. S. Saul, eds., *Socialism in Tanzania* (Nairobi, 1973), vol. 2; also in *The Silent Class Struggle* (Dar es Salaam, 1972). Both of these carry articles commenting on Shivji's piece. In addition, see his *Class Struggles in Tanzania* (New York and London, 1976).

On the *state* in Tanzania, see John S. Saul, "The State in Post-Colonial Societies: Tanzania," in this volume, which contains a critique of Shivji's writings.

On *planning* in Tanzania, see *Towards Socialist Planning*, Tanzanian Studies No. 1 (Dar es Salaam, 1972). Especially relevant to this article are the essays by myself, "Planning for Socialism in Tanzania: The Socio-Political Context" and by John Loxley, "Financial Planning and Control in Tanzania."

On *workers*, the following include valuable case studies of workers' struggles: Henry Mapolu, "Labour Unrest: Irresponsibility or Worker Revolution," *Jenga*, no. 12 (1972); and "The Workers' Movement in Tanzania," *Maji Maji*, no. 12 (September 1973).

On *participation*, see Mapolu, note 4 above, and I. J. Maseko, "Workers' Participation in Management in Tanzania," Political Science Paper 7b, mimeo. (Dar es Salaam, 1972); Pascal Mihyo, "The Workers' Revolution in Tanzania," *Maji Maji*, no. 17 (August 1974); and Shivji, *Class Struggles in Tanzania*.

On *workers' organization and NUTA*, see especially the *Report of the Presidential Commission on NUTA* (Dar es Salaam, 1967); and M. A. Bienefeld, "Workers, Unions, and Development in Tanzania," in R. Cohen and R. Sandbrook, eds., *Towards an African Working Class* (London, 1975).

On *foreign experts*, see David Ransom, "The Berkeley Mafia and the Indonesian Massacre," *Ramparts* (October 1970), for an account of the reactionary role played in Indonesia by various "academic" foundations and institutions, including the Development Advisory Service of Harvard University. This is also an excellent study of the "modernization" theory underlying their approach. See also F. Ackerman, "Who's Afraid of Development Economics?" *Upstart* (Cambridge, Mass.) (1971).

The model of the "self-centered" economy referred to in the article is at the core of Samir Amin's magisterial *Accumulation on a World Scale* (New York and London, 1974). He has neatly summarized his argument in his "Underpopulated Africa," *Maji Maji*, no. 6 (June 1972). On the relevance of this model to the discussion of Tanzanian development strategy, see A. M. Babu, the then Minister for Economic Affairs and Development Planning, in the Tanzania supplement to the *Financial Times*, December 9, 1971. His article argues for an "inward-looking" development strategy, and should be compared with the argument for greater emphasis on primary exports by the Minister for Finance, Hon. A. H. Jamal, in his budget speech in June 1971.

10

TANZANIA'S TRANSITION TO SOCIALISM

The debate about the precise nature and significance of Tanzania's flirtation with socialism over the past decade continues. To date, it has thrown up a scholarship—much of it self-consciously Marxian in its orientation—of a very high quality and this has made an important contribution to the emergence of a solid radical perspective on African developments more generally considered. In addition, the intensity of this debate has had the virtue of forcing the various analysts involved to put their political cards on the table, to bring their various commitments closer to the surface of their work rather than half-burying them in the unquestioned premises of the models with which they work. In consequence, the calculated blandness—concealing much, much more than it illuminates—of American-sponsored development studies has done somewhat less damage to Tanzanians (and others) in their understanding of that country's progress than might otherwise have been the case.

Moreover, the heat of the debate about Tanzania seems, if anything, to be increasing (even as, in the opinion of some radical observers, the embers of Tanzania's actual experiment in socialism are cooling—could this be another case of Minerva's owl?). We have recently had Issa Shivji's militant *magnum opus*, the excesses of whose ultra-left critique of Tanzanian practice I have discussed elsewhere.[1] Now there is a fresh addition to the

---

This essay was first published in the *Canadian Journal of African Studies* (1977–78).

debate which is, quite simply, the most polemical contribution of all, Cranford Pratt's *The Critical Phase in Tanzania 1945–1968: Nyerere and the Emergence of a Socialist Strategy*.[2] Of course, in Pratt's case the polemic is directed not against "Tanzanian socialism" but precisely *against* the entire range of radical critiques of that socialism and of Tanzanian realities. But polemical his book certainly is!

Indeed, it will be argued here that Pratt permits polemic to so crowd out analytical rigor as to greatly reduce the positive enlightenment which might otherwise have been expected from a work so painstakingly researched and so carefully written. Not that this criticism should be seen to imply that Pratt's book is insignificant. It is, in fact, likely to be highly influential, coming, as it does, from the pen of one who has been a confidant of President Nyerere over many years and providing, as it does, a virtually definitive statement of the left-liberal *cum* social-democratic analysis of, and *apologia* for, Nyerere's brand of socialism. If only for the latter reason, therefore, it requires some kind of confrontation by Marxist students of Africa, confident of the superior power of their own perspective and their own tools of analysis. There are two additional, more political, rewards to be gleaned from such a confrontation, however. First, and somewhat ironically, it will become apparent that Pratt's concern for assuring the centrality of "democracy" to any transition to socialism is at once so crucial to his argument and so misconceived by him in its theoretical elaboration and concrete application that the revolutionary socialist is encouraged, in response, to reiterate and to refine even more clearly the manner in which democratic participation is central to his/her own socialist concern. For, of course, it is the unfailing arrogance of social democrats (Pratt included) to pretend that they alone, among "socialists," are genuinely concerned to safeguard "democracy."[3] Nothing could be further from the truth. Secondly, as we shall also see, Pratt's careful documentation of those themes which preoccupy him ultimately sheds real light on the Tanzanian experience, albeit light of a rather disturbing and discouraging sort. For what Pratt manages is to present Nyerere as being quite as moralistic, wishy-washy, and utopian as his sharpest left critics would have us believe. Is this an accurate picture? Does Nyerere perhaps deserve to be defended from such friends at least as vigorously as from his enemies? Where, in this book, does Nyerere begin and Pratt leave off? Answering such questions—reviewing Pratt's evidence and assessing its adequacy—thus promises to contribute significantly to the ongoing evaluation of the strengths and weaknesses of Tanzania's efforts.

I

Vulgar socialism (and from it in turn a section of the democracy) have taken over from the bourgeois economists the consideration and treatment of distribution as independent of the mode of production and hence the presentation of socialism as turning principally on distribution. After the real relation has long been made clear, why retrogress again?

Karl Marx, *Critique of the Gotha Programme*

Obviously, these two areas of inquiry—more generally, the place of "democracy" in a transition to socialism, and more specifically, the strengths and weaknesses of Nyerere's leadership under the concrete conditions extant in Tanzania—do not exhaust the investigation of Tanzania's own possible "transition to socialism." Unfortunately, however, there is a severe limit to what can be learned on this latter subject from Pratt's book, since so much else is missing from it which might be relevant to such a task and which might then make a critique of it more broadly instructive.

Most seriously, there is no explicit discussion of the economic system even loosely defined, much less of the mode of production more rigorously defined. At one stage something more seems promised. Thus, at the conclusion of a strong and convincing first section of the book (much the best section, as it happens) on British policies in the late-colonial period, the British are seen, in the end, to be seeking the establishment in power of "a [African] political elite which would accept a continued major dependency on Britain" (p. 58). And Nyerere himself is presented as having, in the short run and for various good reasons, to make "the deliberate choice of a neo-colonial dependence upon Britain" (p. 88).

Promising, but a promise that is scarcely delivered upon in succeeding sections. For when the terms of such dependence are spelled out by Pratt, they involve no very extended commentary on the structure of the inherited economy—trapped as it was in the posture of primary producer within the Western market system, robbed of internal linkages and domestic economic dynamic, subordinated to imperial sources of finance, technology, and management systems—but rather a virtually exclusive preoccupation with the questions of (1) the continuing prominence of British officers within the independent Tanganyikan civil service; and (2) the heavy, very nearly unilateral, reliance upon Britain for loan finance and development grants. The alternative for overcoming a dependence so defined? Self-reliance.

Indeed, the latter has been a central ideological theme in Tanzania since the mid-1960s. What, then, is "self-reliance"? Primarily, it would seem to connote the movement away from an inordinate emphasis upon ties with Britain and a diversification of sources of aid! Pratt's descriptive phrase for this is "positive nonalignment" (p. 249); both his account of the emergence of this trend in Tanzanian policy and his evaluation of it are instructive. In the first place, Pratt is at great pains to demonstrate that Tanzania's "nonalignment" is to be seen primarily as a *nationalist* response, not only to domestic political pressure for an accelerated rate of Africanization, but also to a range of foreign-policy excesses on the part of Western countries during the mid-1960s: the evident disinterest of these countries in the liberation of Southern Africa and especially Rhodesia for example, their intervention in the Congo, their troublemaking over Zanzibar's link to the G.D.R., and the like. Criticizing Catherine Hoskyns's earlier account of the interface between Tanzania's domestic and foreign policies, he documents carefully that any more self-reliant "development strategy" largely *followed from* this forced rethinking of external linkages, rather than these external readjustments themselves manifesting the existence of such a coherent strategy. Most important, Pratt argues, there was certainly no hint of a systematically anti-imperialist perspective at play at any stage of this process.[4]

This finding suits Pratt very well, of course, and he is more than happy to slide over the difficulties which the phrase "positive nonalignment" encapsulates. He does so by means of a kind of intellectual sleight-of-hand, which is all too common in his book: the setting up of a false dichotomy. Clearly, he implies, the alternative to nonalignment is *alignment*. But, as is true for most social democrats, Pratt's is basically a Cold War model of the international arena. What could be worse, then, than the specter of "alignment," however skeptical of the West events may have made President Nyerere? In consequence, Pratt is at great pains to confirm that cooler heads have prevailed in Tanzania and that no headlong rush to the East has followed. Indeed, four pages are devoted to a careful demonstration of the weaknesses of Soviet aid and Tanzania's skepticism about it, five to exploring the slightly more mixed blessings of Chinese proposals. In contrast, virtually no space (one very general sentence, in fact, pp. 156–57), is given over to a comparable evaluation of the costs and benefits of Western aid. Substantively, when the latter is discussed at all it is quantity, not quality, which is front and center. And his conclusion (p. 167): in 1968 "the four most important sources [of capital assistance] were the U.S.A., Sweden, the I.D.A. and China. It is a list which seems appropriate to a country seeking to be nonaligned in international politics."

A staggering bias, all the more attractive to Pratt because, as we have stated, he has no model of what the structure of a socialist economy for Tanzania might ultimately look like. Naturally, then, he can feel under no particular obligation to evaluate Western aid (not to mention any other Tanzanian entanglements with the West) in terms of its *qualitative* contribution to any real shift in the country's mode of production. Yet isn't it obvious that Tanzania's state of dependence has been defined by its historical subordination to the logic of Western capitalism? Even if the record of Western aid, trade, and investment were not already so damning,[5] would there not remain important theoretical grounds for questioning whether that logic has been reversed (in the cases, say, of aid from the United States, from Sweden, from the World Bank), and for carefully evaluating the ways in which such aid concretely does or does not sustain dependence? But Pratt is not interested in this. For to press such a question would be to hint at an anti-imperialist perspective, something which Pratt has already laughed off the page and conflated, all too glibly, with the demand for "alignment" (with "the East").

Yet, to repeat, the nature of Tanzania's historically conditioned dependence (broadly conceived) clearly dictates the necessity of such a perspective. Moreover, *pace* Pratt, this anti-imperialist perspective, not "alignment," is the true alternative to the "positive nonalignment" which he praises so immoderately. To adopt this perspective is not to lose one's critical faculties with regard to so unsavory a regime as that of the Soviet Union, or even with regard to China. Nor is it necessarily to preach *autarky* and demand the immediate ceasing of all interchange with "the West." It is merely to insist that any steps be taken with eyes open and with a clear perspective on the absolutely crucial role of the metropolitan bourgeoisies in defining and structuring the problem of Third World underdevelopment in the contemporary period. Serious discussion of the transition to socialism *must* take this as an absolutely essential starting point. Pratt, of course, is so indifferent to these matters that he does not even bother to refute the case, merely restructuring it, as we have seen, to meet his own purposes. But Pratt, in any event, can safely be left to the servicing of his own muse. What is more disturbing is the substantial evidence he adduces to demonstrate that the Tanzanian leadership has been as little preoccupied with such an essential socialist undertaking as he is.

Since the productive process—international and domestic— has virtually disappeared from Pratt's Tanzania, it becomes concomitantly difficult for him to locate the country's class structure.[6] Yet Pratt is aware that he must make some bow in this direction since Nyerere, whatever his pregnant silences regarding imperialism, has had much to say about the ongoing process of stratification in Tanzania. Pratt is visibly uncomfortable with class analysis, however. In consequence, his categories slither uneasily across the page, now revealing the existence of classlike entities, now all but denying their existence, the emphasis to be adopted at any one time depending upon the way in which it services the broader arguments which he is making. Thus, classes surface in Pratt's book when Nyerere mentions them and when some of the latter's statements are then unavoidably to be elaborated upon; they disappear when it is necessary to downplay any hint that there might be struggles either within a class or between classes. At all costs we are to have a transition to socialism without tears: no class struggle.

Certainly there is to be no upsurge from below by the workers and peasants (whom one might have thought to have the greatest interest in a genuinely socialist solution to Tanzania's development problem). On this subject, Pratt, in his introduction, cleverly deploys his only direct quotation from Marx: in order to bring the latter's authority to bear against the very notion of class struggle! Any attempt to raise class consciousness in Tanzania is, apparently, to be equated with what Marx assailed as "crude communism," with "universal envy setting itself up in power." If, says Pratt, "techniques of 'crude communism' are used to accelerate socialist change, if, for example, the greed of men is aroused in order to mobilize them against their class enemies, then the result will be an intensification of values which are opposite to the values envisaged for a socialist society. That will surely render more difficult the achievement of a genuine socialist society" (pp. 7–8). Again the false dichotomy, as if the individualistic greed of the mob, rather than the collective demands of the class, were the only alternative to the judicious snail's pace of elite-sponsored "socialism." (As if, too, socialism is primarily about the distribution of goods and services, not about power and control over the production process—a theme to which we will return.) Not surprisingly, the confusion so sown is sufficient for Pratt to conclude, on his very last page, that "the deliberate intensification of mass antagonisms towards the bureaucracy and the successful peasant farmer" would (along with "a vanguard party") "increase the risk of authoritarian rule [!] and of serious economic and governmental failures" (p. 264). No hint, of course, that it might release popular energies or provide from below the democratic guarantee of leadership commitment to the socialist cause.

Indeed, since Pratt is so little concerned about the powerless in Tanzania developing class consciousness, he can even turn the argument around in a rather startling manner—using his assumption of the absence of such consciousness in Tanzania as proof of the virtual *nonexistence* of classes. He thus soft-pedals the importance of the "political and bureaucratic leadership" in 1967 on the basis that "their incomes were not being extracted from a resisting society which rejected their legitimacy. Their salaries were part of an income and salary structure which were not challenged within the society" (pp. 220–21). No thought as to the nature of the dominant class's hegemony in class societies, which so often serves to legitimize such distinctions; at a stroke important dimensions of the class structure are merely conjured away. Such a formulation has obvious political implications: it might well be asked from whence, in the absence of class consciousness, resistance to such stratification would ever be likely to come. For Pratt there is no such problem: lacking any pressure from below, "the politicians and civil servants had no reason to feel either guilty towards or threatened by ordinary critizens." In consequence, "they were able to respond to a variety of professional, nationalist, democratic and ideological considerations and motives which, to varying degrees, operate to keep governments reasonably committed to the public good" (p. 222). This benign interpretation is, as we shall see, central to Pratt's political formulations. Here it must be reiterated that the "legitimacy" of the elite's position is one more reason adduced by Pratt for not taking it very seriously as a class in the first place.

The ground has been well prepared for this by Pratt, of course. Many examples could be cited. Thus, where others might spot African entrepreneurs emerging in colonial Tanzania, Pratt sees "self-improvers." Similarly, most informed observers would be prone to interpret Paul Bomani, one of Tanzania's more conservative ministers during the Arusha period, as opposing the government's 1966 intervention into the cooperative movement (and especially into the Victoria Federation of Cooperative Unions [VFCU], an organization first started by Bomani and one from which he had, many suspected, made his fortune) in order to protect his own record from too-close scrutiny and to safeguard in lucrative offices members of his own family (including his brother, the autocratic general manager of the VFCU, whose gross malfeasance ultimately led to his being pushed out of power by the government). All of this was common knowledge in Mwanza, headquarters of the VFCU, where I was living at the time, and elsewhere in Tanzania. Yet for Pratt, Bomani resists because he is a "pluralist-minded minister," concerned about the dangers to democracy arising from too great a government encroachment upon the autonomy of a grass-roots institution like the cooperative movement (p. 191).[7] Here, as so often elsewhere in Pratt's book, the juice of Tanzanian political and social life is boiled away into a porridge of bland naïveté, and as a result real interests and real conflicts are consistently denatured.

In short, whenever the fact of class does rear its ugly head— Nyerere and the Arusha Declaration, as noted, having sanctioned the countenancing of that reality—it is a very soft interpretation of the phenomenon that Pratt produces. Despite his assertion that "by 1967 there was real class stratification within Tanzanian society" (p. 221), such stratification seems to make no substantive difference whatsoever to the process of transition to socialism. To be sure, I have myself argued elsewhere that the dominant elite/petty-bourgeoisie was still very much a class-in-formation during the Arusha Declaration period and that Issa Shivji's interpretation underestimates the fluidity of the situation in seeing a dominant domestic class as being already fully formed at that time.[8] However, for Pratt any such a class is not merely characterized by a certain "plasticity," but is almost evanescent. To a man, it seems, those "with political and governmental power responded positively to Nyerere's call for a collective endeavour to achieve a socialist transformation of Tanzanian society," pledging themselves to "committed endeavour to advance the welfare of the whole society" (p. 242).

Classes, then, when Nyerere says so, but not when radical commentators query the credentials of the petty bourgeoisie to carry socialism forward. Classes, but no real class interests (despite some unhappiness concerning the Arusha Declaration leadership code noted by Pratt), and ultimately a uniformly positive response from the "elite" to the request that it commit class suicide. In the course of arguing this case Pratt does rehearse, albeit quite eclectically, some of the peculiar features which did make some kind of positive response to progressive policies a potential one within this class-in-formation. Moreover, alongside familiar attributes like the relatively unconsolidated position of the "elite," the peculiar strength and popular character of TANU, and the "moral quality of Nyerere's leadership," Pratt even includes such a factor as elite alarm occasioned by "the appearance by 1967 of political discontent on a fairly widespread basis" (p. 242). Yet once again the overriding emphasis is not upon this kind of hint concerning the existence of contradictions within Tanzanian society, but rather upon the smoothness of the transition under discussion. Consequently, Pratt is much more interested in stressing some presumed logic of nationalism which ineluctably bears everyone forward toward the countenancing of socialist solutions,[9] or (supported by extensive quotations from Nyerere) in emphasizing the persistence and vitality of "traditional communal values" which move "politicians, civil servants and urban dwellers . . . to acknowledge the moral legitimacy of the restrictions being placed upon them" (p. 239). How this latter fantasy, in particular, could survive even the briefest of discussions with any significant number of Tanzanian politicians and civil servants is hard to imagine.

For in spite of such emphases, real struggles were taking place in Tanzania during this period. Ironically (and despite the title of his book), it is precisely the absence of a discussion of strategy meaningfully conceived which makes it easy for Pratt to ignore them. For "strategy" cannot be reduced, as it is by Pratt, to noting a few chosen dimensions of Nyerere's concern—equality, self-reliance, democracy—abstracted from the realities of the world economy and from the neocolonial biases inherent in all Tanzanian institutions. Nor should it be considered as established once a few dramatic initiatives—the leadership code and the nationalizations of 1967—had been sprung upon the nation as *faits accomplis*. If real autonomy of economic processes (Samir Amin's "self-centered economy") and genuine control of the productive process by the producers themselves were to be realized in Tanzania, it remained to be fleshed out as a series of consistent and interrelated programs in every sector—housing, health, transportation, industrial structure, cooperatives and rural development, and so on. Yet surely there was already considerable evidence even during the few post-Arusha years with which Pratt concerns himself (1967 and 1968) that realizing any such integrated strategy was going to be an enormously difficult task—precisely because of the profound resistance within the "elite" to that kind of denouement to Nyerere's grand initiatives. In fact Nyerere, while providing a real opening for progressives in Tanzania, had, on Pratt's own evidence, advanced much less by way of concrete strategy than the latter's book implies. To then picture Tanzania's "political and bureaucratic leadership" as enthusiastically seizing the opportunity thus provided and settling down creatively to the task of constructing socialism in the post-Arusha period is to rewrite history. Some members of that leadership did so, but a struggle ensued nonetheless, a struggle which, unhappily, progressive elements often lost. [10] Pratt's monolithic cadre of socialist leaders is thus the perfect pendant to Shivji's monolithic, self-aggrandizing oligarchy: neither of these militant analytical postures can tell us much about the very real political infighting, centered precisely on the issue of whether or not there was to be a "socialist strategy" at all in Tanzania, which marked this period. [11]

Thus, even if the full playing out of relevant trends is primarily a feature of the years following those chosen by Pratt for the main focus of attention, it must be confirmed that his book, in the end, provides little basis for understanding such trends as they did emerge. Instead, Pratt succeeds primarily in shifting attention away from the most relevant variables. We have seen already that much of the drive to overcome dependence collapses, on his account, into the fatuities of "self-reliance," narrowly defined. Now, as Marx might have predicted, Pratt's conclusion finds any debate about the capacity of the dominant domestic stratum (petty bourgeoisie, "nizers," "leadership," or "elite") to transform Tanzania's mode of production diverted into distributive consideration and into a debate about "equality." [12] Indeed, writing as if the main concern of left critics of Tanzania lay in some form of latter-day leveling ("crude communism"?) rather than focusing as it has done on the questions of class power and strategic location in the production process, Pratt finds little difficulty in arguing that demands for complete equality of income would be hopelessly romantic and adventurist. As he correctly observes, quite significant progress has, by any comparative African standard, been made in this sphere: who could reasonably ask for more at this time? And besides, tactically, to push too hard would be to run too great a risk of backlash.

A sensible enough argument, perhaps—if the issue were first and foremost one of income distribution. However, the calculations are much different and the urgency greater if one does question—on both theoretical *and* empirical grounds—the ability of this group (those who, in terms of distribution, are to be allowed to be somewhat more equal than others) actually to flesh out a strategy for socialist reconstruction in the absence of increased pressure by classes which have most to gain from a radical transformation of the situation. Pratt can, at worst, conceive of the "political and bureaucratic leadership" only abusing their position by demanding rather too high salaries (or possibly by engaging in rather too arbitrary a range of political practices). He cannot conceive of their various acts of omission and commission actually serving to sabotage those significant changes in the Tanzanian social formation which might lead to socialism (such changes as might ultimately serve to make them the real, rather than notional, servants of the people). Because of this failure of imagination (and observation) the real costs of a failure to harness the "elite," to strengthen the hand of such progressive members of it as exist, and to guarantee people's power, evaporate from his model, and we find instead a politics of the "transition to socialism" which is virtually devoid of content.

II

To say that a transitional social formation follows the socialist road is tantamount to saying that this formation is engaged in a revolutionary process of transformation which enables the laboring masses to gain increasing control over their conditions of existence, i.e., which strengthens their ability to *liberate* themselves. To say that a formation follows a capitalist road is tantamount to saying that it is engaged in a process which increasingly subjects the laboring masses to the requirements of a process of production which they do not control and which ultimately, therefore, can only serve the interests of a minority which uses the state apparatus to establish and consolidate the conditions that enable it to become dominant.

Charles Bettelheim, *On the Transition to Socialism*

The final sentence of the preceding section represents a strong charge, for even if Pratt's claim to present Nyerere's socialism as exemplifying a coherent strategy were to crumble, he would be left, some might feel, with his political hole card. It is, in any case, the card he has really come to play. For Nyerere's socialism is, Pratt insists, *democratic*. It is this crucial political dimension which, ultimately, establishes Tanzania's claim to our attention, and which also distinguishes it from models of the transition to socialism held by those nefarious "Marxists" (the present author included) whose work on Tanzania Pratt has set himself, none too subtly, to attack. In point of fact, this is an argument which he can pretend to sustain, as we have already begun to see, only by *oversimplifying* many of the cruel dilemmas which confront Tanzanians concerned to make such a transition, but also by *caricaturing*, willfully or otherwise, the perspectives on socialist politics put forward by writers more radical than himself. It seems important, therefore, to turn to the documentation of such charges against Pratt while at the same time taking advantage of the opportunity thus provided to further illuminate aspects of the politics of the transition to socialism left unclear (if only to Pratt) in earlier Marxist writings on Tanzania.

Even Pratt is vaguely aware that there are two terms to the socialist political equation: leadership and popular self-assertion. Occasionally, too, he does present the reconciliation of these two dimensions as being somewhat problematical. Thus, on the one hand, he is quite prepared to accept that some degree of "leadership" is a legitimate requirement, given the necessity to arouse people for the task of national reconstruction; yet this very necessity to provide leadership may also tempt said leaders toward authoritarianism. On the other hand, such assertions as are forthcoming from the mass of the population may be directed toward irrational or counterproductive ends; nevertheless, a

commitment to democracy which is both philosophical and practical (the need precisely to check authoritarian-minded leaders)
requires that the people retain the final word. In light of these
complexities, Pratt is even moved, at one point, to speak of "the
balance" which Nyerere must strike between "the leadership
strand and the democratic strand in his thought" (p. 255). Clearly
there is a problem here, a contradiction with which the best
writing on socialist politics has consistently been preoccupied and
one which, *pace* Pratt, has figured prominently in the Marxist
literature on Tanzania. For Pratt, however, the contradiction is,
ultimately, conjured away.

There are two ways in which this is done. One is, in effect, to
excuse the necessity for leadership (especially to skeptical Western liberals, Harvey Glickman being one such to whom Pratt
refers several times in the text) by sketching a context which may
be thought to legitimize any seizing of the reins that Nyerere has
had to undertake. Ironically, in so doing, Pratt manages to present the case as having almost nothing to do with Tanzania's
struggle to realize socialist objectives. On the contrary, it quickly
becomes apparent that, at bottom, Pratt's is the very conventional model of underdevelopment common to the most orthodox versions of Western social science, a model to which has
been added, thanks to the prodding of Nyerere's example, a rather
thin veneer of preoccupation with quasi-socialist concerns. Thus
the need for leadership reveals itself as being, first and foremost, a
function of Tanzania's backwardness:

> Nyerere has never seen himself as a cipher, whose role is simply to
> transpose the wishes of the people into laws and government ac-
> tions. His populism has not been a simple judgment that the people
> are always right. Neither has Nyerere seen his primary function as
> that of finding effective and lasting compromises between the main
> interest groups in Tanzania. Such a conception of democratic
> leadership is a product of economically developed plural societies.
> It is inappropriate in countries such as Tanzania which still lack the
> institutions and skills that would make it possible for their peoples to
> lift themselves from their present extremely low living standards.
> These societies need more than the provision of services, the main-
> tenance of law and order, and the negotiation of working com-
> promises. They need new enthusiasms, new capacities for collec-

tive action, a new receptivity to innovation and a new attitude towards work. They need new political institutions and wider loyalties, and a more acute awareness of the international dimensions to the continuance of their poverty [!]. They are, to put it briefly, societies that need to be transformed. They are societies which need leaders who are men of vision, who can see a way forward for their people, can define a path that will win the understanding and support of ordinary men and women and can lead them towards it. (pp. 255–56)

Yet the bias in this passage is particularly revealing. Presumably the "economically developed plural societies" of which Pratt seems to approve (but whose example is at present not quite relevant to Tanzania) are the class-ridden advanced capitalist societies with which we are all too familiar. Presumably, too, not even Pratt would argue that there exist in such societies "traditional communal values" which encourage their leaders to adhere instinctively to the common good. Might one suspect that a dose of class consciousness transcending the pluralistic categories in which we find ourselves enmeshed in Western societies would facilitate the struggle for socialism here? Yet the "conception of democratic leadership" to which Pratt alludes as being virtuous for such settings is precisely the kind which registers the lowest common denominator of fragmented opinion and *never* facilitates the crystallization of a social base capable of confronting consciously the capitalist status quo. At one important level then, and despite important differences in the socioeconomic terrain upon which they operate, a socialist leadership in both advanced and peripheral capitalist settings faces a similar challenge: finding the class base which is necessary to wage an effective struggle for socialism. That Pratt can miss this point even with respect to advanced capitalist countries and can see fit to measure Tanzania's virtue, first and foremost, against the phantom canons of liberal democracy, suggests how far down on his list of priorities a facilitating of the emergence of socialist relations of production really lies. As hinted earlier, we are far closer to the fetishes of the American-sponsored literature on "political development" than to a discussion of the politics of socialist reconstruction—in Tanzania or anywhere else.[13]

The above quotation is even more instructive on a second level, however. For Pratt's poetic invocation of the scope for innovation which such leadership apparently connotes presents what is really a rather intimidating image—Nyerere as Rousseau's Legislator. Here it is crucially important to confirm the obvious about such a passage: it suggests quite strongly that the assertion of any such leadership inevitably involves a very real measure of *control* over the political process on the part of the Legislator/Educator. After all, leadership does not assert itself in a political vacuum nor, in real life, does it realize its ends instantaneously. Surely it is obvious that, to at least some degree, the parameters of popular choice are being structured during a process of education, so defined, and that institutions are being constructed and strategic options selected in various spheres even before the exercise in education is completed and the people in full accord. Ironically, when so considered, it becomes apparent that the risk of authoritarianism is even greater than Pratt cares to admit.

Not that Pratt ignores this point altogether. At one stage in his book he goes so far as to characterize Nyerere as having

> been able to manipulate the circumstances of politics in order to lead his people to moral perceptions which as yet they only imperfectly comprehend. . . . In doing this Nyerere has been willing to use the opportunities which are his as President to set the stage for decision-making, to influence its timing and to define the issues in ways that will increase the likelihood that the people will decide along the lines he feels are necessary. . . . He has guided and he has manipulated, in addition to merely teaching and advocating. For some, perhaps, this will mean that he is not a democrat. But in a society that needs transformation someone must strive to define the society's needs for it. In a society in which national political institutions are still imperfectly structured and inadequately rooted in the life of the society, strong leadership may be the only way in which a national consensus can be obtained on essential issues. To be a political leader in such a society is inevitably to be open to the charge of elitism. (p. 256)

Nonetheless, Pratt's basic response is to blunt this reality by feats of rather astonishing intellectual sleight-of-hand. Thus, negatively, he proceeds to a parody of other socialist perspectives on this issue, pretending thereby to shift the burden of proof of democratic intent from Nyerere to the "Marxists." To a consideration of this particular ploy we shall return. Arguing more positively, however, he falls back upon a formula which might be designated, for want of a better term, "Mwalimuism" (p. 256). Problems related to the institutionalization of the leadership function disappear, and *Mwalimu* Nyerere—the teacher—is coolly assigned the task of educating fourteen million people, more or less by himself! And since we know that we can trust Nyerere not to be authoritarian—numerous quotations being assembled from the president's writings to demonstrate his soundness on this score—the leadership problem is solved. Pratt can then, with an easy conscience, turn his attention to the democratic term of the socialist political equation (though there too, as we shall see, the narrowness of his preoccupations can afford little insight).

It must be insisted, then, that a more radical analysis does not ignore the problems Pratt raises; it merely takes them seriously. For such an analysis is aware that "Mwalimuism"—the "man of vision" solution—provides no fully satisfactory set of answers to the leadership question. Firstly, as hinted above, this "solution" tends merely to evade the full range of implications that follow from the agonizing admission that leadership implies a measure of control and that such control, even when unavoidable or creative, is also inherently dangerous. Secondly, such a formulation evades the inescapable reality that any program of socialist leadership must be fleshed out in a systematic manner and grounded as a broad-gauged method of political work if it is to be at all meaningful. In contrast, it is merely foolish to imply that one person can be expected to generalize awareness of the direction of movement of a society for a whole nation. The answer suggested by socialist experience is, of course, that this function be carried out by trained cadres who themselves have such awareness and can find the means of making it real and vibrant to a much broader range of people in the most varied of settings. Yet whisper this and Pratt snaps down his trump: "vanguard," he charges.[14] And with vanguard, "authoritarian." However, given the shakiness of his own formulations regarding "leadership," these charges represent a particularly unilluminating line of attack—a point to which we shall return.

As for the popular, democratic dimension, we have already noted Pratt's attempt to drain off much of the positive content of the people's intervention in the political arena by denying the advisability of their attaining to either anti-imperialist or class consciousness. Paradoxically, he seems, in this connection, to be calling for mere *lack of leadership*, the avoidance, as cited earlier, of any "deliberate intensification of mass antagonisms."[15] Radicals, in contrast, would argue that the workers and peasants have a rather different, and much greater, stake in democracy than is apparent from Pratt's reading of the Tanzanian situation. Here they would take some of Nyerere's own statements far more seriously than does Pratt (and perhaps, on Pratt's account, more seriously than does Nyerere himself):

> President Nyerere has called on the people of Tanzania to have great confidence in themselves and safeguard the nation's hard-won freedom. He has warned the people against pinning all their hopes on the leadership who are apt to sell the people's freedom to meet their lusts.
>
> Mwalimu [i.e., Nyerere] warned that the people should not allow their freedom to be pawned as most of the leaders were purchaseable. He warned further that in running the affairs of the nation the people should not look on their leaders as "saints or prophets."
>
> The President stated that the attainment of freedom in many cases resulted merely in the change of colours, white to black faces, without ending exploitation and injustices, and above all without the betterment of the life of the masses.
>
> He said that while struggling for freedom the objective was clear but it was another thing when you have to remove your own people from the position of exploiters.[16]

Why is Pratt so suspicious of popular intervention, which springs from a generalization of this kind of insight? As we have seen, one's reading of the propensities of the "bureaucratic and political leadership" is important here, and Pratt's naïveté in this regard does little to encourage his lending any such content to the democratic forms which he prizes so highly. But no doubt he would be less prone to fear the workers and peasants if he were as confident as his "Marxist" antagonists that socialism is a solution to the Tanzanian development problem which the broad mass of the country's people *can know to be in their own best interests and can act to achieve.* Indeed, the Marxist affirms (in spite of Pratt's sustained innuendo to the contrary) that the workers and peasants really can trust no one but themselves to defend such "best interests."

It is precisely this confidence in the people's stake in socialism (and in their ability to understand that stake) which gives point to the radical's further, and most central, set of political formulations. Accepting that both leadership (involving, as it does, at least some measure of control from above) and democracy (involving, as it must, a large measure of control from below) are essential features of the transition to socialism, they argue that the tension or contradiction between these two realities will not quickly or easily be transcended. Yet this remains a contradiction which it is possible to *resolve*, on a continuing basis, by the mediation of effective methods of political work. Charles Bettelheim, in his important writing on the transition to socialism, has circled in on this political reality by emphasizing that "the role of the party . . . consists not only in defining sound objectives, but also in grasping what the masses are prepared to do and leading them forward *without ever resorting to coercion*, and by advancing slogans and directives which the masses can *make their own*, elaborating adequate tactics and strategies, and helping the masses to *organize themselves*."

The key to such a resolution is, to repeat, the crystallization of a necessary level of class consciousness and commitment to socialism on the part of the mass of the population, but this is not just some kind of arbitrary *deus ex machina* for Bettelheim. He also emphasizes the extent to which democratic pressure from the workers and peasants is necessary *throughout* this process in order to insure that the leadership does not itself degenerate even as it is, ostensibly, working toward this kind of denouement (i.e., toward the congruence of both leadership aspiration and mass consciousness at a higher level of socialist awareness and commitment).[17] It may be that even Bettelheim's political formulae understate the degree of control which is inherent in such leadership and underestimate the "irrationalities" which can impede the clear and rapid emergence of mass understanding of the objectives involved. At times there does seem to be a bit too close (and ironic) a parallel in atmosphere to Pratt's approach as regards the smoothness with which a judicious balance between leadership and democracy can be struck. In consequence, something of the agony involved in any transitional society's attempting to keep *both* dimensions alive *simultaneously* is in some danger of being abstracted away. Nonetheless, unlike Pratt, Bettelheim has located such political contradictions firmly on the terrain of class struggle, where alone their resolution can be sought; in addition, he manifests a profound concern for realizing socialist relations of production. His formulations therefore speak to the real world and remain most suggestive ones.

My own earlier writings on Tanzania moved over similar terrain, though it seems fair to say that the harshness of the challenges inherent in the politics of the transition to socialism are somewhat closer to the surface than in Bettelheim's work.[18] Thus I argued that Tanzania's politics involved a struggle

on two fronts: to expand the numbers and efficacy of the progressive petty bourgeoisie, and to release the energies of a more conscious and vocal mass of workers and peasants. A . . . likely danger . . . is the creation of a vicious circle within which a petty bourgeoisie, on balance still relatively untransformed, demobilizes and instrumentalizes the mass of the population and guarantees, at best, a stagnant quasi-state capitalism, thereby checking further progress. . . . The alternative to such a vicious circle is to struggle effectively on *both* fronts and, even more important, to see that effort on one front is likely to fail without simultaneous effort on the other—to see, in short, that the two fronts are closely, indeed dialectically, interrelated. Effectively achieved, the interchange between a petty bourgeoisie which increasingly allows itself to be radicalized, and the mass of the peasants and workers whose consciousness is rising, must at some point become self-reinforcing: the petty bourgeoisie working not only to serve the masses but also to mobilize them and raise their level of consciousness (a necessity), even as the masses increasingly move to put pressure on the petty bourgeoisie and thereby guarantee the latter's further solidarity and commitment (equally a necessity).[19]

Moreover, like many other Marxists, I was well aware (Pratt's opinion to the contrary notwithstanding) that the mounting of such an "alternative" was not something to be solved merely by the invoking of some talismanic "vanguard." As I argued in a second article, it is unfortunate that

> much discussion about the party has focussed upon the misleading juxtaposition of two presumed alternatives—an "elite" or "vanguard" party on the one hand, a "mass" party on the other. Yet such a way of structuring the problem of the party obscures precisely the crucial necessity that both control and participation (vanguard and mass in effect) co-exist at the very heart of the party. It is essential, for example, that party cadres raise the level of mass consciousness even while feeling the prod of the masses' class interests; choice must be structured for the system even while any vested interests which lurk behind the premises of choice so structured are being exposed; and so on. These are not mere paradoxes; rather they are the grim necessities of Tanzania's present situation.[20]

The formulations quoted above are not perfect, of course. The politics of the transition to socialism—holding together, as it must, imperatives which pull in opposite directions—is almost as difficult to write about clearly as it is to realize in practice.[21] Yet such writing can scarcely be said to manifest a penchant for authoritarianism *tout court*. Readers will therefore be surprised to learn that in Pratt's book my position is presented, virtually without qualification, as exemplifying just such a bias. Indeed, this is the justification for citing my own articles and quoting from them here: because they provide the chief target in Pratt's demagogic attempt to portray a Marxist approach to Tanzania as being overtly dictatorial in its presuppositions. Moreover, it is on this basis—the sharp contrast which such an approach can then be claimed to strike with Nyerere's own exemplary dedication to democracy—that Marxism is to be shrugged off the Tanzanian stage once and for all. Obviously, then, the stakes are high. All the more unfortunate that precisely here Pratt's polemical intention leads him furthest away from a consideration of the real issues raised by the problem of the transition to socialism. Here, too, his lack of understanding of these issues borders most closely upon intellectual dishonesty in debating with his peers.

To get the full flavor of this point, it is necessary to quote Pratt at some length. In his version,

> the authoritarian socialist takes an instrumental view of participation, valuing it to the extent that it will contribute to the achievement of the socialist objectives as these are identified by a committed and ideologically sound elite, the benevolent leadership, to use John Saul's flattering phrase. In contrast to that position, Nyerere regards democratic participation as intrinsically valuable and strategically essential. . . . [Saul] suggests that, to the extent that the party becomes more tightly ideological and its leadership more firmly committed to socialism, there will be a correspondingly increased justification for a greater degree of authoritarian rule and for a lessening of the democratic component in the electoral system. (pp. 257, 252–53)

Putting it quite bluntly, there is no such argument to be found in the articles of mine which are cited by Pratt. To be sure, it is stated that struggle within the leadership stratum (the "petty bourgeoisie") can make some significant differences in rendering its internal composition and its exercise of leadership more progressive. But the further point is made, quite unequivocally, that without a powerful input of popular, democratic pressure from the workers and peasants of the society, that leadership stratum will inevitably degenerate, whatever the potential it might otherwise have for playing a progressive role. It is also stated that, under certain circumstances progressive leadership might run marginally ahead of rising mass consciousness as a key to socialist advance, but that it cannot do so for long without great cost to socialist goals is also made painfully clear. Certainly increased authoritarianism by an ideologically committed leadership is never represented as a meaningful resolution to the contradictions inherent in the politics of socialism. Resolution comes, as spelled out above, only to the extent that progressive leadership and rising mass consciousness strike an increasingly harmonious balance. Not an easily achieved resolution, to be sure, but there is certainly no hint that democracy, real and active, is anything but an essential ingredient to realizing such an advance. Yet here is Pratt again:

> All these positions, the colonial, the nationalist, the administrative and the Marxist, . . . are in agreement that for an indeterminate period, hopefully finite but of significant length, a group in power must be ready to override the wishes and sentiments of the people. Popular recognition of the wisdom and historical necessity of this elite's role will come later. For the moment however that elite must rule according to its own prescriptions and pursue its own vision of the future.
>
> A group of American political scientists took a position close to the classic defense of controlled participation under the direction of an administrative state when they declared, "The problem remains one of increasing the feeling of participation without necessarily increasing the local input into decision making." This in turn could easily be a paraphrase of the position taken by John Saul who has argued that the pursuit of socialism in Tanzania is likely to require that a socialist leadership be ready to act without popular support in order to promote social change which will, he hopes, then lead to a situation of "congruent socialism," a happy situation in which the socialist leadership and the mass of the people are in agreement on the objectives of social and economic policies. (p. 262)

This is the crudest conceivable paraphrase of the notion of "congruent socialism" as advanced in my analysis of Tanzania's electoral process (this being the article upon which Pratt focuses the bulk of his attention). For it should by now be evident that in this and other Marxist texts the "leadership phase" and the "democratic phase" are not presented as being merely consecutive, as Pratt implies. They must, to repeat a point made earlier, be *simultaneous*, difficult a reality as this seems to be for Pratt to grasp. Thus the reader would never suspect from Pratt's account that the article on the electoral process which he chooses to parody does *not* come to the conclusion that greater authoritarianism is called for. Instead, it epitomizes the electoral process as having worked primarily to diffuse such popular assertions as might have been forthcoming and bemoans the fact that, while " 'government' or 'the leadership' needs other kinds of [popular] pressure to guarantee its continued commitment to the popular cause," elections in Tanzania have done little to facilitate expression of "the sort of consciousness which could be expected to weigh heavily upon the actions of the holders of privilege." The same article concludes with a discussion of the ways— through genuine workers' participation and strong rural collectives—in which a more effective popular term for the Tanzanian political equation might be grounded in that society.

Sadly, Pratt is not about to be troubled by such uncomfortable facts and reverts, once again, to the tactic of the false dichotomy:

> There is on this issue a key divide which separates the socialist whose primary commitment is to a doctrine (however much he feels that this doctrine reflects the true interests of the people) and the socialist whose primary commitment is to the people themselves as they now are, warts and all. No state can achieve its communal objectives without relying upon political, administrative and technological "experts." Yet to rely upon "experts" is to risk oppression by these "experts." Some socialists would seek to minimize the risk primarily by an emphasis on ideology, arguing that if "experts" are ideologically well trained and the leaders are a committed socialist vanguard the risks will be minimal.
>
> At this divide in socialist thought, Nyerere takes, instead, the democratic path. He would prefer to run the risk of the people misusing their power than the risk of a "benevolent leadership" abusing its power. (p. 260)

Clearly the "man of vision" argument (itself a rather startling evocation of "benevolent leadership," as we have seen[22]) has been bracketed off for another part of the book—that directed toward forestalling the most zealous of liberals. Now we have the democratic argument—intended, apparently, to forestall Marxists. Unfortunately for Pratt, however, Marxists have long since transcended his position, working much more effectively than himself to hold these two strands together. Indeed, they are merely likely to murmur "Right on" to one other outburst by Pratt which he must imagine, in his confusion, would outrage them:

> For [Nyerere] it has always been an unacceptable paradox to suggest that the people might have to be coerced into a socialist

society. "A people cannot be developed: they can only develop themselves." Nyerere's rejection of an authoritarian imposition of socialism thus rested firmly and fundamentally upon a profoundly felt conviction that in statesmanship no great thing can be accomplished without the people. (p. 253)

It is, of course, true that Marxists would probably prefer the substitution of the phrase "class struggle" for the empty word "statesmanship" in the final sentence of this quotation!

Pratt does make two final attempts to patch up his argument as his book draws to a close. On the next-to-last page he asserts that the Marxists pursue the establishment of checks only upon the "senior officials of the public serivce." There is sense to this, he now rather belatedly admits:

> They [the Marxists] fear that the senior officials in the public service are increasingly hostile to socialism and are determined to bend the policies of government to suit their interests as an emerging dominant class. This certainly is one of the risks that must concern the political leadership in Tanzania. It is an almost unavoidable risk in any third world country that seeks a peaceful transition to socialism. (p. 263)

A deathbed reprieve for the Marxist approach? Hardly, for the Marxists are now to be found guilty on other grounds, that of "ignoring the tendency to authoritarian rule which still persists within the middle and senior ranks of TANU and which the politicization of the army and the greater emphasis on social discipline may be intensifying." Yet there is *no evidence whatsoever* that Marxist commentators generally (e.g., Bettelheim), or when writing about Tanzania, drew such a line, no evidence that they either underestimate the dangers of party-sponsored authoritarianism or downplay the need to thwart oligarchic tendencies within even the most apparently committed of socialist parties. Pratt's assertion here is merely gratuitous. Not accidentally so. For such a distortion is also necessary to Pratt in order to set up his parting shot (quoted in the previous section), that "Marxists emphasize the need for a vanguard party and the deliberate intensification of mass antagonisms towards the bureaucracy and the successful peasant farmer," all of which will, astonishingly, "increase the risk of authoritarian rule." (Pratt also argues that this combination will increase the risk of "serious economic and governmental failures," an argument to which we will return.) This latter prediction is true by definition only if such "mass antagonism" (read "class consciousness" and "democratic self-assertion") is not brought to bear upon the so-called vanguard party itself. Yet who would argue that it should not be?

Secondly, one also finds evidence that, toward the end, Pratt has had a slight case of cold feet regarding his willful caricature of the Marxist approach. Such evidence is to be glimpsed on the final page of footnotes (p. 293, footnote 83, to the eighth and final chapter). Here we discover a somewhat humbler tone and the argument that

> Marxist analysis is, of course, not intended to reinforce oligarchic tendencies within the party. We are however talking of an area of political practice where the slippage between intention and reality can be very great. If the effort were in fact made to convert TANU into a vanguard party the result might very well be the full entrenchment of a political oligarchy free of the encumbrance of the existing democratic constraints, an oligarchy which utilizes a socialist rhetoric without real commitment to it.

Yet he has written throughout the book as if Marxian analysis is indeed directed (with whatever good intentions) quite consciously toward the reinforcement of oligarchic tendencies both within the party and within the society as a whole. Both charges are false. Obviously it is the case that if we leave aside Pratt's continuing confusion over the notion of the vanguard, he can be seen to make a crucial point: "This *is* an area of political practice where the slippage between intention and reality can be very great." If only Pratt had written his entire book with this kind of empathy for the dilemmas involved, then he might have made some genuine contribution to illuminating the agonizing political problems which socialists must face in transitional societies. However, coming so late in the book as it does, and appearing in such an obscure corner of it, it is hard not to read this sentence as an afterthought, one designed to cover himself if ever he were to be pressed to defend himself from reviews such as the present one. Any such defense will not be an easy one, since further supporting evidence for the criticism embarked upon here is readily available. In citing it we run the risk of carrying Pratt beyond the historical period he has taken as his primary subject. Yet this is something he is prone to do himself, particularly in his conclusions. In fact, further evidence of the manner in which he manipulates the parameters of debate in favor of his own views lies precisely in his discussion of such post-Arusha initiatives as workers' committees, *ujamaa* (collective) rural villages, and decentralization. These he interprets as facilitating "the creation of a socialist environment," and in the following terms: "Each hopes to achieve meaningful mass participation within structures which will encourage broader and more responsible attitudes and will aid the development of social relationships and a work ethic that is more appropriate to a socialist society" (p. 251).

This is a rather tame (and, dare one say, somewhat "instrumental") view of such initiatives. Ironically, it is the Marxists—Pratt's diabolical authoritarians—who have welcomed these undertakings most enthusiastically in their writings and stressed, even more than Nyerere perhaps, the *democratic* potential which they might have on a national scale in focusing the more coherent and conscious pressure of organized workers and peasants upon the leadership. In a similar vein it has also been Marxist commentators who have emphasized the very real promise of *Mwongozo*—the TANU Guidelines of 1971—to facilitate popular control from below. As noted earlier, these are prominent themes in my own writing, themes which Pratt sees fit *not even to mention* in extracting what he feels to be the authoritarian kernel of my approach. These are also the central themes of those indigenous Tanzanian Marxists who have written in recent years to condemn the many rollbacks of such beginnings of effective democracy: the crushing by the "bureaucratic and political leadership" of the Ruvuma Development Association (this being an early exemplar of radical democratic pressures arising from a rural collective milieu) in 1969; the smashing of the industrial workers when they attempted to give *Mwongozo* a concrete expression at their workplaces during the wave of strikes and factory occupations in 1972–73; the routing of students in high schools and at the university (1971) when they resisted the high-handed (and substantively reactionary) authoritarianism which has remained so prominent a dimension of the style of leadership manifested within Tanzanian institutions.[23] Perhaps it is Pratt's narrow conception of democracy, one which hovers primarily around the formal electoral system,[24] which permits him consistently to overlook such themes in the writings of those with whom he disagrees. Perhaps it is, once again, his suspicion of anything that might seem to facilitate the more militant expression of a class-conscious political force in Tanzania. Can it be that he would consider the abovementioned activities of the leadership as manifesting merely its legitimate resistance to the unseemly demands of "crude communism"?

There is one further theme, closely related. It arises from Pratt's own presentation of developments in one important policy sphere—the *ujamaa* village program. Here Pratt begins by reiterating the familiar point, that Nyerere has not been prepared to adopt "an authoritarian short-cut to socialism," has not, in this case, been moved to force Tanzanians to take up communal agricultural practices, despite his commitment to the establishment of *ujamaa* villages. On the other hand, "he has simultaneously insisted that strong pressure be applied to get the peasants to live in villages. This, he feels, is such a basic requirement of progress that some coercion may be justified to overcome initial opposition to it" (pp. 254–55). Pratt is uneasy with this, though not as uneasy as he should be. Apparently he can draw some solace from the fact that the motive is, in his words, "a nationalist's conviction that his country must develop." Again the excuse of backwardness: "The coercion which Nyerere appears to accept here is an expression of an impatient nationalism not a coercive socialism." This excuse, and the bogey of "coercive socialism" (p. 259)! When measured against the latter specter, Nyerere can be forgiven anything:

> . . . it does appear to be the case that despite this readiness to use coercion to bring the peasants into villages, it has still remained

Nyerere's view that the creation of a socialist environment, which is an important component of Nyerere's strategy for the transition to socialism, must still be accomplished with the support and cooperation of the people. . . . The balance between the leadership strand and the democratic strand in his thought has thus been sustained in that area of policy in which it was, perhaps, most severely strained. (p. 255)

Surely it is obvious that Pratt is here splitting hairs—and missing the real implications of the degeneration of Tanzania's *ujamaa* program into a kind of enforced villagization. We have quoted the final page of Pratt's book above; we can cite it here again to conclude this section. On that page he continues his efforts to caricature the Marxist's simultaneous emphasis upon the need for a more committed socialist leadership (presented by Pratt as "the vanguard party" solution) and upon the need for a class-conscious base of workers and peasants (presented by Pratt as the "deliberate intensification of mass antagonisms"). We also find him ignoring once again the Marxists' effort to think through creatively the manner of resolving the tension between these two terms of the socialist equation: he attempts to package their program as the willingness to contemplate, with a fair degree of equanimity, "authoritarian rule." On that page, however, he adds a second string to his bow. Apparently the Marxist project (so caricatured) also invites another risk besides that of authoritarian rule, the risk of "serious economic and governmental failures." Yet this implication too is largely spun out of thin air, since it is precisely the opposite case which can more easily be argued. The villagization program now under review is a case in point.

Thus a Marxist approach to the rural areas structured along lines sketched by Bettelheim or myself would be unlikely to find itself advocating the forcing of Tanzanians into villages (whether or not those villages were immediately to have the appurtenances of collective endeavor which would fully qualify them as *ujamaa* villages). Instead, for reasons which we have discussed, it would emphasize the use of more effective methods of political work than sheer force, while also assuming the possibility of a real release of creative energies and demands for socialist solutions from the rural population itself if such methods were found. Nor is this alternative some mere abstraction standing outside the bounds of the contemporary African setting. It happens to define the kind of political context which one now finds to be premising independent Mozambique's fledgling efforts to launch its own program of rural collectivization.[25] Recent experience in Tanzania stands in sharp contrast to this, and it is hard not to feel that Nyerere's willingness to fall back upon coercion as a guarantor of only half his program in the rural areas (the village *without* the socialism) epitomizes the end and not the beginning of socialist endeavor in Tanzania. Indeed, it is tempting to see this as the last desperate act of a *Mwalimu* who finds himself, all too predictably, isolated, without either the cadres or the conscious mass base which together might have sustained a socialist dialectic in his country.

Such a Tanzania may remain a scene of good intentions (at least on Nyerere's part), but it also exemplifies a great political misfire. More than that, it is characterized by an economic misfire, the "serious economic failure" which the disastrous course of the villagization program represents having been documented by a whole host of contemporary observers.[26] Other of Pratt's words ring in our ears; it could well be argued that this is the very kind of failure which is "of such an extent as finally to alienate mass support and leave the leadership prone either to self-transformation into an authoritarian oligarchy, or to replacement by a new set of men who would constitute such an oligarchy" (p. 263). Yet it would be fruitless to seek the reasons for such failure where Pratt is, apparently, tempted to look. It seems clear that a real release of popular energies would be not merely the best possible political solution for Tanzania's rural areas, but the key to their economic regeneration as well. And if this is the case, it can be confirmed that the economic failure in Tanzania's rural sector (as in too many other sectors) has not been occasioned by too much socialism but by too little.[27] It might well be the most telling comment of all upon Pratt's book that a reader armed only with Pratt's concepts and his vision could never even begin to understand why this should be the case.

III

A good man fallen among Fabians.

—Lenin on George Bernard Shaw

Pratt's picture of Tanzania is a sobering one, in important respects much more damning than Issa Shivji's celebrated account. For Shivji, at least as regards his historical analysis, presents something of a caricature of Tanzanian reality, summarized more or less accurately by Pratt as follows:

> Shivji extends [his point] beyond the credible and into the realm of radical mythology when he suggests that the bureaucratic bourgeoisie sought through the nationalizations to bring the economy under its control for its own class interests and for the protection of the interests of international capitalism with whom this bourgeoisie remains intimately linked. Nationalization in his view was thus but an alternative, equally nefarious, to the development of an African bourgeoisie which associated directly with the foreign corporations in order similarly to advance their common interests. In this interpretation Nyerere becomes the agent of the bourgeoisie and the Arusha Declaration, far from being a product of nationalist and socialist concerns, was a selfish, class-motivated intervention manipulated into being by the bureaucratic bourgeoisie.[28] (pp. 241–42)

In fact, the articulation of Tanzania's left turn was much more complicated than Shivji allows, and Nyerere's input a much more positive one. At the very least it must be affirmed that the president certainly felt he was beginning to build socialism, and so did others of the petty bourgeoisie who were prepared to back his play.

It is important, then, to note that Pratt does capture something of the ambiguity of the petty bourgeoisie (though this stratum is never so identified) in its stance toward the socialist initiatives propounded by Nyerere, just as he confirms the seriousness of Nyerere's intention. All the more significant, then, that his account lends such credence (albeit unintentionally) to the profound concern felt by many observers—by those skeptical about Tanzania's undertakings but less prepared than Shivji to write them off on the basis of an abstract and ahistorical argument—as to the excessively *ad hoc* nature of the country's policy and as to the weakness of Nyerere's own formulations for launching, much less sustaining, a genuine transition to socialism. In short, Pratt's account goes some way toward confirming the suspicion that the original problematic of Tanzanian socialism was much too unregenerately petty bourgeois—too lacking in an understanding of imperialism and of the nature of economic dependence, of class struggle and of the political imperatives attendant upon it—to stay the course. Indeed, this is precisely the position summarized sharply and succinctly by so careful an observer as Leys in his own recent contribution to the debate about Tanzania:

> These initiatives [of 1967 and 1971] reflected an appreciation of some of the class *implications* of the existing social and economic system, as revealed in a succession of policy contradictions (neutralism versus dependence on bilateral aid, egalitarianism versus the elitist educational system, etc). This appreciation was very partial, however. In particular it was assumed that the dominance of a local bourgeois class, and of foreign bourgeoisies, could be prevented by legislative and administrative action taken by the existing state. This ignored both the bourgeois character of the existing state (its adaptation to the task of defending bourgeois interests) and the fact that the penetration of Tanzanian society by capitalism was far too advanced to be checked, let alone prevented, by juridical measures. . . . To check, let alone eliminate, the dominance of the capitalist class could only mean mobilizing the working class and the poorer peasants to a struggle against it at all levels. This was excluded, partly by Nyerere's resistance to the idea that class struggle was involved in the "building of socialism". . . . Distortion and "neutralisation" of the initiatives taken by Nyerere and his supporters within the state apparatus clearly played a part in reducing their impact. . . . But it needs to be emphasized that this process itself reflects the limitations of the original initiatives taken. . . . These ideas mark the limits, not of one man's ideology, but of the broadly "populist" form of consciousness of the wing of the original nationalist leadership most sensitive to its mass base.[29]

As Leys also notes, this is, by and large, the position which I have myself articulated in earlier writings, though I must confess that a reading of Pratt has tended to reinforce the skeptical side of my own somewhat hesitant reading of the auguries regarding Tanzanian socialism!

Of course, there does remain the additional possibility that accepting the "Pratt version" may be somewhat unfair to Nyerere. We return to a question raised at the very outset of this essay: Where does Nyerere leave off, in *The Critical Phase in Tanzania*, and Pratt begin? My judgment would be that, even though Nyerere's socialist project has been weak in many of the ways Pratt's book reveals it to be weak, and even though it is unquestionably subject to Leys's strictures as quoted above, it nonetheless has had rather more spine and substance than a reading of Pratt's account would suggest. Unfortunately, any such conclusion is in large part a judgment call and one which would, in any case, require a book at least equal in length to that of Pratt's to affirm. Nor, written without the benefit of the fervent certainties of a Pratt or a Shivji, would its composition be an easy task. The evidence is ambiguous, certainly, the probable conclusions equally so. Thus, on the one hand it is hard to escape an awareness that, in Tanzania, economic stagnation, continued imperial penetration, and bureaucratized authoritarianism are rather more prominent features than socialist development, a self-centered economy, and people's power. Yet at the same time, there is undoubtedly a firm measure of truth in Bienefeld's conclusion:

> On balance, it is wrong to suggest that the efforts of the progressive fraction of the Tanzanian bureaucracy have been of no consequence. They have made a considerable impact on the consciousness of workers and even of some peasants; they have changed the relative size and influence of various classes to the detriment of the emerging capitalist class; and finally they have made critical contributions to the broader struggle, as when they assisted in the resolution of the internal conflicts within FRELIMO and helped the progressive wing of that movement to assume the undisputed leadership of the movement. It is no accident that a progressive denouement to Portuguese colonialism was much easier in a neighbour of Tanzania than in a neighbour of Zaire. Neither is it an accident that those actively engaged in the Mozambiquan struggle can appreciate both the weaknesses and the undoubted strengths of the Tanzanian situation.

Bienefeld does take this point a stage further, arguing against various ultra-left critics of Tanzania's efforts that

> to suggest . . . progressive forces [in Tanzania] can dispense with Nyerere as an ally is to misjudge the present strength of these forces disastrously. To suggest that Nyerere has always been a reactionary force in Tanzania is both factually and politically wrong. It is politically wrong because it plays into the hands of those forces which have always opposed the more progressive elements of Tanzania's policies. Because it contributes to the view which equates bureaucratic excesses with policies. Because it will lure people into the belief that a Ghanaian coup would make no difference. Indeed some analysts may even believe this themselves but they are sorely mistaken.

One can be much less sanguine than Bienefeld about the extent to which the struggle to save Tanzania from following the conventional African path of neocolonialism can now be furthered within the terms of the political problematic defined by Nyerere, without losing sight of the fact that there is also some sense in this latter formulation![30]

In any case, the debate implied here will be a continuing one—with the evaluation of the Tanzanian experience likely to remain a fruitful arena of controversy for some time to come. This is particularly true, of course, for Tanzanians struggling to define their own futures, but it is also the case that, whatever the immediate fate of Tanzania's undertakings, these have been sufficently significant to demand that they be incorporated by progressives in Africa as part of a continental learning experience. Certainly such undertakings permit the raising of questions and the exploring of ambiguities about the transition to socialism at a more advanced level than that permitted earlier by discussion of the cruel contradictions characteristic of Nkrumah's Ghana. Carefully interrogated, Tanzania has much to teach all— Bienefeld mentions the Mozambicans as an example—who would undertake the struggle for socialism elsewhere on the continent.

Yet as we have seen it is precisely the real meaning of Tanzania's undertakings—the questions and the ambiguities—which Pratt's formulations serve to conjure away. The more promising approach remains, despite Pratt's caricature of it, Marxism. The lineaments of such an approach both to understanding and to practicing socialism—"scientific" in the best sense—have at least been implied here, and are also the subject of a growing body of literature. On this basis, what can be affirmed is that the Marxist alternative provides the crispness in the definition of the terms of African underdevelopment, in the articulation of a forward strategy for socioeconomic transformation, and in the elucidation of the realities of democracy and class struggle which Nyerere's approach, however morally admirable and tactically adept, has so often lacked. In this light, it is sobering to note how often, over the years, advisors like Pratt (the latter's stewardship of the University College, Dar es Salaam, in its early years, and his more recent specially commissioned report on the decentralization of the Tanzanian government are examples) have had the president's ear rather than those (especially Tanzanians) more firmly rooted in a Marxist methodology. "A good man fallen among Fabians," indeed.[31]

This much may be affirmed, then, and it is of no small importance. However, there is another reason for discussing Pratt's book at what otherwise might seem to be inordinate length. Better, perhaps, to have spent the equivalent amount of time and energy in, say, a critique of Bettelheim, and in fleshing out, more concretely, what his formulations might mean with reference to Tanzania. Yet books do have consequences. One of the crosses which those of us who lectured on politics in Tanzania in the late 1960s and early 1970s had to bear was the ready access of students to mystifying books on Tanzania by Tordoff and Bienen. Not only did such texts virtually ignore the crucial realities of imperialism and social classes, but their discussion of politics was redolent with the biases of Western liberalism and crude anticommunism, making *no bow whatsoever* to such political complexities of a transition to socialism as have been alluded to above.

Pratt's book, as will now be apparent, is of the same mold, though fortunately, for reasons noted earlier, its biases are even closer to the surface than those written by his predecessors. What emerges is a particularly graphic case of the devil trying to have all the good tunes: As noted at the outset of this article, it epitomizes the attempt by Western liberals and social democrats, both in the press and in the academy, to corner the market on the praiseword "democracy." For many Africans, students and otherwise, who are tired of the specter of quite so much authoritarianism in quite so many countries on the continent, the seductiveness of this appeal may be more immediately apparent than the narrowness of the definition of democracy with which such theorists are working. Moreover, Pratt's careful delimitation of the debate about democracy in Tanzania in the interests of moderation may be only the thin edge of the wedge in another sense. For we can expect a parallel approach to be a growing part of the effort to caricature and to isolate regimes in Africa which are much more revolutionary than Tanzania's and which give promise of being even more radically democratic; in these cases too the goal will be the legitimization of the "moderate solution."[32] Hence the imperative that radicals not be discomfited by attacks like that of Pratt against "Marxist authoritarianism." It is true that the Marxist analysis of politics—including the analysis of the politics of the transition to socialism—has tended to lag behind its analysis of economic and social structures. It is equally true that many regimes outside Africa which have presented themselves as being "Marxist" have lapsed into the crudest of authoritarianisms. But it is also the case, as this essay has argued, that a genuine transition to socialism is about a dramatic democratization of the development process or it is about nothing. Indeed, democracy in Africa is not really Pratt's tune at all. It is the revolutionary socialist's, the Marxist's. There is an important theoretical project involved in further proving and elaborating this point. And, of course, there is an even more important *political* project involved in exemplifying it.

Notes

1. See my "The State in Postcolonial Societies: Tanzania," in this volume. Issa Shivji's volume, entitled *Class Struggles in Tanzania* (London and New York, 1976), makes available in monograph form his widely circulated work.

2. Cranford Pratt, *The Critical Phase in Tanzania 1945–1968: Nyerere and the Emergence of a Socialist Strategy* (Cambridge, 1976).

3. As we shall see, this bias informs the text throughout, but it is made explicit in one footnote (p. 289) where "Western Marxists" who worked in Tanzania are juxtaposed to others characterized as "Western democratic socialists" (note the use of lower-case letters in the latter phrase).

4. To take merely one example, Pratt quotes approvingly Nyerere's expression of the faith of the period that, in spite of all the evidence to the contrary, "the basic philosophy of Western democracy has its own life and its own power and that the people's concept of freedom can triumph over their materialism," thereby leading Western countries to cut their links with the white-minority regimes and support a nonviolent path to genuine liberation in Southern Africa. A touching naïveté, but one which is paralleled by Pratt's own injunction to the Canadian government in another of his writings that "in our judgment it is enormously important that some rich, white countries should stand aside from the scramble to cash in on the profit-making opportunities provided by a racist regime in South Africa in order to demonstrate actively and effectively that the Western liberal tradition has not become empty rhetoric" (Cranford Pratt, "Canadian Attitudes Towards Southern Africa: A Commentary," *International Perspectives* [Ottawa], November–December 1974). Such a parallel suggests that in certain respects Nyerere may, regrettably, have found his ideal commentator in Cranford Pratt!

5. On this subject, see Peter Lawrence, "Socialism, Self-Reliance, and Foreign Aid in Tanzania: Some Lessons from the Socialist Experience," published as "Socialist Experiments: Lessons for Tanzania" in *Third World Forum* (Montreal) 1, no. 3 (December 1974–January 1975).

6. Pratt invariably identifies such classes as he is willing to admit into his discussion in terms of income differentials, not in terms of their differential position in the production process, *viz.*: "If those with political and governmental power have significantly higher incomes than ordinary citizens, they are likely to constitute a 'new class.' " See also his assertion that Nyerere has sought to "minimize the risk of oppression by 'experts' by assuring as best he can that they are not so well rewarded as to constitute a separate class . . ."!

7. Pratt does ultimately make the point that the cooperatives were not operating effectively as any sort of admirably grass-roots organization—but too late to cast any retrospective doubt on the exemplary

intention of Bomani already enshrined on earlier pages. In fact, Pratt is a great one for playing favorites: conservatives are invariably "pluralist" or soberly "administrative," as opposed to more suspect "political" ministers. Conversely, a document by A. M. Babu, then minister of commerce and cooperatives (though now in detention) in Tanzania, written around 1965, which foreshadows the multipurpose cooperatives of later years, is dismissed out of hand as "a rather doctrinaire paper." Pratt is also prone to conflate crude and power-hungry thugs like Oscar Kambona, who were not averse to laying on a patina of radical rhetoric to sweeten their authoritarian designs, with more genuinely progressive members of the unofficial Left "opposition" in Tanzania.

8. For this reason, I am rather startled (as Shivji, I'm sure, would be outraged) to find our positions on this subject crudely bracketed together by Pratt (footnote 100 to p. 221). See my essays "The State in Postcolonial Societies: Tanzania" in this volume, and "African Socialism in One County: Tanzania," in G. Arrighi and J. S. Saul, *Essays on the Political Economy of Africa* (New York, 1973). In my interpretation, this fluidity can be seen to give rise to a significant struggle within the "petty bourgeoisie" over the direction of Tanzanian development.

9. This argument, ignoring the more usual functions of nationalist ideology throughout the African continent in the postcolonial period, quickly became a staple of much post-Arusha historiography in Tanzania; for a commentary see "Nationalism, Socialism, and Tanzanian History" in this volume.

10. I will document this argument, in detail and from first-hand experience, for one important sector of the society in a forthcoming monograph on the University of Dar es Salaam. In fact, 1967–68 were crucial years in witnessing the failure really to attempt to transform the university into a socialist institution. The profound reluctance to countenance the fleshing-out of socialist strategy during these years on the various "working parties" created to develop the Second Five-Year Plan (on one of which I served) is another case in point. The problem is further defined, overall and for various sectors, in J. F. Rweyemamu, et al., eds., *Towards Socialist Planning* (Dar es Salaam, 1972).

11. I have attempted to illuminate something of the character of this struggle in my various writings on Tanzania (though the argument is perhaps theoretically most developed in "The Unsteady State: Uganda, Obote, and General Amin," in this volume). Also Colin

Leys has recently suggested one possible hypothesis on the subject, arguing that "the origins and course of the struggles inside the state apparatus" in Tanzania "evidently lie in the links—personal, organizational and ideological—with the workers and peasants which some of the party-recruited elements bring into the state apparatus with them. Individual career officers identify themselves with their outlook, but the impetus comes from the party elements, and it was in the party executive, by then largely composed of holders of state posts but still organizationally and ideologically distinct from the state, that the initiatives of 1967 and 1971 were taken" (Colin Leys, "The Overdeveloped Post-Colonial State: A Re-Evaluation," *Review of African Political Economy*, no. 5 [1976]). This formulation probably underestimates the extent to which contestation between fractions within the petty bourgeoisie cut across political and civil-service categories, but it at least has the virtue of talking about the real world. What can be confirmed is that, in spite of the efforts of Pratt and Shivji, the Arusha Declaration period awaits its historian.

12. Pratt's narrow approach to the problem of class—insofar as he approaches it analytically at all—is best epitomized by his assertion, noted above, that "if those with political and governmental power have significantly higher incomes than ordinary citizens, they are likely to constitute a 'new class.' " Ergo, "greater equality as between ruler and ruled is an important restraint upon such a development. If ruler and ruled are of the same class, if the leaders are truly of and with the people in their daily living, then government is more likely to be responsive to popular needs." Of course, this is not to deny that there remain great problems in perfecting a class analysis relevant to Africa, but merely to note that Pratt does not treat the problem with anything like the breadth and clarity which is required.

13. Take another example: "It is not what distinguishes Nyerere from the pure populist or from the liberal democrat that is important so much as what distinguishes him from the ideological authoritarian." One would have thought that the socialist would be at least as suspicious of "liberal democracy," given the capitalist relations of production generally associated with it, as of "ideological authoritarianism." In fact, most genuine socialists are quite suspicious of both, although you would never know this from Pratt, who is, as we shall see, quick to label almost anyone with whom he disagrees an "ideological authoritarian."

14. Mention that these cadres (or even the people more generally) might also be expected to have a clear and systematic understanding of the

problem of imperialism, class structure, and the transition to socialism in Tanzania, as well as of the ramifications of these realities for concrete policy making in various sectors, suggest, in short, that they might have some clear idea of overall socialist strategy which they can both communicate to the people and bring to bear critically upon programs being articulated in those sectors, and Pratt has another scare-word for us: "scientific socialism." Once again, one is left with the promise of Nyerere doing all the strategic thinking for Tanzania and, in place of strategy, the familiar litany of equality, self-reliance, democracy. It is also worth noting the incantatory use to which Pratt puts words like "vanguard" and "scientific socialism"—again and again all too demagogically cutting off debate with a phrase which, he strongly implies, pinpoints the sinister intent of his opponents. There is but one explanation for this: Pratt, like so many social democrats, seems almost to have been preserved in amber, still exclusively preoccupied with fighting the shade of Stalin (whose negative example does, to be sure, present real challenges to socialists) rather than dealing with the problems of the transition to socialism in all their concreteness in a variety of contemporary settings or grappling with the theoretical arguments of Marxists who are at least as free from the charge of Stalinism as Pratt himself.

15. That these "mass antagonisms" might take on a real (and legitimate) life of their own without benefit of much prodding from "leadership" or "vanguard party" is another possibility never really contemplated by Pratt (in spite of his rather Delphic reference, quoted above, to the existence, around 1967, of "political discontent on a fairly widespread basis"). Yet this reality (with workers in particular manifesting a high level of class consciousness) was to become an ever more prominent dimension of the Tanzanian situation in subsequent years.

16. *The Nationalist* (Dar es Salaam) September 5, 1967. On another occasion he is reported as saying that " 'African leaders have their price these days. The moment one becomes a minister, his price also gets determined. The price is not even big; some are bought only for £ 500, or a simple house.' Mwalimu said that although it was possible to buy ministers, there was one section of Africa that could not be bought. 'The people,' he said, 'could not be bought.' " (*The Standard*, July 8, 1967).

17. "In brief, a ruling party can be a proletarian party only if it refrains from *imposing orders* on the masses and remains the *instrument of*

their initiatives. This is possible only if it submits fully to *criticism on the part of the masses*, if it does not try to *impose* 'necessary' tasks upon the masses, if it proceeds from what the masses are prepared to do toward the development of socialist relationships." Note that this is rather far from Pratt's grotesque formulations concerning the penchant of Marxists for vanguardism. Regarding Pratt's other bogeyman, "scientific socialism," another of Bettelheim's formulations may be instructive: "In order for the Marxist-Leninist principles to which a ruling party is committed to remain alive, and not to 'function' as a frozen dogma abstracted from life, the party and its members must reject authoritarian practices, criticize those who engage in such practices, and constantly subject themselves to criticism by the masses." The quotations from Bettelheim found in this essay are all taken from his contributions to Paul M. Sweezy and Charles Bettelheim, *On the Transition to Socialism* (New York and London, 1971).

18. The line between a focus upon "party" on the one hand or "petty bourgeoisie" on the other with respect to the leadership term of the socialist equation is also less straightforward in my writing, but the logic of the argument remains a similar one, nonetheless.

19. In this essay ("African Socialism in One Country: Tanzania"), written in 1972, I concluded that "the core of Tanzanian achievement lies in the fact that leadership, and especially President Nyerere, has sought to mount precisely this imaginative alternative," though the essay was quite skeptical as to whether a resolution along these lines was really likely to be achieved.

20. "The Nature of Tanzania's Political System: Issues Raised by the 1965 and 1970 Elections," reprinted in Lionel Cliffe and J. S. Saul, *Socialism in Tanzania* (Nairobi, 1972). In this essay, in "African Socialism . . . ," and in "The Tanzanian Elections in Post-Arusha Perspective," coauthored with Jonathan Barker as Chapter I of Election Study Committee, University of Dar es Salaam, *Socialism and Participation: Tanzania's 1970 National Elections* (Dar es Salaam, 1974), I have presented in much more detail an analysis of Tanzanian politics which makes the complex dialectic established between the two terms, leadership and democracy, central to an analysis of Tanzanian politics during the period they cover.

21. In addition, this is notoriously a sphere in which the unity of theory and practice is of the essence. Within any such dialectical process, the outcome of which is beyond the capacity of any one man or group *completely* to determine, the socialist must merely continue

to struggle to see contradictions resolved in a progressive and democratic manner. One weakness of my earlier articles was to sometimes give the impression, like Pratt, that Nyerere remained an arbiter of these contradictions, somehow slightly above the battle. To the extent that this is an accurate criticism, it probably reflected the milieu of political activity in which one moved at the time in Tanzania, where appeals to the authority (or the ear) of Mwalimu was, correctly or not, a tempting strategy to adopt.

22. Pratt makes great satirical play with my phrase "benevolent leadership." It is true that it does appear now to have been rather too evocative and imprecise a formulation, but Pratt is content in any case to wrench it brutally out of context. As used in one of my early articles, it was designed to pinpoint the "ideal type" of a committed leadership within a theoretical model of the politics of socialist transition. In its pure form, it was given no empirical referent, but it was made perfectly clear that mounting democratic pressure was an absolutely necessary complement to ensure the growing "benevolence" of any such leadership. Pratt has little time for noting such subtleties when meting out justice to "Marxists," however.

23. On these themes see Issa Shivji, *Class Struggles in Tanzania* (New York and London, 1976); Henry Mapolu, "The Workers' Movement in Tanzania" in *Maji Maji*, September 1973; Paschal Mihyo, "The Struggle for Workers Control in Tanzania" in *Review of African Political Economy*, no. 4 (November 1975); Karim Hirji, "School Education and Underdevelopment in Tanzania" in *Maji Maji*, September 1973.

24. It is tempting to see an example of this in Pratt's discussion of the Arusha Declaration leadership rules when, outside the context of any reference to the electoral process, he states that "to the extent [these rules] are enforced they lessen the risk that leaders will develop interests which will conflict with those of the ordinary *voter*" (emphasis added). Yet it is a conception of democracy that narrows the definition of participatory citizenship only to the act of voting that most socialists are fighting against.

25. My own observations in Mozambique have suggested that the same blending of cadres and consciousness which contributed to an effective guerrilla struggle there has begun to be a hopeful feature of the move toward collective endeavor in the rural areas. The picture on the ground there is significantly different from that to be seen in rural Tanzania and suggests, in practice, the possibility of a genuinely socialist resolution to the contradictions which we have been dis-

cussing, one that also promises, despite the difficulties, economic success, not failure.

26. On the grossness of the bureaucratic compulsion which has characterized this program, and on its economic consequences, see, for example, P. L. Raikes, "Ujamaa and Rural Socialism," and A. C. Coulson, "Peasants and Bureaucrats" in *Review of African Political Economy*, no. 3 (May–October 1975).

27. Jonathan Barker has come to a similar conclusion in an important recent survey of the *ujamaa* village program: "One fears that the political-administrative leadership may be drawing the over-hasty and under-researched conclusion of many production liberals that somehow rural socialism has failed, when in fact only an inspiring [*sic?*], but in practice very incomplete and tentative socialist effort was attempted." It is worth noting that Barker emphasizes that a more genuinely socialist program would not only be more effectively political (in the sense we have been exploring) but also more *scientific*—in the sense of facilitating a more precise understanding of the context within which such programs are being implemented and of the social forces which might facilitate or hinder their implementation. But what other meaning would one want to give to the phrase "scientific socialism," a phrase which nonetheless so frightens Pratt. See Barker, "Socialism and the Rural Sector in Tanzania," paper delivered to the 1976 Annual Meeting of the American Political Science Association, Chicago, September 1976.

28. It should be noted that this victory over Shivji is nonetheless a rather Phyrrhic one. For the crushing of the workers in Tanzania is also a major theme in Issa Shivji's "The Class Struggle Continues," one of Shivji's texts which Pratt cites (later *Class Struggles in Tanzania*). Yet Pratt, in his zeal to scotch Shivji's (admittedly overstated and ahistorical) critique of Tanzania's petty bourgeoisie, makes no mention of this particular theme, even though it is the primary evidence advanced (and advanced quite unhysterically) by Shivji as to the *contemporary* debilitation of the Tanzanian leadership. All the more easy, then, to dismiss Shivji out of hand.

29. Colin Leys, "The Overdeveloped Post-Colonial State: A Re-Evaluation." Leys also mentions the possibility that there is some sign of tactical moderation in Nyerere's stated socialist intentions in order to avoid "running the risk of a reaction from the right within the state apparatus." Weighing the importance of this factor has always been a difficult aspect of the task of evaluating Tanzania's

ideology, though, like Leys, I think this ambiguity does not negate the broader criticism to be made of Nyerere's formulations.

30. See M. A. Bienefeld, "The Class Analysis of Tanzania: A Comment on the Debate" in *Review of African Political Economy*, no. 4 (November 1975). Indeed, one might wish to interpret the recent demotion of (former) Vice-President Rashidi Kawawa and many others of his ilk as a sign of a revivifying of the leftward impulse in Tanzania, though there are many more indications of the continuing strength of the rightward trend. "African Socialism in One Country: Tanzania" represents my own early attempt to strike a convincing balance.

31. Obviously Nyerere has been only one factor—although a particularly important one—in the Tanzanian socialist equation. His passing over of the Marxist option—and his choosing of moderate advisors—reflects a whole host of objective and subjective factors which have defined the Tanzanian conjuncture (just as Mozambique's opting for a specifically Marxist-oriented approach to their problems reflects a very different historical and sociological moment); it is not merely a matter of some arbitrary whim on Nyerere's part. In any case, the point is not to speculate about what might have happened had Nyerere become a Marxist, but rather to underscore the missed opportunities inherent in a radicalism which is not grounded in an adequate methodology and ideological perspective.

32. Indeed, this kind of rhetorical offensive seems already to be part of the new Carter/Young strategy—within the broader framework of their facile "human rights" crusade—for facilitating the emergence of "moderate solutions" in postcolonial Zimbabwe and Namibia.

PART III
EASTERN AFRICA: SOCIAL FORCES AND POLITICAL ALTERNATIVES

This section has a somewhat broader focus than the preceding two, emphasizing more general considerations regarding class analysis in Africa (albeit considerations which are grounded with reference to concrete Eastern African experience). The first two essays (numbers 11 and 12) discuss the role of the popular classes—the peasantry and the proletariat. As noted earlier, their political input as class-conscious actors must be preeminent if "socialism" is to be something more than the utopian whim of a handful of petty-bourgeois leaders. Yet this is not something that comes to pass spontaneously. Essay 11 examines the nature of the African peasantry and, against the vapidities of some "left" analyses, affirms that this peasantry is quite capable of assuming a revolutionary vocation. However, a comparative analysis of Mozambique and Tanzania suggests that the processes which can facilitate this outcome are complex and the terrain treacherous, especially since the scope for initiative by petty-bourgeois leadership in shaping peasant action is wide and such a petty bourgeoisie's role, even if potentially positive, is not readily so.

The problem of the class base for the African revolution is further complicated by the fact that the proletariat in Eastern Africa, a class that might be expected to develop an ever more self-consciously socialist project, remains small and, in its predispositions, somewhat ambiguous. The presence of such ambiguities was one of the reasons why Arrighi and I, in our earlier writings, were led to emphasize the concept of "labor aristocracy" when discussing some segments of the African proletariat. Essay 12 speaks all too briefly to the controversy to which our use of that term has given rise, while providing the opportunity for me to qualify somewhat my advocacy of such a conceptualization. The activities of the Tanzanian workers discussed in essay 9 in the previous section would be one good reason for doing so; moreover, as one's analytical and political focus shifts farther south, many of the apparent ambiguities regarding the role of Africa's working class may seem to drop away. Yet even if this brief piece does strike a note of necessary self-criticism, it is not by any means the retreat several commentators read it to be when first published. For it also reiterates some of the reasons why any form of "proletarian messianism" is still to be eschewed in contemporary Africa.

The essay on Uganda (number 13) which follows in this section is a particularly important one. It is, of course, of substantive interest, for General Amin looms large in the Western media—a constant (and quite illegitimate) point of reference for those who would demagogically cast doubts on the claims of the liberation movements farther south. For this reason, as well as by reason of solidarity with those Ugandans who are struggling to liberate themselves from such a tyranny, it is important to have an understanding of where Amin springs from: as an explicable, though not inevitable, product of the syndrome of African dependence and underdevelopment. As emphasized in the general introduction to this volume, it is also in this essay that the nature of the African petty bourgeoisie is most elaborately theorized and the diverse implications of its important role spelled out. The formulations here presented are very much "work in progress," but it does seem possible that an ongoing preoccupation with the nature of the state in Africa and with the dynamics of "petty-bourgeois politics"— both being themes which this Uganda essay attempts to elaborate upon—is a potent growth point for the scientific understanding of Africa's dependent social formations.

As the latter essay concludes, such a scientific understanding is likely to have important political implications as well, not least because the patterns of petty-bourgeois politics interpenetrate with the politics of the subordinate classes. Though left-wing fractions can sometimes emerge to prominence within the petty bourgeoisie (especially, as was seen in Part I, under the conditions provided by a full-fledged liberation struggle) the more familiar scenario is an intense and opportunistic jockeying for power within the overarching framework of continued imperial domination. In the course of rallying popular constituencies for purposes of advantage within this kind of political process, petty-bourgeois fractions have often had the effect (as in Uganda or, from Part I, as in the Zimbabwean liberation camp itself) of further politicizing various vertical divisions—ethnic, regional, religious—which cut across the possible class identifications of African workers and peasants. Obviously this kind of development can serve (alongside such more straightforward instruments as the repressive apparatus of the state) to blunt the thrust of subordinate classes into the political arena; it is a reality which renders quite complex the terrain upon which the revolutionary socialist must work in order to rally a more class-conscious constituency for fundamental change.

Yet, valuable as it is to make this point, it is also necessary to avoid the temptations of a crude class-reductionism. The interplay of class and "tribe" in particular is a subtle one, and the final essay is designed to underscore some additional aspects of the way in which ethnicity comes to the fore in the African political arena. In doing so, such an essay reinforces our awareness of the difficult challenges—and very real opportunities—which present themselves to socialists on the continent. At the same time it underscores the importance of conceptualizing more precisely the manner in which the emergence of Africa's class structure interacts with a simultaneous polarization between imperial center and dependent periphery, the coexistence of these two processes within the framework of global capitalism's penetration of the continent being often noted but not always taken sufficiently seriously. And this, in turn, refocuses our attention upon the complex—and creative—politics of the popular classes themselves, the latter being no mere passive objects for instrumentalization by the petty bourgeoisie! Such emphases thus give promise of grounding our comprehension of the class struggle ever more firmly in African realities. Fresh questions are raised, with the result that, far from providing a neat conclusion to our exploration of the postcolonial state and the revolutionary prospect in Eastern Africa, this essay quite correctly points the way forward to the vast amount of scientific work which remains to be done by Marxists in Africa.

11

AFRICAN PEASANTRIES AND REVOLUTION

In the past, many social scientists have been reluctant to utilize the term *peasant* with reference to African cultivators. More recently, a body of literature has emerged which, in seeking to theorize the most important trends in rural Africa, has found the notion of the peasantry to be a particularly illuminating one. Some brief reference to this latter emphasis, and to the rationale which sustains it, will need to be made here. But the main thrust of this paper lies elsewhere—in a discussion of the conditions (socioeconomic, ideological, organizational) under which the African peasantry, so identified, becomes a force for radical transformation of the status quo of colonialism and neocolonialism in contemporary Africa. It is worth emphasizing at the outset that the latter is no mere academic concern. In the two concrete situations which we shall explore—these being the Portuguese colony of Mozambique and the independent country of Tanzania—it is the conscious attempt to engage the peasants in precisely such revolutionary activity that has been one of the most striking features of recent political and socioeconomic developments there. In Mozambique, the success of this strategy has been crowned by the presentation of a particularly dramatic challenge to Portuguese colonial hegemony. In Tanzania, the ultimate effectiveness of that country's challenge to neocolonialism is more open to doubt, but the intense interest of

This essay was first published in *Review of African Political Economy*, no. 1 (1974).

the effort to construct a new, socialist Tanzania on a popular base of active and self-conscious "workers and peasants" cannot be denied.

Peasants and Revolution

Revolutionary theory has evinced much skepticism concerning the peasantry—a skepticism rooted in the classics of Marxism and, most dramatically, in Marx's own oft-quoted description of the peasants as being merely like a "sack of potatoes," divided and demobilized.[1] Yet peasants in the twentieth century have become a revolutionary force in ways that Marx necessarily could not predict. There are those who cling steadfastly to the classical view, of course—arguing that the proletariat, by virtue of its participation in the centralizing and collectivizing logic of modern industry, remains the sole and indispensable guarantor of genuine revolution. Those who, like Nigel Harris, press the point most fiercely, are aided in so doing by a definition of socialism (the end-product of any such genuine revolution) which excludes every existing country from that category.[2] Others, less concerned to ignore the claims of, say, a country like China to revolutionary achievement, are, concomitantly, more charitable toward the peasantry. Indeed, Malcolm Caldwell, vigorously criticizing Harris's position and making, among other points, "the simple factual assertion that the peasantry played the decisive role in the Chinese Revolution," has gone so far as to conclude:

> We may be sure that the peoples of Africa, Asia, and Latin America themselves alone can transform their own lives. Since the vast majority of these people are peasants, the future must lie in their hands, whether it accords with one's preconceived theories or not . . . In the world of today, the poor, the dissatisfied and the unprivileged are peasants: therefore "the peasants alone are revolutionary for they have nothing to lose and everything to gain."[3]

It is not necessary here to exhaust the general debate being rehearsed (and, it would seem, unduly polarized) in the exchange between Harris and Caldwell. As a first approximation, it is sufficient to remind ourselves of Trotsky's dictum: "Without a guiding organization the energy of the masses would dissipate like steam not enclosed in a piston box. But nonetheless what moves things is not the piston, or the box, but the steam."[4] For one cannot examine the course of recent history without affirming that peasants have provided much of the steam for revolutionary challenge to the status quo in this century. Why should this be so? Many Marxists emphasize that the expansion of the international capitalist system into less developed areas of the world has been such as to displace certain crucial contradictions of that system from its center to its periphery.[5] And even a growing number of non-Marxist thinkers seek for answers to such a question in an understanding of imperialism. Thus, Eric Wolf, summarizing the lessons drawn from a careful survey of peasant wars of the twentieth century, concludes that the historical experience which situates such wars "constitutes, in turn, the precipitate in the present of a great overriding cultural phenomenon, the worldwide spread and diffusion of a particular cultural system, that of North Atlantic capitalism."[6] Moreover, we shall see that it is precisely a concern with the historical emergence and further evolution of capitalist imperialism which is crucial to an identification of the peasantry (and other relevant actors) in an African setting.

Nonetheless, many misgivings expressed by Marx and others about the peasantry's likely contribution to revolution also have some validity. Parochialism cuts deep in the rural areas; the outlines of the broader exploitative environment, worldwide and territorial, which oppress them, are not easily perceived by the peasants and as a result "the aggregate of small producers" constitute themselves only with difficulty as a group capable of "a shared consciousness and joint political action as a class."[7] Even if peasant political action (rather than apathetic resignation or preoccupation with quasi-traditional involvements closer to home) is forthcoming, it may still prove either to be quite localized and isolated in its spontaneous expression, or else be forced too easily into channels of mere regional and ethnic self-assertiveness by a territorial leadership which divides in order that it may continue to rule. Moreover, most twentieth-century revolutionaries aim at some kind of socialist transformation of the existing system, this being, ultimately, the only effective response to imperialism. The peasants' temptation to seek a resolution of the contradictions which confront them either by shoring up "traditional" aspects of the peasant economy or by attempting "petty-bourgeois" solutions which would further service their isolation—a redistribution of land designed to guarantee their own individual tenure and possible economic aggrandizement on that basis, for example—may make them a risky ally for such an enterprise.

This seems all the more likely to be the case when one considers the findings of Wolf and of Hamza Alavi—that it is the middle peasant rather than the poorest of peasants who is "initially the most militant element of the peasantry."[8] Yet counterrevolutionary results are not inevitable. Alavi does observe that "when the movement in the countryside advances to a revolutionary stage they [the middle peasants] may move away from the revolutionary movement" since "their social perspective is limited by their class position." Nonetheless, he suggests that this is only true "unless their fears are allayed and they are drawn into the process of co-operative endeavour." Moreover, poorer peasants, who have an even greater stake in structural transformation, gradually can become mobilized for action as well—and carry the revolutionary process further.[9] Indeed, what is demonstrated by the introduction of various qualifications to the more roseate picture of the peasantry painted by Caldwell is merely the need to avoid falling back on romantic illusions about the inevitable and unequivocal spontaneity of peasant involvement in revolution. It becomes clear that if peasant action is to service such a revolution—to manifest full confidence and a sense of efficacy, to acquire effectively national focus, and to set in train a comprehensive transformation of society—political work must come to mediate it and help to define its thrust.

We return by this route to Trotsky's metaphor: a "piston box" is also necessary in order to harness the steam of peasant discontent. Again, one of Wolf's formulations is suggestive: "Peasants often harbor a deep sense of injustice, but this sense of injustice must be given shape and expression in organization before it can become active on the political scene; and it is obvious that not every callow agitator will find welcome hearing in village circles, traditionally suspicious of outsiders. " Like Wolf, we must be "greatly aware of the importance of groups which mediate between the peasants and the larger society of which he forms a part." However, this emphasis too would be misleading if the capacity of the peasants to play an active role in the process of politicizing their grievances were to be understated. In fact, the vital contradiction between organization/leadership on the one hand, and participation/spontaneity on the other, is not one that can be evaded or suppressed—both aspects are essential. If effective methods of political work are used, it is merely a contradiction which can be resolved, over time, in a manner that contributes to further revolutionary advance.

In recent times, "people's war" has been the technique which has most satisfactorily realized this goal, this effective blending of both leadership from above and spontaneity from below. Selden has stated this point clearly with reference to Vietnam and China, and his formulation is worth quoting at length.[10]

Out of the ashes of military strife which enveloped China and Vietnam in protracted wars of liberation emerged a radically new vision of man and society and a concrete approach to development. Built on foundations of participation and community action which challenge elite domination, this approach offers hope of more *humane* forms of development and of effectively overcoming the formidable barriers to the transformation of peasant societies. In the base areas and consolidated war zones in which the movement enjoyed its fullest growth, the redefinition of community began in the resistance to a foreign invader and continued in the struggle to overcome domestic problems of poverty and oppression. People's war implies more than a popular guerrilla struggle for national independence; it impinges directly on the full scope of rural life. In the course of a people's war, local communities defined in response to the imperatives of defense and social change may be effectively integrated in national movements. The very intensity of the wartime experience contributes to rapid development of consciousness and organization. In people's war peasants cease to be the passive pawns of landlords and officials or to fatalistically accept the verdict of a harsh natural environment. Where the primary resource of insurgent movements is man [*sic*], and where active commitment is the *sine qua non* of success, the sharing of common hardships and hopes creates powerful bonds among resisters and between leaders and led. In the new institutions which emerge locally in the course of the resistance, to an unprecedented degree peasants begin to secure active control of their economic and political destinies.

We shall see that this is precisely the pattern that has emerged in Mozambique in the course of the liberation struggle against Portuguese colonialism. In Tanzania the situation is more complicated. There the leadership (or one section of it) has also made some effort to forge "new bonds of unity in which the very definitions of leader and led are recast and the beginnings of a new social base are created." But it is doing so in cold blood as it were—from within the framework of established structures, rather than in the heat of a convulsive upheaval. It is obvious that the making of a peasant-based revolution under such circumstances presents anomalies—and, as we shall see, it is indeed proving to be a difficult task.

African Peasantries

Who are the peasants in Tanzania and Mozambique, then? Indeed, "are African cultivators to be called peasants?" as a well-known article on rural Africa once asked.[11] It is worth noting that this has been a subject of some controversy in the literature, though it is a controversy which easily degenerates into a mere word game. In the first instance, the debate has seemed most concerned with the nature of "traditional" Africa; moreover, the latter has all too often been ossified and discussed by social scientists as some kind of "anthropological present" in a manner which can foreclose discussion of the real present of colonialism and neocolonialism. Even with reference to pre-contact Africa, there may have been more peasant-like dimensions of the rural situation than has sometimes been assumed.[12] But the more immediately relevant argument of a number of recent writers is that, whatever the case for an earlier Africa, the incursion of imperialism and particularly of formal colonialism has gradually forced a large proportion of rural dwellers in Africa to take on the characteristics of a peasantry. As Woods and I have argued elsewhere,[13] this way of construing the majority of rural Africans is important, firstly because it fits neatly within the kind of broad analytical framework which seems best suited to identifying and explaining the overall patterns of change and development in contemporary Africa. Secondly, the concept quite accurately pinpoints characteristics of rural Africans which bear a family resemblance to peasant characteristics as identified elsewhere; it thus enables students of Africa, and political activists there, to collect data and theorize experience alongside others concerned about the problematic of the peasantry in other parts of the world. These two points can be briefly documented.

The key historical factor in defining the shape of contemporary Africa has been its forced insertion, as a dependency, within the broader Europe-centered imperial system.[14] And, as Woods and I wrote, "Despite the existence of some pre-figurings of a peasant class in earlier periods, it is more fruitful to view the creation of an African peasantry . . . as being primarily the result of the interaction between an international capitalist economic system and traditional socio-economic systems, within the context of territorially defined colonial political systems." Ken Post has described the process of "peasantization" in West Africa in similar terms, citing Trotsky's "law of uneven and combined development" and emphasizing the economic, the political, and the cultural dimensions of the process which subordinates "communal cultivators and such pre-colonial peasants as there were" to that broader system:

> Whatever their differences, it is true to say that all the colonial powers in Western Africa greatly extended the market principle to the point where the impersonal forces of the world market dominated the lives of millions and imposed a state where none had been before or to supersede indigenous ones. The African quest for western education and the issue of assimilation amply demonstrate the presence of a new "great" culture. It would appear, then, that many of the conditions for the existence of a peasantry were suddenly created, but from outside and quite independently of the processes of internal differentiation in origin, though the internal factors had important influences upon the final form of these conditions.[15]

In validating this perspective, Post is particularly concerned to demonstrate that "surplus" is extracted from the African rural population within such a structure by the "levying of taxes and other dues by the state," for example, and by unequal terms of exchange for agricultural produce.[16] Finally, Derman has made closely related points—with reference in particular to the role of the state in peasantizing cultivators—when he criticizes the views of those anthropologists who continue to withhold the term "peasantry" from such rural dwellers and instead see them as "subsistence-oriented cultivators in the process of becoming farmers"! In Derman's view, this ignores the fact that "the state—both colonial and post-colonial—remains highly exploitative of the rural peasants or cultivators. African peasants are coming to form an increasingly subordinate segment of the population, a trend which began during the colonial era." This too is a suggestive perception—and is entirely accurate.

Balancing the fact of such structural subordination within the wider political and economic systems of Africa is a second feature, one which is equally necessary in order to confirm the peasant character of such cultivators (particularly in comparative terms)—"the importance to the peasantry of the family economy." Woods and I wrote:

> Thus peasants are those whose ultimate security and subsistence lies in their having certain rights in land and in the labour of family members on the land, but who are involved, through rights and obligations, in a wider economic system which includes the participation of non-peasants. The fact that for peasants ultimate security and subsistence rests upon maintaining rights in land and rights in family labour [is] an important determinant shaping and restricting their social action. It is also the characteristic which peasants share with "primitive agriculturalists," though not with capitalist farmers. For while the capitalist farmer may *appear* to depend upon his land, and even upon family labor in some cases, he is not *forced* to rely upon these in the last instance; he has alternative potential sources of security and investment. What the peasant does share, in general terms, with the capitalist farmer (though not with the primitive agriculturalists) is his integration into a complex social structure characterized by stratification and economic differentiation.

In Africa it is also possible to keep the term "peasant" flexible enough to include pastoralists since they "are subject to the same kind of political and economic forces as their predominantly agricultural brethren and since their productive economy (in as much as it involves rights to, and control over, family herds) is based on a similar kind of homestead principle." And, more controversially, to include migrant laborers. The latter inclusion is justified by the stake which such migrants retain in, precisely, the family economy. While some peasants will seek to guarantee the surplus demanded by the broader social structure by means of attaching a cash-crop component to their basically subsistence-oriented cultivation, others will seek to do so by periods of time spent laboring in mines, plantations, and urban centers. But they will do so without relinquishing their family's claim to an agricultural stake in the rural community. The logic of the migrant's position within the overall system remains same as that of the cash-cropper—at least in the short run—while both remain peasants.

Note the latter point. It is important, for the logic of continued capitalist penetration should be, of course, to phase out the African peasantry even as it creates it. At the one end of the spectrum peasants who start to generate surpluses in the sphere of cash cropping may become, in time, capitalist farmers. And migrants (as well as those who start to sell their labor power locally to supplement their subsistence agricultural activities) may become, in time, more definitively proletarianized. In short, these two tendencies "can chip away at the peasantry, pulling it in different directions." At the same time, the pace at which this apparent "logic" now works itself out must not be overestimated. The reality of Africa's continuing dependence means that peripheral capitalism in Africa tends to produce merely further underdevelopment rather than a total capitalist transformation of countries there. As a result, and as Colin Leys has written in demonstrating the increased rate of peasantization in Kenya (itself one of the most seemingly dynamic of dependencies in Africa):

Analytically speaking, the peasantry in Africa may be best seen as a
transitional class, in between the period of primitive cultivators
living in independent communities and that of capitalist development in which peasants are restratified into capitalists and proletarians; but under the conditions of growth of neo-colonialism it
seems clear that in Kenya at least the stage during which the
peasantry itself goes through a process of development, and develops its own pattern of relationships with the elite, may be fairly
prolonged. [17]

It could be argued, therefore, that the African peasantry is not
composed of peasants quite like those in earlier, historically more
progressive, capitalist systems (as analyzed by Barrington Moore)
"over whom the wave of progress is about to roll." [18] Perhaps this
will give them more of an opportunity to shape their own futures. [19]

Two main points follow from the analysis thus far presented.
There is a peasantry in Africa—large numbers of rural Africans
caught, by international capitalism and colonial and postcolonial
state structures, between subsistence cultivation and the fates
which capitalism might eventually hold in store for them. In this
reality of common "peasanthood," there is the potential ground
for "shared consciousness and shared political action" against the
broader structures which have come to dominate and exploit
them. The multinational corporations and the national elites
(along with their representatives in the rural areas themselves)
would be the legitimate targets of action to redress such a situation. It is in this reality that there lies the promise of a peasant
revolution and possibly the seeds of socialism—a promise to the
analysis of which we will return in the next section.

But what we have said so far also suggests that there are
peasantries in Africa—these representing the wide range of variation in the way the peasantized have become involved in the
broader imperial system. Or, in terms used by Lionel Cliffe, the
presence of varying "articulations of modes of production": different ways in which "historically and geographically specific and
varied modes" of production in Africa have "articulated," or
interacted, with "the increasingly dominant capitalist mode."
This variation means, in turn, as Woods and I wrote, that

. . . in each territory we can distinguish a number of peasantries who are differentiated according to locality—some localities being labour exporting, some food-crop exporting, some cash-crop exporting and some with varying proportions of each . . . [In addition] the dynamic of capitalist development tends to introduce a further element which cuts across the differentiation of peasants by locality with a differentiation based on the degree of involvement in the cash economy. This involves . . . the possible movements towards proletarianization of migrant labour on the one hand and towards capitalist agriculture on the other.

Since, unlike certain other parts of the globe, African territories lacked some broadly comparable precapitalist structure (e.g., feudalism) spread over a large area, but instead comprised an extraordinary range of precapitalist social formations, it seems probable that the range of "articulation of modes of production" which springs from capitalist incursion is, if anything, more varied in Africa than elsewhere. To elicit even a roughly common response and common level of consciousness from "peasants" so diversified is concomitantly difficult.

Revolution in Africa

What of revolution, then? In the first section I quoted Malcolm Caldwell's general conclusion to his argument concerning "the revolutionary role of the peasantry": "In the world of to-day, the poor, the dissatisfied and the unprivileged are peasants. Therefore 'the peasants alone are revolutionary, for they have nothing to lose and everything to gain.'" Significantly, the quotation which Caldwell uses here is from Fanon—and Fanon was writing about Africa.[20] But Fanon's enthusiasm is not fully shared by others—the late Amilcar Cabral, one of Africa's outstanding revolutionaries, for example. "Obviously," he says, "the group with the greatest interest in the struggle is the peasantry, given the nature of the various different societies in Guinea . . . and the various degrees of exploitation to which they are subjected." However, this cannot merely be left to rest there, for "the question is not simply one of objective interest." Cabral then proceeds to broach one key problem which is of enormous importance for us, as we are a country of peasants, and that is the problem of whether or not the peasantry represents the main revolutionary force. A distinction must be drawn between a physical force and a revolutionary force; physically, the peasantry is a great force in Guinea; it is almost the whole of the population, it controls the nation's wealth, it is the peasantry which produces; but we know from experience what trouble we had convincing the peasantry to fight.[21]

Leys, the academic observer, states a related point even more forcefully in concluding his analysis of Kenya and of revolutionary prospects there. For "as writers such as Moore, Alavi and Wolf have shown, it generally requires a rare combination of tyranny and misery to produce a peasant revolt, let alone a peasant revolution; short of which the clientelist political structures characteristic of peasant society have a resilience that can easily be underestimated."

Many of the grounds for skepticism about the revolutionary vocation of the peasantry which were asserted in general terms in the first section apply to Africa—in some instances with even greater force. In many parts of the world, rural dwellers are, in effect, peasantized twice over, first by the workings of some form of feudal system and secondly by the further structural subordination which arises from the insertion of that feudal system within a colonial-cum-international-capitalist framework. However, exploitation and subordination are rendered more intangible in many (though of course not all) African settings because of the absence of landlords and quasi-feudal relationships at the point of direct production. This can have the result of depersonalizing and distancing the overall exploitative system, thus diffusing discontent.[22] Secondly, population pressure on the land has not been as great in rural Africa, relatively speaking, as on other continents, and the visible threat to peasant status (especially to prospects for guaranteeing subsistence) from that quarter not quite so pressing.

Thirdly, while it is true that few but the most isolated of Africans remain untouched by the peasantization process, the unfulfilled nature of this process, its unevenness and its relative recentness, has left standing, perhaps more firmly than elsewhere, important vestiges of precapitalist social networks and cultural preoccupations—particularly a range of variations on kinship relationships and upon the theme of ethnic identification—which mesh closely with the survival of the subsistence agricultural core of the system. At the same time some of those who do begin to break more definitively with the attributes of peasanthood do so under the influence of burgeoning pettycapitalist aspirations, rather than as moved by notions of the collective improvement of the rural dwellers' lot. In making links with the world beyond the village, such elements may find their most natural allies among the new elites who control state power.

But this—the aligning of itself with energetic capitalists-in the-making in the villages—is only one way in which the neocolonial state defuses the possibility of peasant class consciousness. Equally important, the quasi-traditional attributes of peasanthood can also be warped in such a way as to service the functioning of Africa's neocolonial systems by those who benefit from them. The key, as Leys has argued, lies in the politics of patron-client relationships, broadly defined. In the first instance, peasants can be tied into the system by links with others above them in the hierarchy (these often being more privileged kinsmen) and by such small benefits as trickle down to them in this manner. In addition, politicians operating in the national arena have often come to play what is, in effect, a similar role over a broader terrain—that of superpatrons with their tribes as their clients. For "tribalism" (the politicization of ethnicity which is all too characteristically a pathology of dependent Africa) does not spring primarily from the bare fact of the existence of cultural differences between peoples. Rather, it has been teased into life, first by the divide-and-rule tactics of colonialism and by the uneven development in the economic sphere which colonialism also facilitates, and secondly by the ruling petty bourgeoisie of the postcolonial period. The latter, too, seek to divide and rule—better from their point of view that peasants should conceive the national pie as being divided, competitively, between regions and tribes, rather than (as is in fact much more clearly the case) between classes. Moreover, as individuals, they are moved to mobilize tribal constituencies behind themselves, using this as a bargaining counter in the struggle for power against other members of the ruling circles.[23]

Can African peasants come to be something more than mere pawns in the unattractive game of underdevelopment? Certainly peasants have not always been passive elements in recent African history. Their discontent often flared into overt action, revealing in the process ironies which Fanon has pinpointed (and Kilson and others have documented):

> What is the reaction of the nationalist parties to this eruption of peasant masses into the nationalist struggle? . . . As a whole they treat this new element as a sort of manna from heaven, and pray to goodness that it'll go on falling. They make the most of the manna, but do not attempt to organize the rebellion. They don't send leaders into the countryside to educate the people politically, or to increase their awareness or put the struggle on to a higher level. All they do is to hope that, carried onwards by its own momentum, the action of the people will not come to a standstill. There is no contamination of the rural movement by the urban movement; each develops according to its own dialectic.[24]

Of course, the very diversity of peasantries also makes the "putting of the struggle on a higher level" a crucial necessity. For different peasantries have felt, immediately, different kinds of grievances against the colonial system. The nationalist movements described by Fanon tended merely to accumulate the support of such aggrieved peasantries around the lowest common denominator of a demand for political independence, rather than generalizing their grievances into a critique of imperial and capitalist reality more adequately defined. The leadership elements, so soon to inherit the established structures, had little interest in encouraging the development of a broader vision, of allaying fears and drawing peasants "into the process of co-operative endeavour" (as Alavi suggested to be one possible denouement of peasant upsurge effectively politicized).

Instead, the mere Africanization of peripheral capitalism proceeded apace. Yet, as Nyerere has argued, this has had little, ultimately, to offer the vast mass of the peasantry:

> . . . sooner or later, the people will lose their enthusiasm and will look upon the independence government as simply another new

ruler which they should avoid as much as possible. Provided it has been possible to avoid any fundamental upset in their traditional economic and social conditions, they will then sink back into apathy—until the next time someone is able to convince them that their own efforts can lead to an improvement in their lives.[25]

Moreover, this latter possibility suggested by Nyerere has occasionally become a reality. The Congo of the mid-1960s providing an example—glimpsed in Pierre Mulele's activities in the Kwilu and in the People's Republic of the Eastern Congo. Of the latter Gerard-Libois has written:

> . . . the insurrections which led to the creation of the People's Republic were first of all a revolt of impoverished and exploited peasants for whom the enemy was not only the foreign colonialist but above all those Congolese who had monopolized all the fruits of independence, and also those policemen, administrators and even teachers who served the new class and sought to imitate its style of life . . . The rebellion was . . . for all its limitations, the hope of a new independence, fundamentally different from the first, and through which the wealth of the Congo would accrue to the poorest and in which a new, genuinely decolonized African society would come into being.[26]

Such activities easily lost focus, and the character of the Mobutist denouement in the Congo (now Zaire) is well known. Whether more recent attempts to revive a revolutionary challenge in that country (seen in the work of the Congolese Marxist Revolutionary Party, for example) will be any more successful remains to be seen, but something of the nature of the "steam" which does exist at the base of contemporary African societies could be discerned in Kwilu. In addition, broad trends like the growth of population pressure may come, over time, to further exacerbate such tensions in rural Africa.[27]

At base, then, the contradiction between the peasantry and established structures, worldwide and continental/territorial, remains. We quoted Cabral at the outset of this section. It is worth continuing that quotation, drawn from his analysis of the Guinean peasantry: "All the same, in certain parts of the country and among certain groups we found a warm welcome, even right from the start. In other groups and in other areas all this had to be won." Nevertheless, it has been won: in Guinea-Bissau the peasants have become an active agency for a deep-cutting revolution. Of course, the overall structure within which the achievement of Cabral and his PAIGC has been realized is a particularly anomalous one. Portuguese "ultra-colonialism," even more cruel and unyielding than other colonialisms in Africa, provided precisely that "rare combination of tyranny and misery" which Leys mentioned as being an important prerequisite of a peasant revolt. Moreover, it is obvious that anti-colonial nationalism could be used as an initial ideological rallying cry for revolution in Guinea much more unequivocally than in a postcolonial situation; in Nyerere's words, it is "another thing when you have to remove your own people from the position of exploiters."[28] Yet Cabral emphasizes again and again that, despite even these "advantages" in Guinea, hard *political work* has still been necessary in order to realize a peasant base for struggle. How much more is this likely to be the case elsewhere in Africa?

Cabral describes the nature of such political work carefully and suggestively in his writings. Particularly important have been the cadres who came to play the role of catalyst of the Guinean revolution. They were drawn initially from the petty-bourgeois stratum and from semi-proletarianized urban hangers-on, beginning their work as what Gorz has termed an "external vanguard" vis-à-vis the peasants. But they have become, with time and with the effective resolution of the contradiction between leadership and participation, much more of an "internal vanguard,"[29] a development which has also meant the sharing of authority with new leadership elements thrown up by the newly mobilized peasants themselves as the peasants' own confidence and commitment to the struggle has grown. Obviously, a number of further questions arise from this: How are the *different* peasantries likely to be geared into such struggle (note that some provided a "warm welcome" to Cabral and his colleagues, others not)? What kind of "piston box" of organization and ideology, constructed by the revolutionaries themselves, can most effectively facilitate this process? By turning to an examination of the situation in Mozambique, similar in certain important respects to that in Guinea, we can begin (though only begin) to answer these questions.

Mozambique

The two questions just mentioned are not separate, however. The Mozambican case demonstrates the importance of examining both the nature of the peasantry as a potential base for revolution and the nature of the presumed revolutionary organization—in this case, the Mozambique Liberation Front (FRELIMO)—in considering recent developments there. But it is probably even more essential to examine the dialectical relationship established between the two—between peasantry and political organization—for it is this relationship which has defined the forward momentum of the Mozambique revolution.

That the peasants are an essential base there can be no doubt. Eduardo Mondlane, the first president of FRELIMO, who was assassinated by the Portuguese in 1969, made this point clearly:

> Both the agitation of the intellectuals and the strikes of the urban labour force were doomed to failure, because in both cases it was the action only of a tiny isolated group. For a government like Portugal's, which has set its face against democracy and is prepared to use extremes of brutality to crush opposition, it is easy to deal with such isolated pockets of resistance. It was the very failure of these attempts, however, and the fierce repression which followed, that made this clear and prepared the ground for more widely based action. The urban population of Mozambique amounts altogether to less than half a million. A nationalist movement without firm roots in the countryside could never hope to succeed.[30]

More recently, Marcellino dos Santos, FRELIMO's vice-president, has described that countryside along lines which are essentially similar to those elaborated upon in this paper. Beginning with a juxtaposition of "two societies" in Mozambique, that which "contains capitalist relationships" and that of "the traditional type—a sort of subsistence economy," he proceeds to dissolve this distinction in his subsequent discussion.

> But these two societies do not exist in isolation from one another; they are entirely linked. Why? Where do these people who work on the plantations come from? All those people who work within the capitalist sector come from the traditional sector. And most of them do not remain permanently outside the traditional sector because,

for instance, many of them go to work on the plantations for a maximum of two years and they then come back to the village and to the traditional system. So that is the main link—going back and forth. Then there are those people who do not become absorbed into the capitalist system but who are nevertheless related to it. For instance, the people who produce for themselves must sell their produce in the market, mainly food like grain, cashew nuts. They are forced into the market system to find the cash for colonial-imposed taxes and to purchase commodities which they do not produce themselves. So these two societies are linked and on many levels the persons comprising the two societies are the same.[31]

It will be readily apparent that dos Santos is here discussing what we have seen to be the African peasantry.

It has been an African peasantry pitchforked into existence and sustained in its "transitional" state by methods even more brutal than those employed by other colonialisms. Mondlane documents many of these methods in his book, discussing cash-cropping peasantries for whom the enforced cultivation of cotton and the rigging of government price schedules have introduced great hardship, and labor-supplying peasantries, even more mercilessly exploited over the years by a complex system of virtual forced labor. It is precisely the systematic nature of such repressive practices that led Perry Anderson to speak of "Portuguese ultra-colonialism."[32] Small wonder that peasants periodically had given expression to their grievances even before the mounting of a comprehensive political challenge to colonialism. Thus, in Mondlane's words, "some developments in the countryside which took place in the period just preceding the formation of FRELIMO were of enormous importance." In the northern region around Mueda, for example, such activity centered upon efforts to organize a cooperative and obtain better terms for produce delivered to the colonial government; when peasants demonstrated peacefully in support of this program at Mueda town in 1960, five hundred were shot down by the Portuguese.

Grievances there certainly have been and continue to be. Nor does it require any very elaborate proof to demonstrate that they provide tinder for peasant action. Nonetheless, my own experience in the liberated areas of Mozambique in 1972 permits me to speak with some added confidence on the subject.[33] Traveling among the people of Tete province with FRELIMO guerrillas, I had the opportunity to attend a number of political meetings and to hear the themes stressed both by FRELIMO militants and by ordinary peasants. A pinpointing of the economic linkages mentioned above—forced labor, a prejudicial system of cultivation—was joined with a precise enumeration of the abuses directly perpetrated by the Portuguese administration. Of the latter, Portuguese taxation was a theme given particular prominence, its historically heavy role in the daily life of peasants being elucidated by FRELIMO cadres alongside an explanation of its importance in sustaining Portugal's ability to support economically its continued military presence. In effect, Mozambican peasants seemed themselves prepared to validate both Post's and Derman's earlier emphases—economic exploitation on the one hand, state power on the other—in defining their essentially subordinate position within previously established structures.

FRELIMO personnel also hinted at the existence of a range of variation in the response of different peasantries to revolutionary imperatives. In fact, it was obvious to me that this has been the subject of much serious analysis by the movement, since its strategy is precisely to establish deep political roots among the people of a given area by means of careful political work prior to launching armed activity. For this to be done, considerable knowledge of the stresses and strains in the local community under consideration is necessary. So much became particularly clear from discussions which I held with cadres who had long been active in such preparatory political work (as well as in the subsequent tasks of constructing FRELIMO-type social institutions in areas once they have been liberated). But, necessarily, concrete and detailed information on these matters was not forthcoming. It was suggested to me that the work of mobilization had gone much more easily in Tete than in Cabo Delgado and Niassa "because the people had had more experience of exploitation"— especially of the push of labor to other parts in Mozambique and to Rhodesia and South Africa.[34] This might seem to be evidence in support of Barnett's thesis that the "labour-exporting peasantry" has a "relatively high revolutionary potential" compared with the "cash-cropping peasantry" and the "marginal-sub-sistence peasantry."[35] But one cannot be categorical in these matters. Certainly the revolution has also advanced dramatically in Cabo and in Niassa, where the latter types of peasantry are much more prominent, as well as in the cash-cropping areas of Tete itself. Similarly, in more immediately political terms, some chiefs seem to have reconciled themselves easily to the novel situation created by FRELIMO's presence, presenting few obsta-cles to the political involvement of "their people" on an entirely new basis, while others have defended themselves and Por-tuguese overrule with vigor. Historians will one day have impor-tant work to do in reconstructing more precisely such realities and the reasons for this range of variation.

Peasant "spontaneity" has been important, then, and will probably become all the more important as peasants both re-spond negatively to such new and desperate last-ditch Portuguese strategies as the enforced strategic-hamlet program and respond positively to the promise which life in the liberated areas increas-ingly exemplifies for them. Nonetheless, peasant spontaneity has not been a sufficient driving force for revolution in Mozambique. It has also taken an effective movement—FRELIMO—to bring the potential peasant base into meaningful and effective exis-tence. I have discussed elsewhere the evolution of FRELIMO itself, which has determined its character as a revolutionary movement. It was not inevitably so: "All those features charac-teristic of the brand of nationalism which has facilitated false decolonization elsewhere on the continent have been present in the Mozambican context."[36] There were elements in FRELIMO who were quite prone to aim primarily at their own elitist and entrepreneurial aggrandizement under the guise of nationalism and to refuse to integrate themselves with the peasant masses, preferring instead to demobilize the latter with ethnic and racial sloganeering.

However, from the point of view of conservative members of the petty-bourgeois leadership of the Mozambican independence struggle, there has been just one flaw in all this: in the context of a genuine liberation struggle this kind of nationalism, quite liter-ally, *does not work* as it did for African leadership groups elsewhere on the continent. Portuguese intransigence meant that a stronger link with the people had to be forged in order to undertake effective guerrilla warfare. It was with this reality in mind that Sebastião Mabote, FRELIMO's chief of operations (with whom I traveled in Mozambique), could say that the Portuguese had given Mozambique an opportunity other African states had missed—the opportunity to have a revolution. And that Eduardo Mondlane could say, shortly before his death, and only half-jokingly, that it would almost be a pity if the struggle were to succeed too quickly, "we are learning so much!"

Learning, for example, the necessity of enlisting the peasants more actively in conscious support of the movement so that they would willingly undertake such *positive* tasks as maintaining the secrecy of FRELIMO activities in the face of colonialist pressure, as carriage of material and supply of produce, direct enlistment in the army, reconnaissance, and militia support work. But the peasants will not embrace such tasks if the leadership does not appear to present a genuine and less exploitative alternative than does the colonial system itself. They thus exercise a kind of passive veto over the movement and over those who lead it. Moreover, the establishment of participatory institutions throughout the liberated areas has enabled the peasant also to play an active role in helping to arbitrate the issue of the movement's direction. This fact became particularly important in 1968–69 when the contestation within FRELIMO's petty-bourgeois leadership—this group drawn initially from classes like those cited by Cabral with reference to Guinea—reached its boiling point. Then the progressive elements closest to the popular base of the struggle carried the day for their conception of the direction which the movement should take.

The popular base was significant. At the Congress of 1968 it was the delegates representing the people in the rural areas and those representing the army working inside the country who supported Mondlane; similarly, in 1969 when Simango broke with the movement, his defection found little or no echo in the liberated areas. It became clear that it was those who could work with the peasants as cadres—resolving in their own methods of political and educational work the contradiction between leadership and peasants' participation—who had been able to consolidate their positions within the movement while others dropped by the wayside. It was also such cadres who could be expected to carry the revolution forward. For in the very process of this contestation the movement was encouraged to develop a new ideology, to move from "primitive nationalism," as Marcellino dos Santos has termed it, to "revolutionary nationalism."

In short, the popular, peasant base of the struggle has become the key both to FRELIMO's military success and to its own internal clarity as a revolutionary movement. And this, in turn, has encouraged its cadres to return to the people with even more searching solutions for the problems of the peasantry: not merely genuine democratic involvement at village, circle, district, and regional levels, but also a comprehensive and practical program of socioeconomic transformation.

> In our case the necessity to define a revolutionary ideology with greater precision emerged when we started to build the liberated areas, to engage ourselves in national reconstruction. As always, the task of building a society economically poses the problem of the type of production and distribution, and especially who is going to benefit from what the society produces. This life process also raises more sharply than in the classroom the deeper question of the type of ideology to embrace. So to summarize, there comes a stage when it becomes clear why everybody in the nation should accept the idea that the main aim of the struggle is to advance the interests of the working people. In the field of organizing the people we follow collectivistic ways as is the case, for example, with our co-operative movement in the liberated areas. [Marcellino dos Santos]

It is precisely here that peasants begin to be drawn "into the process of co-operative endeavour" (Alavi). The further radicalization of the nationalist movement, and the need to consolidate its rural base, create this kind of momentum. In the words of Samora Machel, FRELIMO's president:

> . . . we leaders, cadres, fighters and militants must work hard to make the masses adopt and live by the collective spirit, using collective methods of production, which will make it possible to enhance the spirit of collective living, thereby increasing the sense of unity, discipline and organization. Adopting a collective consciousness in

work means renouncing individualism and considering that all the cultivated plots belong to us, that all the granaries and houses are ours, the people's. It means that I must unite with others in a co-operative, a production brigade. We will cultivate, harvest and stand guard together, and together we will protect that which belongs not to me or you, but to us. The field is not mine or yours, but ours. The pupil in the school, the soldier in the base and the patient and the nurse in the hospital all have collective consciousness. No one looks upon the school, the base or the hospital as their private property, and everyone therefore takes an enthusiastic interest in advancing the work in the school, base and hospital. As a result, progress is made, the work advances and the enemy cannot so easily attack. Where there is collective spirit we are more organized, there is better discipline and a proper division of labour. There is also more initiative, a greater degree of sacrifice and we learn more, produce more and fight better, with more determination.[37]

This step is in some ways more difficult than laying the initial bases of armed struggle. Joaquim Chissano of FRELIMO suspects that "peasants are generally rather conservative and you have to go step by step. In our case there are traditional ways of cooperation, such as mutual help, and at the first stage we encourage them. Later we establish district committees to administer the area, and groups within this framework to look after agriculture. In their discussions within these committees, little by little the members come to understand the benefits of working collectively."[38] In other words, given the quality of FRELIMO cadres and the general participative atmosphere in the liberated areas, striking results can be achieved. When, for example, I visited one village inside Mozambique where this process had been underway for only a year or two, I discovered a division of labor which incorporated a significant proportion of collectively farmed fields, work on these being recorded in a logbook against eventual distribution of the proceeds. I found metalworkers and basketmakers, who had originally worked as mini-entrepreneurs in the village, now working as part of this collective division of labor, their time spent also being recorded in the village book. Such dramatic developments may eventually inspire social scientists to write books like *Fanshen;* for the present we must rely on twentieth-century versions of travelers' tales. But the latter evidence is impressive and does begin to suggest that in such a peasantry, increasingly well organized and now working self-consciously against various forms of exploitation, there can be seen some guarantee of the continued forward momentum of the Mozambican revolution, even after independence has been won. This is also the underlying thrust of dos Santos' comment in his recent interview:

> I accept that [communal effort] is partly made easier by the demands of war. But does that mean that once we have independence the approach will be changed? In the particular conditions of fighting against Portuguese colonialism, revolutionary attitudes are not only possible but necessary. If we do not follow collectivist attitudes we will not be able to face the enemy successfully. In this sense it is true to say that the internal dynamic of the struggle is such that the conditions generate collectivist thinking. But one should also say that even if the origins of such attitudes are partly pragmatic, it can, nevertheless, provide a basis for the growth of real social revolution. There is certainly a strong possibility that in the course of the collectivist effort a situation is created from which it will be difficult to withdraw. If our organization maintains a true revolutionary leadership, the special circumstances of the process of our liberation open up real possibilities for an advance from liberation to revolution.

How to make certain that this is achieved? "The main defence must be to popularize the revolutionary aims and to create such a situation that if for one reason or another at some future time some people start trying to change these aims, they will meet with resistance from the masses."

Tanzania

For Tanzania, the future is now. In consequence, that country reveals much more clearly some of the problems of peasant-based structural transformation. The absence of "tyranny and misery" of the proportions offered by Portuguese colonialism means that those features which tend to divide and to differentiate the peasantry become far more prominent aspects of the terrain of struggle than in Mozambique. At the same time, the leadership which has emerged in Tanzania has not been moved to cleanse and rededicate itself to anything like the extent of that in Mozambique. Despite the Arusha Declaration and *Mwongozo* (the TANU Guidelines of 1971), it is the more conservative wing of the petty bourgeoisie which seems increasingly to be consolidating itself, with the result that the cadre-based methods of work which might serve to crystallize and focus peasant discontent and positive aspirations are not so well developed. From both points of view, Tanzania falls short; rather than a dialectic being established between leaders and led which reinforces forward movement, the gap between them seems to be growing.

Still, what is striking about Tanzania is that it can be discussed in these terms at all. In most of independent Africa the break between nationalist parties and peasantry was of a kind described above by Fanon, often from a point even prior to the winning of independence. In Tanzania, on the other hand, an attempt has been made to resolve such a contradiction within the framework of the country's policy of "socialism and self-reliance." "Peasants" were to become (with "workers") a crucial agency for transforming established structures from within—for a "quiet revolution," in effect. I have traced elsewhere the background to this attempt, and some of its continuing strengths and weaknesses.[39] Here it is relevant to note three themes which have defined the rural dimensions of Tanzania's socialist project.

First, there has been President Nyerere's oft-repeated emphasis on the necessity that, territorially, the masses—"the workers and peasants"—become responsible for their own socialist development, distrusting their leaders and holding them firmly to account.[40] Though not always clearly defined in the language of class struggle, the point was thus being made that *the peasantry* has an interest in confronting those elements who might work to sustain its continued subordination.[41] Moreover, this aspiration found some reinforcement in subsequent policy initiatives. *Mwongozo* further called upon the people to check their leaders.[42] It is true that this invitation was, in the first instance, taken up most actively by the workers in the urban areas; nonetheless, *Mwongozo* confirmed the general emphasis upon the peasants' own positive role. And the whole process of decentralizing planning processes closer to the villages in 1971-73, however much disfigured in practice, was designed to redress a situation where "to the mass of the people, power is still something wielded by others." With decentralization, "more and more people must be trusted with responsibility—that is its whole purpose."[43]

Second, there has been a desire to preempt the further development of capitalist relations of production in the rural areas themselves:

> . . . as land becomes more scarce we shall find ourselves with a farmers' class and a labourers' class, with the latter being unable either to work for themselves or to receive a full return for the contribution they are making to total output. They will become a "rural proletariat" depending on the decisions of other men for their existence, and subject in consequence to all the subservience, social and economic inequality, and insecurity, which such a position involves.
>
> Thus we still have in this country a predominantly peasant society in which farmers work for themselves and their families and are helped and protected from exploitation by co-operative marketing arrangements [sic]. Yet the present trend is away from the extended family production and society unity and towards the development of a class system. It is this kind of development which would be inconsistent with the growth of a socialist Tanzania in which all citizens could be assured of human dignity and equality, and in which all were able to have a decent and constantly improving life for themselves and their children.[44]

In this respect, too, socialism was seen as a way out of the peasant condition. By becoming "socialists" peasants would avoid the other possible fates discussed above—their continued subordination as a peasantry or their destruction under "the wave of [capitalist] progress."

Thirdly, there has been a desire to improve the quality of rural life by raising productivity and by slowly but surely making available necessary services and amenities. Implicit was an agreement with Raikes's formulation:

> It has been shown time and time again that tremendous resources of productivity and creativity can be released in peasants and other producers once they take control of their own production process and control democratically its planning and implementation.[45]

The mechanism chosen to realize these goals has been the "*ujamaa* [socialist] village" policy—an attempt to structure collective agricultural communities at the base of the Tanzanian system which would give concrete expression to the peasants' involvement in the tasks of socialist construction. In working to build rural socialism, peasants could be expected to transform themselves.

Moreover, *ujamaa* communities, once established, could also be expected to provide more effective rallying points for critical action by an increasingly radicalized and organized peasantry, and hence the greater likelihood of a "real, rather than a theoretical, check upon the petty-bourgeoisie of party and bureaucracy, at local and national levels, by the mass of the population in the interests of socialist development."[46] And this on a nationwide scale. It is true that much of the original emphasis seemed to lie on the formation of brand-new villages in marginal-subsistence areas, but this was by no means an exclusive emphasis. Already, in the first major policy paper which launched the *ujamaa* approach, the president made clear that in established cash-cropping areas the move toward collectivism was equally to be fostered—even if, of necessity, by more subtle and graduated means:

It must be accepted . . . that socialist progress in these areas will be more difficult to achieve, for when vacant land is not available there is only one way to create a community farm; that is by individual farmers coming together and joining their pieces of land and working them in common . . .

It may be that the way to start under these circumstances is to operate first on the basis of working groups, but with the individual plots retained—that is, on the basis of mutual help. This would be simply a revival, and perhaps an extension, of the traditional system of joint activity, making it applicable to existing farms and not just to land clearing or house building. By working together on their private farms, the farmers will be able to finish different jobs more quickly, or to do things which would be too difficult for any of them individually. They will then have time to do other useful things— either by themselves or co-operatively.

This first step of mutual help can be followed by others. The farmers could buy certain essential goods co-operatively—things like fertilizers for example—or they could together build a store for their coffee, or something else which is of use to them all. By doing such things together the farmers will be gradually moving towards an acceptance of *ujamaa* socialism.[47]

Reference was also made in that paper to the peculiar problems of bringing collective agriculture to "animal husbandry" areas. In short, the initial formulation was not a crude one: it began with the firm recognition that Tanzania contained a markedly diverse range of peasantries.

The original guidelines for the policy seemed also to strongly emphasize peasant spontaneity as a key to progress. Thus Nyerere argued that "any citizen who understands the principles of *ujamaa* is encouraged to take the initiative"[48] and stressed again and again that the transition to collectivism was to be a voluntary one. Discussing his paper "Socialism and Rural Development," he noted that

> it is directed to all the people of Tanzania—or at least all of those who live in the rural areas. It is an outline of a policy of inter-linked, self-governing village communities which are *of* the people, and which therefore cannot be created for them or imposed on them. The paper, therefore, calls for leadership, but not for orders to be given; it directs the people along the socialist path, but excludes any attempt to whip them into it—saying clearly that you cannot force people to lead socialist lives.

But the call for leadership is equally crucial. Nyerere in fact sought the key to success in leaders who will be, arguably, those very cadres whose importance we discussed earlier, persons who "will lead by doing."[49] He specifies some of the methods of work of such people, and concludes: "The members of an *ujamaa* village must control their own affairs—I say it again! But the role of a leader is crucial and good leadership will make all the difference to the socialist success and the material success of such a community."

Spontaneity and leadership—with cadres who will resolve that contradiction! Let us again check both terms of that equation. In Tanzania, peasant protest was an active ingredient in the nationalist movement; moreover, the party (TANU) which gave a focus to nationalism was linked more closely to this peasant base than other parties in Africa. This was one factor which facilitated the forging of the progressive program of socialism and self-reliance by one wing of the territorial leadership in the postcolonial period. In addition, there have been some significant peasant actions subsequent to the winning of independence—not least the taking of a number of local initiatives to establish rural collectivization in scattered parts of the country—notably in remote Ruvuma region. In the latter case, the Ruvuma Development Association (RDA, with its small attendant organization of cadres, the Social and Economic Revolutionary Army—SERA) was established formally under the umbrella of TANU, but more spontaneously than that fact might tend to suggest. In important ways it became a prototype for Nyerere when he moved to generalize this and other "unofficial" experiments into a national *ujamaa* villages policy. Moreover, the potency of such rural collectives in institutionalizing a peasant challenge to class formation—in particular a challenge to those whose power and privilege had begun to crystallize around the apparatuses of state and party—can be seen in the history of the RDA's struggle with the bureaucracy and with local notables over a number of years in Ruvuma. It can also be gauged from the fact that the RDA was dissolved by the party, possibly against the president's better judgment, in 1969.[50]

Despite the example of the RDA, it is nonetheless clear that "spontaneity" has been an inadequate source of rural transformation in Tanzania. A potential is there, but to trigger off peasant consciousness around a national program of socialist reconstruction and to give this program its local embodiment in collective units requires the sort of leadership identified by Nyerere. It could of course be argued that in the period after 1967, when Nyerere and his colleagues launched their overall project of transforming the economy and consolidating a progressive leadership, some of the preconditions for drawing peasants into the process of cooperative endeavor did exist.[51] Yet the inability of Tanzanian leaders to cope with the reality of a mobilized peasantry when it had sprung to life (witness the RDA experience) is suggestive of a lingering problem. Not surprisingly, they have been equally unsuccessful in becoming active agents for mobilizing such a peasantry into existence and releasing its energies elsewhere in the country where this is necessary.[52] On balance, the trend toward the *bureaucratization* of the leadership (or, more accurately, its crystallization as a privileged class around the apparatus of the state) has begun to outpace any countertendency which would serve to transform it into a complement of socialist cadres.[53] Raikes argues that this degeneration has in turn determined a running-down of the *ujamaa* policy into one marked by coercion, by the uneconomic and demobilizing reliance upon solely material incentives, and by compromise with the locally privileged who have most to lose from collectivization. Thus, even if other, more radical alternative approaches existed in theory,

> it would be unrealistic to paint a picture of what "might have been" in a political vacuum. The change in emphasis of *ujamaa* was not simply the result of a neutral judgement . . . [T]he *ujamaa* strategy was changed to conform more closely with the preconceptions and interests of the bureaucratic bourgeoisie who controlled its implementation. Similarly, their judgement cannot be considered neutral concerning the question of socialist transformation of the economy. Just as they tend to distrust the intentions and capabilities of peasants and are concerned to maintain their own status in relation to them, so do they distrust the major political changes which would have to occur before and during a socialist transformation. Large numbers of democratically controlled *ujamaa* villages would pose a real threat to their status, and should the next logical step be taken, to form democratically elected local councils of village leaders, this would go further to threaten their very reason for existence.

This at a territorial level. The consolidation of a more radical overall tendency there would, as in liberated Mozambique, have been reflected in more adequate methods of political work at the local level as well. For despite Nyerere's emphasis, cited above, on adapting the policy to suit the situation of diverse peasantries, little has been done to follow up on this insight. Yet the need to generate detailed knowledge both of political "stresses and strains" at the local level, and of the realities of productive potential there, is at least as crucial to those engaged in facilitating the transition to collectivization in Tanzania as it is to those engaged in mobilizing a base for guerrilla warfare in Mozambique. If anything, it is even more important, for the range of variation of the articulation of modes of production is vast in Tanzania, while the necessity to give the struggle for socialism a concrete and meaningful expression at the local level is even more pressing in the absence of a direct, physical threat to the peasantry like that provided by the Portuguese colonialists.

Several writers have addressed themselves to these realities,[54] Woods discussing a range of "area-based peasantries in Tanzania" and Cliffe pinpointing six different "broad types of rural situation" which need separate consideration: highland high-density areas, medium-density, cash-crop areas, marginal subsistence areas, frontier areas, settler/estate areas, pastoral and semi-pastoral areas.[55] Furthermore, Cliffe, in a number of his writings, has spelled out some of the implications for socialist construction of this range of variation by identifying differing strategies for engaging the peasants of each such area in collective activity. He finds one key, particularly in advanced areas, in premising strategies upon the opportunities for struggle offered by class divisions internal to the areas themselves. In the absence of such strategies, those peasants who have shifted furthest toward a capitalist posture may seize the day, as in Bukoba where, as Cliffe shows in his article on rural class formation,

> in the contemporary period when the Tanzanian government is attempting to restructure the modes of production into co-operative forms in order to avoid class differentiation, the policy was preempted by a coalition of bureaucrats and the locally privileged. They translated the policy into terms which safeguarded the existing positions of rich and middle peasants by removing poor peasants who had little or no land to so-called *ujamaa* villages in resettlement areas.

Nor is the latter case an isolated one: Raikes would see it merely as a further example of a more general phenomenon—the class alliance of bureaucrat and "kulak":

> Thus communal labour for *ujamaa* villages required communal land-holding, something which required careful political education for peasants both large and small if they were to give up all or part of

the private plots on which their livelihood depended. More particularly, of course, the larger farmers plainly stood to lose, and this could have led to some difficult choices in view of their considerable local political influence. The discomfort would have been the greater since by training, inclination and previous practice, the administrators were accustomed to work through precisely these local leaders and specifically through "progressive" (i.e., large) farmers. This had been a stated objective of colonial agricultural policy, and was largely continued through the first six years of independence. Concentration of advice, credit and membership of co-operative and other local committees upon such groups had led, in many areas (and especially the richer ones) to the emergence of fairly small and tight groups of relatively wealthy and influential peasants and capitalist farmers whose relations to government staff were much closer than those of the mass of the peasantry.[56]

Is there added "steam" to be drawn upon in such a situation? The work of the Iringa regional commissioner, Dr. Wilbert Klerru, in emphasizing class contradictions in the Ismani area, isolating the "kulaks," taking over holdings, and releasing the energies of poor and middle peasant strata might seem to suggest so, though in the event it led to Klerru himself being assassinated by a "rich peasant."[57] And Ismani is a frontier area where capitalist relations are the most fully developed in Tanzania and the least muted by quasi-traditional identifications and solidarities. Where "middle peasants" are a more dominant proportion of the rural population than in Ismani, the precise blend of class struggle, exemplification of collectivity, and technical innovation to be encouraged would have to be a more nuanced one.[58] Of the need for such effective and militant local struggles, however, there can be no doubt.

But, to repeat, the methods of work which might generate such strategies have not been forthcoming. The one effort (in 1967) to develop, systematically, a core of cadres who could be expected genuinely to release peasant energies around the promise of collective action foundered on the reef of bureaucratic and political hostility to such a program.[59] Instead, quite dubious alternative policies have been mounted, some of which have already been mentioned: a frontal approach directed by civil servants (generally themselves from more developed regions) toward backward areas least able to defend themselves and reduced in content to mere "villagization," rather than collective enterprise; a ceding of other *ujamaa* experiments (in tea and tobacco) to the purview of World Bank experts little concerned to guarantee socialist relations of production; and so on. Meanwhile, amidst the degeneration of his policy, President Nyerere seems only to have become more shrill and desperate in an attempt to recover the ground which has been lost. His latest utterance on the subject has struck a particularly uncharacteristic note: "To live in villages is an order," in the words of a Tanzania *Daily News* headline.

> President Nyerere said yesterday that living together in villages is now an order. And it should be implemented in the next three years. This was a TANU decision. And any leader who hesitated to implement it would not be tolerated because he would be retarding national development. Addressing a public rally at Endabashi, Mbulu district, *Mwalimu* [i.e., Nyerere] said there was a need for every Tanzanian to change his mode of life if rapid progress was to be achieved. People who refused to accept development changes were stupid, if not ignorant and stubborn.[60]

There may be more promising countertendencies at the base of the system, though (as noted earlier) it is workers and students who have thus far responded most actively to *Mwongozo's* invitation to take power into their own hands.[61] Nonetheless, in a country so rurally biased as Tanzania it remains true, ultimately, that "the only available class *base* for revolutionary transformation would seem to be a reconstructed peasantry—even if elements from other strata of society provide much of the leadership."[62] Nor is it likely that the peasantry has been entirely unaffected by the experience of struggle over the direction postcolonial Tanzania will take. Difficult though it is to gauge, some measure of consciousness-raising has undoubtedly taken place in the rural areas, even if the *ujamaa* program has yet to give it effective institutional expression. Indeed, von Freyhold seems to argue that the advance has been substantial, though

> while society has changed, parts of the bureaucracy have not yet fully understood that the peasants have emerged victorious from colonial domination. The old vices of bureaucracy—commandism,

hasty decisions without investigation, red-tape and superiority feelings—have survived and it will probably take a cultural revolution—including communal re-education through self-criticism—to readapt the superstructure to its new social base.[63]

Whence such a cultural revolution? In Handeni, von Freyhold does see seeds of growing consciousness even in the rather compromised villages which have emerged from implementation of the *ujamaa* policy there. Furthermore, she feels that the struggle to determine the overall direction of the system is still sufficiently alive to make the opting for a cadre-based strategy—and a consequent strengthening of a rejuvenated party over and against the "staff" or bureaucracy—a continuing possibility. This conclusion is controversial—some would argue that it is the bureaucrats and not the peasants who have emerged victorious—but her perception as to the need "to change the structures of communication between the villages and the outside [in a way] which could bring more knowledge, more motivation and more self-assurance to the common members of the villages" is much less controversial. In the end she returns to familiar recommendations, recommendations which recall the dynamic of developments witnessed in Mozambique.

> The kind of recruitment, training and task-description needed for political cadres will in any case have to change as the party and the peasants gain more experience with each other and with *ujamaa*. What matters at the moment is that the necessity of cadres [should be] realized and that different ways of finding and educating the right kind of people be tried. Strengthening the party at its base would have to be a priority not only because peasants need political guidance but also because the party at higher levels cannot grow into a meaningful institution without confrontation with the real and concrete problems on the ground.[64]

Here would be a rejoining of the dialectic between leadership and peasantry that we have seen to be so important. Time alone will tell whether Tanzania still retains the capacity to reverse all those trends which suggest the running-down of its socialist experiment and whether it can begin again to consolidate a peasant base for itself along the lines thus suggested.[65]

Conclusion

The two cases which we have discussed are important, but they are not entirely typical of the continent as a whole. Southern Africa is crucial in its own right; moreover, successful revolution in Mozambique (using the term revolution in its broadest sense to include a successful challenge both to colonialism and to any prospect of subsequent neocolonialism) would also be a stimulus to developments in the rest of Africa. But, as we have seen, the colonial factor—Portuguese ultracolonialism—has given a point and purpose to nationalism there which has fashioned it, ineluctably and in the preindependence period, into a revolutionary ideology and a revolutionary movement—of peasants. Tanzania, though already an independent state, is also atypical in that some attempt has been made by those already in positions of authority to mobilize the peasants (and workers) to support, even to demand, radical structural transformation.

Even with reference to Tanzania, there are those who would suggest that a point has now been reached which demands a more root-and-branch, from-the-bottom-up, challenge to established structures, and who argue, in effect, that a much less ambiguous revolutionary thrust is becoming a necessity there.[66] Whatever the answer to this difficult question, the fact remains that the situation elsewhere in independent (and neocolonialized) Africa is far less ambiguous and the imperative of such a straightforward challenge to established authority more clear-cut, if the peasants' plight is to be alleviated. There the time has arrived where "someone" operating outside the established structures must attempt again to convince the peasantry, in Nyerere's phrase, "that their own efforts can lead to an improvement in their lives"! Of course, a further exploration of this prospect is not our concern here. Yet if and when mass-based revolutions do become a more characteristic feature of other parts of Africa, there will be lessons, both positive and negative, to be learned by African revolutionaries from the experience of Mozambique and Tanzania—lessons about the precise range of peasantries which exist in Africa and, most important, about the methods which might facilitate these peasantries making the revolution their own. We have begun to touch upon some of these lessons in this paper. More generally, it has become obvious that additional scientific work on the question of African peasantries can be expected to make a positive contribution to the revolutionary process on the continent.

Notes

1. Karl Marx, "The Eighteenth Brumaire of Louis Bonaparte," in Marx, *Surveys from Exile* (Harmondsworth, 1973), p. 239.
2. Nigel Harris, "The Revolutionary Role of the Peasants," *International Socialism*, no. 41 (December–January 1969–70).
3. Malcolm Caldwell, "The Revolutionary Role of the Peasants—2," ibid.
4. Quoted in Daniel Singer, *Prelude to Revolution* (New York, 1970), p. 1.
5. See Paul Sweezy's particularly strong statement of this point in his "Workers and the Third World" in George Fischer, ed., *The Revival of American Socialism* (New York, 1971): "If we consider capitalism as a global system, which is the only correct procedure, we see that it is divided into a handful of exploiting countries and a much more numerous and populous group of exploited countries. The masses in these exploited dependencies constitute a force in the global capitalist system which is revolutionary in the same sense and for the same reasons that Marx considered the proletariat of the early period of modern industry to be revolutionary. And finally, world history since the Second World War proves that this revolutionary force is really capable of waging successful revolutionary struggles against capitalist domination." (p. 168)
6. Eric Wolf, *Peasant Wars of the Twentieth Century* (New York, 1969), p. 276.
7. Lionel Cliffe, "Rural Class Formation in East Africa," paper presented to the "Peasant Seminar" of the Centre of International and Area Studies, University of London, November 23, 1973, mimeo., p. 1.
8. Hamza Alavi, "Peasants and Revolution" in Ralph Miliband and John Saville, eds., *The Socialist Register 1965* (London, 1965).
9. Alavi's emphasis suggests an additional point of crucial relevance to our discussion of Africa: that "the peasantry" is not uniform. Alavi's own distinction between "poor" and "middle" peasant is one of a

number of possible differentiations to be made among various peasantries in any specific historical setting.

10. Mark Selden, "People's War in China and Vietnam" in Lawrence Kaplan, ed., *Revolutions: A Comparative Study* (New York, 1973), pp. 374–75.

11. L. A. Fallers, "Are African Cultivators to Be Called 'Peasants'?," *Current Anthropology*, no. 2 (1961), pp. 108–10.

12. See William Derman, "Peasants: The African Exception?" *American Anthropologist* 74 (1972): 779–82.

13. John S. Saul and Roger Woods, "African Peasantries" in Teodor Shanin, ed., *Peasants and Peasant Societies* (Harmondsworth, 1971).

14. For a general overview of this process see Walter Rodney, *How Europe Underdeveloped Africa* (London and Dar es Salaam, 1972).

15. Ken Post, *On "Peasantisation" and Rural Class Differentiation in Western Africa*, ISS Occasional Papers, The Hague, 1970.

16. William Derman in his book, *Serfs, Peasants and Socialists* (Berkeley–Los Angeles–London, 1973), suggests, following Wolf, a very broad definition of "rent" to encompass these varying realities while maintaining conformity with certain of the literature on peasantries on other continents.

17. Colin Leys, "Politics in Kenya: The Development of Peasant Society," *British Journal of Political Science*, no. 1 (1970), p. 326.

18. Barrington Moore, *Social Origins of Dictatorship and Democracy: Lord and Peasant in the Making of the Modern World* (Boston, 1966), p. 505.

19. This fact also demonstrates the urgency of a peasant-based revolution in Africa, for peripheral capitalism seems unlikely, by its further evolution, to produce an alternative agency, a fully developed proletariat, which could underwrite a socialist way out of the dead end of underdevelopment.

20. Frantz Fanon, *The Wretched of the Earth* (Harmondsworth, 1967).

21. Amilcar Cabral, "Brief Analysis of the Social Structure in Guinea" in his *Revolution in Guinea* (London and New York, 1969). Here he draws an explicit comparison with the Chinese case: "The conditions of the peasantry in China were very different: the peasantry had a tradition or revolt, but this was not the case in Guinea, and so it was not possible for our party militants and propaganda workers to find the same kind of welcome among the peasantry of Guinea for the idea of national liberation as the idea found in China." (p. 50)

22. The "crisis of feudalism" which is often attendant upon the incursion of capitalism and which intensifies a number of contradictions for the peasantry will not, therefore, be so prominent a feature.
23. See the analysis in my essay "The Dialectic of Class and Tribe," in this volume.
24. Martin Kilson, *Political Change in a West African State*, among others.
25. Julius K. Nyerere, "Introduction," *Freedom and Socialism* (London and Dar es Salaam, 1968), p. 29.
26. Jules Gerard-Libois, "The New Class and Rebellion in the Congo" in Miliband and Saville, eds., *The Socialist Register 1966* (London, 1966). Gerard-Libois goes on to note, significantly, that "the rebellion did not find the united, effective and revolutionary organization it required, and it is very doubtful whether the brief experience of the People's Republic made any contribution to its creation." (p. 278)
27. Moreover, it is also obvious that trends in the urban areas (the activities of workers and/or lumpen elements, for example) will be important in determining the nature and extent of peasant involvement in movements directed toward radical social reconstruction.
28. Julius K. Nyerere, quoted in *The Nationalist*, Dar es Salaam, September 5, 1967, and cited in John S. Saul, "African Socialism in One Country: Tanzania" in G. Arrighi and J. S. Saul, *Essays on the Political Economy of Africa* (New York, 1973), p. 248.
29. This distinction is developed, with reference to an advanced capitalist setting, in Andre Gorz, *Socialism and Revolution* (New York, 1973).
30. Eduardo Mondlane, *The Struggle for Mozambique* (Harmondsworth, 1969), p. 116.
31. "FRELIMO Faces the Future," an interview by Joe Slovo with Marcellino dos Santos in *The African Communist*, no. 55 (1973), p. 29.
32. In Perry Anderson, "Portugal and the End of Ultra-Colonialism," *New Left Review*, nos. 16, 17, 18 (1962).
33. For a brief account of my initial impressions, see the article "Lesson in Revolution for a Canadian Lecturer" in *Mozambique Revolution*, no. 52 (July–September 1972).
34. See also Jorge Rebelo's comment on the struggle in the province of Manica e Sofala: "One of the most interesting developments in Manica e Sofala has been the response of the people, which has been even stronger than that in Tete, again, we believe, because of

the experience of oppression which the people here have" (in "Comrade Rebelo's Report to CFM on Current Developments in Mozambique, June 19, 1973" in *Committee for a Free Mozambique News and Notes*, mimeo, New York 1973).
35. Don Barnett, *Peasant Types and Revolutionary Potential in Colonial Africa* (Richmond, B.C., 1973).
36. John S. Saul, "FRELIMO and the Mozambique Revolution" in Arrighi and Saul, *Essays on the Political Economy of Africa*, ch. 8.
37. Samora Machel, "Sowing the Seeds of Liberation" in *Mozambique Revolution*, no. 49 (October–December 1971), pp. 23–24.
38. "Chissano: Within Five Years the Liberated Areas Will Be Developed Ten Times More than Under Colonialism," interview with Joaquim Chissano in *Ceres* (Rome), July–August 1973, p. 40.
39. John S. Saul, "African Socialism in One Country: Tanzania."
40. Thus "President Nyerere has called on the people of Tanzania to have great confidence in themselves and safeguard the nation's hard-won freedom. He has warned the people against pinning all their hopes on the leadership who are apt to sell the people's freedom to meet their lusts. *Mwalimu* [i.e., Nyerere] warned that the people should not allow their freedom to be pawned as most of the leaders were purchasable. He warned further that in running the affairs of the nation the people should not look on their leaders as 'saints or prophets.' The President stated that the attainment of freedom in many cases resulted merely in the change of colours, white to black faces without ending exploitation and injustices, and above all without the betterment of the life of the masses." This statement is from the newspaper account cited in footnote 28.
41. This includes some attack upon imperialism—the confrontation with the "new class" of leaders/bureaucrats is implicity this—throughout, and a wide-ranging program of nationalizations and self-reliance is part of Tanzania's broader socialist policy. Nonetheless, it seems fair to argue that the overall policy has not been sufficiently clear concerning the peasants' role in subordination to international capitalism—especially vis-à-vis the world market system. Strategies for the rural sector have been weak in linking peasant production to a new pattern of demand brought into existence by structural change in the industrial/urban sector, the latter in turn to be facilitated by a more decisive break with dependency. Cf. Saul, "African Socialism in One Country: Tanzania," for a more detailed critique along these lines.
42. *Mwongozo/The TANU Guidelines* (Dar es Salaam, 1971).

43. Julius K. Nyerere, "Decentralisation" in *Freedom and Development* (Dar es Salaam and London, 1973), p. 347. Nyerere adds that "those who cause the new system to become enmeshed in bureaucratic procedures will, as they are discovered, be treated as what they are—saboteurs."

44. Julius K. Nyerere, "Socialism and Rural Development" in *Freedom and Socialism*. This is an important perception of trends in rural Tanzania, though Roger Woods, in his "Peasants and Peasantries in Tanzania and Their Role in Socio-Political Development" (in Rural Development Research Committee, *Rural Co-operation in Tanzania* [Dar es Salaam, 1974]) argues that involution and stagnation may be an equally prominent feature in many such areas.

45. Philip Raikes, "Ujamaa Vijijini and Rural Socialist Development," paper delivered to the Annual Social Science Conference of the East African Universities, Dar es Salaam, December 1973, mimeo. This is a particularly important recent appraisal of Tanzania's rural development policy and practice.

46. John S. Saul, "Who Is the Immediate Enemy?" in Cliffe and Saul, eds., *Socialism in Tanzania*, vol. 2, p. 357.

47. Nyerere, "Socialism and Rural Development," pp. 361–62.

48. Nyerere, "After the Arusha Declaration" in *Freedom and Socialism*.

49. Nyerere, "Implementation of Rural Socialism" in *Freedom and Development*.

50. R. Ibbott, "The Disbanding of the Ruvuma Development Association, Tanzania," mimeo, London (November 1969).

51. For example, "leaders" were sealed off from very gross "conflicts of interests" vis-à-vis the private sector under the terms of the 1967 Leadership Code (although familial links to "kulaks" often remained); moreover, given the stated attempt to undermine elite consolidation and to rally the masses as "workers and peasants," the instrumentalization of the peasants by manipulating tribalism has been significantly reduced, thus encouraging the latter to come into more direct, unmediated, confrontation with structural realities.

52. See Raikes, "Ujamaa, Vijijini and Rural Socialist Development"; Michaela von Freyhold, "The Government Staff and Ujamaa Villages," paper presented to the Annual Social Science Conference of the University of East Africa, Dar es Salaam, December 1973; Lionel Cliffe, "Planning Rural Development," in Uchumi Editorial Board, *Towards Socialist Planning*, Tanzanian Studies, Dar es

Salaam, 1972. For example, as I have argued in my "African Socialism in One County: Tanzania," "it is . . . in the rural areas that manifestations of the hectoring, bureaucratic style of such a leadership are most likely to have the predicted effect of demobilizing the mass of the population, thus choking off that release of popular energies which is the program's ostensible aim" (p. 292).

53. The strongest statement of this position which, in fact, sees the leadership as compromised from the outset as a "bureaucratic bourgeoisie" is to be found in Issa Shivji, *Tanzania: The Class Struggle Continues* (Dar es Salaam, 1973); I have argued the existence of a struggle within the petty bourgeoisie over the direction of Tanzanian development, a struggle which nonetheless evidences the growing strength of conservative elements in "The State in Postcolonial Societies: Tanzania."

54. For an important historical perspective on rural development in Tanzania and on the emergence of a differentiated peasantry, see John Iliffe, *Agricultural Change in Modern Tanganyika* (Nairobi, 1971).

55. Lionel Cliffe, "The Policy of Ujamaa Vijijini and the Class Struggle in Tanzania" in Lionel Cliffe and John S. Saul, eds., *Socialism in Tanzania*, vol. 2.

56. Raikes, "Ujamaa Vijijini and Rural Socialist Development." Von Freyhold even argues that kulaks can sometimes operate within so-called *ujamaa* villages to advance their interests, a point which is also developed in an interesting case study by H.U.E. Thoden van Velzen in his essay "A Case-Study of Ujamaa Farming in Rungwe," in Rural Development Research Committee, *Rural Co-operation in Tanzania.*

57. For an excellent, detailed account of developments in Ismani see Adhu Awiti, "Class Struggle in Rural Society of Tanzania," *Maji Maji*, Special Publication no. 7 (October 1972).

58. Some examples of such possible strategies are presented in the final section of Rural Development Research Committee, *Rural Co-operation in Tanzania*, where both the alteration of relations of production and the expansion of productive forces are equally stressed in exploring the promise of rural collectivization.

59. See the account of this episode in N. Kisenge, "The Party in Tanzania," *Maji Maji* (September 1971).

60. *Daily News of Tanzania*, November 7, 1973.

61. On the recent dramatic rise of worker activism, see Henry Mapolu, "The Workers' Movement in Tanzania," *Maji Maji*, no. 12 (Sep-

tember 1973) and Mapolu, "Labour Unrest: Irresponsibility or Worker Revolution?" *Jenga*, no. 12 (1972). For an attempt to theorize student unrest see Karim Hirji, "School Education and Underdevelopment in Tanzania," *Maji Maji*, no. 12.

62. Cliffe, "The Policy of Ujamaa Vijijini and the Class Struggle in Tanzania," p. 197.

63. Von Freyhold, "The Government Staff and Ujamaa Villages." This is of a piece with my earlier conclusion which, however, now may seem excessively sanguine in light of the analyses by Raikes and others: "The horizon of really dramatic, cumulative change remains a distant one, but there can be little doubt that in the rural areas the *ujamaa* policy has given a content and structure to the struggle for progress in a nonrevolutionary situation around which consciousness can crystallize and a popular base may form" (in my "African Socialism in One Country: Tanzania").

64. Von Freyhold, "The Government Staff and Ujamaa Village." In addition, von Freyhold sees this as a step toward facilitating the emergence of "peasant-experts" from within the village who would carry the process of transformation further; presumably, these kinds of village activists would be precisely those militants who would also feed into the party from the base, helping to transform it from within.

65. Unfortunately, there is little comparative material to go on, since many aspects of the Tanzanian situation are unique on the continent; moreover, despite its title and despite its many other virtues, Derman's book, *Serfs, Peasants, and Socialists*, does not take us far in understanding processes in Guinea-Bissau which might conceivably be comparable, beyond his concluding sentence: "In my view, the transformation of peasants into socialists will be far more difficult than the transformation of serfs into peasants or the transformation of Guiné from colony to independent nation."

66. This might seem to be a conclusion to be drawn from Shivji's essay, for example.

12

THE "LABOR ARISTOCRACY" THESIS RECONSIDERED

The concept of the "labor aristocracy" as previously employed in the literature to facilitate an understanding of Africa's current class structure and revolutionary dynamics has come in for pointed criticism in a recently edited collection entitled *The Development of an African Working Class*, particularly in the chapters written by Adrian Peace and Richard Jeffries.[1] Since the theoretical work jointly undertaken by Giovanni Arrighi and myself which made use of this term was especially singled out for such criticism, some additional brief comment on the subject is in order here.[2] Not by way of self-justification—indeed, it appears that the term as used in that work may do more to conjure up unintended echoes than to clarify the contemporary situation and for that reason the advisability of continuing to use it in quite the way we did is open to some doubt—but rather to suggest directions which further analysis might take. However, one point should be made clear at the outset: that such analysis must not be isolated from political considerations. The "structures of domination" in contemporary Africa are such that only *revolutionary* solutions to the development problem seem promising and viable. Therefore, the main point of interest concerning the role of the working class (and concerning the trade unions which claim

---

A slightly modified version of this essay/comment appeared as a chapter of the Sandbrook and Cohen volume discussed in the text. See Richard Sandbrook and Robin Cohen, eds., *The Development of an African Working Class* (Toronto and London, 1975).

to institutionalize that class's presence in economic and political arenas) must be the extent to which the role so played either facilitates or cuts against a radical challenge to the status quo of underdevelopment and neocolonial domination.

As originally applied to African reality in our earlier essays, the concept "labor aristocracy" had several seeming virtues. To begin with, it fitted neatly into an overall theoretical model designed to highlight the primacy of the contradiction between international capitalism on the one hand, and any given African territory on the other. One historic function of imperial penetration was to force the proletarianization of sufficient numbers of the indigenous precapitalist population to staff the lower echelons of the colonial state apparatus and to work the extractive and (later) semi-industrial sectors developed by such penetration. A pattern of *migrant labor*[3] became the characteristic mechanism by which indigenous societies adapted to these imperial demands for labor power, any "push from behind" (such as might be caused by a drying-up of access to the means of production in the rural areas because of overpopulation and/or expansion of holdings/ enclosure by a rural capitalist class) being a much less prominent factor. For those Africans who chose to stay more permanently in the wage sector, full proletarianization was therefore *voluntary* in a way that it was not for the peasant pitch-forked into the wage system in, say, the classic British case.[4] This was true both for "educated" elements in the state apparatus and for better-paid workers in sectors where international capitalism could afford to pay a sufficiently high wage to encourage migrants to sever most of their ties with a rural base.[5]

The use of the term "labor aristocracy" underscored important points, therefore. First, it pinpointed the similarity, historically, between the structural position of the "elites" (and "sub-elites") in bureaucratic employment *and* of the wage workers, both supplying their labor power to service imperial exploitation and both having objective grounds for developing a stance of conscious opposition to that pattern.[6] At the same time, it took cognisance of the extent to which material benefit—sufficient, that is, to encourage "voluntary proletarianization"—lay at the heart of the choice of roles within the system by bureaucrats and by the better paid, more stabilized, worker. In this way it highlighted the irony of the fact that these elements were, of indigenous strata, at once the *most exploited* (in the scientific sense) and among the most "benefited" by the system (in the absence of a very strong national bourgeoisie and certainly as compared with the great mass of semi-proletarianized or wholly rurally based agriculturalists). And when this social structure became overlaid, as it was increasingly, by a cultural/ideological pattern premised on the centrality of incremental material benefit, rather than on the possibility of systematic transformation of the exploitative linkages with imperialism or with employer, any class (or even national) interest on the part of these urban elements in the promise of such a transformation was even further blurred.

The institutional implications of this situation can be demonstrated in African practice, of course. Not surprisingly, trade unions have come to encapsulate (quite) precisely the bargaining concerns of these strata in their most narrowly "consumptionist" definition.[7] The "more privileged" and better organized workers have been encouraged to identify *upward*—to become partners (albeit the most junior of partners) in the jostling for surpluses among the internationally and domestically powerful (including most prominently in the latter category the elites and sub-elites themselves)—rather than to identify downward with the even more "wretched of the earth," the urban marginals and the average inhabitant of the untransformed rural areas.[8] Faced with explaining both the acquiescence of even the proletariat proper in that "false decolonization" which the attaining of formal independence generally signified, and the absence of any subsequent root-and-branch challenge to the status quo, it was tempting to view the labor aristocracy, broadly defined, as being sufficiently favored to have become the domestic guarantors of the neocolonial solution. And this temptation became all the more seductive when set in opposition to the crude and unrealistic "proletarian messianism" which dotted much of the radical literature on Africa at the time of our writing (1967–68).

Thus the term "labor aristocracy" helped to capture the reality that the most organized and articulate of those proletarianized by the imperial impact appeared to have been "processed" in such a way as to facilitate their material and cultural identification with the system of neocolonial domination. But, as Bertell Ollmann has recently emphasized,[9] concepts are both necessary *and* dangerous in scientific work, dangerous particularly in work directed toward a dialectical analysis of real historical process. Inevitably they freeze a reality which is in flux, and their use may come seriously to distort analysis when this danger is not borne firmly in mind. And as noted, and despite its utility for many purposes, it now seems that the term "labor aristocracy" as used in our earlier work risks producing some such unintended consequences.

In the first place, given the direction of developments in the postcolonial period, our use of the term in its broadest connotation begins seriously to distort the image of the "elites" and "sub-elites" and to overemphasize the continuing similarity of their structural position to that of the working class *per se* (even that of the most strategically situated of this working class). For the elites' self-interest in the status quo congeals more quickly (hardening, in effect, their "relative social autonomy and plasticity"[10]), while at the same time their control over the state increasingly grants them a different kind of position in the production process than that of merely proletarianized "employees" of imperial concerns, whether such concerns be private (corporations) or public ("the colonial state"). After independence, the state becomes, in its own right, an instrument for extracting surpluses on their behalf, and the elite's interest much more that of a dominating class—a "petty bourgeoisie" or "bureaucratic bourgeoisie."[11] Even if certain material benefits continue to encourage the upper echelons of the working class to play the role of junior partners to these indigenous dominants, the workers nonetheless seem more differentiated from, and potentially mobilizable against, such a petty bourgeoisie than the term "labor aristocracy," used most broadly, might otherwise imply.[12]

Secondly, even if the term were to be applied more narrowly to skilled, relatively well paid, organized workers, used carelessly it could still freeze reality in a misleading manner, masking—for the analyst and the radical activist—the contingent nature of such workers' vested interests in the status quo. Indeed, certain of the criticisms of Arrighi's and my formulations suggest that, unintentionally, we may have done precisely this. For the capacity of the neocolonial economic system to deliver payoffs is strictly limited in contemporary Africa; in the absence of structural transformation premised on socialist strategies, crises and/or stagnation are inevitable, and, concomitantly, the cooptation of even the most stabilized sections of the working class is that much more difficult. In such circumstances, the extent of false consciousness will be less dramatic and some of the classic strengths of the urban working class more evident (e.g., the insight into the capitalist system which is made possible by the experience of exploitation, direct and unmediated, at the workplace; the spirit of collective activity which can parallel, for the proletariat, the centralization of production following upon some measure of industrialization). Then too, the upper stratum of the workers will be most likely to identify *downward*,[13] becoming a leading force within a revolutionary alliance of exploited elements in the society.

To be sure, Arrighi and I did not have any illusions about the long-term development potential of peripheral capitalism in contemporary Africa. However, the argument of Adrian Peace's essay is that it has even less viability in the short term than we supposed; in his view, the bankruptcy of this option, in Nigeria at least, is already providing the objective conditions for the radicalization of all strata of workers, and in particular of the most stabilized of them.[14] In addition, he argues (much more explicitly) that the term "labor aristocracy" has indeed encouraged analysts, *by definition* as it were, to underestimate the level of consciousness and revolutionary potential of the proletariat proper in contemporary Africa. As should by now be apparent, the seriousness of such a charge cannot be overstated!

Peace's article offers some evidence that the Nigerian working class has indeed sloughed off certain of the characteristics which might brand it a "labor aristocracy." Much of his evidence (with respect both to their level of consciousness and to their actions) is of interest and begins to underline the *possibility* that all strata of the working class will "go the other way"—from cooptation toward revolutionary challenge—and that the "downward identification" of the more stabilized, better-paid workers can become their dominant characteristic.[15] At the same time, however, it must be stressed that there are serious ambiguities in his evidence. Some of the indications of downward identification which he cites, for example, seem to be as much proof of the existence of a form of patron-client network (dressed out in kinship terms) between paid workers and their hangers-on as they are testimony to the forging of revolutionary solidarity. More important, one may doubt the precise extent of the challenge to the status quo which is really represented even by such dramatic stirrings. Thus Peace asserts in his article:

> The relationship between the political class and the proletariat can serve as the starting point [of analysis]. In itself, it is significant that in this highly inflationary situation affecting the urban masses as a whole, government intervention was specifically directed at wage and salary earners. At least in part this constituted a recognition of the potential political repercussions from the wage-earning class should no attempt be made to alleviate increasingly intolerable economic conditions in the urban areas.

Here the "political elite" seems to be moving, as at various subsequent stages of the "crisis" described by Peace, to preempt too radical a denouement; an implicit bargaining process was underway, in which the peasantry, for example, was virtually unrepresented! It was, of course, fortunate for international capitalism and the Nigerian ruling class that peripheral capitalism retained enough life to deliver the goods to organized workers. However, one wishes Peace had addressed himself more formally to questioning how long this kind of system can continue to do so,[16] and how fundamental a challenge the workers' action really represented under the circumstances. Similarly, Richard Jeffries, who seeks in his own essay in the Sandbrook-Cohen volume to paint a picture of proletarian radicalism in Ghana that stands in sharp contrast to the actions and attitudes of any so-called "labor aristocracy," succeeds primarily in documenting a kind of "populist" outburst (as he himself terms it), the basic demands of which were ultimately absorbed, with only minimal disruption, into a quite conventional bargaining process.[17] In these cases, to be sure, the working class does seem poised to move leftward, and the contingent, open-ended character of its potential roles is more clearly revealed. But revolutionary classes must be made of even sterner stuff. A return to "proletarian messianism" is no answer, therefore. Certainly there are crucial constraints (some of them quite specific to the current African situation) upon the revolutionary spontaneity of a stratum still small and often *relatively* well placed to advance its immediate interests. Thus Peter Waterman's identification of a crucial missing link in Nigeria itself—a revolutionary ideology and the revolutionary intellectuals who could make it relevant to the working class—seems a sound complementary emphasis. [18] Similarly, in Tanzania, struggle *within* the petty bourgeoisie and the attempt by the more progressive tendency within that stratum to (among other things) mobilize the workers and maximize the likelihood of their making a positive contribution to the country's move toward socialism was, at least initially, even more important than any pressure for radical solutions arising from the working class itself. [19] Furthermore, the importance of the vast mass of the peasantry must continue to be stressed, not merely with reference to Southern Africa, where urban marginals and rural dwellers are so crucial to the liberation struggles, but in independent Africa where a new revolutionary alliance must eventually be formed. There is still much to be learned from Fanon (*pace* Jack Woddis)[20]—all the more so when one considers that the stagnation induced by neocolonialism will not soon allow for the proletarianization of vast numbers. Ironically, in most African countries only some form of socialism seems likely to have the economic strength to so "proletarianize" the peasantry as to provide a fully fledged proletarian input to the African future. [21]

But having reinforced these points, we must agree that something of Peace's critique does stand up: there is a danger of *prematurely labeling* the African working class (a danger we may well have courted in using so evocative a term as "labor aristocracy" without due qualification). The role of this class is far from being frozen by history or by any internal logic of the current African socioeconomic structure. What is needed instead is to concentrate attention upon the processes that are at work in specific African settings. This means identifying, analytically, the objective conditions under which a more conservative or a more radical stance toward the neocolonial situation is likely to be adopted by the working class (and further working out a prognosis for African political economies which specifies the likelihood of their providing such conditions). It also means identifying, politically, the organizational and ideological steps necessary to facilitate the emergence of those subjective conditions which are equally essential to the historical assertion of a revolutionary proletariat, and its alliance with other progressive elements, in contemporary Africa. For ultimately, adequate "working definitions," concepts which illuminate processes without denaturing them, will best be forged by those engaged in significant practice.

Notes

1. References to essays by Peace, Jeffries and others (see below) are to their papers as originally presented at the Toronto workshop on "Workers, Unions, and Development," April 6–8, 1973, edited versions of which eventually formed the contents of R. Sandbrook and R. Cohen, eds., *The Development of an African Working Class* (Toronto and London, 1975). I had not had the opportunity to review the final drafts submitted for publication or to take account of any possible revisions in them. Moreover, the present "note" merely summarizes the oral comments which I made in discussion at that workshop.
2. These original papers, cited by Peace and dating from 1967/68, now appear as chapters 1 and 2 in Giovanni Arrighi and John S. Saul, *Essays on the Political Economy of Africa* (New York, 1973).
3. Peace's view (as expressed in his essay, "The Lagos Proletariat: Labour Aristocrats or Populist Militants") that once a worker enters a factory floor he is "proletarianized" seems a vastly oversimplified way of dealing with the processes which continue to define the African labor force; Arrighi's "Labor Supplies in Historical Perspective: A Study of the Proletarianization of the African Peasantry in Rhodesia," in Arrighi and Saul, *Essays on The Political Economy of Africa*, provides a more subtle approach to the urban-rural continuum in Africa.

4. This is not to ignore the fact that use of *force* (ranging from the imposition of arbitrary and compulsory taxes to much more direct methods) was the predominant element in the colonial strategy for drawing Africans into the labor market, but merely to suggest that a "migrant labor" response, with its range of distinctive corollaries, remained the central one. In parts of Southern Africa where sharp encroachment upon African land rights was a more characteristic companion policy, the situation was somewhat different, and the pace of proletarianization to that extent stepped up (cf. Arrighi, ibid.).

5. Arrighi's "International Corporations, Labor Aristocracies, and Economic Development in Tropical Africa," in Arrighi and Saul, *Essays on the Political Economy of Africa*, is particularly suggestive in exploring the calculations of the multinational corporations which encourage them to behave in this manner.

6. Within such a framework, for example, one could attempt to explain "the relative social autonomy and plasticity" of this elite (noted by Roger Murray in his "Second Thoughts on Ghana," *New Left Review*, no. 42 [March–April, 1967], p. 34) and the logic of the situation which led Cabral to expect some of these elements to "commit suicide" (in his famous phrase).

7. This was a tendency all the more likely when it is realized that many of the best organized and articulate African trade unions have been, historically, those representing civil servants—the "bureaucratic bourgeoisie" on the rise, as it were.

8. Nor was it surprising in such circumstances that the encroachment upon trade-union autonomy which has been so prominent a feature in independent Africa generally could be interpreted as much more a political counter in a fairly narrowly circumscribed power game than part of any discernible effort to hold the line on wages and further squeeze the working class.

9. Bertell Ollman, *Alienation: Marx's Conception of Man in Capitalist Society* (New York, 1971), especially Part I.

10. See note 6, above.

11. These elements often spill over into the middle levels of the private sector in their activities, of course—and they remain firmly subordinated to imperial interests as well!

12. In addition, such aspects of the assertion of government control over the trade unions as do in fact represent growing class conflict can also be more easily appreciated; see note 8.

13. Such "downward identification" would be not only with peasants,

but with other, less stabilized, members of the urban work force. One additional weakness of the original concept probably was the tendency which it had to *dichotomize* too schematically that work force as between "labor aristocrats" and semi-proletarianized elements, rather than merely to emphasize the placing of all workers—whatever the differences between them—*on a continuum* between urban and rural settings and identifications. To approach the situation in the latter manner will, in future, make it easier to analyze the *processes* which affect the emergence of class solidarity—or the reverse.

14. Much of this is implicit; unfortunately, Peace does not present clearly the nature of the broader contradictions within the Nigerian political economy, some appreciation of which seems, nonetheless, to premise his argument.

15. It may be that part of the difference in emphasis reflects the differential pace of emergence of contradictions basic to neocolonial development as between West Africa on the one hand and East and Central Africa (where Arrighi and I carried out our first-hand empirical research) on the other; perhaps it is significant that Sharon Stichter's paper on Kenya given at the Toronto workshop argues strongly that the Kenyan organized worker still basically reflects material/cultural attributes of the "labor aristocracy" syndrome—a term she herself uses to describe them. See Sharon Stichter, "Trade Unions and the Mau Mau Rebellion in Kenya," paper presented at the Toronto workshop, April 1973.

16. For example, an assessment of the extent to which it was merely the availability of oil revenues which helped ensure such breathing space in the specific case of Nigeria would have been illuminating.

17. Richard Jeffries' essay, "Populist Tendencies in the Ghanaian Trade Union Movement," presented to the Toronto workshop, is included in the Sandbrook-Cohen volume; see also his "The Labor Aristocracy? Ghana Case-Study" in *Review of African Political Economy*, no. 3 (May–October 1975).

18. Peter Waterman, "Communist Theory in the Nigerian Trade Union Movement," *Politics and Society* 3, no. 2 (Spring 1973). A version of this paper was also presented to the Toronto workshop.

19. On this subject see M. A. Bienefeld's "Socialist Development and the Workers in Tanzania," in the Sandbrook-Cohen volume, and my own "African Socialism in One Country: Tanzania." For an alternative formulation see Henry Mapolu, "The Organisation and Participation of Workers in Tanzania," Economics Research Bureau Paper

72.1 (Dar es Salaam: Economic Research Bureau, University of Dar es Salaam, 1972).

20. Cf. Jack Woddis, *New Theories of Revolution* (New York, 1972), ch. 2, a *locus classicus* of "proletarian messianism"; see also Alex Callinicos" and John Rogers, *Southern Africa after Soweto* (London, 1977).

21. I am well aware that this formulation raises a whole host of further, quite basic, questions which simply cannot be dealt with in the space available.

13

THE UNSTEADY STATE:
UGANDA, OBOTE,
AND GENERAL AMIN

It would be incorrect to see in the replacement of the colonial state by the postcolonial state merely a distinction without a difference. The colonial state provided imperialism with a quite direct and unmediated instrument for control in the interests of "accumulation on a world scale" within the colonial social formation. The postcolonial state, while prone to play a similar role to that played by its predecessor, is something more of an unpredictable quantity in this regard. Unpredictable because of the greater scope for expression given to indigenous elements who now find in the "independent" state a much more apt target for their activities and a potential instrument for the advancement of their own interests and concerns.

In theory, such unpredictability might hold the threat of challenges to the structures of continuing imperial domination arising either from the left (socialism) or from the right (a burgeoning and competitive locally based capitalism), with indigenous classes attempting to use the state in order to realize independent national projects of their own. However, under African conditions, these have been much less prominent than a third, more ironic kind of "threat" to imperial interests: the crystallization in many African settings of a state too weak and too internally compromised to stabilize society and economy and thereby effectively guarantee the ongoing generation of surplus and accumulation

This essay was first published in *Review of African Political Economy*, no. 5 (1976).

of capital. Such weakness, when it evidences itself, certainly reflects economic contradictions as well as specific attributes of the class forces at play in contemporary Africa. Nonetheless, it is a brand of weakness which finds its primary expression in the political sphere, and, as we shall see, only a proper understanding of that sphere can shed real light on the problems involved. Unfortunately, it must also be noted that neither bourgeois political science (as exemplified in the work of countless "Africanists") nor the work of those few Marxists who have undertaken analyses of African politics have yet taken us very far toward such an understanding.

Uganda provides an example of these several points and will be explored in this article in order to illustrate them. Here is the "unsteady state" *par excellence*—a dependent social formation which has not given rise to a revolution, but which has nevertheless *failed to produce a state adequate to the task of guaranteeing the stable environment necessary for ongoing imperialist exploitation*. At its most extreme, this has meant "Aminism," a state "unhinged," representing a situation so unpredictable that it has led, at least in the short run, to a particularly dramatic disruption of the production process—a situation very far, it would seem, from servicing imperialism's most basic interests. At the same time, it must be emphasized that this bizarre denouement to Uganda's development process is consistent with problems and possibilities present within Uganda from a much earlier period, problems which haunted General Amin's predecessor, Milton Obote, and problems which will not necessarily disappear with the passing of Amin himself.

Nor has the nature of such problems been well understood. Not, certainly, by those racists of all colors who either parody or praise Amin with little genuine concern for the havoc he has wreaked—most notably among his own African brothers and sisters. Not by President Nyerere and his advisors, whose ill-fated support for Obote's post-coup adventures served only to set back the emergence of a genuine resistance movement in Uganda. Not by the many Western scholars interested in Uganda, even though they have provided a wealth of data on the various permutations and combinations of factional politics there. And not by Mahmood Mamdani, even though his recent pioneering work (both in an article in the *Review of African Political Economy* and in his *Politics and Class Formation in Uganda*[1]) does represent an important contribution to the Marxist study of Uganda—and of Africa. In short, much remains to be learned—not least by Marxists—about the nature of African politics. What follows is intended, therefore, to suggest some possible directions which further discussion might take.

The Nature of Petty-Bourgeois Politics

Of course, it would be at least as incorrect to overestimate imperialism's difficulties in contemporary Africa as it would be to underestimate them. As a first approximation to African reality, Frantz Fanon's insight continues to serve us well. For it is surely true (despite the fact that his point is expressed in a loose and somewhat metaphorical manner) that in postcolonial Africa

> the national middle-class discovers its historic mission: that of intermediary. Seen through its eyes, its mission has nothing to do with transforming the nation; it consists, prosaically, of being the transmission line between the nation and a capitalism, rampant though camouflaged, which today puts on the masque of neocolonialism.

The lines of neocolonial dominance are etched deeply onto the economic structures of postcolonial society, the productive process having been cast over the years into a mold—difficult to break—which continues to service the requirements of the imperialist system. Moreover, classes nurtured during the waning years of the colonial presence—Fanon refers to "the formation of an intellectual elite engaged in trade"—do tend to play their allotted roles as guarantors of that system. In consequence, the norm for Fanon was that of a fairly smooth transition to the postcolonial phase, the absence in contemporary Africa of any very profound contradiction between the metropolitan bourgeoisie and the indigenously powerful, both parties continuing to enrich themselves at the expense of the vast majority of the population.

This is, by now, familiar—and convincing—stuff, and many subsequent Marxist writers on African decolonization have followed Fanon's lead. To be sure, the term "national middle class" has tended to give way to the potentially more rigorous concept "petty bourgeoisie" in characterizing the locally prominent—this shift further underscoring the point (which was nonetheless made by Fanon) that such a class is nothing like the full-fledged (national) bourgeoisie familiar from Western European development. In contrast to the latter, this is a class of persons small in the scale of their economic operations and/or dependent upon, and auxiliary to, large-scale, particularly metropolitan-based, capital. Not that we can leave the question of definition even here. After all, this is the indigenous class which has gained the most direct and immediate access to the "overdeveloped state" which Africa inherited from colonialism. It is obviously important that its nature be specified further.

Unfortunately, the attempt at further specification is no easy task. Poulantzas has argued that "the definition of the class nature of the petty bourgeoisie is the focal point of a Marxist theory of social classes," this formulation in itself suggesting a challenging enough prospect. Yet it is a prospect made all the more challenging when features of the petty bourgeoisie's development specific to Africa are also added in.

Fanon's own definition of what is, in effect, the petty bourgeoisie—"an intellectual elite engaged in trade"—hinted at one of the problems. In what ways and to what extent do the "intellectual elite" and those "engaged in trade" comprise one and the same social category? As von Freyhold, another writer on Africa, has written, " 'Petty bourgeoisie' has a double meaning: it refers to small capitalists on the one hand and all those who look to the bourgeoisie as their model on the other." The petty bourgeoisie in this second sense refers in turn to that "educated stratum . . . which is directly employed by colonialists or a national bourgeoisie" or which, even "in the absence of such direct employers," remains "subservient to those by whom it has been created." And, in postcolonial Africa, the latter category defines, first and foremost, the salariat which staffs the machinery of the state.

As we shall see, some recent analyses of Africa have laid great stress on this distinction between the two wings of the petty bourgeoisie—small capitalists (traders and kulaks) on the one hand, and bureaucratic salariat (especially the cadre of civil servants whose passports to rank and privilege have been their educational qualifications, i.e., Fanon's "intellectual elite") on the other. Here it is necessary to confirm a prior point: that, whatever the reality and the implications of this distinction, both wings nonetheless may be conceived of as belonging to a single class.

The strongest statement of this argument, in general terms, is that presented by Nicos Poulantzas—though he also makes firmly the familiar distinction between what he calls the "traditional" petty bourgeoisie ("the small-scale producers and small traders [small property]") and the "new" petty bourgeoisie (the "nonproductive salaried employees," including "civil servants employed by the state and its various apparatuses"). What makes it appropriate to see these two elements as comprising a single class? In Poulantzas's view, it is because "these different positions in production and the economic sphere do, in fact, have *the same effects* at the political and ideological levels," namely, "petty-bourgeois individualism; attraction to the status quo and fear of revolution; the myth of 'social advancement' and aspirations to bourgeois status; belief in the 'neutral state' above classes; political instability and the tendency to support 'strong states' and Bonapartist regimes; revolts taking the form of 'petty-bourgeois' jacqueries." Without accepting uncritically the relevance of all the items on this list, one can see that it does go some way toward defining the characteristics which the petty bourgeoisie begins to evidence in the postcolonial period.

Poulantzas suggests that there is something further which can be said about the political practice of a class so defined. For, in his judgment, it will manifest certain crucial weaknesses. Its intermediate position—strung out between bourgeoisie and proletariat—and its "petty-bourgeois individualism" make it "very difficult for [the petty bourgeoisie] to organize politically into a specific party of [its] own." Moreover, both of the groups which make up the petty bourgeoisie "share a politically unstable nature. It is they who 'swing' most often, either to the side of the bourgeoisie or to the side of the working class, according to the conjuncture, since they are polarized around these two classes." In stressing the weakness of the petty bourgeoisie in this way, Poulantzas opens up an important perspective which can be brought to bear upon African realities. For, as stated, it is precisely this class which assumes formal political power in the postcolonial phase. And since, in turn, "political power" in postcolonial Africa means staffing a state at the very heart of the neocolonial production process—a state which is at once *overdeveloped* and *relatively autonomous* [2]—this class's weaknesses (as theorized by Poulantzas) are quite often particularly clearly exposed in practice.

To understand this, we need merely transfer to the level of the state Poulantzas's observation (previously cited) that because of its "unstable nature" it is "very difficult for [the petty bourgeoisie] to organize politically into a specific party of [its] own." How much more difficult, then, for such a class fully to guarantee the stable continuance of the broader state structure inherited from colonialism (and designed, needless to say, to guarantee the smooth functioning of the neocolonial production process)? How much more difficult to organize the terms of a new hegemonic relationship vis-à-vis the mass of the population? We thus find ourselves faced, in an ironic way, with a major qualification of Fanon's model. The middle-class/petty-bourgeoisie, too weak, in his scaring description, to challenge imperialism or manifest any genuine historical creativity, threatens to be too weak even to carry out effectively its role as intermediary! In contrast to the more schematic versions of Fanon's approach, the coherence which the "middle class" requires in order to play such a role is not present *ab initio* or by definition. It is, in itself, something which remains to be achieved and consolidated—and there are great obstacles in the way of any such consolidation. In consequence, what follows the winning of independence is a period of much greater uncertainty than Fanon sometimes seems to allow for.

This point appears particularly pressing if the petty bourgeoisie is now placed even more firmly in its specifically African context.

For, up to now, we have been advancing the argument as if the petty bourgeoisie, whatever its inherent weaknesses, were already a more or less fully formed class in Africa. In fact, this is far from the case, such a class still being very much in the process of formation in many areas. This is even true, to a degree, of the petty bourgeoisie of the private sector. Its members in the agricultural sphere—the "kulaks," as they are sometimes termed—have managed to distance themselves only very slowly and with some difficulty from the broader ranks of the peasantry, in which milieu many of their social relationships continue to be embedded. Similarly, African traders have faced uphill struggles against the competition of well-established alien trading communities (Asians in East Africa, for example), and as a result also have taken shape only slowly as a coherent class fraction.

Even less straightforward has been any crystallization of the "bureaucratic" fraction of the petty bourgeoisie. In an earlier article (included in this volume) on the postcolonial state in Africa I stressed this point, noting that the uncertainty of its predispositions led von Freyhold to employ the term "nizers" to conceptualize such a stratum, a stratum which is not yet unequivocally a class and one which might still "commit suicide" by identifying *downward* with the workers and peasants in the society. No wonder Murray, in a seminal article, felt the necessity of "refocusing class analysis" with reference to the decolonization and developmental process in sub-Saharan Africa by seeking to "comprehend the contradictions inherent in the accession to *state power* of unformed classes." To the extent that Murray's emphasis is correct, the provision of a steady hand at the helm of the postcolonial state will appear to be even more difficult an undertaking.

Focusing on the emergence of the petty bourgeoisie to positions of power in contemporary Africa is a crucial key to our understanding them, but the ambiguity and incoherence of this process must not be underestimated. In a parallel manner, any conceptualization of the various fractions of such a petty bourgeoisie also must be presented with caution. Yet this is a warning which recent Marxist analysts have not always heeded. As noted earlier, a number of them have placed a distinction between two very clearly articulated wings of the petty bourgeoisie at the very center of their analysis. Leys hints at something of this sort when he argues that "the significance of the higher bureaucracy has been somewhat obscured in the literature on African underdevelopment, perhaps under the influence of Fanon, who appeared to run together the idea of the higher bureaucracy and that of the bourgeoisie or would-be bourgeoisie when he wrote of a 'bourgeoisie of the civil service.'" Mamdani makes a similar distinction even more sharply and draws from it implications which premise his interpretation of Ugandan developments. Indeed, they premise his approach to developments throughout the continent:

> The ruling class in independent Uganda was the petit-bourgeoisie. What is central to understanding the "underdeveloped" ruling class, in contradistinction to that in developed capitalism, is its weak economic base and its *fragmentation* at the level of politics. The "underdeveloped" petit-bourgeoisie is *not* a *consolidated* class . . .
>
> It is the struggle within the petit-bourgeoisie that determines the method of accumulation and the manner of appropriation of the surplus. Given that it is located both within the state (state bureaucracy) and outside of it (kulaks, traders), the petit-bourgeoisie has two alternative methods of accumulation open to it: either use the state to create public property which the petit-bougeoisie would control indirectly through its control over the state, or use the state to expand private property which the petit-bourgeoisie would control directly through ownership. . . .
>
> It is the economic base of the fraction that emerges victorious which defines the political character of the state. In Africa today, the petit-bourgeois regimes can be roughly divided into those that use the state to create public property (the so-called "progressive" regimes) and those that do so to create private property (the "reactionary" regimes). This difference in the manner of appropriation of surplus conditions the nature of future class formation. With the creation of state property, the dominant class that emerges is a bureaucratic bourgeoisie; when the emphasis is on the use of the state to create private property, the petit-bourgeoisie transforms itself into a commercial bourgeoisie.

It is one of the contentions of the present essay that any such formulation, while obviously suggestive, goes much too far and has led, at least in Mamdani's case, to the creation of a stark and misleading dichotomy between entrepreneurial and bureaucratic "fractions" of the petty bourgeoisie which obscures much more than it illuminates. There is an essential wisdom in Fanon's admittedly vague formula ("an intellectual elite engaged in trade"). As we shall see in dealing concretely with the Ugandan case, there *is* indeed an interpenetration of the realms of petty-bourgeois activity which substantially qualifies any such dichotomy. Once this interpenetration is lost from view, it is all too easy to misinterpret the role of the postcolonial state and to denature the essential features of postcolonial politics.

This argument becomes even more clear if we introduce one final element into the picture, an element which Roger Murray attempted to conceptualize by using the concept "political class"—a somewhat unsatisfactory term for what is, nonetheless, a vitally important reality. The reference here is to those who staff the state *at the most overtly political level*—including, most obviously, the president or prime minister, his cabinet and immediate circle of advisors, senior officials of the ruling party (or politicized army), even the leaders and senior functionaries of the opposition party or parties (if such there be). It is they who have the most immediate and potent access to the levers of the state; in consequence, they have a quite significant role to play in defining how that state will express itself. Yet they are certainly not to be lumped together straightforwardly with the "bureaucrats" or civil service. Nor are they exactly coterminous with the petty bourgeoisie of the private sector. Instead, this is a stratum which acts as a link between state and private sectors, refracting and reconciling (when it can) the various pressures which spring from the production process—a foot in both camps (bureaucratic and entrepreneurial), as it were, and composed of members with various interests of their own.[3]

What needs to be emphasized here is that this "class"—this circle of political activists—is one which exemplifies particularly graphically the basic attributes of the African petty bourgeoisie identified above, its relatively undefined and unformed nature and its ambiguous overlapping of the various fractions conceivable within such a class. Murray, in particular, has stressed this point, suggesting that such a stratum reflects, quite simply, "the *absence* of a determinate class standpoint in the production process" (emphasis added). This may overstate the case somewhat. Obviously, the standpoint of the "political class" will *tend* to be petty bourgeois. Moreover, insofar as its class character is "partial and transitional" (in Murray's phrase) it will, in this, be reflecting attributes of the petty bourgeoisie as a whole, reflecting them in a manner which is, perhaps, merely an exaggerated version of the norm for such a class under postcolonial conditions. Nonetheless, this does mean that there is even less of an *a priori* reason why the elements who are closest to the state should express the "determinate . . . standpoint" of any one particular *fraction* of the petty bourgeoisie. Nor is there any reason why they should underwrite exclusively *either* of the two policy thrusts which Mamdani has suggested as exhausting the options open to the postcolonial state. The elements are likely to be much too commingled for that! Of course, the full implications of this argument can only become clear when fleshed out with respect to the Ugandan reality. Perhaps enough has been said, however, to suggest that by adding the "political class"—with its "*relative autonomy and volatility* in the political arena"—into our equation, we see even more clearly the dangers of fixing too schematically the nature of the petty bourgeoisie or of oversimplifying the likely characteristics of any fragmentation which it may manifest.

This, then, is the class context of the kind of politics which swirls around the postcolonial state. We must now say something more directly about the nature of these politics themselves. In this connection, a careful consideration of the concept "fraction" itself can prove particularly useful, since it is a concept which has surfaced forcefully in recent attempts (by Poulantzas and Mamdani, for example) to understand the political dynamics of the petty bourgeoisie. For Mamdani, as seen above, such fractions of the petty-bourgeois class are fully defined by the different locations of groups within the production process: kulaks, traders, bureaucrats. He then interprets parties and other political formations in Uganda as quite direct expressions of one or another of the fractions so defined. Yet, in truth, this does not quite work.

As Poulantzas correctly observes, "The problem of fractions of a class is in fact rather complicated in Marx." Indeed, "the effects of the political instance . . . may produce fractions of a class in the field of political class practice alone"! An example, drawn from Marx's *Eighteenth Brumaire*, illustrates the point quite clearly. Writing of the "republican fraction of the bourgeoisie" during that period, Marx states:

> This was not a fraction of the bourgeoisie bound together by great common interest and demarcated from the rest by conditions peculiar to it; it was a coterie of republican-minded members of the bourgeoisie, writers, lawyers, officers and officials. Its influence rested on the personal antipathies of the country towards Louis Philippe, on memories of the old republic, on the republican faith of a number of enthusiasts, and, above all, on *French nationalism*, for it constantly kept alive hatred of the Vienna Treaties and the alliance with England.

If this can be the case for the bourgeoisie—the possibility that fractions will exist which are not explicable merely in terms of their expressing the interests of the various "commercial," "industrial," or "financial" constellations within the broader bourgeois class—how much more likely is it to be true of a class, like the African petty bourgeoisie, which is at once weak (as any petty bourgeoisie tends to be), relatively unformed (in the African context), and not yet divided, in any unequivocal manner, into constituent elements diversely rooted in the production process? The result: we find, within the African petty bourgeoisie a whole range of "fractions" which are produced "in the field of political practice alone." Moreover, the implications of this formulation are important. For it is precisely such a perspective which, in the realm of theory, can lend to the diverse ethnic, religious, institutional, and ideological alignments of Africa's petty-bourgeois politics the *reality* they so clearly possess in practice—while at the same time situating them in such a way as to validate the claims of class analysis to be the crucial key to an understanding of African social formations.

Class analysis? Here we must reemphasize the role as interested "intermediary"—junior but active partner with imperial interests—which we have sketched for the petty bourgeoisie within the context of peripheral capitalism, a role the more clearly enunciated, the more coherent and sharply defined such a class becomes. It can also be reiterated that it is the petty bourgeoisie which will be in direct control of the postcolonial state, this "overdeveloped" state being, in turn, an important prize, well situated to arbitrate for aspirant Africans the terms and methods of capital accumulation in the new economies as well as the uses to which various surpluses and scarce resources are to be put. This, then, is the core of a realistic class analysis of contemporary Africa. What cannot be said with the same degree of certainty is who among the petty-bourgeoisie-in-formation will achieve such control of the state. In fact, this will be decided only by a struggle within the petty-bourgeois stratum itself!

Fractions? A further explanation may now be suggested, for it is precisely this intraclass competition for control of the state and for related economic advantage which activates the diversity of fractions produced "in the sphere of political practice alone." The mechanism? The efforts of members of the petty bourgeoisie to *stitch together alliances* and to *rally constituencies* in order the more successfully to engage in such competition. Here the ethnic and/or regional card is a particularly tempting one to play, and for a number of reasons. At the level of *alliances*, the sharing of a common ethnic background (one which may actually be reinforced by direct ties of kinship) by certain members of the petty bourgeoisie can often serve as a kind of lowest common denominator of trust and communication on the basis of which negotiations toward formation of a political alliance may take place. As regards the mobilizing of constituencies—this referring to the attempt to create some popular base for sustained political activity—a utilization of "tribal" ploys can also seem particularly attractive to petty-bourgeois politicians.

After all, there do exist cultural differences between African peoples, differences which will have been underscored and exacerbated in many instances by the divide-and-rule tactics of the colonial powers. Even more crucial is the fact of *uneven development* between regions and, by an easy transposition, between "tribes." Under these circumstances, it is relatively easy to induce the lower strata of any given ethnic group to interpret the essence of their backwardness as being the result of a zero-sum game over the distribution of scarce resources played out between tribes, rather than being primarily a result of class division, worldwide and local. Petty-bourgeois politicians can then present themselves as their champions! Moreover, even members of the petty-bourgeoisie can themselves become mesmerized by this same kind of construction of social reality, resentful of the "unfair" advantage (or, on the contrary, defensive of their own "deserved" privilege) in terms of entrepreneurial/bureaucratic advancement, education, and the like, seen to have been bequeathed upon their class counterparts in another ethnic group by the unevenness of the development process. Upon these and other building blocks, tribalist ideologies and ethnic political groupings are developed, ideologies and groupings which take on a tangible and undeniable reality and resonance, however spurious some of their foundations may be.[4] Moreover, a quite similar sociopolitical dynamic determines that religious distinctions deposited by the historical process can also become available for this kind of politicization—providing another possible basis for the forging of alliances and the building up of constituencies.

Any student of African politics knows that ethnically and religiously based fractions have been of great importance. Indeed, it is precisely along these lines that the petty bourgeoisie—and the countries which they lead—can crack wide open, failing, as suggested earlier, even to guarantee that minimum degree of stability necessary for the consolidation of a smoothly functioning neocolonial system.[5] In addition, fractions can sometimes crystallize around interests defined, for purposes of the competition for scarce resources, in narrowly *institutional* terms, the army being one obvious example of this in many African settings, the bureaucracy (narrowly, not broadly, defined) being another. Enough to note these three possible bases for fractions here. Each will surface more clearly when, in the following section, we examine the recent politics of Uganda.

But there is one final source of the kind of fractionalization now under discussion which must also be noted. Even less familiar than the other three, it centers on the existence, within the petty-bourgeois class, of partisans of diverse developmental ideologies. To be sure, there is a "conventional wisdom" characteristic of the bulk of the African petty bourgeoisie which does serve, normally, as that class's ideological cement, both rationalizing its subordination to imperialism and crystallizing such internal unity as it possesses. It is a conventional wisdom which blends a fuzzy and opportunistic nationalism (of the sort so trenchantly demystified by Fanon) with a Western-derived developmentalist perspective ("modernization" with its attendant elitism, "capital scarcity" with its attendant "requirements" of increased foreign investment, aid, expansion of the raw-material export sector, etc.). However, what must be emphasized here is that the mold of this ideology—like that of the class itself—is not firmly set. There is also room for ideological maneuver which can, upon occasion, introduce significantly new variables into the petty-bourgeois political equation.

Roger Murray has spoken directly to this feature of the petty bourgeoisie in dealing with "the relative social autonomy and plasticity" of his "political class in formation," discussed above. He argues that

> it is precisely this social *uncertainty* and susceptibility to multiple determinations and influences which makes the dimension of *consciousness* so crucial to the analysis . . . The contradictory situation and experience of these typically transitional and partial postcolonial ruling groups is mediated through the transformations, incoherences, oscillations, "false" and illusory representations and reconciliations at *the level of ideology*.

Murray finds in such a milieu the seedbed of the real (though severely limited) socialist departure which Nkrumahism represented; I have provided elsewhere a parallel explanation for those progressive attributes which have been one dimension of Tanzania's experiment in *ujamaa*. No doubt such left-leaning initiatives, when undertaken by segments of the petty bourgeoisie, also reflect other ambiguities of that class. We have seen that Poulantzas describes the petty bourgeoisie as being "polarized" between classes above and below it, capable of "swinging" one way or the other. Those who do identify *downward*— "committing suicide," in Cabral's expression, and "reincarnating" themselves "in the condition of workers and peasants"—also reflect this potentiality in the situation. Of course, it must also be recognized that even such left ideological expressions will tend to reveal their petty-bourgeois origins, exemplified most often by the absence of the clear perspective on class struggle and the dynamics of imperialism which Marxism might provide. Such ideologies all too easily collapse into a vague, even opportunistic, *populism*—one more ploy in building a broader popular constituency! Nor does this exhaust the range of possibilities. There is also room for ideological predilections of an even less familiar kind to come to the fore and to take on political life. As we shall see, Amin's peculiar contributions in Uganda provide a particularly dramatic case in point.

In contemporary Africa, then, it is fractions based on these diverse grounds—not, as some would have it, fractions more firmly rooted in the production process itself—which most often will be prominent in defining the character of petty-bourgeois politics. Furthermore, the possible permutations and combinations of these fractions in concrete political situations are numerous, the results never entirely a foregone conclusion. Skilled politicians can produce more stability than so treacherous a terrain might seem readily to allow for, suppressing or assuaging populace and petty bourgeoisie alike for considerable periods (Senegal, Kenya). At other times, as noted earlier, any such consolidation of the politics of neocolonialism will be a much more fugitive goal (Nigeria in the 1960s, Uganda). Indeed, the range of possible variation here recalls Murray's admonition of a decade ago to the effect that what is needed is "a much finer discrimination of the variant forms of a 'neocolonialism' which embraces much of the world."

Of course, even this range of variation does move rather straightforwardly within the parameters defined by neocolonialism—the petty bourgeoisie beginning to play, well or badly, the role it is best suited to play. Yet we have hinted (in discussing the ideological variable, above) that there may be somewhat greater leeway than this, that from the petty-bourgeois politics which swirl around the postcolonial state something more unpredictable may emerge. The notion of the "relative autonomy" of the state can be helpful here. Not that, for all its growing usage among Marxists in recent years, this concept is without real ambiguities. Thus, Miliband sharply criticizes Poulantzas for first establishing the relative autonomy of the state as a concept and then blandly and unjustifiably proceeding to subvert such a supposedly autonomous state (in Miliband's words) "into the merest instrument of a determinate class—indeed all but conceptualizing it out of existence." He continues:

> The reason for that confusion, or at least one reason for it, is Poulantzas's failure to make the necessary distinction between *class power* and *state power.* State power is the main and ultimate—but not the only—means whereby class power is assured and maintained. But one of the main reasons for stressing the importance of the notion of the relative autonomy of the state is that there is a basic distinction to be made between class power and state power, and that the analysis of the meaning and implications of that notion of relative autonomy must indeed focus on the forces which cause it to be greater or less, the circumstances in which it is exercised, and so on. The blurring of the distinction between class power and state power by Poulantzas makes any such analysis impossible: for all the denunciations of "economism," politics does here assume an "epiphenomenal" form.

Here Miliband points the way more clearly for us than does Poulantzas. Indeed, when the dominant class concerned is a relatively unformed one (as is the case with the African petty bourgeoisie) the possibility of "state power" assuming a particularly vital importance within the social formation is substantially enhanced. Then it is that the fraction or fractions of the petty bourgeoisie which have managed to establish control over the state can hope to place their own stamp upon events. Needless to say, this does not mean that there are no limits upon their so doing, or that class determinants do not threaten to foreclose on such autonomy at every turn. What it does mean, for example, is that Tanzania, or Ghana under Nkrumah, where the postcolonial state was used for a time for some novel and progressive purposes, are not to be construed glibly as being merely "typical" neocolonial regimes. Nor, for other reasons, is General Amin's Uganda to be so construed. A "finer discrimination" is necessary here, too.

The Ugandan Case

In fact, Uganda offers a particularly illuminating case study, one which demonstrates clearly the possible contribution of the theoretical arguments advanced above. This is even apparent from a simple juxtaposition of writings on the country already available. On the one hand, there is a rich selection of analyses rooted in the conventional methodologies of Western political science. More than is the case for many other African countries, such analyses have succeeded in illuminating Ugandan politics, the area of their main contribution lying precisely in a documenting of the diversity of ethnic, religious, institutional, and ideological strands which have crisscrossed Ugandan political life.

In particular, "the problem of tribal and ethnic diversity and hostility" has preoccupied such writers as Glentworth and Hancock:

> Uganda is uniquely ill-favoured in this respect. The tribes are not small enough to allow a Tanzanian situation where no one tribe or group can effectively dominate as an alliance. On the other hand, the tribes are neither few nor large and cohesive enough to provide an uneasy balance of power, such as appears to exist in Kenya within the shadow of President Kenyatta. A further complicating factor is that the largest and richest and most cohesive group, the Baganda, while not sufficiently powerful to dominate the rest, have by their numbers, ambitions and relative advancement convinced the others of their desire to dominate. The result was that from the late 1950's combinations among other tribes were formed with the object of stopping the Baganda, a development matched from 1963 by amateurish attempts by the Baganda government to form alliances among the southern Bantu peoples. Ethnic divisions, separating the Bantu in the south from the Nilotics and associated peoples in the north, became an added complication. Perhaps these divisions were not sharp enough to convince the anthropologists that there was a real distinction but they were ever present in the minds of the Ugandans and capable in fact of arousing bitter ethnic

rivalry. One reason has been the conviction among the northern peoples, from West Nile to Karamoja, that the southerners received disproportionate economic privileges under colonial rule and that a government led by a northerner should set itself to reverse this situation. The Langi and the Acholi may have feared each other, and may have been divided within themselves, but they had a common aim in overturning the southern emphasis in colonial policy. At the other end the Baganda were concerned about the allocation of government revenue in favour of the north whose backwardness, in the view of a former minister in the Baganda government confided to one of the authors, was a reflection of "barbarianism." The suspicion and hostility engendered by this sort of attitude was hardly a sound basis for national unity.

There is also the politicization of religious diversity. Commenting on the competition between the Uganda People's Congress (UPC) and the Democratic Party (DP) in the 1950s and 1960s, for example, Leys observes that it "was based on religion; unlike nearly all other multi-party systems in Africa, the UPC–DP struggle was not a competition between ethnic groups with their characteristic regional bases. It was a competition between the adherents of the Roman Catholic church, wherever it was established, and, in effect, everyone else." His detailed case study of one district, Acholi, demonstrated the manner in which party loyalties, determined on this basis, defined an all-pervasive jockeying for position within every local institution, such infighting centering, in turn, on questions related to the distribution of various goods and surpluses.

Similar diversity also riddled the UPC itself, as a case study by Cohen and Parson of the UPC's branch and constituency elections of 1970 emphasizes: "One of the main issues was supposed to have been the UPC as a mobilizing force for socialism, but the elections appear to have drawn heavily on other forces. Issues of tribe and religion and old cleavages within the party appear to have dominated many campaigns." All of which leads Twaddle to summarize the situation as follows: "In Uganda, political alliances at the centre of the country sometimes follow an ethnic line, sometimes politico-religious allegiances, sometimes a racial difference. More frequently, they cluster along some combination of these alignments."

Accurate enough at one level. However, what these analyses fail to illuminate is the broader setting—of imperialism and the class struggle—within which such infighting occurs. Glentworth and Hancock, for example, grace their analysis of the Obote period with the startling observation that "the imperialists were absent," this with reference to what is, even by African standards, a dramatically dependent economy and society. Twaddle quite specifically juxtaposes his emphasis upon factional politicking to more radical alternative theoretical frameworks, stating categorically that "recent Ugandan politics are more clearly understood in these terms than in the language of neo-colonial dependence." Obviously, it is here that a Marxist approach shows its strength, a point at least partially demonstrated by the work of Mamdani, cited earlier, which represents the first systematic analysis of Ugandan political economy from a Marxist perspective. Mamdani begins to trace the process by which Uganda was incorporated into the global imperialist system and the seed sown for emergence of an indigenous petty bourgeoisie. And this, in turn, provides the context which alone situates and renders understandable the political realities pinpointed by Twaddle and his colleagues.

Crucial long-term developments are identified by Mamdani: the enforced creation of a peasant-based, cash-crop economy designed, quite specifically, to service imperial requirements; the emergence of an intermediary Asian "commercial bourgeoisie" in the economic sphere—their strategic position in the economy destined to become as much the target of African petty-bourgeois aspirations as the colonial state structure itself. Most graphically of all, the clear beginnings of crystallization of an African petty bourgeoisie, this latter being no mere casual by-product of colonialism but rather a class whose consolidation came to be considered by the British imperial strategists as vital to their long-term interests. Mamdani quotes Mr. Lennox-Boyd, when the (then) "Colonial-Secretary said in the House of Commons in London that an African property-owning middle-class would be 'one of the stabilizing factors in that continent.' He said he would regard himself as 'pretty inefficient' if, at the end of his period of office, he had not encouraged a sense of private profit and public

service among Africans." But the activities of Sir Andrew Cohen
as governor of Uganda during the 1950s speak even more
eloquently of this emphasis as the latter drove to establish the
Uganda Credit and Savings Bank, the Small Industries Development Fund, the African Traders Development section of the
Ministry of Commerce and Industry, and African Business
Promotions. Though the record of success was mixed, it is clear
that through such initiatives a class ready to inherit power was to
be created. And, of course, Africanization proceeded apace
within the interstices of the state structure itself—in both bureaucratic and political spheres. There is no need, then, to repeat
Mamdani's story here. Without doubt, the basic preconditions
for a false decolonization—economic dependence and the presence of an aspirant petty bourgeoisie with interests not antagonistic to such continuing dependence—came ever more readily to
hand as the colonial period wore on.

Given this strong and viable starting point for analysis, it is all
the more unfortunate that the closer Mamdani's account comes
to the political realm—and the closer it comes to the present
day—the more ineluctably it degenerates into an oppressive and
overly schematic determinism. We have hinted at some of the
terms of this analytical anticlimax in the preceding section. Substantively this means that, in spite of the overall vacuum within
which their accounts proceed, Glentworth and Hancock, Twaddle, and their ilk have at least as much to tell us about the terms
of the political process under Obote and Amin as has Mamdani.
A depressing admission if true, and one with which Marxist
observers of the African reality must come fully to terms.

What does Mamdani have to say about petty-bourgeois politics
in Uganda? As he quite correctly observes of the transition to
independence, "the nearness of the event, when state power was
to be transferred to a class situated within the colony, brought to
the fore the contradictions within the petty bourgeoisie. The
question now was simply: Who was to control state power?" What
were the terms of this competition for state power? In the first
instance, he argues, the competitors crystallized into political
parties, "mass-based, petty-bourgeois parties [which]—whether
ideologically nationalist, tribal, or religious—were each based in a

different section of the petty bourgeoisie." For "section," read "fraction" (Mamdani's more normal usage). In short, these parties derived their real meaning from their representing, variably, the "trader," kulak," and "bureaucratic" fractions of the petty bourgeoisie.

In the early period, "whereas the KY [Kabaka Yekka] represented a kulak-intellectual-peasant alliance and the UPC [Uganda People's Congress] a trader-intellectual one, the DP [Democratic Party] was an alliance of chiefs-intellectuals-peasants." The core: "kulaks," "traders," "chiefs." Yet this gives rise to a picture of Uganda which is unrecognizable. Surely the overlap between kulak and trader in Buganda throughout this period was patent, with the interpenetration of African commercial petty bourgeoisie (kulaks and traders) and bureaucratic petty bourgeoisie almost equally so.[6] The UPC? Traders, but also kulaks and bureaucrats-in-the-making, and distinctive, first and foremost, for their coming from areas outside Buganda. This made them not only eager to advance themselves in petty-bourgeois terms, but equally eager to redress the pattern of uneven development which had placed their Bagandan counterparts in the trader-kulak-bureaucratic categories ahead of them in the race. Moreover, in the process of building up constituencies to back their own political plays, they attempted (often with success) to deepen the commitment of the peasantries of their area to this same kind of perspective—in a manner parallel to the Baganda politicians in Buganda. Needless to say, much of the nationalist project of such petty-bourgeois "nationalists" became blurred in the process, as it was by the politicization of religion. For what of the DP, seen as a party of the chiefs? Unfortunately, this formulation is as little illuminating as the others: if ever a division—in this case one premised to a considerable degree on religious difference—cut across any supposed fractionalization of the petty bourgeoisie based on diverse location in the production process, this was it. Clearly, the history of party conflict in Uganda has to be accounted for in other terms.

Mamdani's model is no more illuminating in dealing with tensions internal to the UPC itself, tensions which surfaced all the more forcefully in the wake of the crushing of the Baganda and the gradual decay, under pressure, of the DP. For Mamdani, the UPC undergoes a sea change as it takes control of the state with the coming of independence: "There is a gradual shift in the core of the non-Baganda petty bourgeoisie from traders to the governing bureaucracy." In consequence, he finds "the 1966 UPC reflecting this balance of forces, comprised of two fractions: the 'center,' representing the government bureaucracy, and the 'right,' comprising the petty bourgeoisie proper (small property-owning kulaks and traders . . .)." The former is successful: "The post-1966 UPC was under the firm control of one fraction of the petty-bourgeois class: the governing bureaucracy."

For Mamdani, the immediate results of this are somewhat equivocal. He presents this bureaucracy as at first merely using the state to parachute its members into commercial roles, but before long he has the same bureaucracy pushing the state itself into the productive sphere in its own class interests (see the long quotation above) and *against* the interests of any fraction of the petty bourgeoisie which aspires to any further aggrandizement in the private sector. In a manner which closely parallels Shivji's reduction of Tanzania's Arusha Declaration to the self-interested machinations of Tanzania's own bureaucratic bourgeoisie, Obote's "Move to the Left" becomes the hegemonic policy of a similar class fraction in Uganda. In addition, Obote, with his shell of a UPC, becomes merely the political arm of this all-embracing bureaucracy. And finally, the coup, when it occurs in 1971, is to be explained primarily as a successful attack by the aforementioned "petty bourgeoisie proper" against the hegemony and the self-interested "socialism" of the governing bureaucracy!

Again, all of this is pretty far fetched. Even at the most basic level, it ignores the practices of many members of the "political class" (practices seen at their most gross in the enterprising career of Felix Onama, Obote's minister of defense) and of many senior civil servants, those who operated in the private sector at least as strenuously as in the public one. This reality alone would give one pause before accepting the "governing bureaucracy" explanatory model. We shall see that any such perspective also makes it impossible to understand either Amin's coup or the subsequent vagaries of the general's regime. What may be noted here, however, is the ironic fact that Mamdani himself provides an important clue to an alternative formulation. Qualifying his picture of African politics—"the contending fractions become locked in combat"—he suggests in a footnote in his book that:

> The case of Kenya would seem to be an exception, for there the fragmentation of the petty bourgeoisie was less important than the integration of its various sections: the bureaucrat acquires the shop of the departing Asian businessman and buys land in the countryside; the son of the kulak becomes a bureaucrat; the African businessman purchases agricultural property.

But precisely the same situation has existed in Uganda, the same blurring of the lines between any fractions which might be thought to root themselves in the production process. Moreover, some of the exact same pressures toward the *fragmentation* of petty-bourgeois political unity along tribal and other related fault-lines can be seen to exist—if, to date, in much less flamboyant a fashion—in Kenya as in Uganda.[7] Such a realization makes it all the more frustrating that in Mamdani's Uganda the reality of such fragmentation keeps getting factored away.

All the more tempting to revert to Glentworth and Hancock:

> . . . arising out of the question of uneven development, there was the widespread assumption that the function of government was primarily if not exclusively to benefit the governors. The winner-take-all philosophy was as much a part of inter-tribal affairs as it was of intra-tribal politics. So just as a Muganda in the days before 1966 saw it as his interest to support his chief and the Kabaka's ministers, he looked with mounting anxiety on a national government seemingly controlled by northerners. To be an outsider was to be a loser. The important thing was to have access to government for this meant access to power and wealth and a guarantee of personal security. Ministers, district commissioners and even some permanent secretaries saw themselves, and were regarded, as the chief patrons and protectors for their localities, and in accordance with the system their relatives and clients came to Kampala or gathered at district headquarters to claim their appointments, promotions and financial rewards. All this increased the importance of alliances and accounts for the constant jockeying for positions within and between tribal groups in the period after independence . . . Com-

petition for office and jobs became the nation's growth industry. For Dr. Obote it meant that as chief patron he could widen his power base without ever being completely secure or certain about his following.

"Competition," "jockeying for positions," "access to wealth and power"—such phrases all have the ring of truth for anyone familiar with Ugandan politics, as do the tribal terms in which, in practice, such processes have been so often cast. Nonetheless, this kind of presentation again reveals itself to be onesided, no less so than Mamdani's, oscillating uneasily between an analysis whose chief cornerstone remains "the tribe" and an analysis which hints, all too obliquely, at more basic attributes of the competition for scarce resources. Are "ministers, district commissioners, and even some permanent secretaries" (among many other denizens of the petty bourgeoisie) really to be seen as tribal spokesmen and representatives pure and simple? Of course not. Any such emphasis would merely leave out one half—and the most important half—of the equation. What is missing from the Glentworth-Hancock universe is precisely a sense of "inter*class* affairs" and "intra*class* politics," and, in consequence, a sense of the dialectic which exists between class and tribe (or religion, etc.) in the African context.

A seeming impasse, then, between Twaddle and Co. on the one hand and Mamdani on the other. But, of course, we have already indicated the way out: the utilization of a concept of petty-bourgeois politics which refrains from boiling away the specificity and irreducibility of *political fractions*, while at the same time retaining the necessary bite of class analysis. By now it will be clear that this approach enables us to affirm, with Mamdani, the centrality of that broad process of the structuring of a dependent economy and policy in Uganda which he emphasizes, while also taking seriously the rich texture of petty-bourgeois politics illuminated by more conventional writers. Unfortunately, only a book-length manuscript could do full justice to such an approach to Ugandan politics during the regimes of Obote and Amin. What follows is merely the briefest of sketches of what such an analysis might begin to look like.

Take, first, the Obote era. The terms of politics in this period have already been suggested. Competition for power and resources within the petty bourgeoisie intertwined with what was an extreme form of uneven development even by African standards—characterized, in particular, by Buganda's dramatic historical headstart. And this in turn was overlaid with a highly visible religious differentiation, the politicization of which provided a further building block for petty-bourgeois politicians (the DP). Once the competition was cast in such tribal and religious categories—consolidated in party or factional affiliations and long-term strategic commitments for the petty bourgeoisie, crystallized in diverse fears and aspirations among the populace—this gave a much sharper political reality to these terms of reference than they might otherwise have had. Politics really was about tribe and religion, though it never ceased to be about the petty bourgeoisie as well! Moreover, as the energies released by this kind of competition burst out, it became apparent that the petty bourgeoisie in Uganda was not strong enough as a class to transcend the fragmentation which it had itself invoked. Indeed, the failure of the petty bourgeoisie to act effectively as a class defined the failure of conventional "nation building" in Uganda.

In such a context, as we have seen, further fragmentation and intensified intrigue (especially within the "political class" itself) became the essential stuff of Ugandan politics. Inside the UPC, groups now crystallized which also took on the attributes of fractions defined "in the field of political practice alone." One thinks here of the southern, "Bantu," politicians who banded together against Obote in 1966, while Obote found it difficult to avoid consolidating a northern, "Nilotic," and, toward the end of his reign, even a Langi "fraction" as one crucial pillar of his own support. One sensed, of course, that Obote was never entirely happy with this seeming necessity forced upon him by the dynamics of petty-bourgeois politics, and that he was constantly working to diversify and expand the ruling bloc over which he presided. In fact, one motivation behind his celebrated "Move to the Left" was precisely his desire to escape from the "northern" corner (including strong reliance on the predominantly northern-recruited army) into which he was being pushed.

What of his "Move to the Left"? Unfortunately, it is all to easy to overstate its significance. Throughout the Obote period, an overall petty-bourgeois project did stand out amidst all the attendant turmoil—one which saw as central the servicing of imperialism and the Africanization of the state machine and the private sector (particularly in its Asian-dominated intermediate spheres). Initiatives like the National Trading Corporation, the Trade Licensing Act, "Operation Bringing African Traders into Town" and other attempts to advance the interests of an African business class characterized Obote's regime until the end. Most apparent qualifications to that policy thrust (for example, an item like the Co-operative Societies Act of 1970, of which Mamdani makes a great deal) seem more like methods of correcting for the difficulties and the malfunctioning of such a direction of policy than part of some move made by the bureaucracy against the African entrepreneurial elements (many of whom were, in any case, among the most prominent activists and Obote supporters within the political class).[8]

It is true that toward the end of Obote's reign there began to surface a more marked diversity of perspective on the development problem, one such perspective (Obote's) becoming the aforementioned "Move to the Left." If this was not the bureaucracy's "class project," as Mamdani would have us believe, what in fact was it? Again, the density and complexity of petty-bourgeois politics, as we have been describing them, determined that the "Move" had several layers of significance. In the first section we discussed the possibility of a petty-bourgeois fraction emerging which centered upon the ideological variable, with Nkrumahism and Tanzania's Arusha Declaration cited as cases in point. There may have been something of this in Obote's initiative as well, in his introduction of a more radical rhetoric and a form of nationalization into the political arena. Perhaps this was in part a spillover from Nyerere's policy departures, which Obote professed to admire: perhaps it also evidenced a dash of patriotism which caused Obote to look wistfully toward the image of a united and prosperous Uganda. Certainly it seems difficult to account for Obote's increased militancy in foreign policy—his "relative autonomy" from imperial dictate in that sphere—in any other terms.

Nevertheless, it is perfectly clear that Obote was no socialist; the manner in which he presided over the decimation of the UPC left wing in the early 1960s and his stifling, throughout the years, of any possibility of genuine working-class militancy offer proof of that. Nor was the "Move to the Left" a particularly deep-cutting left initiative, demanding, as Gershenberg and others have documented, only marginal readjustments on the part of international capital and the domestic private sector, and in certain respects even further servicing the latter's interests. Much more clearly, the program suggests a populist ploy in the petty-bourgeois political game, a calculated attempt to leapfrog the fragmentation inherent in that game in order to consolidate a more effective trans-tribal, popular constituency. The new electoral procedures which Obote intended—procedures designed to force candidates to gain support in several ethnic settings—evidenced a similar goal. If this is so, the fact that the content of such an attempt remained far more rhetorical than real need not surprise us. Rare is the petty-bourgeois politician who can commit class suicide and turn to the full-fledged mobilization of a popular base of workers and peasants, as in the genuine African revolutions of Guinea or Mozambique. Such an initiative in Uganda was unlikely to come from the top down, in any case. The story of Obote's last years was much more that of a sometime master of petty-bourgeois politics, the great coalition-builder, trying now to add another string to his bow, that being a broader, more popular base. His main intention: to consolidate himself and his followers in power and in privilege.

Against this background it becomes possible to interpret the 1971 coup in something other that a one-dimensional manner. To be sure, the coup did represent a crisis of petty-bourgeois politics. But it was at bottom a familiar kind of crisis, one fully consistent with the overall pattern of such politics which we have been tracing, apparently just another turn of the wheel of petty-bourgeois coalition-building, despite its dramatic, military character. In this case, facilitating the coup was a kind of *negative* coalition of petty-bourgeois fractions whose acquiescence at least insured that the Obote government would have much too little support to enable it to resist the military's push. The initial positive response to the coup in many Baganda and other ethnic circles (at petty-bourgeois and mass levels), and in DP/Catholic circles, must be accounted for as being, in significant part, the residue of previous historical battles. And such responses were continually being reinforced by the specter of Obote's own apparent political schizophrenia. As noted earlier, even in the course of "Moving to the Left" he was also falling back on a strategy of building up his own team of ethnic defenders: as, for instance, in the promotion of Acholi and (particularly) Langi military officers, as well as their prominence in his refurbished paramilitary General Service Unit, the latter apparently consolidated as a counterweight to the predominance of West Nilers in the army. But this, in turn, merely demonstrated that the unity of any prior "northern" component to Obote's coalition was distintegrating. The negative coalition which could align itself against Obote was becoming dangerously broad.

And then there was the military itself. Not unified, as we shall see, but an important institutional reality nonetheless, and one available for realizing the larger purposes of the senior command. Indeed, Twaddle and others have emphasized that it was precisely the army's interest *qua* army which most crucially determined the launching of the coup—whatever the other *permissive* conditions may have been. It became, in effect, the positive arm of a negative coalition. Samuel Decalo has theorized in general terms a potentially useful approach to this phenomenon:

> . . . it is possible to adopt the conceptual image of the officer corps as essentially an elite body (actually a coterie of elite cliques), primarily concerned with corporate and individual interests, in a societal context of scarcity where other elites (politicians, trade unionists, students) are competing for the same rewards and benefits. In such conditions of scarcity, civilian and military grievances tend to coincide, and the existence of corporate and/or personal ambitions of officers might be the key variable in sparking off a coup. Viewed thus, all the inadequacies of civilian rule usually cited as reasons for African coups become the back-drop against which inter-elite conflict (intra-civil, intra-military, and civil-

military) arises, and the arena within which personal ambitions manifest themselves.

Or, in the more adequate Marxist terms in which a parallel framework was set out above, such an army becomes an institutionally based fraction acting upon the competitive terrain of petty-bourgeois politics. Decalo applies his framework specifically to Uganda (among other cases), and there can be little doubt that his insight does illuminate one crucial dimension of the coup. There is not space here to reprise the terms of the deterioration in the relationship between army leadership and other members of the established "political class" in general, or between Obote and Amin in particular. But it is hard to avoid entirely the force of Decalo's assertion that "this was a classic example of the personalized takeover caused by a General's own fears and ambitions, within the context of a widespread civic malaise and a fissiparous fratricidal army rife with corporate grievances." And Twaddle's emphasis is similar: "The Amin coup is best understood . . . as an internal war led by an army general whose network of followers managed to seize the national armour before anyone else did. It did change the shape of Ugandan political life, not towards parliamentary government rather than dictatorial rule but rather towards a realignment of Ugandan factions along a new axis."

Once again, Twaddle's commonsensical view appears to have more to offer than alternative left formulations, despite the fact that he lacks a theory of petty-bourgeois politics which could alone give his argument analytical resonance. Compare the view of Michael Lofchie who, in a well-known article, has interpreted the Uganda coup as a reasonably pure case of a "middle class" (with the army as its agent) resisting a coherent socialist initiative. There may be something in this. Certainly, Obote's "Move to the Left" was unpopular with most segments of the petty bourgeoisie and perhaps even an effective populist project, if carried off by Obote, would have upset some of the most cherished calculations of the established petty bourgeoisie (of both public and private sectors). Moreover, the outspoken foreign-policy departures which Obote's "relative autonomy" permitted did apparently bring the weight of Israeli and British intriguing down upon him in a manner which undoubtedly facilitated the coup. Despite this, it seems unlikely that any supposed socialist content of that "Move" was a primary cause in galvanizing resistence to Obote;[9] Lofchie almost certainly overstates the extent of that socialist content and underestimates the other variables which were involved.

Similarly, Mamdani overstates the importance of the "Move to the Left," though in his case he sees the coup as evidencing the resistance of the entrepreneurial petty bourgeoisie not to "socialism," but to the aggrandizement of the governing bureaucracy, which he takes the "Move" to exemplify. Unfortunately, within his model there is no reason why the army should be expected to act as part of the entrepreneurial petty bourgeoisie, rather than as part of the governing bureaucracy; in fact, one would more readily expect the latter, not the former, to be the case. Once again, this lack of fit merely testifies to the weakness of the model itself and of the supposed juxtaposition of "fractions" rooted in the production process, which Mamdani continually emphasizes. In any case, the army's response was not monolithic, something which Mamdani himself must concede. His answer: "Factions within the army now reflected the fragmentation within the ruling class."

Even this does not work, however. For the main expression of such fragmentation after the coup was the alacrity with which Amin's group within the army (mainly hailing from the West Nile) set about killing Acholi and Langi officers and men—the latter suspected of "subversive" loyalties to Obote on tribal grounds. Obviously, this was not a case of the entrepreneurial petty bourgeoisie locked in mortal combat with the governing bureaucracy. It evidenced a different kind of fragmentation of the petty bourgeoisie itself, one with which Mamdani's model cannot cope. In fact, what was happening was that Amin, using the military as a necessary springboard and operating from within the bowels of the "negative coalition" which united to permit the overthrow of Obote, had begun already to forge a new petty-bourgeois fraction—one built along ethnic and religious lines—in order to sustain himself in power!

The reality of the post-coup period could be interpreted differently. Was not the way now clear for the African entrepreneurial petty bourgeoisie to establish its hegemony unequivocally, without even the challenge which Obote's populist *étatisme* might have seemed to pose? It is tempting, perhaps, to see the expulsion of the Asians, which came in the wake of the coup, as that fraction's "ultimate solution" to its contestation with the Asian commercial bourgeoisie. Certainly the dramatic steps of 1972 and 1973 had something of this flavor (although the extent to which they represented any kind of sharp break with earlier trends could easily be overstated). Nonetheless, a great many other things were happening alongside this programmatic development which are too important to be bracketed off from the main line of theoretical explanation. For example, the ethnic infighting (within the army and outside it) mentioned in the preceding paragraph, and the reign of terror which Amin's army directed against broad segments of the African population, must not be considered phenomena secondary in importance to the anti-Asian measures. In fact, they have been, in certain respects, even more integral than the expulsions in defining the nature of Amin's regime.[10]

For the killing did not stop with the Langi and Acholi. The weapon of terror was quickly turned against people from most ethnic groups in the country (including the Baganda, who had welcomed Amin with great enthusiasm) and from all the Christian denominations. More instructively, terror has been directed primarily *against members of the petty bourgeoisie*—and at least as often against those who might be deemed members of a commercial petty bourgeoisie as against those of the so-called governing bureaucracy. In short, what was taking place was the dismantling of the "negative coalition" which had comprised the challenge to Obote. And it is another development which Mamdani has difficulty in explaining. For him, such developments become an expression of "Amin's own individuality" and result, paradoxically, in "a rapid erosion of Amin's social base." As he puts it, "The petty bourgeoisie advances as a class, but not necessarily the most advanced individuals within it." The latter, it seems, are too busy being killed!

To be sure, Amin has carried intraclass competition to its logical (and most horrifying) conclusion: the unrestrained physical elimination of rivals, real or fancied. But even if this is unprecedented, we need not be surprised at other aspects of his rule, the aggressive movement of army officers (those whose survival has been premised primarily on the ethnic and religious grounds described above) into the private sector, for example. Naturally enough, those members of the petty bourgeoisie who survive will sustain this project, their aspirations having been one force behind the move against the Asians and their present commercial activities being an obvious result of that move.[11] Not that this is the only explanation for the expulsion. The circumstances and timing of that move also suggest that it had an ironic parallel with the actions of Obote: Amin's attack on the Asian community seems to have been designed, as much as anything, for populist purposes, similar to those which inspired the "Move to the Left." Like the latter, the expulsion was aimed at broadening Amin's popular constituency and thereby further consolidating his position. Moreover, for all that it exploited a particularly racist formulation of the problem, it did build on a real popular grievance. Perhaps that is why, in the short run, it generated at least as much popular enthusiasm as had the "Move to the Left" itself. At the same time, Amin, like Obote, was not one to mobilize the populace in any very fundamental way. Like Obote, too, he was prepared (albeit in a much more ruthless and paranoid manner) to subordinate his search for a populist legitimacy to the forging of a narrower, well-trusted constituency and to the use of force. On these many fronts, therefore, the continuity with the Obote period is apparent. Perhaps Amin is a caricature (and a particularly frightening one) of petty-bourgeois politics, but he is an entirely recognizable caricature nonetheless.

Having said this, it must also be affirmed that Amin's regime *is* unique in Uganda in certain important respects. There can be little doubt that developments there have been anything but satisfactory from the point of view of Western imperialism. The sheer disruption caused by the kind of infighting we have been chronicling, particularly during the Amin period, has slowed the pace of economic activity, and hence of exploitation, to a crawl. This would be bad enough, an almost classic example of the kinds of difficulties imperialism has in establishing its hegemony *efficiently* in the context of petty-bourgeois rule at the periphery (even in the absence of any very serious revolutionary threat from the mass of the population). But Uganda also demonstrates another facet of the unpredictability, from the point of view of Western capitalism, of petty-bourgeois regimes: the danger of their finding, in the degree of *relative autonomy* which is available to them, room for maneuver which can be further disruptive of any smooth and easy marriage between imperial and petty-bourgeois interests in the dependent social formation. By Ugandan standards, Aminism has exemplified this possibility in an unprecedented manner.

We have seen the terms of such a possibility in the first section; we have also noted that Obote, in foreign-policy matters and to a much lesser extent domestically, availed himself of it. But for Amin this "possibility" has become virtually a full-time preoccupation; having knit together his own fraction and being in reasonably firm control of the state, he has placed the stamp of his own (bizarre) personality upon events. Witness, for example, his very personalized manner of turning on the British and, after an initial round of denationalization, launching a fresh assault, one characterized by expropriation and by a steamy brand of anti-imperialist invective. Obviously, such initiatives have not been part of a socialist project, nor have they lifted any of the structural constraints upon Ugandan development. On the other hand, they have not serviced in any discernible way the interests of imperialism. Quite the contrary. It is not good enough to note blandly, with Mamdani, that Amin's distancing himself from the more familiar (and very powerful) centers of imperialism and from time to time linking his fortunes to such countries as the Soviet Union, Libya, and Saudi Arabia merely reflects the fact that Amin has "diversified [the] dependence" of his economy. This is true at one level. As noted, Amin has done anything but create a genuinely self-centered, autonomous economy. But Mamdani's statement is so self-evidently true as to be unilluminating. For the very arbitrariness of Amin's political and economic maneuvers abroad tell us as much about the nature of his regime as does its continuing "dependence."

"Arbitrariness" is a good word to describe Amin's domestic activities as well, despite the fact that (as seen above) they are more broadly consistent with familiar patterns than is generally understood. For if the physical elimination of petty-bourgeois rivals is, in some sense, a "logical" conclusion of the trajectory of petty-bourgeois politics, it is by no means an inevitable one. Amin's privileged access to the instruments of coercion—as springboard to his ascendancy and as cornerstone of his dominant coalition—has rendered him even more "autonomous" than most victors in the African political game. And here, too, that relative autonomy has enabled him to give much freer play to his personal motivations and personal style than might otherwise be the case. It is within some such framework that Mamdani's reference to "Amin's own individuality" makes most sense, for example. Because of that "individuality," this latest turn of the wheel in Ugandan politics has been much more destructive than it need have been.[12]

Mamdani sees signs that any such relative autonomy may be short-lived, however. He cites the consolidation of Amin's fellow army officers in entrepreneurial roles, and suggests that this will lead to a downplaying of arbitrariness and a relative stabilization of petty-bourgeois rule, all in the interests of a stable economic environment. In addition, Mamdani argues that peasant and worker protest is gaining increased focus and militancy, which (if true) provides not only a new revolutionary term for the Ugandan political equation, but also suggests a challenge that might force the petty bourgeoisie to unite more effectively in defense of their own project. Others have argued that the main lineaments of external dependency—those which run in the direction of the Western imperial centers, with their markets for Uganda's crops and their seductive supplies of capital and technology—are also reasserting themselves, and that there are signs of a rapprochement with the United States and Britain. Even if Amin continues to evade assassination, it could be argued that Aminism is being dragged back into line by the determinants of dependency and class, and that it is on the road to stabilization—even if it be, as Mamdani insists, the stabilization before the revolutionary storm.

Nonetheless, there is little room as yet for either imperialism or revolutionaries to be particularly sanguine about Aminism. We must be careful not to ignore or downplay the significance of such a deviation from the norm as Amin's autonomy has exemplified. Just as Nyerere's deviation from petty-bourgeois orthodoxy has left its distinctive mark on the class struggle in Tanzania (however close his brand of socialism may now have come to devouring itself), so Amin's own peculiar deviation continues to scar the Ugandan political situation. Thus, his terror tactics have eliminated many of those members of the petty bourgeoisie who might have staffed the public and private sectors of a more efficient neocolonial system on the one hand—or provided the cadres necessary to a revolutionary movement on the other. And his reinforcing, in a particularly graphic and rapacious manner, of the emphasis upon religious and ethnic calculation (Islam, the "Nubians") within the sphere of petty-bourgeois politics can only have deepened the mystifying hold of these variables upon petty bourgeoisie and populace alike. In sum, such developments not only have constrained the long-run stabilization of a more smoothly functioning imperial dependency; much more importantly, they have also had a seriously negative impact on the prospects for consolidating revolutionary activity by the mass of the workers and peasants in Uganda.

Such an analysis provides a clearer sense of the dynamics of petty-bourgeois politics in Uganda. It also presents the beginnings of an accurate portrait of the Ugandan state: dependent but not dependable, the unsteady state *par excellence*. Of course, it will be equally clear that in so short a space the Ugandan reality has not been probed at sufficient depth. But perhaps enough has been said to validate the strength of an approach to contemporary African politics structured along lines indicated in the first section. If so, we might hope to avoid excessive reliance not only upon the bluff, commonsensical insights into day-to-day events provided by conventional political science but also upon the procrustean, depoliticizing determinism—often illuminating almost in spite of itself—of various recent "Marxist" innovations in the field of radical Africana. Certainly some kind of analytical way forward is necessary if we are to forge an approach to politics adequate to the tasks which face the African revolution. Tragically, the accuracy of this latter statement has nowhere been more evident than in Uganda itself. Take, for example, Obote's adventurist attempt to reinstate himself, with Tanzanian backing, by means of an invasion of the country in 1972. The putschist mentality which this scheme manifested revealed the weakness not merely of Obote's approach to politics, but also of Tanzania's. The superficiality of Obote's populist project while in power was ignored, as was the fact that his (temporary) ruling coalition had itself been based on factionalism, false consciousness (ethnic and religious), and force (thereby earning him at least as many enemies as friends, especially in the southern part of Uganda). Rhetoric rather than reality became the stuff of strategic calculation, and the pressing need to create politically—by dint of long, hard work—a popular base premised on a new level of (class) consciousness was no more grasped by Tanzania's well-meaning petty-bourgeois "socialists" than by Uganda's UPC opportunists-in-exile. The consequent defeat inflicted by Amin upon his enemies was one which both shored up the self-confidence of the general's regime and led to the physical elimination of many additional potential cadres. Indeed, it was sufficiently disastrous to undermine for a considerable period the possibility of any real or effective resistance being offered to Amin.

No doubt the lessons of this incident will have been lost on Obote, and lost, perhaps equally certainly, on the Tanzanian leadership, which backed his play so foolishly. But they need not be lost on others. Thus, at one level, it will be evident that even the unsteady state makes available to the fraction controlling it resources (chiefly military) which can prove most formidable. Equally crucial, it must be clearly grasped that the politics of the unsteady state in a country like Uganda exacts a heavy toll upon the capacity of the mass of the people to resist neocolonial oppression. It does so, as we have seen, precisely because of the kind of politicization of ethnic, religious, and other variables which it facilitates, this encouraging, in turn, the warping of popular consciousness to fit these molds and no other. If the vitality of "fractions" (together with their followers) defined in such terms is downplayed, then the sophistication of the methods of political work necessary for forging a more class-conscious mass base of peasants and workers may also be underestimated.

This was not an underestimation made by the leadership in Guinea-Bissau or in Mozambique in building their revolutionary constituencies, and they approached the *realities* of tribe and religion with concomitant circumspection. In light of Uganda's recent history, Ugandan revolutionaries will have to be even more circumspect. For example, only a vicious circle would be created by drawing, in the next round of Ugandan politics, on Christian *revanchisme* against the Muslim community. Unfortunately, some such card is now all the more available. So, too, is the card of, say, Langi or Baganda *revanchisme*, ready to hand for those who might wish to play it. Obviously any unleashing of these and other propensities would not be a revolution, but would evidence merely the unsteady lurching of a petty-bourgeois politics spinning ever more wildly out of control. Yet for revolutionaries such a vicious circle is a difficult one to break into. Which is merely to underscore, once again, the urgency of developing a theory of petty-bourgeois politics—and of revolutionary struggle—capable of deepening the awareness of such dangers and capable of sharpening the practice which must follow from such an awareness.

Notes

1. For the full citations, see the Bibliographic Note.
2. Concerning the nature of the postcolonial state, see also the papers on the subject by Alavi and the present author which are listed in the Bibliographic Note.
3. As we shall see, this "political class" is singularly absent from the analysis of Mamdani, who tends to present the confrontation between bureaucratic and entrepreneurial "fractions" of the petty bourgeoisie, which he emphasizes as being virtually unmediated by politicians. Reference to such a stratum is also absent from the analyses of others, like Meillassoux and Shivji, whose frameworks parallel Mamdani's. In "The State in Postcolonial Societies: Tanzania," in this volume (especially notes 17 and 22), I tended, myself,

to underestimate the distinction between bureaucrat and politician, noting that Meillassoux merely lumped the two together in speaking of his "bureaucrats" (while also overstating the cohesion of this group as a class) and suggesting that Murray could be interpreted as making such an identification (while correctly stressing the "relative autonomy and plasticity" of such a class-in-formation). I see now that Murray was implicitly touching on an important distinction, despite the fact that he leaves the question of the class nature of the bureaucracy relatively unexplained.

4. There will also be certain instances—and these not uncommon, given the mixed and complex nature of the social formations of contemporary Africa—when, in addition to petty-bourgeois political activists, quasi-traditional and quasi-feudal elements will seek to mobilize "tribalism" in their political interests.

5. And since the overarching framework of dependence and underdevelopment will not permit any very profound expansion of the productive forces, the basis for an ever fiercer competition for scarce resources in these terms is firmly laid.

6. Mamdani expresses some surprise at the fact that the "Baganda petty bourgeoisie failed to secede at independence." This seems less surprising when one considers that prominent members of the Baganda petty bourgeoisie also dominated the central bureaucracy and that these had no difficulty in considering themselves as much Baganda (defending their turf and the fruits of uneven development) as members of any "bureaucratic bourgeoisie." Moreover, it seems clear that they could equally easily consider themselves to be denizens (present or potential) of the private sector!

7. This point is elaborated upon further in "The Dialectic of Class and Tribe," in this volume.

8. There may be a real confusion here, one evident in the work of Mamdani, among others. Actions which negatively affect some individuals or segments of a dominant class (in the African case, the petty bourgeoisie) are not necessarily to be seen as a full-fledged assault upon that class (or even upon a crucial fraction of it). One of the roles of an effective state is precisely to articulate and defend the general interest of the class it represents against the temptation open to various members of that class to seek short-term gains at the expense of the interests and calculations of the class as a whole. The fact that the state actions to which this gives rise are implemented by bureaucrats does not, by definition, make the bureaucrats a class, or even a distinctive fraction of a class. In the Uganda case, the weakness of the

African entrepreneurial element meant that it often had real difficulties in effectively filling the new roles carved out for it by the Africanization program, this shortfall in their performance having to be made up for by the state!

9. Any entrepreneurial backlash was at least as likely to represent misgivings about the precise pace of Africanization and about the northern, even Langi, tilt of such Africanization activity.

10. They are also as important as the expulsion in defining the continuity of Amin's regime with previous phases of petty-bourgeois politics in Uganda. A comment of Twaddle's provides a clue here: "'Langi and Acholi versus the rest' was not only a creation of the post-coup situation: it was also a feature of pre-coup army life and, as such, a timely reminder that the Ugandan armed forces were no more immune from wider political influences before the Amin coup than they were after it."

11. Mamdani observes that "unlike the pre-coup governing bureaucracy, the army officers are *not* transforming themselves into a class, they are not developing an *independent* economic base. Quite the contrary: members of the officer corps are being integrated into the commercial bourgeoisie which is gradually emerging." He does not explain why this should be the case, why the army officers do not become a governing bureaucracy. In fact, it can be repeated here that these activities are fully consistent with the activities of army personnel, bureaucrats, and members of the "political class" in the pre-coup period. From the correct theoretical vantage point, they require no special explanation.

12. Elsewhere, I have argued that a very different set of circumstances in Tanzania enabled Nyerere to find significant room, within the petty-bourgeois political framework of that country, to give expression to his "own individuality" in some kind of socialist impulse. This is not likely to be an application of his concept which Mamdani would welcome, however.

Bibliographic Note

The work of Nicos Poulantzas and Ralph Miliband has been of obvious importance to the writing of this paper. Poulantzas's most interesting writing on the nature of the petty bourgeoisie is to be found in his *Fascism and Dictatorship* (London, 1974) and *Classes in Contemporary Capitalism* (London, 1975). Miliband's article, "Poulantzas and the

Capitalist State," *New Left Review*, no. 82 (November–December 1972) has been particularly helpful.

On the postcolonial state, there is Hamza Alavi, "The State in Post-Colonial Societies—Pakistan and Bangla Desh," *New Left Review*, no. 74 (July–August 1972) and my "State in Postcolonial Societies: Tanzania," in this volume.

Among general works on African politics, Roger Murray's "Second Thoughts on Ghana," *New Left Review*, no. 42 (March–April 1967) is cited on several occasions in the text and remains of seminal importance many years after its publication. Reference is also made to Micheala von Freyhold, "The Workers and the Nizers" (mimeo., University of Dar es Salaam, 1973); Samuel Decalo, "Military Coups and Military Regimes in Africa," *The Journal of Modern African Studies 2*, no. 1 (1973), and Colin Leys, *Underdevelopment in Kenya* (London, 1975), ch. 6, "Neo-Colonial Society."

The works of Mahmood Mamdani are "Class Struggles in Uganda," *Review of African Political Economy*, no. 4 (November 1975) and his book *Politics and Class Formation in Uganda* (New York and London, 1976). This latter Mamdani was kind enough to let the present author read in manuscript form. Mamdani's work is closely linked to that of Issa Shivji, author of *Class Struggles in Tanzania* (New York and London, 1976), whose article "Peasants and Class Alliances" appeared in *Review of African Political Economy*, no. 3 (May–October 1975). Mamdani's writings share many of the strengths—and many of the weaknesses—of those by Shivji.

As indicated in the text, among the more "conventional" writings on Uganda I have found Michael Twaddle, "The Amin Coup," *The Journal of Commonwealth Political Studies* 10, no. 2 (July 1972) and Garth Glentworth and Ian Hancock, "Obote and Amin: Change and Continuity in Modern Uganda Politics," *African Affairs* 72, no. 288 (July 1973) to be of particular interest. Reference is also made to Colin Leys, *Politicians and Policies* (Nairobi, 1967) and to D. L. Cohen and J. Parson, "The Uganda Peoples Congress Branch and Constituency Elections of 1970," *The Journal of Commonwealth Political Studies* 11, no. 1 (March 1973). In addition, there is D. A. Low, "Uganda Unhinged," *International Affairs* 49, no. 2 (April 1973).

The "Move to the Left" itself is critically appraised in Irving Gershenberg, "Slouching Towards Socialism: Obote's Uganda," *African Studies Review*, no. 25 (April 1972), and not so critically in Michael Lofchie, "The Uganda Coup—Class Action by the Military," *The Journal of Modern African Studies* 10, no. 1 (1972).

David Martin's *General Amin* (London, 1974) is an excellent journalistic account, light on explanation but very long on the compilation of suggestive facts, especially as regards both the depredations of Amin and the folly of the Obote-Tanzania attempts to overthrow the general.

14

THE DIALECTIC
OF CLASS AND TRIBE

Marxist and other progressive writers on Africa generally approach the issue of "tribalism" as one would approach a minefield—and with good reason. Colin Leys exemplifies this mood in his important volume *Underdevelopment in Kenya* when he begins his discussion of "tribalism" in that country (the term itself deliberately set off by quotation marks) with the statement: "So far nothing has been said about 'tribalism.' It is tempting to leave it that way." As he notes, "The fact that 'tribalism' is still explicitly or implicitly treated by so many observers as a mysterious independent force in African politics strongly suggests its ideological function. In the past people frankly declared that Negroes had smaller brains. Today it is said more cautiously [that] what bedevils the African scene is the Africans' inveterate attachment to 'primordial sentiments.' " Yet Leys is also shrewd enough to balance this cautionary note immediately with a necessary, if apparently contradictory, observation: ". . . since 'tribalism' is such a pervasive phenomenon in most African countries it does call for considerable self-denial on the part of most outside observers not to explain almost everything in terms of it." Marxists have their work cut out for them if they are to do justice to *both* of the emphases Leys has introduced here.

Leys's reasons for not wanting to explain everything "in terms of it" become clear as his discussion proceeds. Crucial is his awareness of the way in which, contrary to the view of the "primordial sentiments" school of explanation (among others), "class formation and the development of tribalism accompany

391

each other . . . in neocolonial Africa"—a theme to which we will return. Suffice to note here that this concern to link the understanding of the politicization of tribal distinctions clearly to a simultaneous focus upon the process of class formation in Africa, and the effort by Leys to distance himself from alternative modes of approach, is not developed in a vacuum. One need look no further than the slight but widely read monograph on Kenyan politics published by Henry Bienen almost simultaneously with Leys's book for an analytical framework and substantive case study which crudely polarizes ethnic analysis and class analysis—Bienen suggesting the latter to be of little relevance to an understanding of Kenya. Moreover, it is this tradition of scholarly discourse about "tribalism" that Walker Connor is generalizing when he argues, like many other political scientists at large in Africa, that "surely ethnic nationalism is the single most momentous political fact in sub-Saharan Africa." For Marxists like Leys (and the present writer) whose primary focus has been, instead, upon the "momentous" centrality of the dependency syndrome in Africa and upon the defining role within the political realm of those classes, local and international, which guarantee the structures of neocolonialism, the position taken by such writers is challenging. For, as Leys observes, these writers are dealing, despite their penchant for overstatement and false dichotomy, with a real and "pervasive phenomenon." How, then, are Marxists to understand such a reality?

Appropriately, rethinking on the subject has begun with the basics, addressing the question of the very concepts that are to be used. Indeed, this particular concern has been more widespread even among orthodox academic analysts (though not, to be sure, among Western journalists) than Marxist commentators have sometimes cared to admit. Thus, much less is heard these days about "primordial sentiments" than in the heyday of Clifford Geertz and other overconfident proselytizers of the "modernization" school, and more effort is made to locate the full range of circumstances within the complex social formations of the Third World which can move people to seize hold of some tribal (or racial, or religious) identity as a premise for sociopolitical activity. Moreover, it is in such a climate of discussion that the term "tribe" itself has fallen into increased disfavor. Not only has its past role (cf. Leys, above) cast suspicion upon the wisdom of its continued use, but also, as Aidan Southall and others have cogently argued, its present relevance, even rigorously defined, is doubtful. A careful survey of the literature convinces Southall that "whichever particular choice of definition [is] made, empirical divergences are so gross, widespread, and frequent as to render the concept of tribe as it exists in the general literature untenable." A "tribe" can only be (relatively) self-contained and autonomous, an entity predating capitalism and colonialism, predating "the beginning of [that] long transitional period in which their members were in varying degrees becoming incorporated into wider systems yet continued to retain strong elements of their former state." More useful for an understanding of those contemporary and "transitional" sociopolitical processes which can induce the saliency of such identifications, and certainly more assimilable to the comparative study of what are indeed rather parallel phenomena elsewhere, is the concept of *ethnicity*.

As advocated by Southall, Crawford Young, and others, the emphasis upon "ethnicity" still speaks to identifications which hover around such "attributes . . . of commonality" as "language, territory, political unit, and common cultural values or symbols." However, the saliency of such elements, the precise blend of them which becomes politically relevant, and the depth of feeling which attaches to them, are seen to be much more *contingent* than discourse structured around the concept of "tribe" has tended to imply. Expressions of "tribalism" are most often "new institutions and organizations which to some extent take inspiration and definition from the old. Yet they are effectively adapted and harnessed to new tasks, though their charters still derive from 'tribal' solidarities, whether of the 'genuine' or the 'illusory' transformed or colonially induced variety." Clearly, as Barrows summarizes the argument, "anthropologists have come to stress the *situational* nature of ethnicity," ethnicity having "a certain fluidity which allows it to be politically activated and de-activated, depending on the circumstances." From this standpoint, precisely what "tribal" elements—if any—will become politicized is not readily predictable *avant la situation*.

Obviously, then, a rather subtler tone pervades Southall's article or such a book as Crawford Young's recent *The Politics of Cultural Pluralism* than was to be found in the work of Geertz, et al. Still, even when this much has been done, it has merely cleared the ground for more meaningful controversy. For in fact Marxists have long argued that "tribalism," the active political expression of ethnicity in Africa, has been situationally evoked and defined, the "transitional" reality which breathes life into it being the class-structured society of African peripheral capitalism. Indeed, in the past decade something of a left orthodoxy has emerged on the subject. Perhaps the theme was initially broached with greatest clarity by Richard Sklar, who noted (in 1966) that "tribalism is widely supposed to be the most formidable barrier to national unity in Africa" and that "nearly every African state has at least one serious problem of ethnic or regional separatism." Yet "it is less frequently recognized that tribal movements may be created and instigated to action by the new men of power in furtherance of their own special interests which are, time and time again, the constitutive interests of emerging social classes. Tribalism then becomes a mask for class privilege. To borrow a worn metaphor, there is often a non-traditional wolf under the tribal sheepskin." As Sklar concludes, "An analysis along these lines does not underestimate the intensity of tribal conflict. It does suggest that tribalism should be viewed as a dependent variable rather than a primordial political variable in the new nations."

This line of argument has recently been given even more forceful expression by Archie Mafeje, in his attack upon what he terms, significantly, "The Ideology of Tribalism." He first associates himself with the kind of conceptual critique alluded to in the preceding paragraph. The term "tribe" has no scientific meaning when applied not to "a relatively undifferentiated society, practising a primitive subsistence economy and enjoying local autonomy" but to "societies that have been effectively penetrated by European colonialism, that have been successfully drawn into a capitalist money economy and a world market." In fact, to Mafeje it is "a serious transgression" to so use the term "where the new division of labour, the new modes of production, and the system of distribution of material goods and political power give modern African societies a fundamentally different material and social base." Of course, he continues, "this is not to deny the existence of tribal ideology and sentiment in Africa." Instead,

the argument is that they have to be understood—and conceptualized—differently under modern conditions. There is a real difference between the man who, on behalf of his tribe, strives to maintain its traditional integrity and autonomy, and the man who invokes tribal ideology in order to maintain a power position, not in the tribal area, but in the modern capital city, and whose ultimate aim is to undermine and exploit the supposed tribesmen. The fact that it works, as is often pointed out by tribal ideologists, is no proof that "tribes" or "tribalism" exist in any objective sense. If anything, it is a mark of *false consciousness* on the part of the supposed tribesmen, who subscribe to an ideology that is inconsistent with their material base and therefore respond to the call for their own exploitation. On the part of the new African elite, it is a ploy or distortion they use to conceal their exploitative role. It is an ideology in the original Marxist sense and they share it with their European fellow-ideologists.

There is a great deal of strength in this perspective and it has helped give to class analysis tools for fending off the crudest of analytical models (e.g., Bienen) which assign primacy to the ethnic factor. In addition, such a perspective can help situate the closely related vogue for "clientelism," the patron-client relationship, also put forward from time to time as a key to understanding African politics *and* as a claimed alternative to class analysis. Peter Flynn has recently underscored the manner in which contemporary patron-client relationships are themselves contingent upon the established hierarchies of a neocolonial economy:

To propose a description based on clientelism as an *alternative* to class analysis . . . is patent nonsense as soon as one moves from the most limited micro-analysis to ask questions about the system as a whole and in whose interests it works. In the case of Brazil or Greece it is sufficient to ask who benefited from and still benefits from the political systems so strongly marked by clientelist relations. . . . [This] underlines the importance of understanding political clientelism not so much in terms of spontaneous derivation from below, but a deliberately fostered system of political integration and control exercised from above. . . . Far from being an *alternative* to class analysis, an approach to dependent economies which emphasizes clientelism can greatly help to understand some of the mechanisms of class control which help to maintain dependency.

Furthermore, while it is true that the networks of patron and client can sometimes cut across ethnic lines, there is a clear sense in which politicized ethnicity is merely clientelism writ large, local or regional political barons (Kenya being, in fact, a case in point) rallying support for their own undertakings at the center of the system by means of tribalistic demagogy or the promise to deliver some portion of the national pie to their constituents on a regional-cum-ethnic basis. Nor is it coincidental that these efforts tend to preempt the possible crystallization of alternative modes of (class) consciousness (and alternative definitions of the nature of the pie!) which could see the African masses moving in the direction of consciousness of themselves as exploited peasants and workers vis-à-vis the "baronial" class as a whole. In short, once the lineaments of the class structure of neocolonial Africa—including, most prominently, the domestically dominant petty bourgeoisie on the one hand and the dominated classes of peasantry and proletariat on the other—are taken seriously, and the production process given pride of place in the analysis, it is hard to avoid the thrust of this argument about the genesis of ethnicity. In this regard, my own "theory of petty-bourgeois politics" attempts merely to systematize (and render somewhat less mechanical) such an approach by zeroing in on the

intraclass competition for control of the state and for related economic advantage which activates [a] diversity of fractions produced "in the sphere of political practice alone." The mechanism? The efforts of members of the petty bourgeoisie to *stitch together alliances* and to *rally constituencies* in order the more successfully to engage in such competition. Here the ethnic and/or regional card is a particularly tempting one to play and for a number of reasons. . . . As regards the mobilizing of constituencies—this referring to the attempt to create some popular base for sustained political activity—a utilization of "tribal" ploys can also seem particularly attractive to petty-bourgeois politicians. [1]

Given the flexibility and fuzziness at the edges of ethnic definitions, and the fact that their activation is far from being inevitable, it should not be surprising that political processes are crucial to any such activation as may occur. Nor should it be surprising that, under African conditions, it is the politics of the petty bourgeoisie which is the primary stimulus.

Yet, having made these points, Marxists must admit that such a framework also runs the risk of leaving too many gaps in the argument and of allowing too many things merely to be explained away. Further analysis is required of the very *availability* of those elements which can coalesce, "situationally," into an expression of political ethnicity—some explanation, too, of the *availability* of significant numbers of the population to rally to such identifications. If this matter is left open, or the "solution" is seen to be a sloganized one—if ethnic consciousness is pigeonholed as "false consciousness" without further elaboration, for example, or crudely reduced to the more or less straightforward project of a particular fraction of capital (as in Mamdani's work on Uganda)—then idealist explanations can easily be reinserted into the argument and the Marxist framework demonstrated to be wanting or, at best, "one-sided" by its critics. These latter can even make a bow in the direction of class analysis—the better to dispense with it. In fact, this is something Crawford Young does in citing Mafeje's argument (". . . it is not necessary to deny ethnic pluralism in order to assert class"), only to follow up with the rather coy observation that "arguing the objective reality of cultural mobilization in certain times and places, we do not want to adopt the converse position and imply that class solidarity is only false cultural consciousness." No, Young here implies, there must be some attention paid to both—though not, of course, in his book, since his topic happens to be "cultural pluralism" rather than class structure.

Having politely disposed of the materialists and relieved himself of the necessity to locate his concerns with reference to the production process, Young can then proceed to a range of sociopsychological explanations for the prominence of ethnicity, explanations which turn on the problematic nature of "identity" in transitional situations. Not for Young any real dialectic between class and tribe, nor, in the end, any attempt to take seriously the process of the global accumulation of capital or the related reality of emerging African class structures. But even if, for this reason, he is not himself to be taken altogether seriously, no reader of his extended study can doubt that he does, nonetheless, score points off Mafeje in their brief exchange, demonstrating, with a rich array of documentation, what is in any case apparent to any observer of Africa: the great vitality of ethnic identifications in Africa and the depth of feeling which can attach to them. This is a reality which must be explained, and, in light of it, Marxism is challenged to go beyond the insights provided by Sklar and Mafeje—while taking care, needless to say, not to blur the centrality of the point they have made nor to abandon the attempt to understand the ethnic variable as a part of the structure of Africa's peripheral capitalism.

Fortunately, a more sophisticated picture of the workings of global capitalism, in Africa and elsewhere, is beginning to emerge from recent Marxist writings, and in consequence this literature also suggests fresh ways of locating and understanding ethnicity within African social formations. Here only a sketch for such an argument can be presented, but three general areas, in particular, seem worth exploring.

1. *Ethnicity as a response to imperialism.* The most promising complement to an overemphasis upon the class structure, narrowly defined, as an explanation for the politicization of ethnicity is, paradoxically, to take more seriously the most obvious variable affecting Africa: the reality of imperialism. Tom Nairn's recent analysis of nationalism provides a useful starting point for demonstrating what I mean here. Significantly, Nairn himself begins by critiquing the way in which Marxists have conventionally handled the question on nationalism: "The theory of nationalism represents Marxism's great historical failure. It may have had others . . . yet none of these is as important, as fundamental, as the problem of nationalism, either in theory or in practice." This observation is particularly significant for our purposes since the dividing line between ethnic unit and nation is a very blurred one, so blurred that Walker Conner has insisted that "what we have thus far been calling self-differentiating ethnic groups are in

fact nations. Loyalty to the ethnic group therefore should logically be called nationalism." In this respect the counterposing of
"nation-state" to "ethnicity" is "conducive to dangerously under-
estimating the magnetism and staying power of ethnic identity,
for those terms simply do not convey the aura of deeply felt
emotional commitment that nationalism does . . . [the] popularly held awareness or belief that one's own group is unique in a
most vital sense." There is just enough truth in this emphasis to
carry us back to Nairn's thoughts on nationalism with renewed
interest.

What Nairn argues is that "nationalism is a crucial, fairly
central feature of the modern capitalist development of world
history" and that the key link between nationalism and global
capitalism is the fact of "uneven development." As he puts it,
"the most notoriously subjective and ideal of historical
phenomena [i.e., nationalism] is in fact a by-product of the most
brutally and hopelessly material side of the history of the last two
centuries." For, far from generalizing its relations of production
smoothly on a global scale, capitalism has done so in dramatic
measure by means of *conquest*: "the impact of [the] leading
countries was normally experienced as domination and invasion. . . . On the periphery itself, outside the core-areas of the
new industrial-capitalist world economy, people . . . learned
quickly enough that Progress in the abstract meant domination
in the concrete." It was in this context that "nationalism was
obviously generated as a compensatory reaction on the
periphery." Moreover, with the problem so situated, one becomes aware of the extent to which

> the ideological dimension of nationalism has always loomed too
> large in reflection upon the phenomenon. There is a distinct sense
> in which this dimension has been far *too* important for theorists.
> The point is that the ideological overdetermination is itself a forced
> response, and what forces it is a material dilemma—the crudest
> dilemma of modern history. That is, "underdevelopment," the fact
> of not having and the awareness of this intolerable absence.

So far, so good, on a global scale; yet the fact remains that in
Africa, where the broader, potentially "national" territorial

boundaries had been largely jerry-built by imperialism, the ingredients for such a response are quite diverse. Partly they do comprise those elements which can serve to define the "new nation" at the territorial level,[2] but partly also elements which can serve to define that alternative nationlike entity in Africa, the ethnic group. Here, then, we have an insight into the "new tasks" for which ethnicity is generated (in Southall's formulation). They are tasks which, taken together, comprise a response to imperialism: the tasks of resisting imperialism, of controlling it, of drawing from it such benefits as it may have to offer.

We can take the argument one step further. Central here is the aforementioned notion that imperialism's penetration of the world has a crucial duality. There is, on the one hand, the tendency to create globally the production relations and class structures characteristic of the capitalist mode of production *per se*. On the other hand, this process of penetration also tends to polarize "center" and "periphery" within the global system, to create colonial and neocolonial relationships. It is, of course, one of the staples of the literature on underdevelopment that the latter reality (dependency) can impede the full realization of the former (capitalist development).[3] However, the point to be made here is that, for actors in this drama, *both* of these realities spawn realms of "ideological discourse" which can begin to make sense of the world.

Further elaboration is in order. For the implied reference in the last sentence is to the sort of analysis opened up by Ernesto Laclau, who cites, in turn, Althusser's conception that ideology has the function of "constituting concrete individuals as subjects. . . . Ideology 'acts' or 'functions' in such a way that it 'recruits' subjects among the individuals (it recruits them all), or 'transforms' the individuals into subjects (it transforms them all) by the very precise operation that I have called interpellation." As Laclau then puts the point in his own analysis of ideologies, "What constitutes the unifying principle of an ideological discourse is the 'subject' interpellated and thus constituted through this discourse." Laclau's preoccupation is with "interpellations" which cut across class identifications, and he stresses the fact that running through capitalist societies there is, in addition to the class contradiction, a second contradiction, one characteristic of any class society, that between "power bloc" and "people." "The first contradiction is the sphere of class struggle; the second, that of popular-democratic struggle," and Laclau sees populism as being a rather typical interpellation spawned by this latter contradiction, one in terms of which individuals are moved to recognize themselves as members of "the people," and on the basis of which they may then act politically.

Adapting this all-too-bald paraphrase of Laclau to our earlier discussion, we can now pinpoint a somewhat different simultaneity of contradictions as illuminating the ideological terrain created by the uneven development of capitalism: there will be room both for interpellations attendant upon the class contradictions inherent in the global reality of capitalism (e.g., African peasants and workers constituted as "class-conscious" subjects) *and* for "interpellations" attendant upon the "center-periphery" contradiction. And both Third World nationalism and "ethnicity" (Africans constituting themselves as "Kenyans" for example, or as "Luo") can be seen as interpellations which are triggered by this latter contradiction. Nor should it be surprising that, on the specific terrain of the center-periphery contradiction, an ethnic interpellation is at least as likely a possibility as a "new nation" interpellation. For ethnicity can often draw upon much more proximate and recognizable ingredients—language, symbols, ties of kin, both real and imagined—in defining itself and recruiting "subjects." Nor is it surprising that such an ideology often can be brought to bear not merely vis-à-vis the imperial center *per se*, but also vis-à-vis entities conceived as being more proximate agents of "external" incursion—the new nation-state itself, for example, or other ethnic groups whose competitive claims upon "the center" come more clearly into focus as a threat once the world has begun to be defined from a peripheral-cum-ethnic perspective.

This is not to say that such realities make the response of African peasants and workers to an ethnic interpellation—their recognition of themselves as ethnic subjects—more progressive than their responses to a class interpellation. Indeed, viewed commonsensically, the reverse seems generally to have been the case, the salience of ethnicity having served most often merely to reinforce the status quo of both imperial and class domination within the territory under consideration and to give the dominated classes, in the end, little real purchase upon the agents of their exploitation. But whatever the truth in this—and we shall see in due course that such a manner of juxtaposing class and ethnicity is just a little too crude a formula—this section's method of situating ethnicity has at least gone some way toward explaining the actual availability of the dominated classes for such ethnic projects.

2. *Ethnicity and the articulation of modes of production.* Something further can be said to underscore the fact that the ingredients of the "ideological discourse" which constitutes a subject as a member of an ethnic group are not arbitrary. Of course we have stressed the flexibility of these ingredients and confirmed, with Sklar and Mafeje, the kind of political "creativity" (exercised, most often, by petty-bourgeois politicians) which must be central to any effort to blend these ingredients into a coherent political project or to mobilize large numbers of adherents to it. Yet there is recent writing on the social relations of production in the Third World that does help anchor these ingredients even more firmly in real socioeconomic processes and which thus provides additional clues as to what such ingredients are likely to be. As with Nairn's insights, this literature turns on a revitalized awareness of the fact that capitalism does not spring into the Third World full blown, emphasizing (as Cliffe has summarized the argument, drawing primarily upon the work of P.-P. Rey) that

> contemporary rural social formations and the modes of production in which they are involved are not pure examples of the capitalist mode; but the stalled advance of capitalism does not mean, on the other hand, that the production relations are still in their pristine precapitalist mode. There has instead been a combination or complex of relationships, as a result of some synthesis of modes. All the various modes . . . may be distinct from *imposed* capitalist production; but they have to be understood as having combined characteristics. They represent not simple transformations from precapitalism to capitalism, but an interaction between the two. It is in this sense that one speaks of an approach which analyzes them in terms of an "articulation of modes of production."

Obviously, such an approach lends further substance to our understanding that "dependence" has its own logic, somewhat different from the logic of emergent capitalist relations of production *per se*. Meillassoux, for example, has reminded us that in many African settings it has actually best served global capitalism's interests to perpetuate certain aspects of the pre-capitalist modes. His preoccupation is with the question of labor supplies and labor migration, and he argues that

> paradoxically, the capitalist exploiters, who are often better Marxists than Marxist theoreticians, are aware of the potentiality of this contradictory situation. The agricultural self-sustaining communities, because of their comprehensiveness and their *raison d'être*, are able to fulfill functions that capitalism prefers not to assume in underdeveloped countries: the functions of social security. The cheap cost of labour in these countries comes from the super-exploitation not only of the labour from the wage-earner himself but also of the labour of his kin group.

But Rey, Cliffe, and others have also shown that a related syndrome can characterize the incorporation of other Africans on the land into the role of suppliers of agricultural raw materials. Areas where this happens, like Meillassoux's "reserves of cheap labour," are well described as "agricultural communities [which] . . . because of this process of absorption into the capitalist economy . . . are being undermined and perpetuated at the same time, undergoing a prolonged crisis and not a smooth transition to capitalism."[4] For Rey it is the "second stage" of articulation where "capitalism 'takes root,' subordinating the pre-capitalist mode but still making use of it" which is of particular interest, this stage to be distinguished from both an earlier one, the "initial link in the sphere of exchange, where interaction with capitalism reinforces the pre-capitalist mode," and a later one, "the total disappearance of the pre-capitalist mode, even in agriculture."[5] It is this second stage which, in Rey's words, is "the actual condition of most of the ex-colonial countries."

Transition, a sense of historical movement, is inherent in these latter distinctions, of course, but our earlier argument (and indeed Cliffe's own summary of the "articulation" approach—"the stalled advance of capitalism") does qualify this kind of emphasis. For a dependent capitalism does not readily facilitate a transition to the so-called third stage. In consequence, the coexistence of capitalist and precapitalist features of the production processes and social relations in Africa seems fated to continue for some time to come. Not coincidentally, the fact of a "frozen" transition is something that students of African class formation also have had to take quite seriously. Thus, in an important sense, the African peasantry is itself a transitional phenomenon. Yet we have quoted Leys earlier in this volume, and can repeat his formulation here, to the effect that "analytically speaking, the peasantry in Africa may be best seen as a transitional class, in between the period of primitive cultivators living in independent communities and that of capitalist development in which peasants are restratified into capitalists and proletarians; but under the conditions of growth of neo-colonialism it seems clear that in Kenya at least *the stage during which the peasantry itself goes through a process of development*, and develops its own pattern of relationships with the elite, *may be fairly prolonged*" (emphasis added). Similarly, the African proletariat-in-the-making bears the marks of this transition, many of its members being only "semi-proletarianized" in the sense that they maintain solid links back into the rural areas and carry over quite readily many cultural traits, interests, and commitments from one sphere to the other. Under neocolonialism, and in the absence of a full-blown capitalist revolution, these features, too, have staying power.

We find, then, that the same frozen historical moment in Africa defines both the most prominent characteristics of the popular classes *and* the chief features of the interaction of modes of production. Nor is it surprising that, with peasantry and proletariat coming into existence during phase two of the articulation of modes of production (the capitalist and precapitalist modes being precisely the two worlds which peasants, in particular, simultaneously inhabit, the worlds which, taken together, define their existence), these two realities should overlap. Perhaps here we move close to the meaning of Arrighi's evocative, if rather opaque, claim that "the division of the world in nation-states, ethnic groups, races, etc., with unequal power is not a purely superstructural phenomenon, but it is something that strongly influences class interests and must therefore be taken into account in the very process of defining classes." This is a formulation to which we will return in the following section.

Here we can note that it becomes much more intelligible once we place on the table the point which our argument has merely implied heretofore: that the articulation of modes of production has a clear tendency to strengthen ethnicity.

One possible referent here is a very direct brand of political-cum-class struggle, one which renders almost inevitable some mobilization of an ethnic constituency. It is this to which Rey refers, perhaps, when he presents "the articulation of two modes of production, one of which establishes its domination over the other . . . not as a static given, but as a *process*, that is to say a combat between the two modes of production, with the confrontations and alliances which such a combat implies: confrontations and alliances essentially between the *classes* which these modes of production define." Yet African realities complicate this process. Such combat will be most straightforward where the precapitalist society was most stratified, as, for example, in Buganda. There it was not only a matter of the boundaries of the ethnic unit being much more clear cut than in many other instances (given the existence of a centralized kingdom). In addition, the quasi-feudal and monarchical structure inherited (if not entirely untransformed) from the past threw up classes linked to that structure whose struggle not only fits Rey's model but also served, alongside other factors and in conjunction with the struggles of other classes in Buganda, to politicize ethnicity in Uganda to the breaking point. However, such patterns are much less straightforward where the precapitalist modes were less clearly stratified (as has often been true of Eastern Africa, especially outside southern Uganda), and where the privileged classes which have relied on and developed ethnicity (as Mafeje) are more "modern," belonging more directly to the emergent class structure of peripheral capitalism, which cuts across ethnic lines (e.g., the petty bourgeoisie, public and private).

Even under the latter circumstances, however, something of the substance of these precapitalist societies must animate the present, if not always in the most obvious ways. It goes without saying that practices in the sphere of production—the conventions of land and cattle distribution, the allocation of labor, the preeminence of subsistence—will be crucial precapitalist aspects of the infrastructure of "transition" from which ethnicity springs. But it is elements in other spheres which will enter most directly into the process which serves to animate and politicize ethnicity. Sometimes this will take the very concrete form of political networks built around actors who derive some of their influence from their quasi-traditional roles and who serve to mobilize ethnic constituencies; in Kenya, the active role of the *jodong gweng* within the coalition through which Oginga Odinga consolidated his Luo base is an intriguing case in point.

At a subtler level we can note Anderson's observation that, much more than is the case for capitalism, "the 'superstructures' of kinship, religion, laws or the state necessarily enter into the constitutive structure of the mode of production in precapitalist social formations." If this is indeed true, it is quite suggestive, for we can begin to recognize the diverse range of ingredients which are available for the forging of ethnic identifications in "transitional" Africa and also to sense some of the sources of their strength. We thus give greater substance to, and some form of explanation for, our earlier observation that ethnicity can often "draw upon much more proximate and recognizable ingredients" than other ideologies. We also return to the insights of Southall and those of Phillip Gulliver, who has similarly stressed the way in which

> new institutions and new values and symbols have been developed in the colonial and independence periods, but these are attached to and receive strength and validity from the persisting or revived parts of the older culture. . . . Old symbols and old institutions and values are put to new uses and they gain new and different significance to deal with and express new interests . . . Nevertheless, . . . cultural differences in their territorial context are the essence of tribe.

But we can situate the observations of Southall and Gulliver on much firmer ground. Can we doubt that our affirmation in this section—via an awareness of the process of the articulation of modes of production—of the deep roots of ethnicity again locates the latter firmly (to repeat Nairn's formulation) on the terrain of the "most brutally and hopelessly material side of the history of the last two centuries"?

3. *Ethnicity and ideological class struggle.* A quite different set of considerations about ethnicity—though ones that can ultimately be assimilated to the analysis emerging here—is to be found in a suggestive volume on the subject by Cynthia Enloe, *Ethnic Conflict and Political Development.* Enloe, writing in a broadly comparative vein, is not prepared to accept uncritically the negative judgment pronounced upon ethnicity by commentators from either the Marxist or modernization schools of approach. Stimulated, it would seem, by such progressive "ethnic" assertions as those of North American blacks and native people in recent years,[6] she asserts that "taking a close look at ethnic groups as they struggle to use politics to articulate and advance their communal interests may alert us to the pitfalls of development theory and enable us to neutralize it." In this regard she is particularly concerned to argue that

> nation states are not the sole realities. Other political entities are capable of choice and innovation. As ethnic groups are politicized—though politicization is not inevitable—they, like nation states, can pursue political development. It is one thing to acknowledge the existence of national polities. It is quite another to assume that they are the logical goal of all development.

Although, generally speaking, the concept of "political development" has proven to be of little scientific use, as defined by Enloe it is evocative: "At bottom, [it] means men's cultivation of forms of political power and authority that enable them to meet external challenges and internal needs." Using this definition, she can then assert that, even though "the nation may be the logical unit of development . . . the matter is open to question," especially in light of the coercive and exploitative reality of many of the national projects and postcolonial states which are on offer. For Enloe, "ethnic groups are proving that nations do not have a monopoly on political development."

Obviously Enloe's emphasis is rendered much less useful than might otherwise be the case by her lack of interest in specifying, analytically or empirically, the way in which class structures interpenetrate with ethnic units. In consequence the latter tend in her model to act politically *en bloc*, as relatively undifferentiated units, a formulation which is, quite simply, inadequate. As with Nairn we have a suggestive corrective to class-reductionist approaches to the problem of ethnicity which then itself tells only part of the story—albeit a different part. Of course Nairn, unlike Enloe, is quite pugnacious, even demagogic, in his dismissal of class analysis, and as a result finds himself tossed back vaguely upon the national unit as the sole important actor in the underdevelopment drama, with such stopgaps as "the peripheral elites" thrown in offhandedly when a motor is required for his model. These are the perils of not taking the simultaneity of class contradictions and center-periphery contradictions seriously, perils which haunt the Nairns and Enloes as surely as they haunt (albeit in a quite opposite manner) the Sklars and the Mafejes.

Yet even if Enloe does fall short here, her overall emphasis bears further scrutiny. Her approach suggests the possibility that ethnicity can, under certain circumstances, encapsulate progressive rather than exclusively reactionary or backward-looking assertions by large numbers of ordinary people—the dominated classes?—who thus seek through it to control their own lives and advance their condition. Significantly, there is a proposition of Fanon's which hints, if much less enthusiastically, at a similar notion. Aware as he was that the many African territorial nationalisms, with their attendant state and party structures, have been very reactionary and have tended to express, first and foremost, the interests of the domestically dominant "middle class," he suggests that "the masses" will sooner or later demand a program which seeks truly "to free the people politically and socially." "What is dangerous," he continues, "is when [the African people] reach the stage of social consciousness before the stage of [what he considers to be a genuine and progressive brand of] nationalism. If this happens, we find in underdeveloped countries fierce demands for social justice which paradoxically are allied with often primitive tribalism." Leave aside for a moment the "dangers," and also the qualification "often primitive." The crucial point to focus on first is the link which Fanon here pinpoints between "demands for social justice" and "tribalism." It is relevant here to return to Laclau in an attempt to theorize this possibility. The fit is by no means exact, since we are discussing matters to the side of Laclau's own preoccupations, but recall the elements of his argument which were summarized earlier. He pinpointed two central contradictions, the class contradiction and the "power bloc–people" contradiction, in the societies he has studied, and he suggests that these give rise in turn to "class interpellation [=ideology] and popular-democratic interpellation [=ideology]." Class struggle is crucial, but the ideological sphere cannot be reduced to a direct and unalloyed expression of class interests. Instead we find

> popular-democratic ideologies . . . articulated with class ideological discourses. . . . The popular-democratic interpellation not only has no precise class content, but is the domain of ideological class struggle *par excellence*. Every class struggles at the ideological level simultaneously as class and as the people, or rather, tries to give coherence to its ideological discourse by presenting its class objectives as the consummation of popular objectives. The overdetermination of non class interpellations by the class struggle consists, then, in the integration of those interpellations into a class ideological discourse.

In sum, "classes exist at the ideological and political level in a process of articulation and not of reduction. Articulation requires, therefore, the existence of non-class contents—interpellations and contradictions—which constitute the raw material on which the class ideological practices operate."

There can be no doubt that in neocolonial Africa, too, the class structure which is part and parcel of peripheral capitalism is sufficiently formed to be "overdetermining," in Laclau's sense. It is also in a "process of articulation" with "non-class interpellations." Of course, somewhat differently from Laclau, we have stressed that African conditions render the simultaneity of a "center-periphery" contradiction with the class contradiction the most salient feature of "class struggles at the ideological level" there.[7] Yet the thrust of his emphasis remains intact. He has made the point that "popular-democratic ideologies never present themselves separated from, but articulated with, class ideological discourses." What, we may now ask, are the ways in which interpellations and ideologies (including ethnicity) structured around the center-periphery contradiction will be "articulated . . . in the ideological discourses of antagonistic classes." Such an approach would seem to give some promise of clarifying the conditions under which Third World ethnicity (like Third World nationalism) can give expression to the potentially anti-imperialist features hypothesized for it earlier, and also the conditions under which it will play a less savory role. There is another point of Laclau's which also holds promise for a discussion of ethnicity, many of whose ingredients have been thrown up by the past. Thus he states that his perspective "opens up the possibility for understanding a phenomenon which has not received an adequate explanation in Marxist theory: the relative continuity of popular traditions, in contrast to the historical discontinuities which characterize class structures. . . . These traditions are crystallized in symbols and values in which the subjects interpellated by them find a principle of identity." What, then, of the ethnic interpellation?

Two possibilities exist. First there are

> those situations where the non-class interpellations and contradictions in which the individual participates are subjected to the articulating principle of a class distinct from that to which the individual belongs. . . . This is the phenomenon of "alienation" or "false consciousness"—terms with which subjectivist theories have tried to explain the ideological colonization of one class by another and which, since they assigned a class belonging to every ideological element, they could only conceive as a collapse or an inadequate development of "class consciousness."

The Buganda case suggests the way in which quasi-traditional dominant classes can seize the reins of ethnicity in their own interests and hope to rally peasants and workers to their definition of it. Even more importantly, we know that the petty bourgeoisie can absorb both nationalism and ethnicity—anti-imperialist potential or no—into its own universe of discourse and, in the manner discussed at length above (by Sklar, Mafeje, Saul), can shape ethnicity to service its hegemony. Of course, even as regards this class, we should be wary of reductionism. Although the petty bourgeoisie (like the quasi-traditional dominant classes) does engage in a significant measure of self-conscious and intentional manipulation of the ethnic variable, it is also the case that ethnicity interpenetrates with its own class interpellation in a real way; some of such a class's ability to play the ethnic card effectively does arise from the fact that many of its members take it quite seriously themselves. More should be said on this subject; however, our chief preoccupation here is with the implications of this process for the dominated classes.

With respect to the latter, we can observe first off that much of their recruitment to another class's universe of ideological discourse regarding ethnicity will occur at the symbolic level; the use of mass oathings by Kikuyu leaders during tempestuous times in the late 1960s Kenya in order to consolidate ethnic consciousness on their own terms is an extreme case in point. But it is equally important to underscore the fact that the petty bourgeoisie is actually prepared to pay for the "absorption and neutralization" (in Laclau's terms) of the progressive potential of mass interpellations. Since "ethnicity" is genuinely rooted in popular aspirations, a *quid pro quo* for divide-and-rule (the playing off of one ethnic group against another), and for the preemption of class consciousness, is the delivery of some minimal surpluses—to the extent that the straitened neocolonial economy can continue to permit such largesse—to the "tribes." As Bienen's book on Kenya amply demonstrates, this is one of the ways in which the postcolonial state, while first and foremost the preserve of the foreign bourgeoisie and the indigenous petty bourgeoisie, registers within itself the struggles of peasant and proletariat, and thus works to tame them. Equally clearly, this is no substitute (*pace* Bienen) for the establishment of a state which does genuinely represent the needs and the demands of the dominated classes.

What other possibilities are open to these latter classes, then? As Laclau points out, "For the dominated sectors, ideological struggle consists in an expansion of the antagonism implicit in democratic interpellations and in the articulation of it with their own class discourses." In the present context, this could be re-phrased as the "expansion of the antagonism implicit in interpel-lations of a potentially anti-imperialist sort—nationalism and ethnicity." For we have seen that there are "bottom-up" as well as "top-down" explanations for the peasantry and proletariat/semiproletariat constituting themselves as ethnic subjects. We should not be surprised at this. Nor should we assume that this is invariably at odds with the development of class consciousness. It is worth remembering that the initial resistance to imperial incur-sions into Africa was generally carried out along tribal lines, and certain more recent anti-imperialist struggles (e.g., Mau-Mau) have also been deeply rooted in ethnic identity; moreover, in some instances these have given rise to "popular traditions" of continuing importance. We have also seen why, nearer to the present, ethnic discourse is particularly ready to hand in this connection, so much so that one is tempted to assert that the class consciousness of peasant and proletariat as it emerges will almost inevitably incorporate elements of that discourse. In this way, perhaps, we return to Arrighi's assertion that "ethnic groups . . . must be taken into account in the very process of defining classes"; we are also closer to understanding, with Fanon, how "fierce demands for social justice" can sometimes be "allied with . . . tribalism." Could not one argue that in Africa (to again rephrase Laclau) it is the ethnic interpellation (together with the national interpellation) which provides "the domain of the ideological class struggle *par excellence*"?

Of course, we must proceed with caution here. So phrased, the point is suggestive, but it may now tend to *overstate* the positive potential of ethnicity. Not that this would necessarily be a bad thing, if such overstatement were to encourage Marxists to avoid merely blowing the ethnic variable aside, as they have too often done, as some kind of very suspect residual category. Nonetheless, it is no place to leave our argument, for there can be no denying that ethnicity remains, from a revolutionary viewpoint, a deeply ambiguous variable.

Note, first, that even if nonclass interpellations are constantly (and inevitably) being "reabsorbed" by class ideological discourses, they do have a measure of autonomy. In this respect the ingredients which can hang together, in a situationally determined way, as an ethnic interpellation are particularly combustible, capable of taking on a certain unpredictable life of their own. Even Enloe is acutely aware of this point. It is true that, even though she stands to the side of class analysis, she does mount the positive case for ethnicity in a manner which reinforces the points made above: "The grievances of ethnic groups frequently serve as catalysts for what eventually become supra-ethnic revolutions. A community which has been treated unjustly illuminates profound contradictions within the entire political system—contradictions present but unseen until exposed in one group's poverty or oppression."[8] Yet in Africa many of the ingredients which ethnicity introduces into the ideological class struggle are different from those introduced by territorial nationalism—that other related interpellation on the terrain of the center-periphery contradiction. In Enloe's words,

> the ethnic group is defined by its cultural attributes to a greater extent than is a nation. Ethnic groups are collections of people who feel tied to each other by certain cultural bonds. Consequently, an ethnic group's political appeals and goals give primacy to cultural matters such as language, religion, and social mores.

The phrase "give primacy" certainly overstates the nonmaterial character of ethnic demands as activated in contemporary Africa. Nonetheless, with these observations we do draw closer to a specification of the ingredients which can spark ethnicity's autonomy, and closer, as well, to an understanding of the reasons why "communal barriers" can, in and of themselves, become, as Enloe states, "as much a threat to a radical movement as the government's military force."

First, some of these ingredients, especially in the cultural and social sphere, will seem to defy the revolutionary's notions of universality and enlightenment, contradicting a perspective which looks to the *future* and to the social relationships of a "developed" socialist society. It is preoccupation with such ingredients that has prompted revolutionaries to approach ethnicity skeptically, zeroing in on a host of anomalies which can range from deeply ingrained practices of male chauvinism to cramped and debilitating ritual and spiritual perspectives to excessive preoccupation with such "side issues" as the sanctity of language and the like. No doubt it is just such a preoccupation which Fanon exemplifies with his use of the (much too evocative) word "primitive"; he implies that, too readily, any "fierce demands for social justice" which may underlie ethnic stirrings are drawn down a blind alley—mere separatism or "tribal war"—of a sort that even the most manipulative of petty bourgeoisies will have some difficulty in controlling. In this context, nationalism, though itself an ideology subject to gross distortions from the point of view of popular interests, must seem a more promising, somehow more rational, vessel for the socialist project.

Ethnicity can be less than universal in another potentially disruptive way as well. To join a different kind of movement (Enloe mentions "a Marxist movement," but in Africa her point would generally be true of a territorial nationalist movement as well)—or even to define oneself as "subject" with reference to another kind of interpellation—

> one need only adopt a set of goals and abstract premises, whereas to join an ethnic movement one must *belong*, in style, mores, perhaps even language and race. [Also] by being more exclusive and having boundaries more visible, ethnic groups have a difficult time winning the confidence and trust of potential allies.

In this regard, it may seem to revolutionaries something of a virtue that nationalisms in Africa have as little history as they do. For while we have seen that many of the ingredients of ethnicity available in the present are positive "popular traditions" of resistance and the like, some of these traditions will reflect a more checkered history, one of "uneven development" and intertribal competition which may even have surfaced in the period antedating capitalist incursion. Clearly, these are "obstacles" which, in and of themselves, can help "prevent . . . ethnic discontent from being translated into revolution," as Enloe says, all the more so when such "traditions" have been reinforced by colonial tactics and the maneuverings of petty-bourgeois politicians.

Thus it is true that much the strongest case can be made for the preeminence of territorial nationalism as the key interpellation pegged to the center-periphery contradiction in Africa. In Laclau's terminology, ethnicity self-evidently offers less scope for the "expansion" of the anti-imperialist content implicit in it than does nationalism and less scope for positive articulation with the class demands of people who are increasingly defining themselves as peasants and workers. Not that even this assertion is entirely cut and dried. We have seen that ethnicity is sufficiently multifaceted—in particular, sufficiently open to articulation with diverse class ideological discourses—to permit the possibility that in some African territories a particular political expression of ethnicity may well be more immediately "progressive" than any nationalism which is on offer there.[9] In any case, revolutionaries will not necessarily be presented with an unalloyed choice between the two interpellations under consideration; even if their preference runs to emphasizing the territorial-cum-national dimensions of their project in the course of political mobilization, they will find ethnic realities and ethnic assertions that they must try to deal with seriously.

Since there are diverse situations created by the differential articulation of modes of production, diverse situations which, as we have seen, will be in part encapsulated in diverse ethnic molds, taking ethnic realities seriously can enable revolutionaries to shape their strategies for mobilization more sensitively to the terrain upon which they must operate. Thus, the crude and across-the-board application of class labels would not have permitted Amilcar Cabral to make the subtle distinctions within the Guinean peasantry between the situations of the Balante and the Fula which he did. Yet the ability to make these distinctions and to act upon them was crucial to the PAIGC's success. Moreover, the notion of taking ethnic assertions seriously can have an even more *positive* thrust: our argument has suggested reasons why the African revolutionary need not feel compelled to dismiss such assertions out-of-hand, as being by definition merely primordial and/or reactionary. For there also exists the possibility of integrating them into a radical project in such a way as to permit the release of their energies and their antiimperialist content onto a broader terrain of struggle, a terrain where they can overlap positively with both class and national interpellations.

Obviously, realizing such a goal is not easy, as Enloe emphasizes when she states that "it is necessary for [rebels] to win not only fair-weather allies among strategic ethnic groups but long-term political converts who later will promote societal change. Usually this is accomplished with patience, careful cultivation, and minimal emphasis on formal orthodoxy, at least at the outset." But these are lessons of which successful African revolutionaries are themselves aware. Marcellino dos Santos of FRELIMO has manifested that movement's strong sense of the manipulative side of ethnicity:

> In many modern struggles tribalism is just a useful instrument for certain people to advance their individual or group interests. We have had people with some responsibility in FRELIMO who fell into this category. . . . It is not really a power base. No. It is power which has its origins in tribalism and is based on the exploitation of tribal values of the people. Some who exploit these sentiments might say: "Why are we going to fight outside our tribal area?" or "You see, our language is not used as much as other languages," or "You see, in this leadership there are people from our tribe." We have more than forty-two tribes. So, you can imagine how easy it is for opportunistic elements to prey on sectional fears.

Not surprisingly, nationalism—"revolutionary nationalism," for dos Santos himself sharply distinguishes that brand from "primary" or "bourgeois" nationalism—has been the much more valued framework for FRELIMO's project.

Nonetheless, one of the movement's initial statements (1962) stressed that

> it is true that there are differences among us Mozambicans. Some of us are Macondes, others are Nianjas, others Macuas, Ajauas, etc. Some of us come from the mountains, others from the plains. Each

of our tribes has its own language, its specific uses and habitudes and different cultures. There are differences among us. This is normal. . . . In all big countries there are differences among people. All of us Mozambicans—Macuas, Macondes, Nianjas, Changanas, Ajaos, etc.—we want to be free. To be free we have to fight united.

ALL MOZAMBICANS OF ALL TRIBES ARE BROTHERS IN THE STRUGGLE. ALL THE TRIBES OF MOZAMBIQUE MUST UNITE IN THE COMMON STRUGGLE FOR THE INDEPENDENCE OF OUR COUNTRY.

Here no necessary contradiction between national and ethnic interpellations is envisaged once they are located on the proper terrain. Quite the contrary. Since then the movement's theoretical perspective on ethnicity has varied somewhat, the situation becoming the more complicated as the class interpellation, too, has become a more prominent feature of its practice. Thus, one FRELIMO document has spoken of the task of "building a new culture, a national culture which is *negating* and transcending both the tribal micro-culture and the colonial anti-culture" (emphasis added), and Samora Machel has himself written that "if I am a Nyanja and cultivate the land alongside an Ngoni, I sweat with him, wrest life from the soil with him. . . . With him I am destroying tribal efforts, and I feel united with him. . . . With him I am destroying tribal, religious, and linguistic prejudices, all that is secondary and divides us." Yet "negating" is generally too strong a word for Mozambican practice, for to move so unequivocally would be to run the risk of handing over the ethnic interpellation uncontested to those who would seek to manipulate it against the thrust of progressive change; it would also be to strive for a probably unattainable, and not necessarily very rewarding, degree of uniformity in the country as a whole.

More typical is the note struck in a crucial FRELIMO document of 1968–69, "Mozambican Tribes and Ethnic Groups: Their Significance in the Struggle for National Liberation," written during a period when the movement actually was under strong pressure from politicians who were consciously manipulating ethnicity in their own interests. FRELIMO, the document

states, "recognises the existence of tribes or ethnic groups." On
the one hand, "Mozambique, as well as most of the nations of the
world, is composed of people with different traditions and cultures"; on the other, it is "united by the same historical experience and the same political, economic, and social aims, engaged
in the same sacred task—to fight for their liberation."

> Today FRELIMO is engaged in the task of uniting the people
> against the invaders, transforming the energies accumulated dur-
> ing centuries of separation imposed by colonialism, into an invinci-
> ble force against the common enemy, by using the talents of each
> tribe, for the success of the struggle. By using the experience gained
> during the centuries of oppression and exploitation during which
> our people suffered as one, FRELIMO is *fusing together* the ener-
> gies up till now dispersed, and transforming them into national
> energies, an organized fighting force. . . .
>   [In sum] the positive elements of our cultural life, such as our
> various forms of linguistic expression, our music and dances, the
> regional idiosyncrasies in birth, growth, love, and death will con-
> tinue to flourish and embellish the life of our nation after indepen-
> dence. There is no antagonism between the existence of a number
> of ethnic groups and National Unity. [Emphasis added]

Certainly my own experience in visiting the liberated areas of
Mozambique in 1972 and in returning there during the transition
to independence in 1975 revealed to me the manner in which
FRELIMO's careful and open approach to ethnic diversity has
facilitated its work of day-to-day mobilization for the liberation
struggle and for socialist reconstruction. I began to see, also, how
it was underwriting the attempt, in the cultural sphere, to realize
a genuine "fusion" of diverse aspects of the cultures and "popular
traditions" of Mozambique into a novel national and revolutionary form, a fusion which people could be expected to make their
own. How the movement will deal with other diversities which
can have an ethnic edge—those linked to the differing economic
situations created within the territory by uneven development,
for example—remains to be seen. One thing is clear, however:
such an ongoing process does evidence much of the subtlety in
this sphere which Enloe demands of revolutionaries and therefore will continue to repay careful study.

This essay has now suggested a number of interrelated themes and approaches which, taken together, begin to complement the rather balder radical formulations concerning ethnicity to be found in earlier writings of Sklar, Mafeje, and myself. Of course, these remain mere theoretical proposals, proposals which demand to be tested by concrete case studies in order to explore them more fully and to integrate them into an even more adequate set of explanations. Some hints have been given in passing as to the ways in which the role of ethnicity in Kenya's peripheral capitalism—Kenya being the specific focus for the differing emphases of Leys and Bienen mentioned at the outset of this essay—might be further revealed by such explanations. Despite the fact that Leys himself does advance the discussion with his stress upon the interplay of "tribalism" with such variables as "uneven development" in Kenya, it is obvious that much more remains to be done. A case study of the approach of African revolutionaries to the fact of ethnicity—we have mentioned above the undertakings of FRELIMO—would be similarly instructive.

However, perhaps enough has been said to suggest that Marxist scientists and African revolutionaries can only make progress when they take ethnicity (and, for that matter, nationalism—though that would be the subject for another essay) seriously as a *real* rather than ephemeral or vaguely illegitimate variable in Africa. The essay argues that this is most likely to be done when the *simultaneity* of class and center-periphery contradictions is placed front and center as a key factor within our analytical framework. This is an orientation which has not been adequately explored in the literature on the political economy of Africa. Equally important, the fact of class *struggle* must be given even more prominence. The maneuverings of dominant classes—the process of "petty-bourgeois politics," as I have termed it—are important and do contribute to an instrumentalization (via "tribalism," among other means) of the African masses in the interests of capitalist accumulation and class privilege. Yet we have seen that ethnicity only reveals its secrets once we also link discussion of it to a more developed concept of the practice of the dominated classes in Africa and, in particular, to a more sophisticated, less reductionist approach to the question of class consciousness. Unfortunately, this is another broad area where significant advance in our scientific understanding is far from being consolidated. Sympathetic as one must be with Leys's ironic demurrer, quoted at the outset of this essay—"So far nothing has been said about 'tribalism.' It is tempting to leave it that way"— one knows that he does not mean it. Indeed, can anyone doubt that Marxists have barely begun the kind of analysis of ethnicity which is required?

Notes

1. See "The Unsteady State: Uganda, Obote, and General Amin," in this volume. Barrows quotes Maxwell Owusu to similar effect from the latter's book, *Uses and Abuses of Political Power: A Case Study of Continuity and Change in the Politics of Ghana* (Chicago, 1970), stating that "Owusu argues that competition for scarce resources underlay what appeared to be traditional 'ethnic' politics in Ghana: 'The struggle for power between groups—chiefs and the new elites, new elites and the colonial rulers, and so on—was primarily a struggle in relation to the possession of wealth and its distribution and consumption. . . . In this politico-economic competition, individuals and groups had manipulated, whenever suitable and to their advantage, a variety of symbols, beliefs, images and ideologies, some clearly traditional and others European in origin, to advance their interests. . . . This is what lends, in the context of social change, a flavor of "tribalism" to much of the clearly modern political and economic competition in Africa.'"
2. Needless to say, nationalisms, even of the most conventional kind, are themselves shaped "situationally" and quite eclectically, rather than being in any way "primordial" or inevitable.
3. It is equally true that the question of precisely *how much of an impediment* dependency is likely to be is a focus of considerable controversy (e.g., the critique of such underdevelopment literature by Bill Warren and others, and subsequent responses to these writers), but that is another subject.
4. Moreover, this was a pattern which was often reinforced in colonial times at the political level by a complementary attempt to build upon the political structures of precapitalist social formations (indirect rule), the better to consolidate colonial rule.

5. These phases are as defined by Foster-Carter in his presentation of Rey's argument.

6. It is in these experiences perhaps that one may find the source of Enloe's particularly strong conviction "that there are instances in which individual progress toward self-confidence and efficacy depends on an ethnic group's development as a community." It is also worth noting another set of propositions which underwrites her generally positive approach to ethnicity and which structures the conclusions of her book. These involve an emphasis upon the merits of decentralization and autonomy as potential counterweights to what she identifies as the alienation and excessive centralization of so-called modern society.

7. It is probably the case that the choice between interpellations structured around the "center-periphery" contradiction on the one hand and around the "power bloc–people" contradiction on the other is a false one, even if it is of considerable heuristic value in setting up our discussion of ethnicity. In fact, both sets of interpellations are probably in play, and a more thorough formulation would have to encompass this reality. I would venture to add that Laclau's argument, too, would benefit if he were to include the "center-periphery" contradiction in his own model.

8. From the perspective being developed here, this could be better formulated in order to underscore the fact that in Africa virtually all ethnic groups—insofar as they are conceptualized in their articulation with the ideological discourse of the dominated classes—suffer such "poverty and oppression"; this is one of the reasons why ethnicity has a measure of positive potential from a revolutionary standpoint.

9. Clearly, nationalism, in Africa as elsewhere, is an interpellation with its own range of ambiguities and contradictory potentialities, one of which is, of course, its possible absorption by the dominant classes.

Bibliographic Note

The books on Kenya referred to at the outset are Colin Leys, *Underdevelopment in Kenya* (London, Berkeley, and Los Angeles, 1975), and Henry Bienen, *Kenya, The Politics of Participation and Control* (Princeton, 1974).

Books on ethnicity *per se* which are cited in the text are Cynthia Enloe, *Ethnic Conflict and Political Development* (Boston, 1973), and Crawford

Young, *The Politics of Cultural Pluralism* (Madison, Wisc., 1976), while articles and essays include Aidan Southall, "The Illusion of Tribe," *Journal of Asian and African Studies* 5, nos. 1–2 (1970); Phillip Gulliver, "Introduction" to Gulliver, ed., *Tradition and Transition in East Africa* (Berkeley and Los Angeles, 1969); Walker Connor, "Nation-Building or Nation-Destroying," *World Politics* 24, no. 3 (1972); and Walter L. Barrows, "Comparative Grass-Roots Politics in Africa," *World Politics*, no. 26 (1973–74).

The two texts mentioned as providing a first approximation to a Marxist approach to ethnicity are Richard Sklar, "Political Science and National Integration—A Radical Approach," *The Journal of Modern African Studies* 5, no. 1 (1967) and Archie Mafeje, "The Ideology of 'Tribalism,'" *The Journal of Modern African Studies* 9, no. 2 (1971). Peter Flynn's related essay on "clientelism" is "Class, Clientelism, and Coercion: Some Mechanisms of Internal Dependency and Control," *Journal of Commonwealth and Comparative Politics* 12, no. 2 (1974). My own discussion of "petty-bourgeois politics" and its contribution to the politicization of ethnicity is "The Unsteady State: Uganda, Obote, and General Amin" in this volume, which also critiques the approach to ethnicity of Mahmood Mamdani in his *Politics and Class Formation in Uganda* (London and New York, 1976). Frantz Fanon's observation, cited here, is to be found in his *The Wretched of the Earth* (Harmondsworth, 1967), p. 164.

Nairn's most profound discussion of nationalism is to be found in his "The Modern Janus," *New Left Review*, no. 94 (November–December 1975). Pierre-Phillippe Rey's observations on the articulation of modes of production are quoted from Lionel Cliffe, "Rural Political Economy of Africa," in Peter Gutkind and Immanuel Wallerstein, eds., *The Political Economy of Contemporary Africa* (Beverley Hills and London, 1976) and from Aidan Foster-Carter, "The Modes of Production Controversy," *New Left Review*, no. 107 (January–February 1978). Both these articles are helpful in their own right, as are Rey's various volumes, as yet not translated into English. Claude Meillassoux is cited from another useful article, that by John Clammer, "Economic Anthropology and the Sociology of Development: 'Liberal' Anthropology and Its French Critics" in I. Oxaal, T. Barnett, and D. Booth, eds., *Beyond the Sociology of Development* (London, 1975).

Giovanni Arrighi's observation appears in his "The Relationship Between the Colonial and the Class Structures," United Nations African Institute for Economic Development and Planning Paper no. 267, mimeo. (Dakar, 1971) and Perry Anderson's in his *Lineages of the Absolutist State* (London, 1974), p. 403 (it is quoted but wrongly cited in Foster-Carter, "The Modes of Production Controversy"). The work of Ernesto Laclau which is drawn upon so frequently in the text is *Politics and Ideology in Marxist Theory* (London, 1977), especially chapters 3 and 4; this is one of the most crucially important volumes written within the Marxist tradition in recent years.

Amilcar Cabral's reflections are to be found in his *Revolution in Guinea* (New York and London, 1969) and Marcellino dos Santos discusses ethnicity, among other issues, in an important interview, "FRELIMO Faces the Future," *The African Communist*, no. 55 (1973). A key FRELIMO text is "Mozambican Tribes and Ethnic Groups: Their Significance in the Struggle for National Liberation" which appeared in English in the movement's magazine *Mozambique Revolution*, no. 36 (October–December 1968) and additional valuable documentation, some of it reproduced here, is available in Edward Alpers, "Ethnicity, Politics, and History in Mozambique," *Africa Today* 21, no. 4 (1974).

POSTSCRIPT

The general introduction to this volume spoke of Mozambique's attempts to "cast the newly liberated state outside the petty-bourgeois mold and upon a base of consciously active peasants and workers." The first three essays then explored the backdrop to such an attempt—in particular, the radicalizing experience of the liberated areas—leaving Mozambicans, at the moment of independence (1975) as described in essay 3, poised to undertake a new phase of their struggle. It is appropriate, therefore, that this final essay should offer at least some brief overview of the results of the first three years of Mozambique's effort to put such an aspiration into practice. And the appending of this account will appear all the more appropriate when one considers that Mozambique's current activities do indeed continue to distinguish that country's experience sharply from that of the other countries of Eastern Africa discussed in subsequent essays.

Of course, the article reprinted here is at best a mere snapshot. Perhaps more could have been made of the price which the clammy grip of inherited state structures exacts from the regime's revolutionary endeavors and of the impossibility, in the difficult short run, of recasting all such structures, immediately and simultaneously, anew. It is evident that the bureaucratization of state, and of party, in the interests of petty-bourgeois self-interest is not something that has been preempted once and for all in Mozambique; rather, the matter remains a focus of sustained political struggle. I am also painfully aware that much more of the vitality of *progressive* developments in Mozambique could have been communicated had space permitted the recounting, in the original article, of additional anecdotes and the elaboration of more precise descriptions.

This is particularly the case with reference to the interaction of those tripartite structures—administration, party, and mass organization—sketched in this essay's third section. Our Canadian study-brigade, whose trip the article recounts, visited such enterprises as Maputo's steel mill and its Caju Industriel (a cashew-processing plant), Beira's dock complex and its Belita clothing factory, as well as several state farms in the countryside. There it was apparent that, even as party cell and administration were beginning to play an important role in guiding developments, so, simultaneously, the assertions of the "production councils" were bringing real democratic pressures to bear on both those structures and thus molding their activities in crucial ways. Indeed, it was hard not to feel that much of the future of Mozambique's revolution was being determined precisely in the ubiquitous meetings in which all these structures participated and where, in concrete ways, they struggled over the political economy of their enterprise's development. Moreover, roughly parallel attempts to resolve, in a progressive manner, any contradictions which might be expected to emerge between party leadership and the creativity of popular classes were discernible in rural settings beyond the state-farm sector—for instance, in the various cooperatives and communal villages now in the process of formation. It is obvious that a much more extended analysis of the complexities of socialist construction in Mozambique is in order since the country remains, strikingly, a laboratory of ongoing sociopolitical experimentation from which concerned revolutionaries, in Africa and elsewhere, have much to learn.

Yet even as it stands the following essay does provide, as a kind of interim conclusion, the opportunity to strike a balance-sheet on the set of ideas and preoccupations that this volume has brought together. At one level it serves to reinforce awareness of the constraints upon innovation which exist in an Eastern African setting: external dependency and the potential crystallization of wasting hierarchies of power and privilege, factors rendered all the more menacing in Mozambique's case by the even greater proximity of cancerous white minority regimes to its borders. Clearly, there will be no very easy transition to socialism anywhere in Eastern Africa. More important than this, however, is a second consideration: in contrast to the experience of other East African countries explored elsewhere in the book, postcolonial realities in Mozambique also suggest that possibilities exist, despite the odds, for significant, genuinely socialist, advance.

As noted earlier, central to realizing such a possibility is the incursion into the political arena of those popular classes—workers and peasants—who can be expected to develop a conscious class interest in the transition to socialism. And Mozambique's attempts to give ideological and institutional expression to such popular participation—so much more real than anything contemplated for Tanzania, even at the height of its quasi-socialist experimentation—already represent a tangible democratization of the system; they thus bear promise of setting the postcolonial state on entirely new foundations. FRELIMO's leadership role remains important, of course. But it is a leadership which is increasingly Marxist in its overt orientation and which remains committed to facilitating popular creativity at the base. Here, too, there is promise,

promise that potential recruits to petty-bourgeoisdom will find themselves—in the postcolonial phase as in the period of the liberation struggle itself—being redefined within a genuinely popular movement as a cadre of militants, rather than as a ruling class-in-the-making vis-à-vis an alienated populace.

Enough has already been achieved in this respect to guarantee that the worst ravages of petty-bourgeois politics—"tribalism" and the like—remain preempted. And if the struggle to avoid the dangers of a petty-bourgeois-sponsored bureaucratization of the political process does indeed continue, that is no more than is to be expected. It is certain, in any case, that such a struggle now takes place in Mozambique at a much more advanced level than has hitherto been reached anywhere else in Africa. In Mozambique the goal—enunciated by Samora Machel in his 1975 Inaugural Address, and cited in the introduction—of a positive blending of state and revolution remains firmly on the agenda.

15

MOZAMBIQUE: THE NEW PHASE

Living in Tanzania, initial base of the Mozambican struggle for independence, I had the opportunity more than a decade ago to witness at close quarters the dramatic developments which were forging, in FRELIMO (the Front for the Liberation of Mozambique), a strong and exemplary revolutionary organization. A trip to the liberated areas in 1972 enabled me to see on the ground the extent to which such developments were also foreshadowing the construction of a new, independent, and socialist Mozambique. Then, in June 1975, I returned as a guest at the country's independence celebrations to observe the initial phases of the effort to generalize the lessons of the liberation struggle to the entire country and to exemplify these lessons as policy in the many novel spheres which now lay open to FRELIMO action.[1] Small wonder that a trip back to Mozambique this year (1978) seemed an important one to make, offering, as it did, the chance to see how three years of the sobering realities of state power had affected the thrust of those previous initiatives.

The circumstances of the trip were also important. I traveled as a member of a delegation of more than a dozen Canadians, many from the Toronto Committee for the Liberation of Southern Africa (TCLSAC), of which I am a member. This delegation had been invited by FRELIMO and the Mozambique government to undertake a study-hour of the country and we were warmly

This essay was originally published in *This Magazine* (Toronto), March 1979, and in *Monthly Review*, March 1979.

received throughout the four southern provinces in which we traveled. Some of my most vivid memories of the trip are of the greetings of welcome, as Canadians and as comrades, proferred to us by peasants and workers in the communal villages, state farms, and factories that we visited, as well as by state and party activists. As I once again experienced FRELIMO's impressive spirit of humane and nonrhetorical internationalism, I realized that this was just another of the many achievements of Mozambique's earlier struggles which has been carried over, intact, into the country's new phase.

I

Yet I spoke of "sobering realities." These there are, and in abundance. In consequence, the mood in Mozambique was different from the euphoric one I had encountered during the first weeks of independence in 1975. When I asked Marcellino dos Santos, minister of the plan, whether the current efforts at socialist reconstruction or the liberation struggle itself was more difficult, the reply was immediate: unquestionably, the current phase. As many others expressed it, the terrain for action is now so much more vast, the obstacles to progress so much more subtle, the gains so much less tangible. Not that FRELIMO has forgotten its motto: "The struggle continues." But I was struck by the clear awareness among Mozambicans, so familiar from the early days of the armed struggle when I first met FRELIMO militants in the dingy little offices on Nkrumah Street in Dar es Salaam, that they have once again enlisted for a long haul.

In what ways, then, is the context for Mozambique's socialist project a hostile one? First and foremost, the visitor to Mozambique is conscious of entering a war zone. Coverage by the Western media had simply not prepared us for the savagery of the war Rhodesia is waging against Mozambique. There were constant first-hand reports of damaging air attacks all along the border and well inside the country during the six weeks we were there, and on one occasion a bomb of apparent Rhodesian provenance exploded in a restaurant in Maputo itself.[2] The costs of Mozambique have been high, not only in human lives and in the destruction of expensive infrastructure, but also in the need to tie up in military roles many more trained cadres than might otherwise have been the case. The consequent loss to current mobilization efforts of the often highly developed political skills of such people has been important.

Important, too, have been disjunctions caused by Mozambique's implementation of sanctions against Rhodesia. Thus the port of Beira, which we visited, has been reduced to a mere echo of its former activity (although all the dock-workers, even if underemployed, have been kept on the job) and crucial revenues have been lost. Migrant labor to Rhodesia, an erstwhile backbone of the dependent economy along the border, was cut off precipitously, well in advance of the planned rural transformation that might have begun to absorb those workers productively at home. When to all this is added the expense of fielding vast numbers of refugees in Mozambique, an expense which, like other related ones, has never been met to the extent originally promised by the international community (e.g., the Commonwealth), we can understand why many Mozambicans were quick to say that the main contribution supporters outside could make to their development efforts would be to force the Smith gang out of power in Zimbabwe once and for all.

Mention of the erstwhile movement of migrant labor to Rhodesia points toward another crucial dimension of Mozambique's precarious situation. No country in Africa has inherited from colonialism an economy so viciously distorted, even though its warping by the Portuguese to service South African needs was much more dramatic than any subordination to Rhodesia. In order to keep such an economy afloat at all in the short run, the country has had to yield something to the logic of this dependency, looking to continued revenues from southern Mozambicans migrating to work in South Africa, for example, and to port and transport earnings from goods shipped via Maputo from the Transvaal. Moreover, South Africa provides a crucial link for the modern sector of the economy: at the steel mill in Maputo, for instance, I found that fully 95 percent of the inputs—iron ingots, wood and coal, machine parts—came from there, and at present much, much more cheaply than from any conceivable alternative source.

The FRELIMO government is thus faced with the prospect of attempting to do two potentially contradictory things at once: to sustain something of its inherited structure in order to avoid economic collapse while beginning to search out openings toward an economy very differently structured. Nor does time stand still while this attempt unfolds: in the past few years the South African mines themselves have moved well ahead of Mozambique's own schedule for disengagement from South Africa and have disastrously curtailed the numbers of Mozambicans working in them, with severe consequences for the country's balance of payments and for unemployment figures in the south. Paradoxically, the opportunity thus afforded for restructuring the economy merely puts much greater pressure on a government already under severe strain.

The same paradox characterizes other sectors. Colonial Mozambique was firmly mired in the classic posture of supplier of raw materials—cotton, cashew, sugar, copra, tea—to Portugal and the West, and this structure was topped off by a narrow industrial sector directed toward servicing the rather specialized needs of the privileged white population. Here again Mozambique has not been afforded the luxury of time, time to sustain something of the productive contribution of these activities while also working to transform them. Instead, the collapse of production in crucial spheres has threatened to whisk away many of these activities all too precipitously, the key here being the dramatic pull-out, across the board, of the Portuguese (of 250,000 present at independence, only 15,000 to 20,000 remain). Not that this pull-out was ever willed by the government; indeed, every attempt has been made to safeguard the nonracial character of the regime. But the majority of Portuguese have responded negatively to the reality of their obvious loss of special privilege and to the implications for their class position of the nationalization of buildings, of various professional activities (law, medicine, etc.), and the like.

Attended by a considerable amount of economic sabotage,

often of a merely spiteful kind, this departure left gaping holes in the social services (including a fall from about 600 doctors—for a population of 6 million—to 50 within six months) and in productive spheres. In agriculture a number of large estates (in copra, sugar, and tea) were left under the (supervised) control of big foreign companies and have continued to produce, but the wholesale abandonment of settler farms, particularly in the south, posed a very serious threat to food production, their main activity. Equally important was the collapse of the network of commercialization in the rural areas (affecting both the retailing of consumer goods and the purchasing of produce, as well as transport) with the marketing of cash crops by peasants of the north—and so also the balance of payments—being severely affected. And, of course, in the industrial sector there was the threat of disaster in many spheres, as entire complements of owners, managers, and technical staff often abandoned their enterprises. Small wonder that many Mozambicans were tempted to feel that merely weathering such a storm must be the order of the day.

Covering all these technical fronts while also advancing the work of mobilization necessary to draw people outside the formerly liberated areas firmly into the network of FRELIMO-sponsored institutions meant that trained and trusted cadres were soon spread thin on the ground. As we shall see, the release of popular energies which the defeat of the Portuguese and FRELIMO's accession to power facilitated has been important in filling this gap, but considerable reliance has had to be placed not just on technical personnel carried over from colonial days—some of whom are ill-adapted to the tasks of socialist reconstruction—but also on large numbers of "cooperantes." The latter input, like other kinds of external aid contributions, has its virtues: many skilled and dedicated people, including a number of Canadians, are now able to make an active contribution to Mozambican socialism, for example. But there are dangers, too, dangers which arise from the ideological overtones inherent in even the most technical-sounding of aid schemes, and this is not merely a threat from the subliminal liberal-cum-social-democratic influences introduced by, say, Dutch or Scandinavian assistance.

The latter kinds of presence loomed particularly large in the heyday of Tanzania's ultimately abortive socialist efforts, but Mozambique places itself much more firmly in the so-called socialist camp than Tanzania ever did, and thus the problem is posed somewhat differently there. Of course, no serious observer could deny the positive role the Soviet Union has played, past and present, in supporting liberation movements in Southern Africa, and Eastern bloc assistance continues to be important to Mozambique, both substantively in the present phase, and potentially, as a possible "last resort" if white regime-sponsored incursions escalate things even further. But it is difficult to be entirely sanguine about the ideological ramifications and possible impact upon policies of this kind of "socialist" assistance: its technical dimensions are often ensnared, abroad as at home, in the most technocratic and authoritarian definitions of preferred social relations of production and methods of political work, and the whole package is tripped out with a particularly lifeless and demobilizing patina of official "Marxism-Leninism." It will become apparent as this essay proceeds that a substantial and sanguinary innoculation against too great a spill-over of such negative influences has been provided by the continuing vitality of Mozambique's own revolutionary tradition. Nevertheless, what has been said does underscore the importance of the present process of defining more sharply Mozambique's own ideology, a process given fresh impetus at FRELIMO's Third Congress in 1977 when, for the first time, the movement (now to become a party) explicitly proclaimed Marxism-Leninism as its chosen framework.

II

Such difficulties have not preempted creative policies. We had every chance to sound these out, not only in the ministries responsible, but also on the ground in rural and industrial settings, in schools, clinics, and the like. Not surprisingly in a country in which 95 percent of the population lives in the rural areas, agricultural transformation takes center stage. Moreover, there are precedents for progressive developments in this sphere. The emergence of collective production was already an important reality in the liberated areas, as I had observed for myself in 1972, and independence provided the opportunity for parallel initiatives throughout the rest of the country. Unfortunately, this seems to have been, at first, an instance of almost too much "politics in command." The necessary technical underpinnings of such a program did not keep pace, and failures led to some retrenchment. Further, the focus of post-independence attention in the agricultural sphere was almost immediately wrenched away from such undertakings by the retreat of the Portuguese. As noted above, the collapse of settler farming in the south jeopardized food supplies to the cities and a quick response to the emergency was imperative. The decision: to convert these already abandoned agricultural enterprises into state farms and, of necessity, to devote a considerable proportion of scarce energies and resources to keeping their often highly mechanized activities in operation.

Despite problems, this move was a success, but it also involved certain risks, most importantly the risk of, in effect, making too much of a virtue of necessity. To see in elaborate mechanization a solution to rural problems is a temptation for all under-developed countries and to overvalue quasi-industrialized agriculture—the state farm—is perhaps a particular temptation for such of those countries as are in receipt of substantial Eastern European aid. The question of whether Mozambique had succumbed too uncritically to such temptations was one which was being hotly debated while we were in the country, and it was instructive to learn that, shortly after our departure, the minister of agriculture, a senior FRELIMO cadre, had been replaced. The reason: he "had repeatedly shown that his conception of development was wrong and in contradiction to the process of advancing to socialism. He refused to implement the priority defined by the leading bodies in relation to communal villages. In essence, he does not place trust in the people, he does not consider man as the determining element of development."

In fact, such "communal villages"—*aldeais communais*—are already the framework for peasant-based, peasant-led collectivization, and we could see this brand of rural transformation being exemplified in the countryside. True, many such villages reflect their origins in the response to those natural disasters which hounded independent Mozambique's first years: terrifying floods in the Limpopo and Zambezi river valleys provided the initial incentive to group peasants in villages on higher ground. And in the north the need to settle returning refugees and to place "strategic hamlets" created by the Portuguese on a new footing was a pressing stimulus. Most often, the fact of living together, the better to receive essential services, is still the most prominent feature of such villages. But the seed of collective production has also been planted, and the new Commission on Communal Villages, created within the President's Office in 1978 even before the sacking of the agricultural minister, gives promise of encouraging its growth both in existing villages and in such crucial peasant-based provinces as Nampula, where the move toward collectivization has been held in relative abeyance. Though initiatives in this sphere will be equally dependent upon parallel efforts to reestablish rural networks of commercialization and transportation, it was hard to escape the feeling that, in the current revitalization of grass-roots rural transformation, one was witnessing a crucial moment in the Mozambican revolution.

In the industrial sphere, too, policy tended to move in fits and starts, adapting to the paradoxical demands, noted above, of a collapsing, yet profoundly warped, industrial sector. Which of these two realities to tackle first—the collapse or the distortion—remained a dilemma. Party and government have moved quite soberly here, making "best utilization of installed capacity" the watchword, with any more dramatic structural transformation a goal for the future. But not the indefinite future: it was reassuring to learn in various interviews how conscious planners were of the dangers inherent in even the most unavoidable compromises with their economic inheritance. Moreover, the FRELIMO government, despite its relative caution, had begun quite early on to arm itself with the means for a different sort of planning through nationalization of crucial sectors—not merely such preserves of local privilege as the private professions (medicine, law) and ownership of buildings, but also all banking, insurance, and oil installations, as well as that wide range of manufacturing firms of various sizes which have fallen into the hands of workers and the state with the departure of the Portuguese. In addition, even those large multinational firms which continue to operate—they are particularly important in estate agriculture (copra, tea, etc.)—do so under quite firm government scrutiny, a scrutiny so real that when one private firm, the coal mine at Moatize, chose to flout government guidelines on worker safety it was immediately nationalized.

Not that Mozambique has assumed the mere act of nationalization to have established socialism or to have guaranteed the existence of a "self-centered" and autonomous economy. A much more important clue to the future has been the clarity of aspiration and intention manifested in such settings as the country's first National Conference of Planning in 1978 (itself forced into being by the more systematic affirmation of the socialist goal at FRELIMO's Third Congress). Thus it has been firmly enunciated that agriculture, though still seen as a major earner of foreign exchange, must first service local food requirements and industrial development, and that industry is to become the "dynamizing factor" which will slowly wrest away the economy from its neocolonial format. Moreover, the "essential needs" of the bulk of the population are now much more consciously front and center as targets for production, a promising source of direction both for the reconversion of existing industries and for the establishment of such new ones as are to be planned into existence.[3] Indeed, one senses that the next few years will be almost as full of crucial decisions in the industrial sector, and in the overall planning process, as in agriculture. Yet for our delegation the main promise lay in the fact that, as socialists, we were able to ask few, if any, questions in these spheres which Mozambicans were not already asking themselves. We came away with the clear sense that such constraints as the country's links to South Africa and its subordination to the global division of labor were seen as precisely that—constraints, not opportunities, to be bent and ultimately broken.

Things were somewhat more straightforward in the service sector. Intentions, at least, could be quite clear, even if the legacy of several centuries of Portuguese colonialism has been staggering needs and far from adequate means at the new government's disposal. Health is a case in point, the priority of a rural-based, prevention-oriented people's health program, already well established in the liberated areas, continuing to underpin current practice. As one expatriate doctor who had also worked in Tanzania put the point to me: "The socialist premises which some people were struggling, often unsuccessfully, to establish in Tanzania are virtually taken for granted here. The real struggle, difficult enough but representing a much more advanced stage, is to implement them." The most dramatic initial advance in this respect has been the extraordinary vaccination campaign. This program, in which over 95 percent of the population has been given basic innoculations, was deemed unprecedented by World Health Organization officials who participated in it; it also gave ample testimony to the efficacy on the ground of FRELIMO political networks, responsible as they were for mobilizing popular participation in the program. Equally encouraging has been the on-going attempt to attack professional hierarchies and democratize the medical workplace in the interests of releasing human energies. Here the vast Maputo Central Hospital, where several senior officials, including the president, intervened to facilitate the process, provide an impressive example. But, in any case, this merely represented a pattern which is at work much more broadly in Mozambique.

In fact, the efforts made to facilitate democratization of profoundly exclusivist, sexist, and hierarchical institutions were also apparent in the various educational institutions we visited (the colonial school having no equal with respect to the above shortcomings). We found faculty, support staff, and students beginning to pin down ways of actively participating in the definition and implementation of their own program at all levels. Equally impressive was the root-and-branch approach to educational change which was the substance of policy. No doubt the risks entailed by possible error are somewhat less dramatic in education than in more directly productive spheres. In consequence, educationists could tell us of quite coolly and self-consciously scrapping most of the preexisting syllabuses and teaching materials, and then allowing the hard work and creativity of education workers to wrest from the ensuing "crisis" courses, texts, and classroom practices which are much more profoundly Mozambican and, of course, more socialist in content. The method seemed to be working, and in such an environment it became all the more difficult to imagine parallel revolutionary aspirations being lost to view even in the most difficult realms of agricultural and industrial policy.

III

Thus, even more striking for us than the harsh constraints was the way in which the long-term goals of Mozambique's radical transformation kept rising to the surface—to premise policy making and, indeed, to revitalize it. Contrast this with other African countries where such goals, even if enunciated, are drowned in the "pragmatic" and commonsense calculations of the "short-run"; there, structural transformation is merely indefinitely postponed and hence rendered rhetorical. But if, despite the necessity for very real compromises, radical advance remains firmly on the agenda in postcolonial Mozambique, what is the precise source of such promise for the revolution? The answer, it seemed to me as I toured the country, was already firmly rooted in the experience of the liberated areas and, in its current manifestation, is threefold: it lies in the *politicization* of the development process, in the *democratization* of the political process, and in the *concretization* of Marxism with reference to the realities of Mozambique's own history and current circumstances. Obviously, it is difficult to disentangle these threads, which are tightly interwoven, but it is important to try to do so.

First, just as guerrilla warfare came to be seen not as mere militarism but as a political process grounded in the clear statement of long-term goals of societal transformation and in the active, self-conscious participation of the people themselves, so too development is understood as being much more than a technical exercise. True, the often rather baroque structures of the Portuguese colonial state are far from having been completely dismantled. Moreover, bureaucratic "operators" and narrow technocrats—indigenous and expatriate, and, in each category, those of both "Eastern" and "Western" provenance—are not absent from Mozambique. Yet everywhere such elements seemed to be coming under some kind of positive political pressure. General political education is stressed—much of each Saturday morning in each ministry is given over to group study of a weekly text published in the newspaper, for example—but a central key is, increasingly, the party.

Indeed, the past year has seen the beginning of the "structuring" (as the phrase goes in Mozambique) of the new party out of the old, more amorphous movement. This involves the creation of party cells in every sector of the society—in ministries, factories, farms, schools, hospitals, neighborhoods—and these cells are already working to underwrite an on-going debate about fundamentals, a debate which helps to keep long-term socialist priorities, including the priority of socialist methods of political work, front and center in every institution. Nor, in such a context, is party membership something to be lightly undertaken. Complementing our discussions of policy with a number of long, semi-autobiographical talks with young party cadres (and would-be cadres), we were able to see how high the standards are, how much is expected from such people in the way of hard work and commitment, and how impressive is the response of many of the younger generation to the opportunities for revolutionary activity provided by FRELIMO.[4]

Such attributes of "vanguardism" are important: the radical premises of progress are visibly alive in Mozambican offices, factories, and farms—they are the very real currency of discourse—in ways that I had never seen them to be alive in Tanzania, for example. But all this would be much less promising were it not wedded to a second feature, the democratization of the various structures in question. For democracy is quite tangible in Mozambique. Just as real and active popular participation had been a necessary ingredient of guerrilla success in the liberated areas and war zones of preindependence Mozambique, so now we observed it to be at work not only in the hospitals and schools mentioned above, but in all the other kinds of production centers we visited. Before, the *grupos dynamizadores* (literally, the "dynamizing groups"), established throughout the country by FRELIMO as a matter of top priority during the transition period leading to independence, had provided the framework for such popular involvement.[5] But these, although extraordinarily important in the short run, represented a still somewhat unclear blending of political movement and mass organization. In consequence, as the *grupos* began to be displaced by party cells whose functions and membership are more clearly and exclusively defined, so too there had also to emerge a parallel network of mass organizations with a much sharper identity.[6]

There have been, during the past year, elections of representatives to the newly established people's assemblies at local, district, regional, and national levels, and lively mass meetings have been held in every sector to publicly evaluate the qualifications of people hoping to become members of the new political party. With specific reference to the factories and state farms, the pertinent organization of mass action is to be the elected "production council." This institution was often described to us as the "trade union in embryo," but it is already providing for a much more active workers' role in the production process than this term might imply. We had enough talks with factory workers and "responsibles" to see that in most cases the councils, and the ubiquitous meetings of workers attendant upon their operation, have had a quite dramatic impact upon decision making, levels of output, and the improvement of working conditions. The same sense of active involvement was visible in the communal villages we visited; here as elsewhere (including ministerial offices, generally the most hierarchical of undertakings) the *reunião*, or general meeting, providing the center stage for lively political drama. Of course, the strength of the process has varied with the nature of the historical experience of the village in question and with the quality of political leadership in the area. But the democratic ethos seems always to be real, often extremely moving and impressive, especially in a country where, until only three years ago, any active role whatsoever was denied the vast majority of the population.

Indeed, it is more than impressive. It is true that the party plays a crucial part, itself screening candidates, for example, and, in the case of the selection of party members, taking the role of popular scrutiny as being merely advisory to it. The parameters of participation continue to be defined, in part, from the top down, this reality representing, in the eyes of FRELIMO leaders, precisely the measure of leadership and guidance of the development process necessitated by the present situation. In this sense, too—in asserting its role in raising the level of consciousness of workers and peasants and facilitating their full emergence as historical actors—FRELIMO makes no apologies for being a vanguard party. At the same time, we heard enough first-hand testimony to realize that the various meetings and elections mentioned above are scarcely formalities: inputs at the base are vital, they do reach the top, and, as so many activists themselves testified, they create a situation in which party and administrative functionaries must become cadres capable of realizing their goals by political and educational means, rather than by administrative fiat, or be seen to fail. Indeed, a stage seems to have been reached where the assertions of workers and peasants which these structures have actively elicited can be ignored only at the regime's peril.

Not that there was any sense that the regime was proposing to ignore them. Quite the contrary. No one seems more aware than the Mozambicans with whom I talked of how often "socialisms" elsewhere have collapsed into bureaucratized enterprises serving primarily the interests of newly formed elites. There is also much writing in the press of such dangers very close to home, in Mozambique itself. Small wonder that the popular term in the political equation is taken so seriously: as FRELIMO argues, ultimately only the workers and peasants can build socialism. Of course, history has also demonstrated that it is notoriously difficult to strike the kind of balance between leadership and mass action which is required for a genuine transition to socialism. The effort to evade authoritarianism will be equally complex in Mozambique. Nonetheless, there is substantial commitment, genuine institutional creativity, and much political subtlety; it is hard to escape the feeling that the possibility exists for a fully democratic denouement to this familiar political dilemma. Moreover, even as this effort unfolds, one can't deny what is quite visible on the ground: the fact that so many Mozambicans actually do feel that they are engaged in making their own history in novel and unmediated ways. Surely this is one very good definition of democracy. The attendant release of energies is also socialism's basic promise for the realization of *development* in Mozambique, the human essence of the liberation struggle which Carvalho, the former minister of agriculture, had forgotten to honor in the new phase.[7]

Finally, it was important for our delegation to observe the manner in which such advances were being consolidated ideologically: as noted earlier, FRELIMO has now more formally proclaimed its ideology to be that of "Marxism-Leninism." True, there have been Marxists in FRELIMO from an early date and, in any case, the movement's practice came increasingly to coincide with Marxist perspectives as it transformed itself during the armed struggle.[8] But the further, self-conscious systematization of the party's position within the Marxist tradition is now expected to make that practice much more coherent and accessible for purposes of political education and more capable of generalization as a framework for policy making in novel spheres.

This is a correct perception. A Marxist approach has the distinct promise of yielding sharper definitions, both of the complex nature of contemporary imperialism and of the class struggle which must continue within the development process, than FRELIMO's own experience, left untheorized, can provide. But there is reason to fear that such an ideological option may have its costs as well. After all, as argued earlier, Marxism-Leninism has all too often become a hollow and ultimately quite demagogic rationalization for the kinds of bureaucratization of the socialist impulse referred to above. Coupled with FRELIMO's strong ties of aid and inclination to the "socialist countries," this reality brings us to repeat our earlier question: does such an apparent ideological advance merely foreshadow a similar fate?

Long talks with FRELIMO personnel convinced me that this was not the case. As President Samora Machel himself put the point to me, "Africans must use Marxism, but Marxism must not be allowed to use Africans"! "Some people," he added, "seem to think that the development of Marxism ended in October 1917." In a closely related manner, it was striking how often we heard not only the president but Mozambicans at all levels hark back to the liberation struggle itself in setting the stage for the discussion of current policies. Indeed, by the end of our stay our delegation almost felt we had heard the same refrain once too often. But it was not difficult to remind ourselves that these were different people we were talking to on each occasion, and that they did not, in any case, evoke the experience of the liberated areas liturgically. Rather, they were almost invariably drawing the correct lessons—precisely the lessons of politicization and democratization—and then applying them concretely to their own circumstances.

The extent to which this experience will continue to be blended into FRELIMO's Marxism (and into its Leninism!) is not predetermined, of course. I would say that the question of the nature of the country's Marxism—its depth and its openness—is now a crucial terrain for struggle in Mozambique.[9] Nonetheless, the balance of class forces is such as to give promise of vitality rather than sterility in the ideological realm.[10] If this is indeed the case, the movement's ideology will help continue to underwrite progressive policies, including a reinforcement of the country's ability to winnow the wheat from the chaff of Eastern—as from Western—aid. There is even the possibility, in light of what has been said above, that Mozambique will find itself making its own distinctive contribution to the historical experience of Marxism. It is, after all, a tradition much in need of revitalization in the Third World.

Clearly, it is late in the historical day to be naïve about the claims to socialist advance which are made by manifestly underdeveloped and dependent agricultural countries in the hostile global environment of rampant and competing imperialisms. Too often their promise has turned to dust in the absence of global transformations which could help to ease their burden and to clear their path. But it would be equally naïve for analysts to err in the opposite direction and replace the crucial dialectic which invariably exists between will and circumstance with a model premised on the sterile determinism of "objective conditions." Nothing is certain in Mozambique, but what is ultimately impressive is the fact that, under trying conditions, popular classes—

peasants and workers—are in motion and that a leadership is in place which has begun to raise self-consciously all of the questions about a transition to socialism that the most intelligent and/or jaundiced left observer from the West could think of. It was instructive to see some of the answers to these questions taking shape in Mozambique and it will be even more instructive to watch the process unfold in future. Equally valuable was the reminder, as I returned to the North American late-1970s political doldrums and to our own often apparently "hostile environment," that the struggle *can* continue.

Notes

1. These three moments in my own observation and analysis of the Mozambican struggle are recounted in my "FRELIMO and the Mozambique Revolution," published as ch. 8 in Giovanni Arrighi and John S. Saul, *Essays on the Political Economy of Africa* (New York, 1973) and in essays 2 and 3 above.

2. Losing to the Zimbabwean liberation forces on the ground inside Rhodesia/Zimbabwe, Smith and the army have adopted the classic tactic of desperation (à la Vietnam): attempting to pulverize the "base areas"—the latter being very broadly defined, of course. There is also probably a motif of vengeance against Mozambique which is at play and which helps broaden the havoc created. Many of those pulling the trigger for Rhodesia are ex-Portuguese army and police personnel from preindependence Mozambique, as well as right-wing detritus from elsewhere, with their own scores to settle. In addition, some of the Rhodesian terror seems directed primarily at frightening off "cooperants"—expatriates on contract—who are currently helping Mozambique in its reconstruction efforts.

3. No less interesting was another argument heard from planners for the emphasis upon industrialization: it will develop the working class, and this must necessarily be a "political stronghold" of the revolution. But such an emphasis is not surprising in light of the active role that workers are being encouraged to take in the actual running of the industries themselves.

4. Only a detailed recounting of such interviews would be sufficient to really make the point, but, once again, the comparison with Tanzania was instructive for me: one saw an encouragement in Mozambique of precisely the kind of militancy which tended to be feared rather than supported in the former country. As another interesting

point of contrast, it is worth noting the expressed intention that the party headquarters in Mozambique be further strengthened with a fresh complement of technically trained cadres—"red," but quite adequately "expert." Not for Marcellino dos Santos (minister of the plan *and* secretary for party economic policy) the "realism" which has elsewhere suggested that, in light of overall laborpower constraints, this would be an unnecessary duplication of function. For, as he affirmed to me, it is only by so enlarging its capacities that the party can really hope to make specific its broad socialist goals and continue to bring them to bear on the day-to-day policy making of the bureaucracy.

5. These *grupos* are discussed in essay 3.
6. It does seem likely, however, that the *grupos* will continue to have some important role as an institution of neighborhood political organization, especially in the urban areas.
7. Significantly, some of the fresh drive to rethink agricultural policies came from within the ministry of agriculture itself, from younger agriculturalists working in the regions and closer to the peasants.
8. See my "FRELIMO and the Mozambique Revolution," and essays 1 and 2.
9. This is a terrain whose complexity was particularly evident for me at the University of Eduardo Mondlane, where a variety of brands of Marxism are on display, some much, much more promising than others. But this struggle—of necessity an important part of the broader struggle against any trend toward the bureaucratization of the revolutionary impulse—was beginning to unfold in other sectors as well.
10. Not to mention vitality in the cultural realm more broadly defined. On the accomplishments of Mozambicans in this sphere, and on the challenges which continue to confront them, see the excellent account, complementary to the present one, by Rick Salutin, a leading Canadian playwright who was in Mozambique at the same time as our Canadian brigade. This article is also published in the March 1979 issue of *This Magazine*, cited above. In addition to his account of cultural developments generally, Salutin discusses his trip to the formerly "liberated areas" of Cabo Delgado where the revolutionary tradition is, of course, particularly strong.

INDEX